BIRDWATCHER

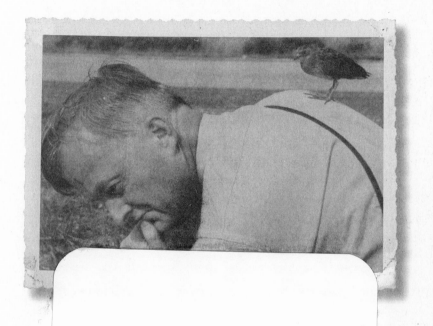

BIRDWATCHER

The Life of Roger Tory Peterson

ELIZABETH J. ROSENTHAL

THE LYONS PRESS
Guilford, Connecticut
An imprint of The Globe Pequot Press

For Stan,

who makes everything possible

The Lyons Press is an imprint of The Globe Pequot Press

Photo on title page: Roger Tory Peterson with sora rail, early 1950s. (University of Iowa)

Text design by Sheryl P. Kober

The Library of Congress has cataloged the earlier hardcover edition as follows:

Rosenthal, Elizabeth J.
Birdwatcher : the life of Roger Tory Peterson / by Elizabeth J. Rosenthal.
p. cm.
Includes bibliographical references.
ISBN 978-1-59921-294-4
1. Peterson, Roger Tory, 1908-1996. 2.   Ornithologists—United States--Biography.
I. Title.
QL31.P45R67 2008
598.092—dc22
[B]   2008008704
ISBN: 978-1-59921-962-2

Printed in the United States of America

10 9 8 7 6 5 4 3 2 1

Table of Contents

Part Six: BIRD MAN OF BIRD MEN

Part One:

FLEDGLING

Chapter One

Boy Rebel to Boy Wonder

I go out into the woods, and every bird and flower I see stirs me to the heart with something, I do not know what it is; only I love them: I love them with all my strength. . . . They are my Bible. This is my nature.

—Ernest Thompson Seton, *Two Little Savages*

In 1908 President Theodore Roosevelt invited to the White House fellow members of the Audubon Society of the District of Columbia, as well as friends and cabinet officials, to watch the first movies taken of wild birds. It had been five years since an executive order established the first federal bird sanctuary in the nation, Pelican Island, in the Indian River near Florida's east coast. Roosevelt's action was an important early response by government to the widespread slaughter of birds—in this case, wading birds such as herons and ibises—in service of the millinery trade, which hired people to kill birds that fashionable Victorian women could wear on their heads.

Roosevelt's local Audubon Society was one of many that had recently sprouted in response to the milliners. Among the oldest was the Massachusetts Audubon Society, founded by women horrified by the destruction of heronries as orphaned nestlings were left to starve. Various Audubon Societies, and some proactive individuals, had cobbled together a wobbly network of local bird protection laws and privately hired wardens to stave off hunters through persuasion, education, and old-fashioned law enforcement.

Frank M. Chapman was one such proactive individual. An ornithologist employed by the American Museum of Natural History in New York, in 1899 he founded *Bird-Lore* magazine, which helped tie the disparate Audubon societies together and spread knowledge of and love for avifauna. One year later, as a nonviolent alternative to the gun-toters' Christmas Hunt, he advocated the establishment of the Christmas Bird Count, a bird population tally by birdwatchers. William Dutcher, an officer of the American Ornithologists' Union (AOU) who steered that organization toward bird protection with limited success, eventually realized that the patchwork of bird preservation groups needed some centralizing force. In 1905, with the help of a benefactor, he founded the National Association of Audubon Societies. That same year a thirty-five-year-old husband and father named Guy Bradley, employed as a warden in the Florida Everglades, was murdered by plume hunters. The Audubon movement had its first human martyr, turning outrage into activism.

Still, by 1908 the crisis in bird protection had not improved; as any social movement will in due time, it engendered a backlash. This one spread conservationists thin as they scurried across states to prevent the enactment of loopholes and the weakening of hard-won legislation. It was a gloomy time for bird lovers and of no particular interest that a boy was born on August 28 in Jamestown, New York, to two immigrants—a Swede named Charles Gustav Peterson and his German-Polish wife, Henrietta Bader. They named him Roger Tory Peterson. The middle name honored his Uncle Tory, of Oil City, Pennsylvania.

The unwise command to give up what was his nature merely made him a disobedient boy—turned a good boy into a bad one.

—Seton, *Two Little Savages*

Jamestown, a southwestern New York furniture-making hub fifty miles from Erie, Pennsylvania, was a magnet for Swedish immigrants who tended to be wood and metal artisans. Thus, Charles Peterson toiled in a furniture plant. (Mrs. Peterson was trained as a teacher but worked as housewife and mother.) Being a provider became a challenge after Mr. Peterson broke his leg and it didn't properly heal. He used alcohol as a painkiller. "Mrs. Peterson's husband was a drunkard," recalls Barbara Coulter Peterson, the woman who became Roger Tory Peterson's second wife. Roger wasn't happy at home, so "he just went his way," she says. "If he wanted to go out, he went out." He had a younger sister, Margaret. Home for the Petersons was a cottage at 16 Bowen Street toward the bottom of a steep hill. (Jamestown was filled with steep hills.)

"He was not formally schooled in anything as far as I could tell, because he didn't go to school very often," says Roger's elder son, Tory. "I mean, that's one of the things he used to brag to me about. He was spanked more times for skipping school than anybody else in his entire school. . . . Not everyone knows what they're going to do when they're eight, nine years old. But he apparently did. So he just decided that school wasn't one of the places where he needed to learn about it."

Truancy doesn't fit with Roger graduating from high school at the early age of sixteen, but he did lean toward disruption, eschewing school rules and falling asleep in class. "Regimentation and restriction rubbed me the wrong way," Roger later remembered.

Roger had a good reason for falling asleep in class. He rose quite early to deliver the *Jamestown Morning Post,* hoping his paper route would earn him enough money to buy his first camera. He needed a Primo No. 9 to take pictures of birds, and he took pictures of birds because he was obsessed with them.

By then, this tall, fair-haired, freckle-faced kid was fourteen. He had had his eyes opened to birds at age eleven, thanks partly to a sympathetic teacher named Blanche Hornbeck. "Miss" Hornbeck, as she was known, had her students join the Junior Audubon Club, a program of the National Association of Audubon Societies. One way to fight the destruction of birds was to educate people about them. Starting with children seemed a good way to ensure a future of conservationist adults. Read an early Junior Audubon Club announcement:

> *To form a Junior Audubon Class for bird study, a teacher should explain to the pupils . . . that their object will be to learn all they can about the wild birds, and that every one who becomes a member will be expected to be kind to the birds and protect them.*

Each student paying 10 cents received an Audubon membership button, a set of color bird pictures, and informational materials.

About Miss Hornbeck, Roger said, "She started a club simply because she wanted to learn, too. And we learned together. It was not a matter of her great wisdom about birds." He had already acquired some bird knowledge, so his fascination wasn't simply because of her dedication. One day on a class trip to the Hundred-Acre Lot, off what is now Curtis Street in Jamestown, he pointed out a common yellowthroat to her. He used Chester Reed's *Bird Guide,* a tiny book featuring color bird portraits and a description of each species.

What really started Roger on birds was an epiphany. It happened on a green elevation called Swede Hill. He later reflected:

> *I can remember the day in early April [1920], even the hour, when I became hooked. On a Saturday morning, during one of*

my youthful explorations, I spotted a bundle of brown feathers clinging to a tree. It was a flicker, tired from migration. The bird was sleeping with its bill tucked under the loose feathers of its back, but I thought it was dead. I poked it with my finger; instantly, this inert thing jerked its head around, looked at me wildly, then took off in a flash of gold. It was like resurrection. What had seemed dead was very much alive. Ever since then, birds have seemed to me the most vivid expression of life.

"I always wondered what the heck it was doing, because that's such atypical behavior for a flicker," natural history writer Scott Weidensaul observes. "It really would be ironic to think that we owe so much to a deathly ill flicker that might not have made it through the rest of the day. I doubt that a healthy flicker would have been doing that. . . . It has the ring of truth. I don't think it's an apocryphal story."

Apocryphal story or not, Roger was smitten with birds. Over time, his passion metamorphosed from a boyish hobby to an intellectual pursuit. He later recalled:

For the first five or six years, I could remember the dates of every field trip I had ever made and could recall just what I had seen. During the first years it was the joy of discovery. Then it became a competitive game, to see how many birds I could identify in a day, to discover rare birds, or to record a bird a day or two earlier in the spring than anyone else, or a day or two later in the fall. This was the listing stage. But as I tore about the countryside, ticking off the birds on my check-list on the run, I gradually became interested in their way of life. At home I pored over ornithological journals like The Auk, The Wilson Bulletin, *and* The Condor.

It was probably a favorite book, *Wild Wings* by adventurer Herbert K. Job, that inspired him to save for the Primo No. 9. Job, like most bird enthusiasts of the time, tended to watch them through a gunsight—until he discovered the joys of bird photography: "Of all the various out-door recreations which I have tried, when it comes to genuine, exciting sport, give me *hunting with the camera*.... It requires more skill than shooting, and hence is a finer sport. The results are of more interest and value, and, withal, the lives of the wild creatures are spared for our further pleasure."

Taking photographs wasn't the only way Roger could memorialize the birds he saw. He had artistic talent. Being a Junior Audubon Club member meant having the opportunity to copy bird art, like that created by the foremost bird artists of the day, most notably, Louis Agassiz Fuertes. Roger pleased Miss Hornbeck with his interpretation of a Fuertes blue jay. "I carefully painted the jay's blue feathers highlighted with white and black, its jaunty crest, and downy-gray breast," he later said.

During the next three to four years he developed an interest in all aspects of nature. Roger reflected: "A year or two later I discovered butterflies, and they eclipsed my preoccupation with the warblers until I ran out of new species of these psychedelic insects in the fields and woods around home. Flowers came later, when I was fourteen or fifteen."

Roger negotiated permission from the local police to stay out after curfew and catch moths. Cocoons he collected outside metamorphosed in the family living room into colorful moths of several species.

A younger schoolmate, Clarence Beal, joined Roger on a "botanical 'big day'" in their home county of Chautauqua, where they "racked up a rough total of 240 [species]," Roger recalled.

Disregard for his health and safety while pursuing nature manifested itself early and continued into Roger's old age. Miss Hornbeck may have thought him gallant when he showed up for a bird walk one unpleasant Saturday morning. Thirty years later, upon learning of his prominence she wrote him a nostalgic letter: "My best recollection of you is on a rainy morning when several from my class were to meet for a bird walk. As I recall it only three appeared. I expressed surprise that any one came and I can still hear you say, 'You can always count on me no matter what the weather, Miss Hornbeck.'"

Besides *Wild Wings* and the ornithological journals, Roger devoured Ernest Thompson Seton's *Two Little Savages*, about a Canadian boy named Yan who yearned to live in the woods (like an Indian, he believed). Upon being sent by his parents to work on a farm, Yan recruited a friend, Sam, to live like an Indian with him as time permitted. The author, who founded the Boy Scouts of America, filled pages with pointers about everything from tepee construction to fashioning bows and arrows. All necessities Yan and Sam gathered from animals and plants around them. Seton's inviting page marginalia depicted wildflowers, paw prints, feathers, tree leaves, and the boys engaging in various escapades.

Birds were prominent in Yan and Sam's story:

> *They passed a barn with two hundred pairs of Swallows flying and twittering around, a cut bank of the road had a colony of 1,000 Sand Martins, a stream had its rattling Kingfishers, and a marsh was the playground of a multitude of Red-winged Blackbirds.*
>
> *Yan was lifted up with the joy of the naturalist at seeing so many beautiful living things.*

Roger was Yan.

He was also impressed with chapter 16, "How Yan Knew the Ducks from Afar," in which the protagonist, in his Indian alter ego of Little Beaver, told a story about the problems posed by the bird guides of the time:

> *He found lots of difficulties and no one to help him, but he kept on and on . . . and made notes, and when he learned anything new he froze on to it like grim death. By and by he got a book that was*

some help, but not much. It told about some of the birds as if you had them in your hand. But this heroic youth only saw them at a distance and he was stuck. One day he saw a wild Duck on a pond so far away he could only see some spots of colour, but he made a sketch of it, and later he found out from that rough sketch that it was a Whistler, and then this wonderful boy had an idea. All the Ducks are different; all have little blots and streaks that are their labels, or like the uniform of soldiers. "Now, if I can put their uniforms down on paper I'll know the Ducks as soon as I see them on a pond a long way off."

The boys traveled to a store in town where all the relevant species of duck were sitting, stuffed, in locked display cases. Yan sketched all the "little blots and streaks" representing each duck species' uniform, and through his creator, Seton, drew two black-and-white plates for *Two Little Savages* showing twenty-four species of river and sea ducks in male and female plumage. All ducks faced in the same direction; all reflected size differences; all featured the markings that a birdwatcher could see at a distance to identify each species.

No such field guides existed during Roger's boyhood. Like Yan, he learned birds the hard way. There were a few bird books like Reed's, but none highlighted the information needed to tell one bird species from another, especially similar looking species. Reed's little paintings were rarely presented so that similar species could be compared, and often showed the birds in artful poses without depicting their trademark uniforms. The side view of the rose-breasted grosbeak showed little of the male's scarlet breast. The female cardinal resembled a cedar waxwing, while the cedar waxwing displayed features of the male and the female cardinal. The descriptions were just as useless. Read this discussion of the cardinal: "Noble in carriage, beautiful of plumage, amiable in disposition and excellent singers are some of the qualifications of these large-billed birds."

Another favorite volume of Roger's, *Handbook of Birds of Eastern North America* by Frank Chapman, the conservationist and founder of *Bird-Lore*, was actually worse. Over five hundred pages of small print and densely packed with enough information for a textbook, the book's narrative tended to overwhelm the otherwise pleasing plates by Fuertes and line drawings by a familiar name, Seton. Chapman described the robin with the same meticulousness with which he approached the rest of the book:

> *Top and sides of the head black, a white spot above and below the eye; rest of the upperparts grayish slate-color; margins of wings slightly lighter; tail blackish, the outer feathers with white spots at their tips; throat white, streaked with black; rest of the underparts rufous (tipped with white in the fall), becoming white on the middle of the lower belly; bill yellow, brownish in fall.*

Roger would later say Chapman took several lines before arriving at the robin's most important field mark, its red breast. With books like these, how could anyone, other than the most dedicated people, learn their birds? The conservationists weren't going to swell their ranks with such impractical works, even if authored by fellow conservationists. Like Chapman, Reed advocated bird protection—and that children be taught about birds: "If our boys and girls are educated to realize the economic value of the birds, and are encouraged to study their habits, the desire to shoot them or rob them of their eggs will be very materially lessened." What were the birds' economic value to man? Chapman explained: "Birds are Nature's most potent checks upon the undue increase of noxious insects and harmful rodents; they devour the seeds of weeds and act as scavengers. . . . Without the services rendered by birds, the ravages of animals they prey upon would render the earth uninhabitable." The trick was how to get this message out. The National Association of Audubon Societies had the right idea with Junior Audubon, but birdwatching in the United States remained a rare pastime.

After graduating from high school in 1925, Roger Tory Peterson worked at the Union Furniture Company in Jamestown decorating lacquered Chinese cabinets. By that November the seventeen-year-old boy had enough money to make his first trip to New York City and attend a meeting of the American Ornithologists' Union at the American Museum of Natural History. He never divulged whether he was nervous to leave home, even for a few days, and meet men many years his senior who seemingly knew everything about his favorite subject.

Roger had been painting birds for a few years—flycatchers, vireos, ducks, geese, chickadees, waxwings, and a species of shorebird much besieged by hunters, the Wilson's snipe. Two of Roger's paintings, a ruby-throated hummingbird and a kingbird, were on display at the museum for the AOU event. He recalled some decades later:

> For three days I attended the sessions. . . . There I met Ludlow Griscom who was then a young man with black hair, [wildlife artist] Francis Lee Jaques who had just started his distinguished career at the museum, Arthur Allen of Cornell, and even . . . Frank Chapman. . . . The climax came when I was introduced to Fuertes. . . . Just what the great man* said about these [Roger's] drawings I do not remember, but I know he was kind. . . . Later,

---

* Roger would eventually be dubbed "The Great Man" by admirers.

as we walked down the broad steps to the first floor of the museum he reached into his inner coat pocket and withdrew a handful of red sable brushes. Picking out a flat one about a half inch wide he handed it to me, saying: "Take this; you will find it good for laying in background washes." I thanked him and before we parted he added: "and don't hesitate to send your drawings to me from time to time. Just address them Louis Fuertes, Ithaca, New York."

The Jamestown teen hesitated to take Fuertes up on his offer. Two years later, the older artist was killed in a car accident at a railroad crossing. Fuertes remained the bird painter whom Roger would cite countless times as his paramount artistic influence. A review by an older Roger of Fuertes's approach could have described his own philosophy of bird portraiture in future years:

The most difficult thing for a young bird artist to master is knowledge of pterylography, or the geometry of feather pattern. It seems complex, and yet, in a live bird it reduces itself to rather simple and beautifully arranged patterns. Fuertes understood this early and made full use of it. . . . His touches of foliage and accessories are always good. He never improvised as much as . . . some of the other bird painters. He apparently used real vegetation to work from, and studied its structure as carefully as he did his birds.

As important as the Fuertes meeting to Roger was his brief introduction to some young men who would become lifelong friends. He long remembered a "special get-together" in Frank Chapman's office at the American Museum of Natural History where Edward Howe Forbush showed attendees Fuertes's original plates for volume one of Forbush's *Birds of Massachusetts*, a favorite of Roger's. "So that all of us could see better, Forbush perched on a small stepladder while he held up one painting after another. At the foot of the ladder were two teenagers, Joseph Hickey and Allan Cruickshank."

High schoolers Hickey and Cruickshank were members of the Bronx County Bird Club, which they and seven other Bronx boys—of Irish, Scottish, Jewish, and Polish extraction—had founded a year earlier. Roger would have to wait before he could join the club. When he did, he made up for lost time.

During the first half of 1926, Roger, a champion letter writer, made the acquaintance of a high school senior and fellow nature enthusiast, Russell Walp, of Youngstown, Ohio. Their long-distance friendship gave the Jamestown youth his first taste of notoriety, albeit among the limited membership of the Nature Correspondent Association, Walp's assemblage of about seventy young people who loved some aspect of nature. The group issued a quarterly newsletter, *Passenger Pigeon*, with Walp as editor and Roger as "curator of birds," then staff artist and adviser to fellow NCA members on issues of art and photography. Walp announced to members in January 1927: "Roger Peterson . . . is going to study art in New York."

Moving that month to New York City, Roger painted furniture in the morning (sometimes evenings too) and spent afternoons in classes at the Art Students League and later the National Academy of Design. He also regularly spent spare time with the Bronx County Bird Club, catching up with them at meetings of the Linnaean Society of New York, a club of amateur naturalists. Home was in Brooklyn with the family of Bernie Nathan, a fellow member of the Nature Correspondent Association.

The Bronx boys' policy was to admit only Bronx residents to their ranks, but they agreed to make an exception with Roger. "I was the first non-Bronx member of this club," Roger said. "In fact, I hung around so much they couldn't get rid of me. They had to let me in." Purportedly because of Roger's "constant and generally disparaging remarks about the avifauna of Bronx County," Joe Hickey teasingly called him "Roger Tory *Jamestown* Peterson."

The club members profoundly affected one another. "They were so particular about how they made their [bird] observations," says Joe Hickey's daughter, Susi Hickey Nehls.

> *Whenever they found something valuable, [they considered] who they should report it to. And I think that there were so few people that found any value in the field of bird study at that time—especially in their age group—that their camaraderie with each other inspired them to continue on, each of them in their separate paths, to . . . take bird study to something unique in each of their lifetimes.*

Birdwatching was for the tough-minded, not the weak-kneed. At Linnaean Society meetings, the Bronx club members subjected themselves and their bird-sighting records to merciless cross-examination by the society's President, Ludlow Griscom, an assistant curator of birds at the American Museum of Natural History. Griscom was as known for his gruff manner as for his field skills. Roger would credit him with his acquisition of the "philosophy and fine points of field recognition," things still in their infancy as bird enthusiasts weaned themselves from the era of shotgun birding. He and his Bronx friends were Griscom's "most apt pupils," he later wrote.

Griscom's 1923 volume, *Birds of the New York City Region*, was the unofficial textbook of the Bronx boys. Not exactly a field guide, most of the book was an "Annotated List of the Birds." The text sometimes provided excellent field marks, other times just a note about the species' distribution, telling where to seek the birds in the Bronx, Central Park, suburban New Jersey, or Long Island.

Still in high school back in Jamestown, Clarence Beal envied Roger's freedom, teasing in one letter: "The Bronx Boys must be a bunch of toughs, certainly not the kind supposed to trip after the dear little birdies, and our Roger may come home with a gat in each hand, shunned by all respectable women and not a few of the other kind. (Hoping I am not painting the facts)."

Like any mother whose only son leaves home, Henrietta Peterson fretted over Roger's well-being, why he neglected to send regards to his father and sister, and whether he was associating with the right sort of young women. Mrs. Peterson also did his laundry via the post office. And, like the typical young man, he was likely reluctant to read her many admonitions.

Periodically, Mrs. Peterson worried about her son's lack of interest in church. "Rev. Lundgren lives in Brooklyn," she observed. "Why don't you look him up & go to church once in a while? I would not keep from church altogether. . . . It will develop the spiritual as well as the physical & intellectual side of one's nature."

There was the Case of the Missing Coat, which amplified an early developing trait in Roger wherein life's practical matters were not his main concern. For some time after Mrs. Peterson mailed him his spring coat in May 1928, she wondered why he hadn't received it, finally ascertaining that it had been lost in transit. He was to make a claim for its insured value at his local post office, but never got around to it. Exasperated, she finally wrote in October: "I had it insured up to $25 so you ought to get something out of it. If you don't need the money I do. By that I don't mean to say that you should give it to me but just to let you know that if you don't want it get it anyway & I could pay off my dentist bill."

Occasionally, although Roger's father—crippled with a bad leg, suffering from rheumatism, drinking excessively—worked as often as he could at the Art Metal Company in Jamestown, there were money problems at home. Sometimes Mrs. Peterson had to borrow from her son's savings. "Roger, I'm going to ask you a favor," she nervously wrote. "If you can let me have it answer at once by return mail. You see, by the 1st of June a large payment is due on the house and I lack $26 to cover it. Also Margaret's [high school] graduation is now on hand and I need extra money. So I thought if you would let me draw $50 or $55 out of the bank from your account just as a temporary loan I'd appreciate it." Roger always gave his mother permission to withdraw funds from his account.

Mrs. Peterson believed that she had to warn her son away from risky female relationships. Roger protested that he ought to be able to date women. His mother responded: "I did not mean that you should have no fun & not go with girls, etc. Only when having that sort of a good time one must be careful of the company one keeps. . . . So have all the fun you want to but still be careful & watch your step."

Roger's mother was proud of his ability to quickly assess his surroundings—something any naturalist must do even in urban areas. A Jamestown friend had been to see him in March 1927 and relayed a favorable report home. Mrs. Peterson wrote to her son: "Stanford wrote home to his mother that you looked awfully nice & clean[,] also your fingernails & that a body would think you lived in New York all your life, the way you found your way about. He wrote that you knew more of N.Y. in 2 months than Adelle did in 3 yrs. That was quite a compliment I thought."

Although Mrs. Peterson often spent several lines asking Roger if he hadn't written because he was sick, she was reassured after he enclosed a recent picture: "Everybody liked your picture you sent home, you seem quite strong & not at all starved in spite of the fact that you always wrote . . . that you did not seem to gain any [weight]. You surely gained some muscle by the looks of things." That's what immersion in the outdoors, hiking for miles on end, and climbing trees did for him.

After a session of the Art Students League in 1927, Roger still had enough money for some traveling. Being a well-read bird student, he wanted to meet a legendary South Carolinian bird man named Arthur Wayne. In looking back at the visit, Roger was nonjudgmental about Wayne's initial notoriety as a procurer and stuffer of wild birds for paying customers. Wayne's biggest client was a wealthy New Englander named William Brewster who had amassed an enormous private collection of stuffed birds that he used for his avocation of bird study and for whom the American Ornithologists' Union named its prestigious honor, the William Brewster Memorial Award. Prior to enactment of protective legislation and Audubon wardens, Wayne and others were able to shoot and collect, in unlimited quantities, all birds, including the dwindling-in-number ivory-billed woodpecker. But Wayne went on to be considered an important ornithologist and wrote the first guide to the birds of his home state. Roger, the keen student, wanted to go where the knowledge was—and where the birds were.

After this trip Roger returned to Jamestown to earn more money so he could continue with art school in New York (he returned there in January 1928). While in Jamestown he and Joe Hickey became dedicated pen pals. His letters to Joe itemized the species and numbers of birds he saw on his field trips; in one letter, Roger described Arthur Wayne: "Mr. Wayne is quite a character—slight of frame, & growing old, red hair cropped close & spinach whiskers, reminding one of [movie comic] Chester Conklin.—Usually he elaborates on his ailments but when he is feeling good he'll tell of his remarkable experiences. . . . He claims to have added more birds to the known ornithology of one particular region than any man living & I don't doubt that a bit."

Wayne had referred the eighteen-year-old to an acquaintance at the Preparation Room of the Charleston Museum, Alexander Sprunt Jr. Sprunt remembered meeting Roger thusly: "Making a somewhat bedraggled appearance, his belongings in a sack slung over his shoulder, he said it was his first trip to the South. . . . His funds amounted to thirteen dollars."

Sprunt and colleague Burnham Chamberlain allowed Roger to accompany them on a three-day trip to Cape Romain in the South Carolina Low Country. Roger later reported to Joe Hickey the guilt he felt in essentially causing the death of a few birds. It was his skill in bird identification, apparently exceeding that of Sprunt and Chamberlain, that led to the birds' untimely demise:

> *Indirectly I was responsible for the deaths of several birds!—Don't tell anyone—I'm ashamed. The taxidermists [Sprunt and Chamberlain] were bent on obtaining specimens for the museum. We were on Cape Island—a fine place. I called their attention to a shorebird coming in across the water—I said, "See that Dowitcher coming in?—hasn't he got a whale of a bill?"—"Danged if he hasn't" said Sprunt.—Chamberlain banged away at it and missed. It lit alongside of two regular Dowitchers and the difference was very apparent—It took off just as Chamberlain fired again.—I myself would hardly have relied on my senses to actually record such a nondescript bird but Sprunt & Chamberlain said that the identification was practically positive—It was a long-billed Dowitcher! . . . It was my fault that a lot of other birds were shot— Sprunt took a look over a bunch of shore birds & pronounced them all Dowitchers. I said there were more Knots than Dowitchers—but only one was in high plumage—I pointed the latter out and as they flew Sprunt banged away at that particular bird & 5 Knots & 2 Dowitchers dropped! I had to turn away. I wish I had agreed that the whole bunch were Dowitchers—anyways they needed them at the museum.*

Here Roger offered his companions not only a glimpse of his birding talents but an early look at the absentmindedness for which he would become known, which often kept him from considering his bodily needs. Birds did this to him. The teen borrowed a skiff early one morning and didn't return till sundown. Sprunt recalled: "We knew he could not have had anything to eat all day. He lived in a sort of trance the entire time and after dinner usually sat on deck, staring with a rapt expression across the waters. . . . After the first day we saw to it that he took food on his solitary jaunts and that he changed occasionally into dry clothes."

After hearing Roger's stories, including tales of Arthur Wayne, Joe Hickey jokingly lengthened Roger's name by another syllable, calling him "Roger Tory *Wayne* Jamestown Peterson."

The following year, Roger met another legendary man in his first trip to Cape May, New Jersey, an ideal place to search out abundant migrants. Roger, Clarence Beal, and a New Jerseyan, Edwin Stearns, hitchhiked

southward across the state of New Jersey. . . . It turned out that Clarence Beal's uncle, Walker Hand, with whom we were to stay at Cape May, was a bird man. And it was at his modest home that we were introduced to Witmer Stone, one of the great field ornithologists of his time. Smiling benignly beneath his white moustache he seemed to enjoy thoroughly the three boys who plied him with so many questions. We heard of great rarities and red-letter days: the time four wood ibises [now called wood storks] were seen at Lighthouse Pond, and the time when he . . . [and others] spotted a Mississippi Kite on the road to Higbee's Beach.

Several members of the Bronx County Bird Club, including Hickey and Cruickshank, attended college while Roger sent himself to art school via jobs in furniture decorating. Russell Walp had enrolled at the University of Michigan in the fall of 1926, majoring in biology. Roger's sister, Margaret, entered college in the fall of 1929. Mrs. Peterson joyfully told him:

> *Margaret is going to Elmira College this fall. She was accepted. You see she got a regents University Scholarship this summer. She will work for her board. It is all arranged through Mr. Persell & the President of . . . Elmira College who is a personal friend of Mr. Persell. Then too she worked as a dining room girl this summer that gave her experience in that line so she ought to see herself through with the aid of a loan that is also offered her through the loan fund of the college. We are all going to help her. Don't you think it is great?*

Later in the fall, Mrs. Peterson advised Roger that "I have been sending . . . [Margaret] a dollar or two off and on. Because every time they turn around they get stuck for something—labratory [*sic*] fees etc. and then she needs little necessaries like paper[,] stamps[,] soap, toilet articles etc."

Roger expressed pleasure to his friends concerning his sister's fortune. But in later years he would complain that he'd been told there was no money for him to attend college and resented that his sister had gotten help, as she never realized her potential. "The first time Roger took me to see his family, we stopped at the house where his sister lived with her family," says Barbara Peterson. "At that time in my life, I was always dressed in a neat, tidy [outfit] . . . . Anyway, Margaret came downstairs with a child in her arms looking a bit frazzled. . . . She looked at me and said, 'Oh, I always wanted a suit.' But she said, 'You know, I've tried to make six of them, and I've never been able to finish one.' That was Margaret. . . . [Roger] didn't have much patience for his sister, I can assure you."

Although in the late 1920s Roger was developing his talents in art and birding, his future was unclear. He confided doubts to Russell Walp, who kindly wrote in response: "No, Roger I think you are doing right, your opportunity will come, don't envy me, because I think you have a bright future before you. Maybe I have gone to [*sic*] far, but by all means don't give up your painting and stick to it and give it all the necessary time."

Of course, Roger had his dreams. When during the summer of 1927 he heard of Fuertes's premature death, he wrote from Jamestown to Joe Hickey: "I guess I'll have to take Fuertes' place now." A month later, he wrote Joe about a letter he received from an Australian pen pal that prompted another wish: "He says parrots of different kinds swarm in the shade trees of the city streets. Believe me, I'm going to go there sometime—(?)—Tis but an idle dream however."

Of all Roger's acquaintances, few were more essential to the fulfillment of his dreams than a local journalist named William Vogt.

His school readers told him about Wilson and Audubon, the first and last American naturalists. Yan wondered why no other great prophet had arisen.

—Seton, *Two Little Savages*

William Vogt, a polio survivor, wrote a nature column that appeared in several Westchester County, New York, newspapers. He made Roger's acquaintance in an unlikely place, the men's room at the American Museum of Natural History. Roger was washing paint from his hands. Vogt wanted to know why. A friendship was born. Later, Roger took credit for teaching Vogt about birds.

Roger took the newspaperman birdwatching on Sundays. "He would show me the flowers, and I would reciprocate by showing him birds," Roger remembered.

Vogt's columns attracted the attention of state officials, who recruited him to manage a bird sanctuary at Jones Beach on Long Island. This he did for several years. It became a favorite meeting spot of the Bronx County Bird Club, to which Vogt had appended himself. Said Roger: "We . . . had parties at the old shooting lodge and then . . . [went] birding around the pond."

On a Bronx club outing along the Hudson early in 1930, searching for eagles and canvasbacks, Roger brought along some of his patternistic sketches to facilitate bird identification in the field. The sketches included little arrows drawing attention to what he thought were the most salient field marks. Roger showed them to Vogt, who was so excited by their potential that he urged his friend to create a field guide—and didn't let up until Roger agreed to embark on the project.

By the summer of 1930 Roger had taken his project to a new place—Maine.

He would strive and struggle as a naturalist. When he had won the insight he was seeking, the position he sought would follow, for every event in the woodland life had shown him— had shown them all, that his was the kingdom of the Birds and the Beasts and the power to comprehend them.

—Seton, *Two Little Savages*

John Aldrich, later a scientist with the U.S. Fish and Wildlife Service, had run the nature program at Chewonki, a summer camp for boys of society's upper echelons, in Wiscasset, Maine. Upon graduating college, he was to take a job with the Buffalo Museum of Natural History. The camp's director, Clarence Allen, knew he would need a replacement. While interviewing at the museum, Aldrich had a chance meeting with a young fellow "who seemed to know something about birds," and recommended the fellow to Allen, who hired the youngster blind.

Allen's first contact with the fellow may have made him think twice about his hiring decision, for Roger Tory Peterson sent him a telegram that read: "If you want your camp naturalist send me $39.40. I'm broke." The camp director obliged and two weeks later:

Roger arrived, on foot, having walked the six miles from the Wiscasset railroad station into camp—for the very good reason that he was literally broke.... He arrived with his two heavy suitcases and dusty from the long walk from the village. It was not his shy smile nor the quietly spoken "I am your nature counselor," but it was something else that set him off from the score of college men gathering to help us launch another camp season.... Looking back after forty years, I have to assume that the effect on my wife and me at that first encounter ... may have astonished us just because the Allens had not been face to face before with undeveloped but potentially great genius.

Allen's son, Doug, was small when Roger arrived at Chewonki but has some distinct memories of him. "He looked like a bird, to be insulting but truthful.... In the evening, sometimes, we'd sit on the back porch of the farmhouse, which was the headquarters, at the camp, ... and Roger would say, 'Okay, I'm going to call in a meadowlark' or a this or a that, and he'd chirp and whistle and so forth, and by God, invariably, whatever he was calling in would show up. He really had a way of communicating with these creatures."

Roger and the elder Allen were kindred spirits. Clarence enjoyed identifying birds by sight and sound. It was only natural that Roger's knowledge of and devotion to nature in general and birds in particular would be embraced by his boss. Says Doug of Roger's influence: "I'd say he reinforced the fact that Chewonki, unlike other camps that I've heard of or visited, was really dedicated to nature and birds. . . . I suspect, before that, at Chewonki, . . . there was no real advocate of birds. That he was the first one who really ran with it."

Chewonki would never be the same, the camp's current director, Don Hudson, confirms. "It's fair to say that . . . the deal was sealed when . . . [Allen] hired Peterson, because from that point forward, it was clear that Chewonki was going to have a strong nature program." The preeminence of natural history at the camp was institutionalized.

It helped that Roger had a way with young people. He'd had no teacher training nor formal higher education other than art school, but "Clarence nurtured that teaching side of him," says Hudson. Allen was the headmaster during the school year at the prestigious Rivers School outside Boston. Roger was the perfect protégé. Hudson adds: "The kids loved him. He was like the pied piper."

One of the activities that Roger instituted, which survives to this day, is "Mystery Corner." The day's programs still begin at the same converted chicken coop where every morning there would be a new natural history mystery. "It may be an animal part, skull, or a feather from a wing, or it might be a plant to identify. Mostly plants and animals, sometimes maybe something geologic as well," says Hudson. Over the course of the summer, the campers who did best at Mystery Corner received a reward.

Lee Peterson, Roger's younger son, followed his father to Chewonki three decades later*, teaching some of the same pro-

---

* By this time, says Hudson, the camp was run by a nonprofit foundation. Boys of different backgrounds attended.

grams. Roger's imprint on the camp was omnipresent: "It was definitely there when I was teaching natural history." Besides Mystery Corner, Lee continued another idea of his father's, still used at the camp. "He'd instituted a program of flow charts where the kid's name would be on the left-hand margin and above there'd be columns of certain disciplines learned, kind of like the Boy Scouts where they have their various merit badges."

More fun for the boys than tracking their growing nature knowledge were other activities, still current. "Roger was a big fan of sort of roaming around in the woods and exploring, learning as you went," says Hudson. "Then he'd come back, and I'm sure they'd use that big chart on the wall of the nature museum to record everything that they'd seen and to quiz people on, 'Well, do you remember this?' We still do a lot of that informal exploration, which kids love to do. . . . Early morning bird walks—I don't think they were done at Chewonki until Roger came along. Now it's an institution. . . . Clarence kept that going after Roger left."

Campers would run delightedly to Clarence Allen to tell him about what they had learned that day with Roger: how to identify the male Monarch butterfly, why it was that goldfinches nest late in the summer, how to distinguish between evergreens. Toward the end of the summer of 1931, Roger had an invigorating experience with a moose, which he shared with campers. He wrote to Joe Hickey:

> *Just before camp broke up I got a slick Graflex picture of a moose— a big bull—within forty feet!—After photographing it I chased it half a mile right thru the center of camp & across the baseball diamond so that every kid saw it!—In fact the thing turned & charged me once when I was tagging at its heels—wow!—was I ever nonplussed! One quick dive into the Hemlock Bushes saved me.*

Roger realized that opportunities awaited him through camp contacts. "Allen introduced Roger who came from, you know, a working family in western New York, . . . to people of wealth who were able to make decisions that could change somebody's life if it had a money component to it," observes Hudson. Among the illustrious offspring who attended Chewonki were relatives of Woodrow Wilson, the Roosevelts, and Charles Lindbergh.

Allen ended up being Roger's benefactor. At the end of Roger's second summer at Chewonki in 1931, the Great Depression was almost two years old and close to hitting bottom. It wasn't a time of opportunity for a young, unemployed male like Roger, however gifted he was. Allen asked him if he'd like to teach natural history at Rivers School. The offer included "bed and board, a quiet place to work, and some pay" and thus the young teacher would have a job year-round. While teaching at the school, Roger could devote free time to his field guide. Allen's secretary at Rivers would be available to type the manuscript.

Now a man of the Boston area, Roger could reestablish contact with birding mentor Ludlow Griscom, who had left New York in late 1927 for the Museum of Comparative Zoology where he became the research curator of zoology.

But Roger was frustrated. Despite uneasiness with Sprunt and Chamberlain shooting birds for the Charleston Museum, he had come to do some licensed "collecting"—or shooting and skinning—of birds himself. This was something that anyone with ornithological aspirations was expected to do; it also helped in painting some species for the field guide. Weirdly, bird protection laws actually conflicted with the latter endeavor. *And* he wasn't getting dates after a clumsy breakup with his girlfriend. Using choice language, he complained to Joe Hickey:

> *Dammit!—I don't like Massachusetts at all—I find that I cannot draw books out of the Boston Public Library because I live in Brookline—I cannot get a collecting permit because bird painting falls under the head of "personal gain"—Hell! A person can't do a goddam thing around here—Can't get along with any of the local*

babes because they're all "debs" & their mamas don't favor school teachers. . . . Just now, my sex-life is the thing I'm worried about.

An employee of the Austin Ornithological Research Station in Cape Cod was birding one day when a car containing several young men pulled up. Spilling out of the car and observing how he went about identifying birds, "they looked down their noses at me," says now retired biologist Roland Clement.

> *They said, "Don't you know the Peterson field mark system?" They were from the Rivers School where Roger Peterson was teaching. Of course, Roger hadn't published his field marks. But these kids had been trained on the field marks. They were showing off. I didn't know the system. I knew most of the birds pretty well. That was my first hearing of Roger Peterson, in 1933, the year before he published the field guide. Because of that experience, I decided to go back to school to see if I could make a living working with birds instead of just watching birds.*

The Nuttall Ornithological Club, dominated by stuffed shirts of Boston Brahman lineage who still tended more toward bird-in-the-hand identification than new member Ludlow Griscom's method of calling a species by sight, was initially loathe to admit the supremely confident twenty-four-year-old Roger Tory Peterson, a mere natural history teacher of humble origins. "The first time I was put up for membership," Roger once said, "I was blackballed by some member who said I was too cocky about the [bird sighting] records I turned in. And so I wrote the field guide and they finally let me in."

Griscom, with the stature of a museum curator, successfully moved to "untable" Roger's membership nomination in 1933. He had a hand in the publication of Roger's guide too, but not before Roger's friend and encourager, Bill Vogt, as a one-time, starry-eyed literary agent, unsuccessfully marketed the finished product to four different, skeptical publishers.

In writing the guide and drawing his sketches, the fledgling author had spent countless hours in the field honing his bird identification skills, and more hours again studying bird skins and laboratory specimens at Boston-area museums and universities. When Vogt failed to interest any publishers, Roger took his manuscript in the summer of 1933 and went to see Francis H. Allen, an editor at Houghton Mifflin at Two Park Street, Boston. Allen (no relation to Clarence) was an avid birdwatcher, head of the Massachusetts Audubon Society, and a Nuttall member, who was as likely to spend time dictating letters about a rare bird sighting as he was actually editing a manuscript. According to Paul Brooks, the young editor who shared his office with Allen, the elder editor liked what he saw in Roger's work and recommended it to his colleagues. But there was another hurdle—Ludlow Griscom's approval.

Roger later learned that Allen "brought in Ludlow Griscom . . . and seated him at the far end of the long table in the Houghton Mifflin board room in Boston. He then held up one plate after another. Without hesitation, Ludlow identified every bird."

That was all Francis Allen needed. But the publisher wasn't going to be rash about compensating the author for a book to be sold for $2.75 at the height of the Great Depression. The (much less useful) Reed guide, which Roger had used as a boy, could still be purchased for only a dollar. Roger remembered:

Houghton Mifflin . . . planned to print 2,000 [copies]. . . . I was told, "It's an expensive book—with four color plates. Therefore we can give you no royalty on the first 1,000."

Well, I was absolutely flabbergasted on the date of publication [April 27, 1934]. It was a wonderful thing to walk through Harvard Square, and to see in the co-op there a whole window full of my field guides! Of course, the book was literally gone on the publication date. Then they scrambled around getting it reprinted, which took several weeks.

It quickly became a new world for birdwatchers. Peterson protégée Fleur Ng'weno, a conservationist-naturalist in Kenya, describes the aftermath of this watershed event:

The Peterson field guides—the first bird books aimed at the general public—opened the eyes of millions of people. Birds became something they could watch and identify and learn more about and travel to see. For many it was (and is) something of a sport, but for most bird-watchers it is more than a hobby—it becomes the doorway to a way of life.

Consequently, says Ng'weno, "Roger should be remembered as the 'father of the environmental movement.'"

In the short term, twenty-five-year-old Roger's *A Field Guide to the Birds,* which covered the eastern United States, served as a springboard to his teaching on a national level, on the staff of the still struggling National Association of Audubon Societies.

Chapter Two

The Boy Wonder
and the Conservative
Conservationist

In November 1934 a new executive director took charge of the National Association of Audubon Societies. John Hopkinson Baker, an investment banker and an arch political conservative, also a birder and a conservation ideologue, was elected the previous year as the association's chairman of the board. He selected Roger Tory Peterson to head the association's education department. Several turbulent years, however, preceded these changes at the association.

The successor to the association's founding executive, William Dutcher, had been T. Gilbert Pearson, a North Carolinian college professor who brought his jeweled tongue and principled passion to bird protection (he founded the International Council for Bird Preservation) and helped pave the way for federal legislation and a landmark treaty that eased the pressure on the association and its allies to be everywhere at every moment defending birds. The Migratory Bird Treaty was signed by the United States and Great Britain (acting on behalf of Canada) in 1916. The federal legislation, labeled the Migratory Bird Treaty Act, was originally enacted in 1913 but had been under court challenge since then. All suits were dismissed once Congress ratified the treaty in 1918. As a result, the U.S. Biological Survey was empowered to ban market hunting and springtime hunting (while limiting the length of the lawful hunting season), establish bag limits, and enumerate bird species, such as most types of shorebirds, which were protected from hunting.

One would have thought that with such a resounding victory on behalf of birds, the association and Pearson wouldn't have to mollify disgruntled members. But there *were* disgruntled members and they courted the sympathy of young Roger Tory Peterson. Back when he was still decorating furniture, attending art school, and roaming the wilds of New York with fellow Bronx County Bird Club members, he and his friends were one day almost literally hauled off the streets to assist a conservationist named Rosalie Edge in toppling the National Association of Audubon Societies.

Edge, a one-time suffragist and a life member of the association, had founded the Emergency Conservation Committee in 1929 with two other dissidents, Irving Brant and Willard Van Name, responding to what she believed were Pearson's ineffectual efforts to restrict bag limits and shorten the hunting season. Action was urgent because wetland draining was accelerating to expand agriculture, placing ever more pressure on waterfowl numbers. Edge and her conspirators accused the association of being in cahoots with gun manufacturers. Wishing to reach out to the association's membership and lure it to her cause, she sued the association for its mailing list and won.

"Like a lot of young men, who were her major acolytes—not women—he was fascinated by her power and her drive to reform the Audubon Society," says Rosalie Edge historian Dyana Furmansky about Edge's recruitment of Roger. "Young men thought she was really something. They were in awe of her. . . . He came to her house at 113 East 72nd Street and he helped her stuff envelopes. . . . She and Willard Van Name were openly talking about undoing the Society. And Peterson was amazed to hear this."

Fifty years later, Roger remembered those days vividly:

During the month of May, I sometimes saw Mrs. Edge. . . . She had her binoculars in the Ramble in Central Park near 79th Street just across from the American Museum [looking for migrant

*warblers]. . . . She'd taken an interest in our small group of teen-
agers known as the Bronx County Bird Club. . . . Several of us
were invited to a couple of the secret meetings chaired by Willard
Van Name in Mrs. Edge's apartment, where they planned their
attacks on Dr. Pearson and the Audubon Society. . . . As a naïve
teenager, a country boy from Jamestown, New York, I sat with
open mouth at these secret meetings, not fully aware of what all
the fuss was about.*

The feud between Edge and the association worsened when
she perceived foot-dragging concerning the carnage at Blue Mountain in Drehersville, Pennsylvania, along the Kittatinny Ridge.
There gunners congregated and shot hundreds—ultimately thousands—of migrating birds of prey for fun or spite. Most of the
birds died quickly; many suffered for days before succumbing to
their wounds. Pearson failed to act because, when he sent Robert
Porter Allen to check reports of the carnage, Allen saw nothing (it
was the wrong time of year). Then Edge leased the land where Blue
Mountain sat, with an option to buy, to keep gunners away. She
beat John Baker, then chairman of the board of the association,
who had moved to act but not swiftly enough. Edge established
the Hawk Mountain Sanctuary. Baker found himself at odds with
her for the next few decades.

Furmansky believes Roger appreciated Edge's activism but,
while devoted to birds, he was "apolitical." Perhaps because of his
love of birds, and the talent she saw in him, Edge forgave him for
accepting Baker's job offer.

"Mrs. Edge somehow continued to accept me as a friend and
not belonging to the enemy camp," Roger recalled. "We were always
good friends. It might have been my youth. I don't know."

"Roger Tory Peterson was so talented that he probably was
going to go wherever he went, anyway, but she was an influence,"
says Furmansky. "She showed him that there was a place for him
to do what he loved with birds." Edge was not just confrontational,

but a firm believer in nature education. "The pamphlets that he helped stuff into the envelopes," Furmansky notes, "He read them! . . . This was all educational material."

John Baker was active in the Linnaean Society when Roger arrived in New York in the late 1920s. But the young artist really came to the investment banker's attention when, in November 1933, Baker took note at the American Museum of Natural History of several color plates and drawings for Roger's upcoming field guide. "It was exactly the sort of thing that he could appreciate—the fact that I was very systematic in my approach to teaching. The field guide is a teaching device, really," Roger said later. "At that point I was teaching school in Brookline, Mass., at the Rivers School. I therefore had teaching experience and he thought a person who had both that and the expertise in natural history was what he wanted."

National Audubon Society historian Frank Graham Jr. regards Baker's decision to bring Roger aboard more cynically. "Baker was rather an arrogant individual, very ambitious to make something out of the Audubon Society under him. And I think he saw that Peterson was almost a tool in doing that. He cultivated Roger. Put him out there in front. Made use of him whenever he could. Because Roger had that ability to attract people to the movement."

By November 1934 Roger was a minicelebrity of rising prominence. It couldn't end with the field guide, with its diagrammatic illustrations and simple language. One could credit Baker with tremendous foresight.

"The magic of Roger was he was able to simplify things," says bird tour leader and author Peter Alden. "He prided himself on being a true word artist, in that he could take the 10 or 20 most pertinent facts, that you most needed for recognition of various birds, and put it all in three or four sentences. . . . Roger was able to pick through the clutter and find out the key differences by word, and then eventually also with his paintings."

Roger wrote in the field guide that the Carolina wren was "the largest and reddest of the Wrens; as large as a small Sparrow; *rufous-red* above and buffy below, with a conspicuous *white stripe* over the eye."* The flamingo, he said, was an "extremely slender rose-pink wading bird, with a broken 'Roman nose'; as tall as a Great Blue Heron, but much more slender."**

In teaching field identification, Roger was "fortunate in possessing sufficient artistic ability to bring out . . . field marks in original drawings, which are in black and white as they should be, while all the species of the same group are represented in exactly the same position which facilitates comparison," read a review in *The Auk*. "The Ducks, for example, . . . we see . . . sitting sideways on the water, while in another [plate] they are depicted on the wing. The Gulls are all shown in a hovering position. . . . In the Sparrow plates little arrows point to characteristic and distinctive markings."

Did Roger think he was contributing to science? Yes, and no. "It is the discovery of rarities that puts real zest into the sport of birding, a zest that many of us would like to interpret as 'scientific zeal' rather than the quickening of our sporting blood," he wrote in the beginning of *A Field Guide to the Birds*, acknowledging that "old timers minimize the scientific value of this type of bird

---

* Frank Chapman's Carolina wren was "above *bright rufous* or *rufous-brown* without bars or streaks; feathers of rump with concealed downy white spots; a long, conspicuous whitish or buffy line over eye; wings and tail rufous-brown, finely barred with black; underparts ochraceous-buff or cream-buff, whiter on the throat; flanks sometimes with a few blackish bars."

**Chapman said the adult was "beautiful rosy vermilion, scapulars and underparts somewhat paler; flanks carmine; primaries and secondaries black; bill red-tinged at base, black at the tip."

work. Truly, it has but little. Recognition is not the end and aim of ornithology, but is certainly a most fascinating diversion—and a stage through which the person who desires to contribute to our knowledge of ornithology might profitably pass."

Pulitzer Prize-winning scientist-author E. O. Wilson once wrote, "The beginning of wisdom, as the Chinese say, is calling things by their right names." Of Roger's first field guide, Wilson says, "The style he introduced of focusing down on the diagnostic traits of each species and indicating them with a clear field mark was brilliant. In other words, he abstracted the bird, to some extent without destroying the reality of it, and brought our attention to how to quickly tell them apart at a glance."

Wilson has immense admiration for him: "Roger Tory Peterson was a great scientist. He was a far better scientist and more productive and influential than the majority of professionally trained scientists. . . . He acquired and transmitted a great deal of new knowledge about birds. . . . He definitely made important contributions to the growth of ornithology and, therefore, science."

Was Roger a scientist—or a sorcerer? Clarence Allen told of a weird display of sensory acuteness that would become familiar over the course of Roger's life:

> *The party [of birdwatchers] was something more than mildly surprised to see the famed leader of the walk lie right down on the ground and close his eyes just as soon as the party reached the appointed place. . . . His well-known sleeping habits* could hardly account for this lack of courtesy and interest in the purpose of the walk. Just as those in charge began to feel some explanation was in order for this embarrassing behavior, Roger got up and then and there reported on a score of birds he had identified by their chips*

---

* Roger was that rare birdwatcher who loved sleeping late. He also was capable of falling asleep anywhere at any time.

and chirps as they flew overhead. Later, for the rest of the walk, he led the party to spots where they found exactly the birds he had picked out of the thin air.

As Baker's underling, Roger suppressed his sorcery. Work at Audubon headquarters, 1775 Broadway in Manhattan, was mundane. At Baker's behest, Roger reorganized the "service department"—the division that sold things like books and birdhouses—and assembled a catalog of its offerings. Next was revitalizing the Junior Audubon Club, which had helped spur his interest in birds as a boy. "In the early 1930s," he remembered, "the . . . [association] lost half of its membership. It was down to only 3,500 when John Baker took over. . . . Someone said it was because of Mrs. Edge's attacks on Pearson and the Society with her pamphlets. Others contended it was because of the Great Depression when eighteen million people were out of work. Many more were hungry. It was probably a bit of both." Attracting children would help the cause and the association.

This meant a field trip. Over a two- or three-week period, Roger visited schools, met teachers, and toured children's museums to get ideas for bolstering Junior Audubon and, especially, for improving the old Junior Audubon leaflets. Reflected Roger: "The leaflets were . . . almost like minor ornithological papers. In other words, written as though the authors expected their peers to pass judgment on them. . . . They were not really written for children." He left his meetings with teachers convinced he would have to rewrite the leaflets twice—once for children up through about age nine, and once for older children. "I had used those same leaflets years ago and it seemed quite extraordinary that 20 years later I should have the task of doing them over. These leaflets sparked me and now they would spark others."

As Roger had been taken with Ernest Thompson Seton's use of marginalia in his writings, he decided to add his own to the new Junior Audubon leaflets. And he devised materials for teachers to use in the classroom. In time he would rewrite and redesign dozens of educational leaflets about different bird species, as well as leaflets focusing on regional avian specialties. By 1939 proving early on his credentials as an all-around naturalist and not simply a bird specialist, he would be responsible for fifteen meaty pamphlets in a series titled Nature Study for Schools, initially premiered in *Bird-Lore* and then reprinted for distribution. Among the topics were marshes, soil, water, grasslands, forests, nature trails, and small nature museums.

Twenty-three of the Junior Audubon leaflets would become the basis for Roger's second book, *The Junior Book of Birds*, published in 1939. It was supplemented with his paintings, as well as those of his artistic forebears—Fuertes, Brooks, Bruce Horsfall—whose works had decorated leaflets he read as a child in Miss Hornbeck's class. It also was decorated by Roger's marginalia, as inviting as Seton's had been a generation earlier. There were birdhouses and bird feeding trays, but also common yellowthroat fledglings nuzzling each other on a branch, starlings swarming a tree, a Baltimore oriole constructing its hanging-sock nest at the end of a twig, a towhee scratching the earth for seeds.

In *The Junior Book of Birds* one could imagine Roger talking to the boys at Camp Chewonki or to children he began teaching on association speaking engagements. None of it was fanciful, and it usually had an ecological message:

> *You have heard people say that so and so is "silly as a Goose." If they mean a tame Goose they are right. But a wild Goose is very clever. It needs to be. With all the trouble it has, a stupid bird could not live very long.*

Can you swim under water? It is slow work, isn't it? A Loon can swim under water as fast as a man can walk on land.

The Bobolink is the bird with the upside down suit. Most birds have the light colors on the breast and the darker colors above. But not Bob. It seems as if he were in a hurry when he dressed.

If you had to travel half the distance around the world each year and change your clothes each trip you would probably be in a rush, too. That is just what Bob does. . . . When Bob starts north he looks like a large Sparrow. He changes his traveling suit as he goes.

Some people are jealous of the bird. They do not like to see it catch fish which they want for themselves. This is selfish. What is more, most of the time the Kingfisher eats fish that you and I do not want—minnows and chubs. . . . Why should we mind, then, if the Kingfisher fishes in our lake?

It is not wise to set birds and animals free where they do not belong—or plants either. Have you ever tried to dig dandelions out of the lawn? Dandelions were brought to the new world by man, and now they are everywhere. They cause us much trouble. [About the starling, introduced in the United States from Europe during the 19th century]

Lecturing to children sometimes fostered surprises. Roger's first teaching engagement outside the Rivers School happened not long before he joined the association staff. Bill Vogt arranged for him to make a presentation to 1,400 people, mostly young-sters, at the Brooklyn Academy of Music—the opening act, as it were, to a Douglas Fairbanks movie. He had his four-by-five glass lantern slides, which he'd meticulously colored by hand, and Allan Cruickshank, whom he'd dragged along, to assist with bird calls.

"I remember starting out with a ghost story about the screech owls that haunted the cemetery at the north edge of Jamestown,"

Roger said many years later. "While telling the story I imitated the screech owl and then I said, 'From a distance came an answer.' Allan Cruickshank, who was in the balcony, then imitated the answering screech owl. That was just fine. The kids thought it was great."

The audience received a few more bird imitations well, too. Then came a mishap involving one of his hand-painted slides. "At one point, I had a slide on the screen of a chestnut-sided warbler. . . . My commentary was a bit long at this point, and I heard the kids tittering and laughing—I looked at the screen—and horrors!—because of the heat of the projector, the chestnut-sided warbler was melting off the screen."

Early in the Baker years Roger was handed a crowded schedule and sent all over the Northeast. Once he had to give five lectures in two days. Another time, he gave eleven lectures in four days. Fighting the flu, he still had to show up for a school talk. On other occasions, because of his packed calendar, he had to turn "mental flip flops," as he would later put it. A garden club, a private boys' school, urban schoolchildren, and an art school all required a different, sometimes a radically different, approach.

It eventually became clear that Roger and other association employees, like new staffer Cruickshank, deserved to have their time managed more wisely. Sometimes, "We would be able to accomplish little else," Roger said. "We had to more or less work things out. And so by trial and error, we found out what would work, what wouldn't work. And eventually we became professionals."

Occasionally, Roger revealed more of himself than he might have intended at these public appearances. Atlanta artist Richard Parks recalls how Roger came to have strong ties to the Georgia Ornithological Society. Two Emory University students started a birding journal called *The Oriole* in January 1936, which became affiliated with the Atlanta Bird Club. One of the students had badly traced a Fuertes orchard oriole painting for the journal's cover. They contacted Roger at the National Association of Audubon Societies for his opinion of the journal. He offered to do an original orchard oriole line drawing for the cover and they accepted. In December 1936 he traveled to Atlanta to speak to the Atlanta Bird Club.

"I don't think he came down just to do a program at the Atlanta Bird Club Christmas Banquet," says Parks, then a lad of sixteen and an aspiring bird artist who attended the banquet. "I assume he was making a tour around the eastern United States— and Atlanta was just one of his stops." During his talk, Roger showed the banquet guests some of his lantern slides. At a breakfast the next morning, he became an honorary lifetime member of the brand-new Georgia Ornithological Society, formed by Atlanta Bird Club members hoping to bring "bird students" together from across the state. *The Oriole,* with Roger's oriole on it, became the official organ of the Georgia group.

Parks wasn't at the breakfast meeting. Roger had given him something to think about the night before: "That's the first time I'd seen him. I talked to him, of course. Told him I was a bird painter. . . . The only thing I can remember that he told me was that he sweat blood when he painted. And I couldn't understand it—why it was such an ordeal!"

"He was a perfectionist," Roger's second wife, Barbara, says of him. "There's no doubt of that. If he was doing a sketch, he worked on it so it would be *right*. . . . He did the very best he thought he could. . . . He worked very hard."

One of Roger's mentors, Frank Chapman, had founded *Bird-Lore* with a conservationist mission in 1899 (its motto was the highly quotable "a bird in the bush is worth two in the hand") and published it since then. *Bird-Lore* was loosely affiliated with the association for many years and allotted space to its activities. When John Baker took over the association he proposed buying *Bird-Lore* from Chapman, who was overwhelmed by publishing duties in addition to his myriad ornithological endeavors. Chapman agreed. Baker hired Bill Vogt to edit the magazine and made Roger its art director, assigning him the task of giving *Bird-Lore* a new look.

It needed one. "The cover of the magazine with its old-fashioned design and Gothic lettering had the look of a religious journal," Roger reflected forty years later. "It fell to me to design the new cover. Although I had once attended lectures by Frederic W. Goudy at the Art Students League, I was not a skilled calligrapher; nevertheless, I came up with some new lettering." From the January/ February 1935 issue onward, Roger provided most of the new, original cover paintings for *Bird-Lore*. The first one was a rough-legged hawk "on the wing over a wintry landscape as viewed from above by another hawk." Each issue's painting also featured his distinctive—rather spooky—signature, R T PETERSON, with paint from the R, T, P, and N eerily dripping. (Roger changed his signature after someone said it looked like bird droppings.)

The transformation of the association didn't end with the Junior Audubon Club and a magazine makeover. In June 1935 Baker sent Roger to the Maine coast to make a reconnaissance of areas suitable for setting up a summer camp. "John Baker felt that the junior clubs could only reach, with considerable effort, a certain number of children," Roger recalled. "His idea was to have a place where we could train the teachers. This would be like the ripples on a pond. One youth leader could influence hundreds of individuals during the course of that person's career."

The place Roger settled on was Hog Island in Muscongus Bay. For promotional purposes (including a screening at the annual association convention in October 1935), he took silent movies with an old Bell & Howell 35 mm camera, while a *Life* photographer named Charlie Jacobs took stills. Roger captured footage of the entire area—spruce trees approaching the edge of rocky shores, waves washing over impressive boulders, nesting colonies of double-crested cormorants and herring gulls (each boasting growing young), and the active, bulky nests of ospreys and bald eagles. The young artist made a cameo appearance in the film, erecting a no-frills blind on Eastern Egg Rock to watch herring gulls from. First, he confidently placed the supporting rods on a precarious-looking surface, threw a dark cloth over them, carried his scope and tripod inside, and disappeared. Roger's then trademark prominent forelock of hair drooping over his face was just visible. On screen, his prose beckoned: "Teachers and other nature students are cordially invited to come to the . . . Audubon Nature Camp—to live among the birds and animals of these north woods. At the camp enthusiastic instructors hold the key to nature's secrets."

Unfamiliar with the concept of film editing, John Baker was upset with Roger for consuming footage just to get things in focus and forbade him from further filmmaking for the association. Unaware of the decree, Audubon Camp director Carl Buchheister, whom Baker had ordered to arrange for the filming of the train arrivals on opening day—June 10, 1936—asked Roger to catch people on celluloid as they disembarked. Later Buchheister meekly informed Baker that Roger had so hurriedly set up the camera at the station as the first train pulled up that he'd forgotten to put film in it.

Roger was the main bird instructor that summer during six two-week sessions. His assistant was Allan Cruickshank. Scott Weidensaul, who teaches at Hog Island in its current incarnation as Maine Audubon's Hog Island Audubon Camp, says, "One of the things we do every summer . . . when we teach field ornithology, we take all the adults to a little town called Medomak which is just across the channel from the island. And there's a . . . walking route that we follow through this little hamlet of Medomak that was laid out in 1936 by Peterson and Cruickshank."

In the 1970s, reminiscing with Roger about that first year at Hog Island, Buchheister said,

I remember one thing, Roger, that used to be a great thing at the camp, was your indefatigable energy and your constant pitch of enthusiasm that you had, even when you weren't teaching. And weren't on so-called duty. . . . Maybe it was 10 minutes before the dinner bell, . . . and all of a sudden you would hear a crossbill . . . up in one of the spruce trees and you would yell out and the next thing you know, everyone in the camp would gather around and you would point the crossbill out to them. And the good thing about that was that there was constant excitement and constant teaching. And at the table you would discuss with the students about birds, and fields and deer and wildlife and conservation. It was all very eager and enthusiastic.

The main bird instructor acquired a reputation for having an eye for the female campers. "I wasn't there, and I know nothing about it," laughingly recalls Virginia Cadbury, whose brother-in-law Joe Cadbury took Roger's place at the camp in 1937. "Except the stories that I'd hear about him. His love of the lady campers. You know? . . . He took them out owling. These were just stories I heard."

Roger cast some blame for his reputation on Allan Cruickshank, later contending that, when a new group of female campers arrived, "Cruicky" would jokingly tell them, "Now, if you're good, Roger Peterson will take you on an owl walk." At least some of the women assumed—perhaps hoped—that Cruicky was serious. After all, Roger was an unattached, tall, lean, physically fit, youth with intense blue eyes and, as his friend Florence Jaques put it, paraphrasing Keats, a "what-can-ail-thee-knight-at-arms" look about him.

He did take women owling, and got into trouble for it. Frank Graham wrote: "At one point Peterson asked for and was granted permission to keep 'some campers' out past ten o'clock at night to go 'owling.' The exemption [to curfew] lasted until Buchheister discovered that Peterson always limited those expeditions to a party of himself and the comeliest lass in camp."

The rumor is that this is why he was replaced the next year by Joe Cadbury.

That Roger could be injudicious when it came to the natural history errors of others didn't help. Five days into the Audubon Camp's first year, John Baker received word of a botany instructor named Young who was becoming known for his mistakes. Despite concerns about the conservation of rare plants, Young dug up clumps of vegetation to use as instructional props. Baker, worried about bad public relations, mentioned in a letter to Buchheister that he just "discovered that Ralph . . . , who got back this morning from the camp, passed word on to Lester Walsh that Roger Peterson had caught Mr. Young misidentifying something. So I had Ralph in and told him he ought to know enough to keep his mouth shut. The same applies to Roger and any other member of the staff there."

Or maybe Roger lost his camp position because he fell in love and became distracted from his duties.

Roger met his first wife, Mildred Washington, at the camp in its opening year. Was she, with her ingenue looks, one of the notorious late-night owlers? No one has said. But she was a blue blood, a great-great-great-great-great-great-granddaughter of George Washington's uncle. She did love birds, an affinity inherited from her mother, Dorothy. Although Virginia Cadbury was of Mildred's generation, "It was Dorothy we knew, who was a very interesting woman. Different. . . . She carved beautiful birds." Mrs. Washington hosted Carl Buchheister and each new crop of campers at her Maine home for mint juleps.

Mildred and Roger married in December 1936, days after his Atlanta Bird Club talk. Physical compatibility didn't mean good communication. They quarreled horribly at their wedding.

A blowup at the camp in the summer of 1937 uncovered Roger's emotions. In an August 12, 1937, letter to Carl Buchheister, John Baker instructed in his authoritarian style: "Roger will come up Friday night, the 20th . . . , and unless you hear from him to the contrary will want to be met at the station Saturday morning, the 21st. He will have my permission to stay at the camp through Sunday, the 28th . . . , but I presume that he may prefer to spend part of that time at the Washingtons. It is to be understood that he is not to be running back and forth all the time but is to stay at the camp while he is there."

On August 28 Buchheister wrote Baker on camp stationery, ironically illustrated with Roger's marginalia, recounting the trouble Roger and Mildred had brought. They arrived on the Saturday afternoon expecting she could stay the week. Buchheister took Roger aside to say that Mildred could not; neither could he travel between his in-laws' home and Hog Island. Roger "became very angry," protesting that Baker had said nothing before he left New York. Buchheister countered that Baker had announced at the summer's start that wives were not to accompany the men.

Roger wouldn't remain unless Mildred could; Buchheister let her stay the night. The next day, the couple absconded to the mainland. Roger returned alone, remaining at the camp without Mildred the balance of the week. But he was furious and told Buchheister that Mildred was, too. Buchheister wrote to Baker:

> I understand that she refuses to come here even for a short visit during the day, for she feels that your rule forbidding wives to accompany their husbands . . . is directly discriminatory against her. For your own information, Roger is quite upset and resents the fact that you did not tell him that Mildred was not to come here. Of course, I did my best to convince him . . . why you, as an executive, wished your men not to have their wives accompany them. . . . Roger felt so upset about the matter that he was in a pretty bad state of mind for three days after he arrived. . . . Roger intends to speak to you about all this Monday morning.

Frank Graham once described Roger, referring to the young artist's time as a wunderkind of the association, as "moody." Graham elaborates:

Hearing some of the old-timers, . . . [like] Carl Buchheister, talk about him, he would have these moods and he would sort of want to be alone. You could hardly reach him at times. That would be in the evening at parties, and so on. He'd go off by himself. They'd all get together in the evening, but he was not a person who would fit in well and tell anecdotes or anything like that at parties. Of course, in the field he concentrated on birds.

Wrote Florence Jaques: "He lost his shyness when birds were concerned and could be eloquent on that subject at any time."

Roger's son Lee remembers his father remarking, while watching an Olympics telecast, "If I had been an athlete, I probably would have been a figure skater." Lee assumed this was "because of his personality that he would do some event that did not involve a team sport." Roger was not a team player. He didn't have the skills for working in an office atmosphere. There was his disregard for bureaucratic requirements.

Wrote John Baker to Carl Buchheister in November 1937: I do hope that the slides sent to you for your talk Sunday will have been satisfactory. Roger pulled one of his absentminded stunts and informed us yesterday . . . that he needed slides to lecture on Monday. It put us in rather a jam." Roger had known for months that this lecture, advertised in an affiliated club flyer, was coming up and didn't request slides until the last minute, a breach of office rules.

The boss had had little regard for any of Roger's office insights well before this, as demonstrated in letters from early 1936 between Baker and association board member Roger Baldwin. The latter commented: "I . . . get the impression that . . . [staff]

initiative is not encouraged, and they do not feel that they are in your confidence as to your plans and purposes or those of the Executive Committee and Board."

Baker thought he was accurately reading between the lines of Baldwin's letter when he responded:

> I gather that you got the impressions that you did from talking with Roger Peterson. I probably don't take him into my confidence as much as some of the others on some matters but purely for the reasons that he is always way behind in the assignments which have been given him and that I want to minimize getting his mind on other things until he gets the artistic and writing work done which has been allocated to him. Moreover, on matters of office system and things of that kind, his ideas are not of much value. Please appreciate that I recognize perhaps more than even you do the full value of Roger's abilities and actual and potential service to the Association, and I am one of his greatest boosters.

Then Baker dismissed Baldwin's concerns about his not encouraging the initiative of staffers as "just bunk."

Days later, Baldwin revealed: "I got the dope about the office not from Peterson but by putting questions to the whole staff committee plus Peterson at a lunch. I'll be glad to go into it with you."

Baker's imperiousness continued as Bill Vogt's revolutionary stripes surfaced. Resenting for some time Baker's autocratic ways, on April 5, 1938, he staged an office revolt with the assistance of staffers Robert Porter Allen, Irving Benjamin, Richard Pough, Lester Walsh—and Roger. They circulated a manifesto in a direct challenge to Baker's authority. This just infuriated their anti–New Deal, Republican chief. In a memorandum to association board president Robert Cushman Murphy, Baker fumed:

> With the Administration in Washington inciting defiance of authority, individual and class hatreds, disrespect for law, and

*strikes, I suppose it was too much to expect that all of our employ-
ees would remain entirely immune to this influence. Throughout
most of the workd [sic] people now seem to be engaged in sub-
mitting to or defying dictators, and claims are loosely made that
any exercise of authority constitutes dictatorship. Mass indiciple
[sic] and incitation of hatreds bankrupt nations, and will likewise bankrupt an association.*

He also recommended, among other things, that the Staff
Committee, comprising the department heads, be dissolved, as
it had given said heads delusions of grandeur; that department
heads not present reports to the board since doing so would
imply "incompetence of the Executive Director to present these
matters"; that all staff take summer vacation at the same time to
ensure full staffing for most of the summer; that "there can be
no such activity in any organization as forthright disobedience;
[that] the alternative to loyalty and obedience is resignation"; and
that the salaries of all "loyal" (i.e., nonrebelling) employees be
increased effective May 1.

The memo led to board president Murphy and board members Roger Baldwin and Guy Emerson meeting with the rebels,
reproaching them, and forcefully suggesting they apologize for the
mutiny. "No words were minced and they [the mutineers] had little
to say in reply," wrote Murphy in a letter to Baker. "All wanted to
go back to work except Roger Peterson, who stated that he wished
to resign from any connection with the Association. We dissuaded
him from this, however, and asked him to stick on the job, forget
the past, and start again from scratch." Murphy urged Baker to
take this squelched rebellion as an opportunity to approach his
staff anew: "I believe that no mutiny ever got in under way unless
there had been some shortcoming in the behavior of the captain."

Baker heard from Guy Emerson, the treasurer, about a pay
raise for the loyalists: "It appears to me like whip-cracking, and
is not consonant at all with the more friendly approach which

you undertook to make, with a view to the specific result of better general office morale, good feeling, friendly cooperation. I'm just 100% against it."

Immediately following the meeting with Murphy, Baldwin, and Emerson, the mutineers issued a written apology to Baker. They pledged to destroy all copies of the manifesto and asked forgiveness for "personal aspersions, whose inclusion was solely the result of the angry mood in which the memo was written." Although even Bill Vogt had signed the apology, Baker quietly demanded his resignation effective the end of the year. To keep Vogt's career intact and without a black mark, board president Murphy had arranged for a grant that would send him to Peru to study seabird guano production. Vogt was, effectively, banished from North America.

"It is so far back in ancient history that I can't even recall the details," Roger said in the 1970s, claiming, "I wasn't close enough to the whole thing. . . . John [Baker] felt somehow that neither [Irving] Benjamin nor I were part of it." Or maybe Baker chose to ignore Roger's role in light of his obvious value to the association.

It should have been apparent to Roger that he was not right for office life and its politics. He likely longed to be his own boss.

By the end of the 1930s Roger Tory Peterson was able to boast being an integral part of the association's "continuous counsel to authors, editors, and writers of radio scripts." In 1938, he became *Life*'s bird artist, a position he maintained through most of the 1940s. His first contribution was several paintings showing many common songbirds and some familiar marsh birds, which were accompanied by basic information about the birds' appearance and habits. He also provided a map of bird migration flyways across

North America. The editors called Roger "one of America's most brilliant young ornithologists and bird painters." Also introducing him as the director of education at the National Association of Audubon Societies *and* the author of a "modern bird classic" could only help the standing of the association and its influence. Given *Life*'s gargantuan readership, Roger became, in effect, the birds' ambassador to America.

In 1939 Roger was especially excited about his involvement in something that would not have been of interest to the average American—the control of the cankerworm, the snow-white linden moth, and other insects in some New Jersey forests by "building up the bird population through management." His role in the project was to census birds on nine plots during the nesting season. This may have been one of his earliest exposures to controlling troublesome insects by biological rather than chemical means.

"This interlude of research each June is very pleasant and instructive," Roger said. For one thing, it got him out of the office.

He must have also thoroughly enjoyed taking attendees of the annual association convention on field trips to Cape May Point and Montauk Point along with people like Bill Vogt (before his unceremonious departure), Allan Cruickshank, Dick Pough, and Bob Allen. Roger was in his element. Members of the Bronx County Bird Club adjunct group, the Sialis Bird Club, traveled with the conventioneers to Cape May Point on October 27, 1935. Sialis founder Bill Weber remembers: "Oh, boy. Standing under that lighthouse at night, we were watching birds . . . against the moon. And Roger could pick out the sounds of the different sparrows. The Henslow's sparrow and the chippie [chipping sparrow] and all of the others. That was amazing! . . . I will never forget that." Barn owls hawking moths around the town's lampposts rounded out the magical night.

Roger gave presentations at these conventions and received further attention with the exhibition of his new oil and watercolor paintings at the events. An undated letter from Guy Emerson to John Baker from this period suggests that Roger was a bit dispirited. Emerson might have meant the paintings exhibited at the 1937 association convention when he wrote,

> I was a little disappointed in the Peterson paintings. They should, perhaps, have been framed before showing. But the birds are accurate, & something more than accurate. The backgrounds & atmosphere reflect a soul a little under wraps—a little dismal & lifeless compared to Jaques or Fuertes. But they're good—& would be much better if he was happy & had not let his painting hand get a bit frozen. Let's turn him loose on Vol. II of the field book. That will cheer him up. And then keep him painting.

Temperamental Roger did revise his eastern guide, perhaps in response to Emerson's encouragement (and because of Roger's meticulous concern with updates and corrections). This Houghton Mifflin published in 1939.

The eastern guide's second edition was fatter than the first. The premier edition had been criticized for lacking range information, but the latest contained range descriptions for all birds—a tremendous effort by Roger. It also featured new plates, such as two beautiful ones showing shorebirds standing. These joined the two plates, imported from the 1934 guide, showing the same birds flying. The revised guide also included new line drawings, such as a wonderfully lifelike depiction of the sleek boat-tailed grackle and another that showcased the long legs of the otherwise diminutive burrowing owl. The second edition further offered the length, in inches, of each bird species from bill tip to tail tip.

Said a review in the *Wilson Bulletin*:

*Peterson's "Field Guide" is too well known to need any introduc-
tion. We received it with acclaim in 1934, recognizing it immediately as the handbook for identifying birds for which we had long
hoped. It is a pleasure to report now a new and enlarged edition
with a number of new illustrations and much additional text. . . .
We are glad to learn that the author is preparing a similar guide
for the western half of the country.*

Despite his growing national stature, Roger's friends of the
Bronx County Bird Club, and its appendage, the Sialis Bird Club
of younger cohorts, remained his friends. But he could still fall
victim to one of their practical jokes in the field, even if he wasn't
the target. There was that pesky "dovekie."

As Roger later recounted in his book *Birds Over America*, the
setting was a Christmas Bird Count. Someone carved and painted
a decoy dovekie and planted it in a nearby lake where the prank's
target, one Danny Lehrman, would be sure to see it and insist
before the assembled birders that night that he had gotten the
first Bronx record for a dovekie, after which the plotters of the
bunch would "roar in derision" and reveal the hoax. As Roger
remembered it, he saw the dovekie first, and then brought it to
Danny's attention, after which they alerted others.

*There was one thing that bothered us, though. The bird listed
slightly, like a leaky toy boat. And it did not move much or dive,
but just stayed in one place, slowly turning in the current. I
explained to my less experienced companions that its presence so
far inland could be accounted for by the heavy wind and fog that
had blown in from the ocean two days before. As an afterthought,
I added that the bird looked rather sick and probably wouldn't
live through the night.*

Some birders thought they saw the bird's head move. Roger agreed. He, Danny, and others were thus prepared to claim the bird for the census that night, and did so, to their regret.

Roger was proud of his birding abilities and obviously didn't enjoy being shown up. Even so, like a good sport, he admitted his fallibility for all the world to know in *Birds Over America*. A version of this story appeared as late as the end of 1989 in *Bird Watcher's Digest*. This latter-day remembrance caught the attention in early 1990 of Bill Weber, by then a longtime botany professor at the University of Colorado, who had been tangentially involved in the prank. He wrote an account of the incident, which he sent to several friends, including Joe Hickey, who was there on that embarrassing night in December 1937:

> *The deception arose from the suspicion . . . that Danny Lehrman had a vivid imagination, and when he found himself alone along a path in the Bronx Botanical Garden, he usually was able to see some rare bird that no one else saw. . . . When we gathered at the beer garden . . . , we, the deceivers, had arranged that, if Danny were to announce the sighting of a Dovekie, all of us . . . would pound the table ten times and yell "Horsefeathers!" . . . After dinner, . . . we went around the table for each bird so that every party could give its number [seen of the species] and all of that went smoothly. . . . When we started the list of new birds for the census, one could see that Danny was getting puffed up, and we sensed what was coming. Sure enough, . . . Danny stood up and reported the Dovekie. And we all pounded the table ten times and yelled "Horsefeathers." (Nowadays we would not be so genteel.)*
>
> *The group was absolutely stunned, and Danny got all red in the face and began to stutter. What we were not prepared for . . . was that Danny protested that he had witnesses. This is when the whole thing became a disaster. Alan [sic] Cruickshank got up and explained that he . . . saw the bird and watched it for a while. . . . He*

then said that he called Peterson over. Roger got up and said that he watched it for a very long time (two hours was what I seem to remember) because the bird did not move, and he needed to know whether the bird was alive or not. After watching it for such a long time, he finally was convinced that he saw the neck move, and felt that it was safe to record it for the census.

Each time an expert . . . got up, the same table-thumping happened and the shout went up. Peterson, especially, was terribly nonplussed when it came his turn, and it was then that someone . . . explained the whole thing.

In the accompanying letter to Hickey, Weber mused, "After 53 years, the Dovekie story is still alive and well. . . . Amazing, isn't it, that Roger can't seem to lay the ghost of this terrible embarrassment of so many years ago."

Said Roger when Hickey broached the subject in the 1980s, "Well, at least we identified the species correctly."

Chapter Three

Spreading His Wings

With nearly twenty years of experience, Roger took pride in his knowledge of photography, something that would eventually become more than an avocation, bringing him gratefully out from behind the drawing board. In the early 1940s his passion for taking pictures began to spill over into his everyday interactions. In September 1941 Virginia Cadbury had been married to Bart, bird instructor Joe's brother, for about a year. She and Bart, along with Joe, Mildred, Allan Cruickshank, and Roger, were helping close up the camp at the end of the season. According to Virginia,

> We all went out to Pemaquid Point. I was into photography with a Brownie . . . , a little box camera. I had just met Roger. He meant nothing to me, really, except he was a nice guy. . . . All of us were looking at the birds. I pointed my little box camera at some gulls, and Roger came over to me and said, "Wait a minute. Let me show you how to do this." He took my arms, with my box camera, and put me in the right position. I was embarrassed to death. . . . Then we laughed about it. . . . He said, "You know, I do take pictures."

By then, Roger and Mildred were nearing the end of a passionate but stormy marriage. In the preface to his *A Field Guide to Western Birds*, published in 1941, he credited many dozens of scientists and birdwatchers with advice, hospitality, or some other kind of assistance. Amid the lengthy list of names were Mildred's mother ("Mrs. Whiting Washington"), who had provided "notes, suggestions, and other aid," and also "Mildred, who has assisted with much of the research and detail work." He also wrote, "[I owe] completion of this guide to Guy Emerson, who constantly urged me on, and to my wife, who spent altogether too many lonely nights at home during the last three years while I burned the midnight oil in my study."

Over thirty years later, Mildred would say that she and Roger were always arguing; she wanted children and he didn't, plus, while he loved her, he also loved himself. She had interests he apparently didn't share, including singing madrigals with a vocal group and volunteering at a hospital for the underprivileged, but these activities kept her busy while her husband worked and traveled. Still, they had birds in common. Mildred claimed they had had many happy times in the field, but she wasn't along in 1937 when Roger searched with others for the nearly extinct ivory-billed woodpecker in the Santee Basin of South Carolina and failed to find it. Finally, in May 1942, acting on a long-held desire to see the bird, Mildred joined Roger when he and Bayard Christy again searched for the ivorybill in the legendary Singer Tract of northeastern Louisiana, where James Tanner had done his comprehensive study of the bird's habitat and habits under the auspices of Cornell University. The Singer Tract was suspected of being the last stronghold of the giant woodpecker but was still an unprotected area increasingly threatened by logging. Roger, Mildred, and Christy found two females. About the first bird, Roger wrote in *Birds Over America*: "This was no puny pileated; this was a whacking big bird, with great white patches on its wings and a gleaming white bill. By its long recurved crest of blackish jet we knew it was a female. We were even close enough to see its pale yellow eyes. Tossing its hammer-like head to right and left, it tested the diseased trunk with a whack or two as it jerked upward."

The fact that Roger's party found no male ivorybills meant that the bird, at least in the Singer Tract, would soon vanish.

Because of the remote, inhospitable swamp where the ivorybills lived and the fact that no one had been able to find the bird elsewhere, Roger believed it might be impossible to learn when it became extinct: "Unlike the last passenger pigeon, which officially expired at the Cincinnati Zoo at 1:00 p.m. Central Standard Time, September 1, 1914, no one will know the exact time of the ivory-bill's passing."

Mildred was absent from the ivorybill story in *Birds Over America*, because by the time Roger wrote it, he was remarried.

Barbara Coulter was born in Seattle in 1919 to parents descended from Revolutionary War veterans. In the eighteenth century, her mother's side of the family had settled in western New York from Massachusetts, while her great-grandparents on her father's side had gone much farther west with the wagon trains in 1849, making the Oregon Territory their home. The Coulters lived temporarily in Atlanta until Barbara was about ten; summer vacations were spent at her maternal grandfather's farm in Spencerport, near Rochester, New York, where she developed her lifelong fascination with wild and domestic animals and horseback riding. Upon returning to the Pacific Northwest, her parents built the new family home on Bainbridge Island, across Puget Sound from Seattle, where she spent the rest of her youth until high school graduation.

"I cannot remember a time as a youngster when the old Chester Reed Guide was not on the windowsill of the family breakfast room," Barbara reminisced. "Every bird going through my mother's garden was checked and hopefully identified—poor as the

Reed guides were. We didn't know of the Peterson bible in those days. I might add that during these days I belonged to a . . . [Junior] Audubon Club. . . . [In Puget Sound] all the sea-going ducks, gulls, etc., were part of my normal daily life."

Things became less idyllic when Barbara graduated from high school. She had to make a living, but how? "Now my father was out of work, my mother was home—but somewhere my mother must have squirreled a nest egg." Mrs. Coulter used it to take her daughter to New York City and enroll her in the Katharine Gibbs School. Being a student at Katharine Gibbs meant living at the Barbizon for Women hotel. Barbara had little money. "I got breakfast & dinner," she later wrote, "& was always hungry." Nevertheless, she had to comply with the dress code, which required high heels, gloves, and a hat.

The first year at the Gibbs school focused on academic subjects, the second, chiefly secretarial skills. Upon graduation, Barbara was a "trained secretary." After two short-lived jobs, she was hired as secretary to Robert Porter Allen at what was now known as the National Audubon Society, with offices, since 1938, at 1006 Fifth Avenue.

Bob Allen was finishing up research for a book, *The Roseate Spoonbill,* about the large wading bird whose numbers plummeted in the days of the plume trade but was slow to rebound since then in Florida, one of its native habitats. "Bob was a great person to work with—and I thoroughly enjoyed taking dictation and my job," Barbara later remembered. "Roger Tory Peterson's office was right next door to Bob Allen's office. And Mr. Peterson was artistic director for the Audubon Society—was re-writing all the Audubon Club leaflets, as well as [doing] the magazine covers for the Audubon Publications and listening in on the ongoing conversations between Bob & myself as we finished the spoonbill book. . . . He told me sometime later that Bob Allen & I sounded so cheerful as we worked together—he was most envious!"

Early in 1942 and Barbara's Audubon employment, Roger and Mildred were still together, albeit shakily. Several years Mildred's junior, Barbara, with her big, all-American smile, delivered some Audubon papers along with two pastrami sandwiches to the Petersons at their apartment one day. Mildred suspected that Barbara was attracted to Roger. He was working ever later at the office. The deterioration of their marriage continued. After a final argument later that year, Mildred moved out.

Toward year's end, when Bob Allen enlisted in the army, Barbara took charge of Audubon's Photo and Film Department, renting out films and enhancing Audubon's library of black-and-white stills. Mateless Roger became interested in her, as his marriage "was not successful. He felt free to court me. One thing led to another and I married him." That was on July 29, 1943, not long after Roger had divorced Mildred. Only now, Uncle Sam had him.

Camp Chewonki was still a part of Roger's life in the early war years before he married Barbara. He missed no opportunity to teach kids about birds. By this time, Bill Vogt was back in North America and the main nature instructor at the camp. Roger visited and took small groups of boys out to look at birds. One of them was a fifteen-year-old New Jerseyan, Al Nicholson.

"Roger Tory Peterson showed me my first Blackburnian warbler," says Nicholson, who had used the Peterson guide from a young age and is today a devotee of raptors. "He was a very patient and deliberate man. He just stood transfixed, studying the . . . [trees] for small bird movement. I would never have been able to find it on my own."

At thirty-four Roger was still a dedicated teacher. "He was very kind and anxious to instill enthusiasm in young birders," Nicholson reflects. "I don't remember that he talked a lot. It wasn't like a running narrative that you have with somebody like [birding guru] Pete Dunne. . . . He was very focused when he was looking at things and [didn't make] . . . a lot of chitchat. . . . We had exchanges. They were lovely exchanges."

Would Roger's love of nature, and teaching about it, be discouraged in the army? Not if an admirer, assistant secretary of the Smithsonian Institution Alexander Wetmore, had his way. Wrote Wetmore to naval commander Charles Bittinger:

> *Herewith I enclose a brief memorandum regarding Roger Tory Peterson concerning whom I spoke to you at luncheon at the Cosmos Club two days ago. Peterson is an excellent naturalist with extended field experience. He has written two standard manuals on birds, one for the eastern states and one for the western states, so excellently that they have the full approval of his fellow ornithologists. This means that he not only paints well but faithfully as to details.*
>
> *Should you be able to mention him for some work in the service for which he is specially qualified I believe that this would be well worthwhile. He has special qualifications that I would think could be utilized to advantage.*

The attached memorandum, identifying Roger as a private serving at Fort Belvoir, Virginia, noted his authorship of "several standard books on birds and various other papers in which nature concealment plays an important part."

Wetmore's letter set off a networking chain reaction. Commander Bittinger contacted Lieutenant Colonel Julian Sollohub of the Engineer Corps' Camouflage School at Fort Belvoir, prefacing his recommendation of Peterson with an endorsement of

Wetmore's wisdom: "I have known Dr. Wetmore a great number of years and I have implicit confidence in his opinions on science and his judgment of scientists. . . . I thought you would like to know of Private Peterson's education and experience and perhaps utilize his talents in the interesting Camouflage Manuals which the Army publishes."

Sollohub informed Commander Bittinger that he was referring the matter to the Department of Training Publications. "I do know that they will attempt to find a place for him in their organization if it can be done," wrote Sollohub.

"You wouldn't think the army would be that smart," says son Lee. "They put him in a position that he was highly qualified to do." Roger had friends in high places, but his good fortune resulted from his extraordinary abilities and his collegiality.

Private Roger Peterson worked for the Army Corps of Engineers at Fort Belvoir on instruction manuals, including ones on defusing land mines and building roads and bridges. Most intriguing was his camouflage work. He designed a pattern for bridges that made them disappear. He turned sorcerer again, making soldiers vanish. Roger demonstrated these skills after the war to Ohio businessman Herbert Brandt, who took multiple ornithological expeditions to Arizona and invited top naturalists along. For periods in 1947 and 1948, Brandt had Roger's company. The younger, more knowledgeable ornithologist enabled Brandt to watch wild turkeys congregating at dusk to roost:

Selecting a spot on the abrupt slope opposite the roosting trees, and somewhat higher than their lowermost limbs, we proceeded to arrange a hide. Behind a few, low pine saplings a small log was placed, and along this I stretched out my sleeping bag. Roger Peterson and Nelson Carpenter then proceeded to cover me with newly cut pine boughs. During his . . . years in the armed forces, Peterson had served as an expert in the army camouflage section,

and he assured me, when they were finished, that even the most
suspicious turkey would not detect me there.

The scheme worked. "From my cozy place of concealment the
retirement procedure of the turkey was a thrilling, noisy affair,"
wrote Brandt. "It was a novel adventure to lie there at the keyhole
to the bedchamber of these grandest of birds, and witness their
retiring behavior."

The newlywed Petersons lived near Fort Belvoir in Alexandria. In
early April 1945 diplomat Louis Halle, strolling in Mount Ver-
non, came upon the serviceman photographing flowering red-
buds. Halle would write: "Peterson told me the flower and foliage
was between two and three weeks ahead of last year's dates, basing
his calculation on the blooming of the magnolias, now over. Who
could remember such an early spring as this, with everything so
far ahead of schedule? At Fort Belvoir young horned larks had left
their nest two weeks ago."

The Fort Belvoir horned larks haunted Roger for years. Their
saga can be traced to a short letter he sent *Audubon* magazine (the
name change from *Bird-Lore* came with the streamlined appellation of the National Audubon Society) in 1944 about a family of
horned larks. "Sirs," Roger began. "Spring birds are coming thick
and fast now. Found a prairie horned lark's nest on our drill field
at camp last week. We routed the regimental parade so as to avoid
the nest."

In a Book-of-the-Month Club news item inserted in *Audubon* magazine four years later, the horned larks metamorphosed

into upland plovers (now called upland sandpipers); other words inserted in Roger's mouth made him seem a different person than he was. Instead of the parade being rerouted in 1944 as his letter had stated, the news item claimed it was rerouted on V-E Day, May 8, 1945. The erroneous story then alleged that when Roger heard of the parade's route, he supposedly "pushed his way into the presence of the Commanding General. They mustn't march there he shouted.... That field was covered by the nests of the upland plover. The eggs would be shattered. Ornithologically speaking it would be a tragedy." When the general brushed Roger aside, Roger allegedly went to the newspapers; only then did the general, publicly humiliated, agree to reroute the march. Roger was also described as being impatient with bird lovers; he supposedly believed birds are "stupid creatures . . . [which] merit no affection."

This short piece of fiction upset Roger and apparently caused a stir among members of the Audubon Society of the District of Columbia who believed the story was true. Friend Louis Halle urged Roger to write a letter to *Audubon* to keep the tale from spreading further. In a letter to editor Eleanor King, Roger said, "I don't mind the nonsense about the upland plover and the general so much as the statements that I have no patience with people who 'love' birds and that I think that birds are 'stupid creatures.' This comes close to being damaging as my livelihood is involved here. Furthermore, it is a back-handed slap at many readers of *Audubon* magazine."

A guilt-ridden King apologized in the next issue of *Audubon*. "I made the grievous error of thinking that this item played up our Roger in a delightful and flattering way. . . . Please do not berate Roger. Reprove me, for having reprinted it. Or, if you enjoyed the story, if it made you love Roger even more (as was the case with me), let us know."

Roger explained in the magazine's letters section that he was not impatient with bird lovers. Wrote the man who admitted throughout his life that he was "obsessed" with birds: "I merely think that the term 'bird lover' like 'our feathered friends' is an unfortunate cliché, to be avoided." He attributed the false claim that he thought birds were "stupid creatures" to his "frequent assertion that bird psychology cannot be interpreted in terms of human psychology." As for the horned lark nest ("I know of no upland plovers nesting within a hundred miles of Fort Belvoir"), he noted that he wouldn't have opposed a superior officer "in such undisciplined fashion. . . . I would have been slapped in the guard house pronto. . . . We merely approached our captain with our proposal, and being a reasonable fellow, he gave orders to change our line of march."

The members of DC Audubon, which once boasted the allegiance of President Theodore Roosevelt, were an illustrious bunch. Besides U.S. Department of State insider Louis Halle were Roger's ally Alexander Wetmore; Ira Gabrielson, head of the U.S. Fish and Wildlife Service; Paul Bartsch, keeper in the early 1900s of one of the last Carolina parakeets; another senior, Millicent Todd Bingham, who had sold thirty-three acres of Hog Island, Maine, to the National Association of Audubon Societies in 1935 for its camp; John Aldrich, Roger's predecessor at Camp Chewonki and since then a high-ranking ornithologist at Fish and Wildlife; and, before too long, a young marine biologist, also with Fish and Wildlife, named Rachel Carson.

Shirley Briggs, another DC Audubon member and a close friend of Carson's, credited many of the distinguished associates of the organization with generating a "clear idea of the kind of natural history society that could be built on the tradition of the second-oldest Audubon society, with all the resources and scientific expertise in Washington on hand. All were long since using Roger's original *A Field Guide to the Birds*. But field trips were just the beginning. They soon generated ways to educate members and the general public to a broad ecological approach far beyond bird-listing."

The membership of the group grew considerably during the war years, with so many servicemen and -women converging in the nation's capital. Robert L. Pyle had been a student at Swarthmore College when he became concerned about the draft and dropped out for meteorological training, then went to work for the National Weather Service in Washington, DC. There he awaited the dreaded induction letter. During that brief period, he pursued his avocation of birdwatching, joining DC Audubon.

"You couldn't go anywhere, you know, with gas [rationing] and everything like that," recalled Pyle in 2006, adding,

> *Many of the trips were along the C&O [Chesapeake and Ohio] Canal. . . . The C&O Canal goes all the way along the Potomac River from the Washington area, all the way up along into western Maryland and West Virginia. . . . It was a tremendously great birding [site], because you had this great promenade right along the canal with the woods on one side and all the warblers were coming, and it was just terrific. Anyway, Roger would lead trips and that was one place we went. We couldn't go many, many other places because of the travel restrictions.*

Pyle remembered Roger as a "nice, quiet person always willing to help . . . [DC Audubon] members (including me) with bird identification questions."

Given everything he had already accomplished, thirty-something Roger was an automatic VIP among VIPs at DC Audubon. He was quickly recruited to lead spring walks, which he did in April and May 1944, to Rock Creek Park, and Kenilworth Aquatic Gardens. He was the star lecturer at the group's annual dinner on October 26, where he presented *A Color Cinema of Bird Life,* described in the *Washington Evening Star* as a film showing "several hundred birds of America, many species found in Washington, and one reel was devoted exclusively to rare birds of Florida." Before year's end, Roger had received his first major ornithological recognition, from the American Ornithologists' Union—the William Brewster Memorial Award.

"Roger was a recognized scientist even though he wasn't really trained as an ornithologist," says C. Stuart Houston, a diagnostic radiologist and Officer of the Order of Canada and a widely respected amateur ornithologist. "He was recognized by the museum people and the professors of ornithology in the universities all across Canada and the United States as one of them." In those days, being an amateur was not a hindrance to stature. The largely self-taught Roger Tory Peterson, a young man of humble background, whose opinions were sought by trained and untrained scientists alike, was a logical recipient of the Brewster Medal, named for a similarly iconic, untrained scientist, but of privileged background.

DC Audubon did what any self-respecting birding organization of gilded heritage would do—it instructed its secretary to write Roger a congratulatory letter.

Shirley Briggs noted that the DC Audubon members held Roger in high esteem: "We knew him as a person whose keen observation and broad comprehension led him to a remarkable range of accomplishments: painting, photography, lecturing, and writing. His skill at grasping essentials and creating logical organization of ideas showed in all his endeavors. His fresh viewpoints kept discussions lively, just as his way of seeing appealing aspects brightened his painting and writing."

During this period, Barbara worked full-time in Washington, initially as Department of Conservation head Bill Vogt's secretary at the Pan-American Union; later, she was secretary to Vogt's colleague, Jose Colom, chief of the union's Department of Agriculture. Her job metamorphosed into purchasing agent for another arm of the organization, the Inter-American Institute of Agricultural Sciences.

When Barbara became pregnant, she left outside employment. "Little by little, I became the resident secretary to/for RTP," she noted.

Barbara says, "[I] took over the minutiae of life. In the early days, when we didn't have any children, I did everything. Number one, he was a perfectly horrible automobile driver. He was scary! So I did all the driving. I did all of the managing. I did all of the food." Taking care of day-to-day, practical things enabled her husband to "stay focused."

Toward the end of his military service, Roger was assigned to do some research in Florida on a pesticide of purportedly wondrous powers against what was viewed as an insect scourge. This pesticide was DDT. Barbara recalls: "He had a WAAC [Women's Army Auxiliary Corps] who drove him around." His job, she says, was to "see how many birds fell dead" after the army sprayed the chemical. Given the small doses used by the army in these early experiments, Roger and his partner, fellow artist/ornithologist George Miksch Sutton, didn't find much of concern.

It would be a mistake to assume that Roger was not yet attuned to the problems posed by pesticide use. In 1941 he seemed to predict battles to come when he wrote: "Spraying kills the insects, but the effects are temporary. In short, we must choose between the two: to have some insects and some birds, or to spray and have no insects and no birds."

In October 1945 Roger was discharged from the service. It was a whole new world—not just for the rest of the world once war ended in September, but for Roger, who was professionally independent for the first time in his life. The seeds of his independence had been sown in the 1930s, first by his groundbreaking field guide, then by an awareness of what he could do apart from Audubon.

Through the war years he contributed to *Life* magazine. Some months before his discharge, he had depicted the mating displays of a variety of birds, from the commonly seen mallard to the less-observed ruffed grouse. Still to come were mockingbirds in April 1946, and bald eagles that July. His mockingbird feature was groundbreaking because although it was for mass consumption, it showed something that, according to the *Wilson Bulletin,* had never before been painted or photographed: the bird's stunning use of its bright, silvery-patched wings in "wing flashing" behavior, a "curious habit," Roger wrote, in which it "runs along, flapping wings when feeding." He advised readers that "ornithologists are not sure why [these] birds do this." The message? Bird behavior holds mystery worth exploring.

The bald eagle feature was significant because it presaged some of the content of Roger's first non-field-guide tome two years later, *Birds Over America,* with its spread about the life of bald eagles and their Floridian champion, a retiree named Charles Broley, who spent his free time banding the birds. It also was an early conservationist piece in a mainstream American publication. Roger pointed out that this avian symbol of the United States had been the subject of wanton slaughter for a number of reasons until finally in 1940 federal legislation was enacted protecting it.

Through the war, Roger also painted birds for the Quaker State Corporation. They weren't quite the "painterly paintings" Roger would yearn to do in his later years, but they served to acquaint the general public via mass-produced prints with the looks and names of various species.

A book published in 1941 with most of the text written by Roger, *The Audubon Guide to Attracting Birds,* seems to have provided the basis for most popular backyard birdwatching manuals since then. While the book was a National Audubon Society product with John Baker editing, Roger's writing was founded on his years of research on all manner of ecological issues housed in reader-friendly prose. As Robert Cushman Murphy wrote in the preface, "Mr. Peterson, the author of the bulk of the book, needs no introduction to bird lovers; his prowess as an artist, indeed, represents only one facet of an extraordinarily keen and scholarly student of birds and their place in nature." Roger's mental acuity in the study of birds and their environs, his devotion to the subject, and his strong desire equal to his marvelous ability to share his knowledge gave him that crucial springboard to launch his solo career.

A leading field guide author of today, David Sibley, sees Roger's "desire to educate people, to share his excitement about the natural world," as paramount. "His illustrations in the field guides were one method of doing that. Photography was one method. Lecturing was one method. Writing was another method. They were all just ways to convey his excitement. He didn't do any of those things exclusively. All of them [were] mixed together."

Much of Roger's advice in *The Audubon Guide to Attracting Birds* is detectable in the mantras found today in birding magazines and other birding guides:

> When a bird's nest is discovered do not disturb it. *The person who finds a nest should feel some responsibility for it. Frequent visits to a nest are likely to draw the attention of cats or other predatory animals.*

> *In brief, a good glass for average use is a well-built pair of binoculars of about eight power with a wide field and good light.*

A woodland with a few dead trees harbors a greater variety of birds than a more verdant unbroken timber lot. Some people despise the sight of dead trees, but the ecologist knows that it is the natural thing for every forest to have a certain percentage of dead or dying timber.

As fresh water is so scarce along the ocean shore, the few spots where this condition occurs often become concentration points for ducks, gulls, sandpipers and herons.

Roger paid homage to his mentor from afar, Herbert Job, with this passage about bird photography: "There are no open or closed seasons, no protected species, no bag limits. The same bird can be 'shot' again and again, yet live to give pleasure to others beside the photographer."

One of Roger's sources for his chapter "Attracting by Planting" was the 1939 Margaret McKenny volume, *Birds in the Garden*. Interestingly, McKenny used Roger's writings, including his 1934 field guide and the *Junior Book of Birds,* as well as his Nature Study for Schools series for the then National Association of Audubon Societies, as sources throughout her book. In citing McKenny as a source Roger was, in a sense, crediting his previous works.

In referring to his pamphlet on birdhouses, McKenny brought Roger's concern—among the earliest expressed—for the bluebird's plight to audiences beyond teachers and pupils: "He says everybody puts up houses for the wren, but it is really the duty of the conservationist to encourage the bluebird as due to the persecutions of the English sparrow and the starling it is a diminishing species."

McKenny would play a role in Roger's solo career. Upon publication of his *A Field Guide to Western Birds* in the spring of 1941, Roger wrote to Paul Brooks at Houghton Mifflin that he had "been giving considerable thought to the future extension of the series." Brooks recalled that Roger was to be the "overall editor," while the two of them would "ferret out the leading authority on each subject, and an artist to match." He parenthetically noted that "Few, like Roger, were both." Work began in 1941. The first nonbird volume in the series was to be on wildflowers, with Margaret McKenny as author. Roger became the artist by default. The artwork was an enormous undertaking—flowers tend to be seasonal. The book took decades to complete.

Other volumes on topics as diverse as mammals, butterflies, shells, trees and shrubs, rocks and minerals, and amphibians and reptiles came more quickly. Serving in World War II gave Roger the courage to "break loose and depend for his living on his royalties," as Brooks put it. He left the National Audubon Society because he had to; he was drafted. At war's end, he didn't return.

Once a month, Roger rode the train to Boston to execute his editing responsibilities, working with copy editor Helen Phillips. He was already becoming known for his nocturnal tendencies. "An owl rather than a lark," Brooks recounted, "he would not yet be fully awake, often belaboring some irrelevant subject while Helen gently but firmly brought him back to the matter at hand."

In January 1946 Roger and Barbara's first son, Tory Coulter, was born. He was a "difficult baby," she noted. Because their Alexandria apartment was so tiny, with one bedroom, a living room, and a study; Roger faced deadlines with further revisions of the eastern guide and work for *Life* magazine; and the impending summer heat could be a challenge, Barbara decided to fly with the baby to her parents in Seattle where they stayed the summer.

Roger may have sensed competition approaching. In April his former colleague Dick Pough, still an Audubon research associate, published his first in a new series of field guides to birds of North America, *Audubon Bird Guide: Eastern Land Birds*. John Baker finally could lay claim to a field guide to birds, one with the imprimatur of the National Audubon Society. (After all, Roger's guides were Roger's.) Over time, the Pough series would encompass guides to western land birds; water, game, and large land birds; and various permutations of Pough's initial three categories of guides. Pough's books were much more detailed than Roger's. While they didn't burden the birder with florid or confusing language, they went into greater depth regarding bird habitats and nests.

They couldn't really compete with Roger's guides, as he covered North America in only two volumes. He treated his water and land birds together, meaning that birders need only carry one of his guides in the field. Also, while Pough was the author, the artist for the first volume was an up-and-coming young fellow named Don Eckelberry, whose birds were entertaining and animated but not diagrammatic like Roger's. Birds were not all in the same pose on the page, nor were their salient field marks highlighted. For now, Roger's primacy in the area of field guides was secure.

Even so, behind that faraway look in his eye, Roger was an ambitious guy. "He told me that he'd set himself certain goals at certain ages, achieved them, and set another goal," says Rolph Blakstad, who filmed birds and other wildlife alongside Roger in the 1960s.

"He was never content," says Lee Peterson of his father. "He always needed to do more."

The first order of business was revising the eastern guide. But he didn't just revise it. He completely redid it! The second edition had had forty plates, four of them color, while the third, published in 1947, included sixty plates with thirty-six in color. All the text too was rewritten. He could do all this for a 1947 publication date because of his tremendous energy and a capacity to concentrate for long periods. Barbara had kept the noise down by whisking Tory to Seattle.

"He worked as hard as any human I've ever seen. And he was unbelievably prolific," says Arthur Klebanoff, president of the Scott Meredith Literary Agency, who knew Roger later in life. "He wasn't motivated . . . by money. He wasn't really directly motivated by fame—although he was famous. He definitely had a mission motivation. He definitely wanted to change the world. And he wanted to educate. But I think he did also want to prove that he was the best at what he did. That was very, very important to him."

The increase from 180 to 290 pages allowed Roger to do much more educating. For the first time, the book showed twenty-eight Roadside Silhouettes on the inside front cover, twenty-six Flight Silhouettes on the inside back cover, and twenty-three Shore Silhouettes following the main part of the book, with an answer key identifying each lifelike shadow. As a review in the *Wilson Bulletin* mused, these constituted a "ready-made quiz program for a bird club entertainment." They also showed how identifiable many birds are by their shapes and postures, regardless of field marks, which, depending on variables such as lighting conditions and distance, are not always visible in the field. Roger also for the first time used silhouettes for four small flycatcher species that were virtually impossible to distinguish in the field—the least, the Acadian, the alder (formerly Traill's), and the yellow-bellied—except he showed that the truly distinctive characters of the birds were found in their habitat and the sound and pattern of their call.

This page has evolved along with succeeding editions of the eastern guide.*

"The significance of a book like this is tremendous because its greatest influence is felt among the rapidly expanding group of people who are taking their first steps in bird study," observed the *Wilson Bulletin*.

In the next few years, Roger produced prodigiously. Some of his new bird paintings had found their way into Herbert Brandt's self-published 1947 tome, *Arizona and Its Bird Life*. Roger was the sole illustrator—of thirty-two color plates, forty line drawings, and a charming, bird-filled map—for *The Birds of Newfoundland*, in the making since 1941, which exhaustively treated 227 species of Canada's newest province. He was also credited with providing "continued suggestions and assistance in the preparation and assemblage" of the volume. Roger donated drawings to the Rocky Mountain Nature Association for a pamphlet it circulated, *The Birds of Rocky Mountain National Park*, in which he was credited with giving "invaluable critical comment on the text."

There were more Peterson books besides the field guide—coming in nearly annual succession. Roger came into his own as a writer.

---

* Since the flycatcher page debuted, the alder flycatcher has been split into two species, the alder and the willow. According to Clarence Allen, this was thanks to Roger. When Roger first met John Aldrich at the Buffalo Museum of Science, where Aldrich thought to recommend him for Camp Chewonki, Roger mentioned a Traill's flycatcher conundrum. He had noticed that the Traill's "sang one song around the shores of the Lake Erie plain and quite a different song on the hills" near his Jamestown home. At Roger's urging, Aldrich commenced a study of the flycatcher that eventually resulted in the species being split in two.

Most notable was *Birds Over America,* published in 1948, the same year as the depressing but uniquely insightful *Road to Survival* by Bill Vogt in which Vogt warned of the perils of human overpopulation and mankind's almost pathological misuse and abuse of the Earth's natural resources. While Vogt's prose dragged the reader into a maelstrom of hopelessness, Roger's uplifted by emphasizing in almost every line the beauty and the worth of the natural world and the spirituality it engendered.

Said Vogt:

And to think of "soil erosion" simply as "soil erosion" is dangerously elementalistic. Not only is soil washing into the seas but, as Jay Darling points out, bread and pork chops and potatoes. The Gulf of Mexico, off the mouth of the Mississippi, is stained with the substance from which our children build bone and muscle and blood. Those tawny waves are drowning the future of America.

Said Roger:

On some misty evenings hundreds of small birds can be seen fluttering through the brilliant lights that illuminate the tall towers of Radio City. . . . On autumn nights, when the wind is in the northwest, I sometimes take the elevator to the observation platform, sixty-odd stories above the street. There, far below, the city lights are strung like jewels to the hazy horizon, while close about me in the blackness I can hear the small voices of southbound migrants. For a few brief moments I feel as if I were one of them.

Said Vogt:

Above all, we must realize that every grain of rice he puts into his mouth, every bit of potato, every piece of meat, and every kernel of corn, must be replaced by another bit from the earth. . . . We must realize that not only does every area have a limited carrying capacity—but also that this carrying capacity is shrinking and the demand growing.

Said Roger:

We invent systems, Socialism, Fascism, Communism and Capitalism. Each despises the other. Yet, as Professor Aldo Leopold of the University of Wisconsin pointed out, they all espouse one creed: salvation by machinery. *Is it any wonder that when these systems prove faulty and men detect the synthetic nature of the civilization of their devising they turn to nature? In a world that seems to have gone mad is it any wonder birds have such appeal? Birds are, perhaps, the most eloquent expression of reality.*

Birds are the most eloquent expression of reality. This statement, or some variation of it, would be a central part of Roger's lectures and interviews for the next many decades. This is what made him want to know more about birds no matter how many hours he had already spent with them in the field. This is what made him want to share what he knew.

Birds Over America didn't just gush about how wonderful birds are. It was substantive, encompassing every aspect of birding (listing, bird censuses, studying individual species), man's relationship to birds and their environment (falconry, urban birdscapes, America before Columbus, egging, monitoring threatened birds), and bird life (migration, habitats, bird populations, pelagic life). Roger was a writer of graceful prose, as well as a historian, and a knowing but optimistic observer of the natural world.

Roger's foreword began with an acknowledgment of a by-product of birdwatching: interest in conservation. This concept, too, Roger would tout for decades to come:

One cannot give a large share of his life to this carefree hobby without soberly reflecting on the mechanics of the well-integrated world

of nature. One inevitably becomes a fervent conservationist. . . .
Such understanding comes slowly, but it does come if one inquires
more deeply into the lives of birds and is not satisfied solely with
being able to identify them.

Having received an inscribed copy of the book from Roger, Bill
Vogt congratulated him, noting that more of this sort of work was
needed to turn the tide of American society's seeming indifference
to the natural world. "We need a great many more books of this
type," said Vogt. "The lack of interest in, and appreciation of, our
outdoors . . . is growing, I am afraid, in relation to our population
and our mounting emphasis on the 'practical' aspects of survival
. . . . If we could have fifty books a year as interesting and attractive
as yours, I'd feel a lot more hopeful about our natural riches."

It's not that Roger didn't employ a serious tone where necessary in *Birds Over America*. He hadn't forgotten the struggle to save
birds from plume and market hunters. That was the world he was
born into; that changed as he grew into it. In the chapter "Sand
and Tide," the title signifying not just shorebirds but also the ebb
and flow of bird fortunes, he wrote: "Milady had to have feathers for her silly-looking hats, so the terns were shot. Two men out
of Freeport, Long Island, killed 600 in one day. . . . By 1884, the
last colony of common terns on the south shore of Long Island
was gone." Once the conservationists grew in numbers and power,
things changed:

In 1927, on the new fill of sand and shell that was pumped onto the
marsh at Long Beach, I found two least tern's nests, the first to be
seen by mortal eyes in New York State for forty-five years. There
are now at least three hundred pairs along the south shore of Long
Island each summer and at least fifteen colonies of common terns.

Optimistic Roger wrote elsewhere in the book: "More birds
have adapted to a changing world than have failed. Very few have

the narrow tolerance of the ivory-billed woodpecker or the Bachman's warbler." Between the resilience of many birds and the education of people about the needs of birds and their environment, things were looking up. Roger pointed out: "Conservation is not just an ideal that we read about; it works."

Birds Over America wasn't filled just with references to legends of the past like Arthur Wayne, but also tributes to regular people dedicating at least part of their lives to studying specific species. There was Charles Broley, the "Eagle Man," whom Roger had briefly introduced in a 1946 *Life* article. There was also Roger's good friend from the Bronx County Bird Club, Irving Kassoy, whose life's passion was studying the barn owl. In a chapter called "Ghoulies and Ghoosties," Roger wrote: "In the past few years he has dispelled more notions and unearthed more new facts about the barn owl than any man before him."

"Irv was very proud of that chapter," says Steve Kress, a Cornell University ornithologist and author mentored by Kassoy. "I mean, he was not a professional ornithologist. Of course, neither was Roger. And Irv never did write up his work on barn owls. He always wanted to. But, like a lot of things, it never really happened."

Birds Over America was Roger's first book completely illustrated by his photography. A postscript portended a rich future behind the shutter: "Photography is not as grim a proposition to me as my painting, hence I enjoy it more—more, in fact, than anything else that I do with birds."

Read a 1950 news item in the *New York Herald Tribune*:

Roger Tory Peterson, one of the country's outstanding field ornithologists and the author of several noted books . . . [on] birds, will receive the 1950 John Burroughs Medal, awarded annually by the John Burroughs Association for exemplary nature writing. . . . Mr. Peterson, forty-one, who is recognized for his ability to identify any bird in the United States by sight, will receive the award for his last book, "Birds Over America."

In accepting the medal Roger remarked, "A writer must be read, otherwise it is as if he were writing with a stick in the sands of the desert. But even if a writer *is* read he always wonders whether or not he has succeeded. This medal, therefore, gives me the greatest encouragement I have ever had, because it means that you have approved."

Roger wasn't treated like an award-winning writer, artist, and scholar at home. There was now a fourth member of the family, Tory's younger brother, Lee Allen. Barbara imposed a strict rule: "No painting in the living room." Since November 1947 home was a single-family structure in Glen Echo, Maryland, just above the towpath of the C&O Canal, at woods' edge where the "spring flush of advancing warblers can be heard from indoors," as a friend observed.

Barbara got little help from Roger around the house. "I tried him just once," she remembers. "I wanted to paint the windows in the kitchen. . . . Roger was going to help me. He got out some of the brushes. He was so meticulous—oh, egads! It was perfection. . . . I ended up doing it, because I couldn't stand waiting to get it done!"

Household hubbub didn't keep Roger from either the easel or pen and foolscap. A year after the 1948 publication of *Birds Over America,* his *How to Know the Birds* appeared in bookstores. This latest, filled with richly detailed line drawings of dozens of bird species as well as scenery typical of different habitats, was intended for children or anyone else who might have been intimidated by Roger's field guides, however user friendly they were, and who needed a primer on where and how to look for birds.

Another volume, of wider focus, followed in 1951—*Wildlife in Color,* sponsored by the National Wildlife Federation. Roger had become art director of the organization's wildlife stamp series and was making his debut known with a new book examining the entirety of the natural world in simple writing suitable for kids. *Wildlife in Color,* illustrated by more new Peterson line drawings as well as paintings from seventeen artists besides himself, profiled American habitats and regions and the wildlife living there: birds, butterflies, moths, reptiles, amphibians, warm-blooded mammals, trees, plants, and fish. If people still thought that Roger was a one-note Johnny, obsessed with birds (yes) to the exclusion of all else (no), this book should have disabused them of that notion.

Some parts of *Wildlife in Color* might have been inspired by Vogt's *Road to Survival,* given its serious treatment of the importance of healthy soil and water to all life, including human life. (Of course Roger had written on soils and other basic components of nature in his Nature Study for Schools pamphlet series for Audubon.) Somehow, Roger's educational tone regarding the sober subject of soil erosion doesn't quite bring futility to mind, as similar writing does in Vogt's book, but encourages thoughtful action:

> *How different is the journey of many a raindrop in this, the twentieth century! It falls with a splash, unchecked by leaves or grass. It finds no litter of humus to hold it until it can sink into the parched earth. Joined by an army of other raindrops it wets the surface of the ground, seals it, and trickles into the nearest rivulet. Rushing headlong, the uncontrolled water cuts away the banks, which add their brown mud to the torrent. Where the beaver dam used to be there is nothing to slow the rushing water. The beavers were trapped off long ago. The swamps which once acted as pockets for the high water to back into have been ditched and drained. So by the time our muddy creek reaches the big river there is a great flood. High water from a hundred brooks and tributaries have reached the same place at the same time. Houses are swept away and lives are lost.*

By the next page, the relieved reader has discovered an attractive tool against soil erosion—the tree: "Trees are the guardians of our streams."

In *Wildlife in Color,* Roger debuted a favorite reflection on the state of nature-ignorant modern society:

> *Many men go through life as though they wore horse blinders or were sleepwalking. Their eyes are open, yet they see nothing of their many wild neighbors. Their ears, attuned to motorcars and traffic, seldom detect the music of nature—the singing of birds, frogs, or crickets, or the wind in the leaves. These men, biologically illiterate, often fancy themselves well informed, perhaps sophisticated. They know business trends, or politics, yet haven't the faintest idea of "what makes the world go round."*

The idea was to expose the virtual wall between blinded modern man and the natural world around him—and do something about it. Roger seems to have adapted this idea from his friend Louis Halle's portrayal of the "hive" in which humankind found itself stuck in *Spring in Washington:*

> *It is curious how the preoccupations of the hive fill us. . . . Perhaps the whole human race may be said to suffer from amnesia, not knowing whence it came or why it finds itself here. . . . We have forgotten that we live in the universe, and that our civilization itself is merely an elaboration of the palm-leaf hat that one of our ancestors tried on ten thousand years ago to ward off the sun, a more complicated and ample version that now not only wards off the sun but shuts out the view.*

A call placed by salesman Robert Lewin of Brett Litho in Queens, New York, to the National Wildlife Federation concerning its stamp program brought Roger into contact with someone who would quickly become one of the most important people in his life.

Bob Lewin, born in 1911, was the grandson of eastern European immigrants who settled in the Midwest before Ellis Island was built. Lewin's grandfather and great uncle came to America as small children, alone, with notes pinned to their jackets delineating their destination. Granddad, a can-do sort, rose from itinerant peddler to banker and, finally, department store owner, until he was put out of business by a competitor. Lewin's father was sickly and died in middle age, so Mrs. Lewin ran the family shoe store in Chicago. By the 1930s Bob began shifting between odd jobs and stints as a college student. An uncle, a prominent New York orthopedic surgeon, got him a position organizing medical conventions. Like his grandfather, Lewin was a can-do sort. "It was a natural for him," says daughter Laurie Lewin Simms, "because he was very good at the big picture and putting people together and anticipating what might go wrong."

Between medical conventions Lewin got a job delivering pies at the 1939 New York World's Fair. This ended embarrassingly. Simms laughingly recounts how Lewin was "wheeling" pies when "all of a sudden something happens, the cart shifts, and the whole load of cream pies is everywhere."

By America's entry into World War II, Lewin hadn't yet found his calling. He served in the army and was assigned stateside to the Aerial Photography School, giving slide talks around the country. One such talk to a sorority at the University of Michigan brought Simms's parents together. Bob and Katie were married in May 1944.

Postwar, Bob's positive personality led him to his most important employer, Brett Litho in New York, where he became the company's star salesman. "He was actually a modified salesman reporting to a president, part of a large corporation that did a lot of printing for things like Whitman Candy Samplers and liquor labels," explains Simms. "Before it came in fashion, he was naturally an up-seller. He said, 'Well, if you're doing this, why not do this, too?'" Before long, Lewin had obtained the National Wildlife Federation's stamp program account for his employer. This meant contact with Roger Tory Peterson.

"Roger's job was to assemble this [stamp] sheet, which became very famous, for the National Wildlife Federation," says Simms.

When Roger came along as art director, he was supposed to call all the various artists, arrange for them to submit their work on time, get it photographed, assemble the images, just so, on a sheet. . . . Dad knew that Roger was tearing his hair out trying to assemble all this, and according to what Dad told me, he finally said to Roger, "Go paint. I'll call all the artists. I'll get it done.". . . I think they began this little tradition [where] Roger kind of quietly assigned the project to my father. . . . It was the coordination that was so hard for Roger—to figure out how to tell somebody that the painting they sent in wasn't going to be suitable. There were all these dynamics that go on when you are engaged in working with talent. Roger left all that to my father, from the contacts, to the coaxing, to the cajoling, to the assembly of the sheets to the enforcement of the deadlines. . . . This went on for many, many years. I remember clearly running around the halls with the Peterson kids, as we would go to National Wildlife Federation conventions in Washington. We were all very small. We were those bratty kids who ran through the halls together. My brother and I and the Petersons. The relationship began way back then—close to 1950.

What made Bob Lewin want to help Roger? "We were very much interested in nature and the preservation of the environment," recalls Katie Lewin. "So we identified with Roger and Barbara right off the bat."

"I think Bob respected the fact that Roger was so knowledgeable about not only birds but the whole field of nature," Lewin adds. "Roger knew so many fascinating people that we were delighted to be with Roger and meet his friends."

Bob believed in Roger. By that time Roger had done more than explore the Atlantic coastline. He had crossed the ocean and begun to establish an international reputation.

Part Two:

INTERCONTINENTAL MIGRATION

Chapter Four

International Range

For the next twenty-odd years Roger shared his art director duties for the National Wildlife Federation with Bob Lewin, while concentrating on writing original text for educational booklets, which featured federation stamps, and contributing occasional artwork.

Roger's old friends remained important to him. He was sentimental about Joe Hickey, who had taken a difficult path to professorhood. Joe went from coaching cross-country and track at New York University in the early 1930s to tedium as a wholesale power salesman at Consolidated Edison, New York's power provider, for the rest of the decade. He spent lunch breaks at the then National Association of Audubon Societies where he met Peggy Brooks, who edited *Bird-Lore* after Bill Vogt's ouster.

"I used to take Peggy out birdwatching before she knew her husband, Joe Hickey," Roger fondly recalled. "I used to go up to Old Greenwich, to Todds Neck, near Peggy's home. So I have known all these people from way back."

Hickey remained active in the Linnaean Society, as had most members of the Bronx County Bird Club. Roger eschewed the more administrative Linnaean posts in favor of service on the Field Work Committee, while his friend ascended more than once to the group's presidency.

A seminar studying ornithological papers with evolutionary biologist Ernst Mayr at the American Museum of Natural History proved pivotal for Joe. With Mayr's encouragement, Hickey began ambitious bird censuses, including one of all the peregrine falcon aeries in a ten-thousand-square-mile area of the Northeast. This he worked on with Cornell's Walter Spofford and BCBC mate Dick Herbert. When it came time for a promotion at Con Ed requiring an electrical engineering degree, Joe returned to school, but took twenty-two credits of biology instead. A fateful meeting with University of Wisconsin professor of wildlife management, Aldo Leopold, led Leopold to offer Hickey an assistantship at Wisconsin. Under Leopold's tutelage, Hickey earned his master's, writing a thesis that became *A Guide to Birdwatching,* a minor classic upon publication by Oxford University Press in 1943. Roger often quoted from the book's first paragraph:

> *Bird watching is old enough to have stood the test of time, young enough to lie within the age of exploration. By some, it is regarded as a mild paralysis of the central nervous system, which can be cured only by rising at dawn and sitting in a bog. Others regard it as a harmless occupation of children, into which maiden aunts may sometimes relapse. The truth is that it is anything you care to make it. It is unquestionably a hobby that can be thoroughly enjoyed for an entire lifetime.*

In 1941 Joe married Peggy Brooks. Despite his closeness to Leopold, Hickey studied for his PhD under a less-supportive luminary, University of Michigan's Josselyn Van Tyne. Joe was still writing his dissertation when Leopold asked him back to Wisconsin to work in the Department of Wildlife Management. Hickey intended to learn all aspects of Leopold's work over the next three years when the latter planned to retire. Horrifyingly, Leopold died four months after Hickey's arrival. Joe later said, "It was a disaster to *me* to lose what were going to be three wonderful years of working under him." He became Leopold's replacement, prematurely becoming teacher and administrator. Paying tribute to his mentor, he arranged for the posthumous publication, through a referral to his Oxford editor, of a collection of Leopold's nature essays under the name *A Sand County Almanac.*

Despite Roger and Joe's geographic separation, their paths would professionally and philosophically intersect at a watershed moment in environmental history during the 1960s.

Roger's old ties swept his thoughts back in time, even as late as 1949 when he began serving on the board of the Hawk Mountain Sanctuary Association. Despite the lofty stature he had enjoyed for some years, he still felt intimidated by Rosalie Edge. As fellow sanctuary director Joe Taylor recounted:

> *Roger Peterson and I were elected to the board in 1949, and since these fall meetings were to begin at noon the two of us would spend the mornings on the Lookout, coming down just in time for the meeting's start. (Peter Edge says we were always late, but he is wrong. It's just that we were never early.) Now and then, when discussions at the meetings became long and, to us, tiresome, Roger and I would quietly start our own conversation about birds—any birds. Suddenly, we would become aware that there was absolute silence in the room, and we would look up to find Mrs. Edge's imperious eagle-eyes staring down at us. No word was spoken, but our little "subcommittee meeting" was over at once.*

But Roger wouldn't be like his mentor, Mrs. Edge, and stay put. Something happened on Hawk Mountain in 1949 that would extend the range of his legend across the Atlantic Ocean to Europe and eventually all the world's continents. No longer could his life be viewed in a linear fashion. It was now starlike, an explosion of experiences and work in countless directions. On Hawk Mountain, he met British naturalist Guy Mountfort, who reminisced:

I first met Roger, appropriately enough, on Hawk Mountain in Pennsylvania in 1949. I was using Roger's Field Guide *and we fell into conversation. Within two hours we had decided to produce an equivalent European version,* A Field Guide to the Birds of Britain and Europe. *Knowing that Phillip Hollom, already working on* The Popular Handbook of British Birds, *was thinking along similar lines, we decided to invite him to collaborate. Roughly speaking, the idea was that Roger should do the illustrations, I the text, and Phil the distribution details and maps.*

What an important meeting this was. "Until 1954, we had no field guides!" exclaims British birder-lecturer Trevor Gunton, retired from the Royal Society for the Protection of Birds. "Up to then, our field guides had been virtually nonexistent and very, very poor—the things that had been produced before the war, with a lot of inaccuracies. . . . A lot of the early guides were actually painted from birds mounted, almost kind of after John James Audubon. And they were in ridiculous positions."

Rob Hume, who has worked in bird conservation for the RSPB since the 1970s and is now editor of its *Birds* magazine, also tells of that bleak time when Britons had no Peterson guide to identify their birds. "Before that, you could find information on how to identify birds, hidden away, in books like *Birds of the British Isles,* by T. A. Coward. But his was a long narrative. . . . It was a general, nice, easy read, a readable essay about each species. Within that you could find out how to tell them apart. But you had to read five pages to get there." As for H. F. Witherby's *Handbook of British Birds:* "Not many people could afford it, quite frankly. Five big, expensive volumes."

But Roger Tory Peterson was American. He'd grown up with American birds. One might have wondered how he could promptly acquire, while still mainly residing in America, the expertise necessary to do for British and European birds and birders what he had done for North American birds and birders.

All he had to do was go birdwatching. "He was very, very smart," says biologist-conservationist William Conway, former president and general director of the Wildlife Conservation Society. "Roger had a very good brain. . . . He was absolutely phenomenal . . . if you wanted to try someone out in terms of memory, as to what was here, there or elsewhere. . . . He might have been absentminded about where he put his umbrella, but he really had a wonderful mind."

Conway witnessed an awe-inspiring display of Roger's birding prowess at the 1958 International Ornithological Congress in Helsinki, Finland.

> We went birding, actually with a big pile of people—very distinguished European ornithologists. I think Guy Mountfort was there. . . . We were walking around on the grounds of the University of Helsinki, which had beautiful forests, and was a great place to bird in June. And the amazing thing to me was that . . . a bird would call, and everybody would turn to Roger to ask what it was! He had such a marvelous ear. He was better than any European birder there, with European birds. It was just astonishing to me. I couldn't get over it!

In studying all the birds of Britain and Europe, Peterson, Mountfort, and Hollom traveled across the continent, "from Arctic Lapland to Southern Spain, from Britain to Turkey, putting the final touches to their field notes and contacts with foreign ornithologists, and combing through all the relevant literature," acclaimed humanist-biologist Sir Julian Huxley wrote in his introduction to the resulting field guide. Mountfort was intrigued by Roger's work habits, noting that after their travels,

> Roger then settled down to begin painting the 1,250 required illustrations. He borrowed [bird] skins from the British Museum and I arranged for him to stay at my club in London. Roger was

*enthusiastic, dedicated and often not a little eccentric. He had
very little regard for time. I used to drop in to see him on my way
to work and, on several occasions, found him fast asleep on his
drawing-board having been painting all night.*

Birdwatching in Europe changed forever. "It became the absolute
bible," says Roger's old friend Keith Shackleton of the 1954 field
guide. "Roger was probably the best bird illustrator that's ever
been, in that he knew exactly how much detail to put in, and what
to leave out. I remember Max Nicholson, who was then head of
Nature Conservancy*, wrote the review of that book, of the European Guide, and it was one of the most laudatory reviews you
could possibly see, because what Max Nicholson said was, 'This
book is so special that if I had to part with all my library of bird
books and keep just one, it would be the *Field Guide to the Birds of
Britain and Europe*.'"

"Fifty years on, the standards that he set are still what field
guides are judged by," says Trevor Gunton. "In my opinion, and
the opinion of a lot of other field ornithologists over here, the
original book has never been beaten. It made the identification of
birds so simple! It was really groundbreaking. . . . Ordinary people
like me"—Gunton pauses to chuckle—"could actually start confidently going out in the field and identifying birds."

"Did you know it was kind of a bible for a lot of us?" muses
John Fanshawe, head of strategic development at BirdLife Interna-
tional (formerly the International Council for Bird Preservation).
"Looking through it now, I can see that a lot of his illustrations

---

* An arm of the British government established in 1949.

basically have hardly ever been bettered. They're really excellent. There's nothing wrong with them for identifying birds at all! . . . I'm just looking at the buntings. This business of placing the male and then the female partly obscured behind, using the male and female symbols on the plates—the whole thing is very similar to what is done now [in more recent guides by others]."

Rob Hume remarks:

> *Roger's book simply said, "This one has got this." "That one has got that." "You can tell them apart because of x, y, and z." And it told you exactly what you wanted to know. The sideways poses—later on, of course, I realized . . . how incredibly valuable they all are to have the birds all in the same view, the same conditions, the same scale, and so on. . . . [In the competing* Collins Pocket Guide to British Birds, *by Richard Fitter and R. A. Richardson, they would have] one bird perched, and a similar one would be flying away, and another one would be diving into the water or whatever. They were very nice, but they were not so easily comparable. It was less practical. But I thought, at the time, "These look more real to me.". . . Only later did I get the Peterson guide and realize how very good it was.*

Fanshawe believes that in Britain alone the new Peterson guide had a tremendous impact. "The growth of the Royal Society for the Protection of Birds . . . went through a massive increase in membership. . . . The popular membership of the RSPB grew dramatically, I think, in the 1960s and '70s. . . . It is possible that the arrival of accessible and easily understood field guides had a big impact on that."

According to *Birds* magazine, when the guide came out in 1954, the RSPB had 7,000 members. By the early 1980s membership had swelled to over 350,000. Was this dramatic increase in membership really because of the Peterson guide? "I'm sure it's true," Rob

Hume remarks, thoughtfully, but adds a couple of caveats. "It's a little difficult to know how things would have gone without that book, because there were at that time other people, like Peter Scott, on television in Britain. He was a sort of pre-David Attenborough, if you like. . . . He was on television popularizing wildlife." The postwar standard of living was also rising; fewer people worked weekends, more were buying cars and traveling. "Leisure time, a bit more money, a few years after the war. That sort of thing. I mean, it would be wrong to say it was just the Peterson book, but it must have had a huge, huge impact in every way, because it gave everyone a chance to tell what they were looking at!" Hume says.

The Peterson-Mountfort-Hollom *Field Guide to the Birds of Britain and Europe* was practical and portable, albeit the longest Peterson to date at 318 pages. It was also the first Peterson to include range maps. Translated into thirteen languages, it was the first truly international Peterson and not just because it covered European birds. Each species description included not only the English name but also the name of the species in Dutch, German, French, and Swedish (and, if the species occurred in North America as well, like the "little tern" did, its English name there—in this case, "least tern").

The man who did the Spanish translation is Mauricio González, a Spanish nobleman whose ancient *palacio* in the Coto Doñana of southwestern Spain was the site three times during the 1950s of expeditions by some of the world's most noted naturalists, including Roger. As a young man during the 1950s, González had been interested in birds for some time and searched for other like-minded Spaniards.

We couldn't find many people interested in birds, . . . But we did get together six fellows from six different places in Spain. . . . and we . . . decided to found an ornithological society. . . . One of us, fortunately, really knew quite a lot about [birds]. He was a real pioneer of birding in Spain. . . . Anyhow, the first thing we did was make a list of all the birds of Spain and try to establish what their proper names were, because in the '50s, well, the birds had names depending on what region they were from. . . . Or even the locality. So [for] the first job, which took about a year, we established a list of the birds of Spain, and their names, and actually we invented some names, because we couldn't find a name for them in Spain.

While this earnest group succeeded in having the Agricultural Ministry publish the list of Spanish names of Spain's birds, they wondered how these names would be accepted by the average Spaniard. In speaking with Roger and Mountfort at the start of what was probably the 1956 expedition into the Coto Doñana, González posed the question to them.

I think it was Mountfort and Peterson at the same time—they said, "Well, look—this is our book we've just put out, which is the birds of Britain and Europe. All you have to do is translate this book into Spanish and put in all your Spanish names. You'll find that people will slowly adopt your names because it's the only book out in Spain." I thought that was a very good idea and I got down to it and translated that book. . . . I had fairly recently married. I always used to tell this story that the translation nearly produced a divorce for me. . . . Every evening I was working at this book, trying to get the voices of the birds written in Spanish. . . . My wife used to get quite cross and say, "If somebody turns up and they hear you chirping away, well, they're going to think you're absolutely mad!"

González found an editor in Barcelona to publish the book. The editor later thanked him, noting he'd gotten rich off a series of nature guides because of publishing the Spanish translation of the Peterson book. "He became the only editor in Spain who was publishing field guides of all sorts. Seashells, or stars and planets, or flowers, or trees." Since publication of the Peterson guide, González says, "Spain has become really interested in birds. In nature in general, but in birds very specially. . . . Nothing much else had been published, and none with good illustrations like that, in that special way."

Roger met fellow artist Peter Scott (later Sir Peter Scott) around 1939 when Scott was visiting the United States.

Scott was an athlete and an adventurer, as well as an artist and a naturalist. His amazing versatility prompts a mutual friend, William Sladen, to call him an "all-round man," unlike Roger, whose interests and abilities were narrow by comparison. But Scott's social pedigree was steps above that of the son of working-class immigrants to America. Sir Peter Scott was the son of British naval captain Robert Falcon Scott, an explorer who died in 1912 at age forty-four with his exploration team in Antarctica after having reached the South Pole, "immobilized," as Roger put it, "by blizzards and swirling drifts." Captain Scott's instructions to his soon-to-be widow were that his baby son be "interested in natural history" and made into a "strenuous man." In 1957 Roger acknowledged his friend's myriad accomplishments without any hint of jealousy:

> He is undoubtedly the world's first authority on waterfowl, but
> he could have been almost anything he chose. He has been junior
> doubles ice-skating champion of England, an Olympic contender

in sailboating, a national naval hero in battles of the North Sea, a telecaster, directing one of England's most popular TV programs, a portrait artist of ability, an explorer, a writer of charm and an artist whose bird canvasses bring a greater price on New York's 57th Street than any American bird artist can command.

There was no gulf between Roger and Peter, who, despite the seeming incompatibility of their backgrounds and some of their interests, shared a passion for natural history.

Lady Philippa Scott didn't meet her husband's friend Roger until perhaps 1951, when as newlyweds they dropped in on the Petersons in Glen Echo. "He was very serious-minded, Roger," says Lady Scott. "He was much more serious-minded than my husband. I don't think he laughed as much as we did," adding, "They talked about birds all the time."

Even if they couldn't compete in sports, they could compete intellectually. Lepidopterist Robert Michael Pyle was fortunate to have been a friend of Peter's and Roger's and bore witness to a rivalry between the two men. Pyle and his then wife, Sally, were guests in the 1970s at the Peterson home in Old Lyme, Connecticut. He remembers:

Sally noticed first, I think, that he had a stupendous collection on the book shelf of the English series of hardback natural history books called the New Naturalist, *published by Collins. . . . He had a whole bookcase devoted to them. . . . They're very, very striking, semiabstract natural history portraits of the animals and plants they pertain to. . . . Sally and I actually had a modest collection of them, but Roger had a whole lot of them, and we both exclaimed upon that. . . . He laughed and said, yes, that he and Peter Scott had an ongoing competition to see who could get a complete series of the* New Naturalist. *He said that the two of them were the only two people they knew who were close to having a complete series of it. They were not all in print, and they were very collect-*

ible and very desirable. . . . When we went to Slimbridge and saw
Peter's collection, I recounted that episode to him and he laughed
also and said, "Oh, yes. I'm not sure which of us has more now,
but we're both pretty close." So it was a friendly competition.*

Keith Shackleton was a painting protégé of Peter Scott's in the
early 1950s, and also descended from an Antarctic explorer. His
uncle was Sir Ernest Shackleton, who explored Antarctica four
times early in the 20th century before dying of a heart attack in
1922 in the sub-Antarctic.

Roger first met Keith in April 1952, writing: "For years I had
wanted to spend a night in a lighthouse when the birds are flying;
to see the hordes of small travelers pouring out of the darkness
into the dazzling beams." He had that chance while in England
working on the European field guide. Guy Mountfort had said
the perfect time to look at migrants from St. Catherine's Light in
the English Channel was the third week in April. They decided to
take a break and go. The recently wed Shackleton, a World War
II Royal Air Force pilot, flew his wife, Guy Mountfort, and Roger
to the lighthouse. There they watched the birds fly past the light
overnight and banded those caught by nets.

Shackleton laughingly remembers:

*Roger used to dine out on the fact that he'd slept with my wife on
our honeymoon, because he'd sort of embellished the facts a little
bit. It wasn't our honeymoon. It was about three months later.
The fact is that both of them went fast asleep in the lamp room.*

---

* A wetlands preserve in Gloucestershire and home of the Scotts.

Roger used to go to sleep at the drop of a hat. In spite of the presence of these birds that had to be ringed and identified and all, he would still pass right out, and he and my wife were fast asleep in the lamp room.

Roger must have been awake long enough to get material for the first installment of his new *Audubon* magazine column, "Roger Peterson's Bird's-Eye View." He observed that most of the birds were whitethroats, a species of European warbler.

Weighing less than an ounce these tiny mites had crossed 60 to 80 miles of water by dead reckoning to be met by head winds, turbulence and rains. So tired were they when we scooped them from the air that they closed their eyes and fell asleep in our hands. This was the second sea crossing they had made on their northward pilgrimage from Africa. They had crossed the much wider Mediterranean and some would continue on across the North Sea.

While he was sending ripples throughout Europe, Roger could also cause a stir north of the U.S. border. Canadian Stuart Houston was twelve in 1939 when he received as a birthday present from a pair of Manitoba aunts *Birds of Canada* by P. A. Taverner. "Taverner was sort of standard text at the time," says Houston. "It didn't have all the little features that helped identification." One day, he was stumped by the birds he saw in his yard: "I had a little difficulty identifying some little brown birds eating dandelions on the lawn." He later learned that they were nondescript looking because they were female and immature American goldfinches, whose dull plumages were not depicted in Taverner.

"Then Peterson's guide came out and I was given one," says Houston, referring to the second edition of Roger's guide to eastern birds, which "covered almost everything into the eastern part of Saskatchewan where I lived.

"Right from the start, I didn't go anywhere without it," he recalls. "You couldn't carry Taverner. It was too big. So I carried Peterson everywhere I went, as did a million other people." Was it helpful? "Oh, it was the bible! 'Help' is too soft a word."

Houston says that in 1959 Roger Tory Peterson changed the face—even the faces—of ornithology in Regina, Saskatchewan, site of that year's American Ornithologists' Union meeting. "People were afraid that nobody'd come to Regina, Saskatchewan," he remembers. "Most people had not heard of Regina, Saskatchewan."

But they came. "We had more farmers, more students, come to this meeting than any other AOU meeting. Roger Tory Peterson was their big attraction."

The aftereffects of the meeting were astonishing. Houston marvels:

> What this AOU meeting did for ornithology in Saskatchewan—this set it on fire! . . . These young people who came to that meeting went on to distinguished careers in ornithology. Now, here's backwoods, rural Saskatchewan getting turned on to ornithology by the AOU meeting. Spencer Sealy, who is now the editor of The Auk, . . . was a high school kid from Battleford [Saskatchewan]. Glen Fox, who is a distinguished [research scientist] from Canadian Wildlife Service in Ottawa and who published a paper on the life history of the clay-colored sparrow, [also came]. When in high school, Ross Lein, who has been secretary of the AOU even though . . . he's a Canadian from Calgary, was turned on. And so it goes.

One of the youngsters attending, nineteen-year-old Frank Switzer, went on to a career in electronics. However, he remains a devoted birder and does a biweekly "seven-minute bird column" on the CBC radio *Afternoon Edition* with host Colin Grewer in which he discusses places where people can find birds all around Saskatchewan.

During that 1959 AOU meeting Switzer had the jolt of his life on a field trip to a federal migratory bird sanctuary at the north end of Last Mountain Lake:

> *Every fall we have great, huge congregations of sandhill cranes come down from their nesting grounds in northern Canada. . . . Some years, there's a tremendous grouping of cranes at the north end of the lake before they migrate farther south. . . . Sometimes, it's almost like a traffic jam . . . because you can see thousands and thousands of them. . . . It's really quite spectacular.*
>
> *Anyway, [the convention attendees] were having lunch, as I recall, and I was sort of on the outside of the group. I wasn't part of the inner circle, so I was having my boxed lunch sandwich on the edge. I could hear what was going on, and I heard this great calling of cranes overhead, grabbed my binoculars, and had to look straight up and here was a large cloud . . . of cranes circling overhead. . . . It's very difficult to look straight up with a pair of binoculars, even for a young fellow. So I looked for a convenient place to lay down . . . , and a few yards off was a badger mound. . . . It was just the right size for me to go and lie down and look straight up at this great pinwheel of cranes that was circling overhead.*
>
> *As I was lying there, this voice came, and said, "May I share the pillow with you?" I said, "Sure." I never took my binoculars away from my eyes. I didn't know who was there. And this person lay down, we lay head to head, and I . . . heard such a string of exclamations [from him] like, "Magnificent! Tremendous! Gosh—how many layers are there?" We started counting the layers of cranes that were circling one above the other and we counted up to seven or eight of them. Then he said, "Look! They're peeling off the top!" . . . The top layers were always peeling off and heading south. That's when I was informed by this individual that they would do this—circle up—that it was a very efficient way of*

migrating. So I sort of got a little bit of a history of sandhill crane migration.

He lay there for, for I don't know how long, and finally, he says, "Well, I guess everybody's moving off. We'd better get up and catch up with them." I really didn't want to leave, because these cranes were just sort of coming in at the bottom of the thermal all the time and stacking up. Anyway, we got up and dusted the badger mound dust off our caps and he stuck his hand out and said, "By the way, I'm Roger Tory Peterson." And that was it! He could have dropped me with a feather. I had my field guide with me, but I was so thunderstruck, I didn't even get him to autograph the darned thing. . . . Then we both sort of walked together to catch up with the rest of the group that was moving off to look at something on one of the fingers of the lake that stretches up into the sanctuary, and he . . . got caught up with other people, and I got caught up with what I was looking at. I don't think we were even on the same bus. . . . But it was one of those encounters that a young guy just absolutely goes brain numb on.

Stuart Houston was no less thrilled to meet Roger. "Oh, this was Seventh Heaven!" he gushes. "This was like meeting God himself! . . . You can be turned off by meeting famous people who are disdainful of you. That's happened to me. But not with Roger. I mean, he just treated people as equals, and respected people for knowing . . . something he didn't know about some minute aspect of distribution or whatever."

Roger's friend James Fisher also attended the meeting. They, along with Houston and possibly—Houston isn't positive—Ernst Mayr were interviewed by CBC radio. "I was phenomenally honored to be with these great men," he reflects. "But I was sort of the token local birder on the program."

Of Roger and James, Houston affirms, "Oh, they were just bosom buddies. They were like brothers."

At the start of the meeting on August 25, 1959, Roger and James went in search of the greater prairie chicken (best identified in Saskatchewan by its subspecies name of *pinnated grouse*) and were able to report a rare sighting of the bird at Old Wives' Lake. The two men had been looking for some of the species they had missed on their *Wild America* trip six years before. Wrote Roger: "The northern plains had been the greatest omission on our lethal tour and therefore [James] expressed a desire to see six or seven species which would be new to him." These birds included the lark bunting, Baird's sparrow, chestnut-collared longspur, McCown's longspur, Sprague's pipit, sharp-tailed grouse, and pinnated grouse/greater prairie chicken. Roger advised his friend that they "had a fair chance to see all but the latter bird," as its numbers had steeply declined.

As Roger would later recount, three-quarters of a mile from the side of the lake they noticed habitat that should have harbored the pinnated grouse. But Roger and James had Baird's sparrows on their minds. "Trying to flush sparrows from a patch of very low shrubs," Roger wrote, "I jumped a cock Pinnated Grouse. It was within 100 feet of me when it flushed and close enough to see its handsome barrings." Ever devoted to his system of identification through field marks, he "yelled to James Fisher who was off to one side and told him to take note of the short rounded dark tail."

James Fisher was a brilliant, extroverted Brit, a fellow ornithologist, and the best friend that Roger would ever have. Fisher was Roger's brainmate, the man he would share a twenty-year intellectual love affair with until the Englishman's untimely death in 1970. Their *Wild America* trip was the most famous and influential of any twentieth-century documented journey through much of unspoiled—and somewhat spoiled—North America.

Chapter Five

Anglo-American Mates in the U.S. Wild

Roger Tory Peterson and James Maxwell McConnell Fisher met at the 1950 International Ornithological Congress in Visby town square, Gotland, Sweden. "I was on my very *best* behavior because I had been warned that James was very much of a scholar and did not suffer fools or innocents gladly," Roger later said.

One might have imagined Fisher an intimidating overachiever. Four years younger than Roger, he claimed to have become interested in birds at two. He was educated at two venerable institutions: Eton and Magdalen College at Oxford. Initially studying medicine, he switched to zoology after a rewarding expedition to the Arctic in 1933. Thereafter, he worked as a schoolmaster and at the London Zoo. At twenty-six he became secretary of the British Trust for Ornithology. He published his first book, *Birds as Animals,* at 27, and his second, *Watching Birds,* two years later. Soon he commenced authorship of a series of practical birding handbooks titled *Bird Recognition.*

In the preface to the first edition of *Watching Birds* in November 1940, Fisher wrote with Churchillian flair just as the Battle of Britain was ending:

> *Some people might consider an apology necessary for the appearance of a book about birds at a time when Britain is fighting for its own and many other lives. I make no such apology. Birds are part of the heritage we are fighting for. After this war ordinary people are*

going to have a better time than they have had. . . ; many will get the
opportunity, hitherto sought in vain, of watching wild creatures and
making discoveries about them. It is for these men and women, and
not for the privileged few . . . that I have written this little book.

James continued his stoicism in chapter 1. To him, birdwatching was "primarily scientific. . . . Those of you who want passages,
purple or otherwise, on the aesthetics of bird watching, will not
find them here."

But there was a different side to James, represented in another
passage from the same chapter in *Watching Birds,* which Roger
would often quote: "The observation of birds may be a supersti-
tion, a tradition, an art, a science, a pleasure, a hobby, or a bore;
this depends entirely on the nature of the observer." In fact, birding *was* a pleasure to James, with aesthetics to spare. He later
wrote of seeing his first roadrunner: "There it was, running over
the prairie, swerving round a bush with one rounded wing thrust
out for balance, dashing across a gap with the speed of a sprinting
man. With a flick of its long, slim tail, it disappeared completely
into a patch of scrubs." Upon obtaining his first closeup of a California condor, he couldn't contain his excitement. "Tally most
incredibly ho!" he yelled. (For less spectacular birds new to his life
list, he called a mere tallyho.)

Yet there was that thing about James Fisher being frighten-
ingly brilliant. "James Fisher was probably one of the most intelligent men I've ever known," says James Ferguson-Lees, a fellow
Brit who, at fifteen circa 1940, met Fisher as they were both birding in the same spot. Fisher became his longtime mentor. "He
worked like a government minister," Ferguson-Lees adds.

Someone once said that he was the only person he knew who
worked like a government minister, all hours, and that sort of
thing. But he was greatly intelligent on an enormous range of sub-
jects. . . . He had a view and a well-backed-up view on almost

anything. I'm not talking about birds, but natural history now. And his knowledge of birds was enormous.

This description would also have fit Roger. So could James Fisher really have taken Roger for a fool or an innocent? Roger reflected, "I was not quite sure what category he would put me in, but we got on just fine."

During that first outing in Gotland, Roger asked James, then the natural history editor at publisher William Collins, if Collins might publish the book that would become the *Field Guide to the Birds of Britain and Europe.* Fisher thus became editor of the first overseas Peterson guide. (He was also *New Naturalist* series editor.) But the professional aspect of their relationship barely scratched the surface of their connectedness.

Their personalities were different. James Fisher was not stand-offish. "My recollection is that James, whom I knew much better, . . . was a very extrovert personality," discloses James Ferguson-Lees. "Roger I always found a quieter personality. James would do much more talking than Roger, who was probably thinking about what he was going to do the next day, or something like that . . . James was the noisy one."

Even if they generated different noise levels, they ideally complemented each other. "I think they started to talk about birds while they were on—I think it was a boat trip, actually," says James's daughter, Clem, curator of birds and mammals at the Liverpool Museum. "And they never stopped talking about birds after that."

Roger fell in love with England during his time there working on the European field guide. To him the average English person had a "passionate curiosity about the outdoors and wild things." BBC programming and press attention on these subjects certainly helped. And he had made "friends who seemed as completely devoted to the study of the natural world" as he was. One such "obsessive," of course, was James Fisher.

James had shown Roger great hospitality, taking him to such places as the Swedish Lapland, the Scottish highlands, the Narvik Fjord in Norway, the Camargue in the south of France. Together they paid respects at Selbourne in southern England, where eighteenth-century bird observer Gilbert White, an Anglican rector, had learned and written about everyday birds and their habits. They visited a reclusive woman in Sussex, Len Howard, who literally lived with wild birds and was writing her first book based on this experience, *Birds as Individuals*. "Both James and I experienced something of a Hansel and Gretel sensation as we approached the mysterious 'Bird Cottage,'" Roger wrote in a foreword to the American edition of Howard's book.

One day while taking determined strides through London's St. James Park, for once (and probably only once) barely noticing the abundant birds around him, Roger thought intently about a way of reciprocating James's generosity.

"I think they were both real scholars," says Clem Fisher. "As well as being ornithologists, they were very interested in the history of ornithology—who had discovered what and when, and the people-history of ornithology, as well as of birds. I think Roger really appreciated my father's insights into Old World birds. . . . Roger said, 'Come over to America and I will show you American birds.' That developed into this huge trip."

A huge trip it was. Over a period of exactly one hundred days— fourteen weeks—commencing in April 1953, the two traveled from Newfoundland to Alaska via Mexico, hugging the North American coastline as much as possible because of James's fascination with seabirds. But this was no haphazard journey. Roger was not known for administrative abilities but could conceptualize a field guide that perfectly boiled down the essentials for bird identification. He used the same principles here. That is, he boiled down the when, where, and how of North American bird finding, plus all manner of appreciating North American natural history, and planned their itinerary accordingly.

"Fisher talks . . . in *Wild America* . . . about stopping at some sort of anonymous pinion-juniper hillside in northern Arizona, stepping out of a car, immediately picking up two or three new species of birds, and realizing that this was not the result of happenstance," marvels Scott Weidensaul.

This was the result of Roger laying all this out in [Glen Echo] Maryland the previous winter. The amount of planning that went into this, in the days before the Internet and even now—it was real work and also a testament to the enormous contacts that Peterson had across the country. That he could kind of whistle up a couple of motor yachts to take them out to the Dry Tortugas. Everywhere they went . . . he just had people that were happy to help.

Wrote Fisher: "I was gradually beginning to realize the planning and care and experience behind Roger's conducted tour of North America; scarcely a mile was wasted. Our apparently casual stop in these pinelands of northern Arizona had, I suspected, been contrived, quite deliberately, at Roger's desk in Maryland the previous winter."

"I've learned not to engage Roger in an interesting conversation when he's driving," James Fisher wrote to Barbara Peterson from "near Miami." The traveling pair was en route to the Dry Tortugas.

As Roger was a terrible driver—something that Barbara learned early in their marriage—it is shocking to know that he drove at all on this critical cross-continental trip. But he and James shared chauffeuring responsibilities. This didn't mean there were no rough patches for the duo on the roads of America in this time before the interstate highway system.

"You read the book and it says they had one fight," Scott Weidensaul says.

> *One disagreement. When they were driving through Arizona, James is telling Roger that he's driving too close to the middle of the road. Roger's arguing, "No, I don't want to drive on the outside of these gravel mountain roads because you get forced off by a truck and I lost a friend that way." Of course, the next thing you know he almost gets hit head-on by a driver who was also driving on the inside of the road. James says, "I think you're a bloody bad driver!"*

Roger and James took turns writing passages for the book. The former made a point of admitting to one argument with James, offering, "I record this conversation exactly as I remember it, because it was the only time in thousands of miles that tempers flared. But I suspect James was not really too nervous about my driving, because he often dozed peacefully for hours on end when I took the wheel." As each dropped footnotes on the other's passages, James contributed a pithy "no comment" to the part about his not being "too nervous" about Roger's driving.

Their trek could have been a Bob Hope-Bing Crosby *Road* movie, sans Dorothy Lamour. The book is filled with humorous banter. When Weidensaul was a boy, jealously reading of the Peterson-Fisher exploits in *Wild America*, it "was mostly like [seeing] a buddy movie—these two guys having this incredible adventure, seeing all these birds." What comes through for Weidensaul today, after having done some *Wild America* historiography for his recent book, *Return to Wild America*, is how strong their friendship was.

> *If I'd been either of those guys, I'd have killed the other one. Oh, yeah—it [their friendship] must have been tremendously strong, which is all the more remarkable, because they hadn't really*

known each other all that long. They'd only known each other for about three years. . . . Some people are just perfectly matched with each other. To spend three and a half months in a 1953 Ford station wagon with another person; I couldn't do that with my wife, and I love her deeply! . . . They just seemed to thrive on it. They really did. That comes through reading Fisher's field journals. He also kept a diary. . . . Whether he said, "Almost killed RP today. Can't stand the sound of him chewing his food one more day"—if that existed, I didn't see it.

Instead of killing each other, Roger and James kidded each other.

After Newfoundland, they motored down the New England coast. In Boston Roger introduced James to his first birding mentor, Ludlow Griscom, as well as his editor at Houghton Mifflin, Paul Brooks. They attended a meeting of the Nuttall Ornithological Club, the group that had been so reluctant in the early 1930s to admit Roger to its ranks. While there James was asked to speak of the fulmar, a favorite seabird he had published a lengthy study on for the *New Naturalist* series. He gladly obliged. "You needn't read *all* 496 pages of your book," Roger needled.

James admired Roger's ability to instantly identify any bird by sound or sight ("his magic ear and skillful eye"), including migrating warblers in the thick of a forest in the Great Smoky Mountains. And while they may have been in the forest, as far as being picked on goes, Roger was not out of the woods. "Several times," James noted, he heard a Kentucky warbler call to Roger "from low growth at the edges of wet woodlands or bogs—*tory-tory-tory-tory*. Roger called back, once or twice." Then there were the similar songs of the golden-winged and blue-winged warblers. It was time to make fun of Roger's encyclopedic ways, as James did when he wrote: "'Both species occasionally sing the song of the other,' murmured Roger casually (afterwards, I checked his *Field Guide* and found R.T.P. was quoting from it—he must use it a lot)."

The Brit was not immune to Roger's idea of a joke. They were still listening to warblers in the forest when James realized, "There were other sounds too: a sharp rattle like a wooden ratchet-rattle, and a ubiquitous *chuck*. I looked hard for these birds, and Roger let me hunt them for a mile or two before slyly telling me they were mammals." (They were red squirrels and chipmunks.)

There was one-upmanship. When Roger had visited James's home in Northampton, James took him on a bird walk that brought him under a thousand-year-old Saxon tower, Earl's Barton. Could America have anything that ancient? On the *Wild America* trip, Roger got his revenge. In New Mexico's Canyon de Chelly National Monument, the American pointed to the Anasazi pueblos, dating from AD 900. "That White House [pueblo] is older than Earl's Barton," Roger boasted. *Touché*.

In America Roger could flaunt what he'd learned while traversing Europe. This especially came in handy in Newfoundland, which got a number of the birds Europe saw. However, these birds had a sometimes markedly different English name in Europe. Some of these dual-named birds included white-winged crossbills (two-barred crossbills in Europe), mergansers (goosanders), horned larks (shore larks), and loons (divers). "Just to be polite—and knowledgeable—I called out the birds by their British names while James used the American names," said Roger. "It was most confusing at times; but we kept this up for a hundred days."

The running gag was how many Cokes they consumed, especially in such hot places as the desert southwest and areas in Mexico where the water was not safe to drink. Coca-Cola received so many mentions that James felt compelled to drop a footnote: "This book, I hasten to add, is not sponsored by the Coca-Cola company."

Despite all the jollity, *Wild America* was not just a succession of funny anecdotes. There was a lister's concern—the matter of beating Guy Emerson's record for the number of birds seen by one individual in North America in one year. Emerson, a banker, arranged his business trips in 1939 to set a record with 497 species, unbeaten until the Peterson-Fisher trek. Thanks largely to their hundred-day cross-country sojourn, the two men ended 1953 by having what is now called a Big Year, setting a new record. Roger's number was 572; James's, 536. (Neither counted the 65 species they had encountered in Mexico.) Birding would never be the same again.

Much more important was what Peterson and Fisher found and wrote. Says Scott Weidensaul:

> *I think for a lot of people, as it was for me, they were lifting the curtain on parts of the country that were not all that well known. . . . And not just [in] the U.S. I'm sure few Americans had much familiarity at all with Newfoundland. It hadn't been part of Canada until just a couple of years before. . . . It was very difficult to get there. Very exotic. The same thing with the areas of Mexico that they were traveling in, the swamps of Florida. I think we tend to overlook from this perspective today how otherworldly a lot of the Deep South was, particularly a lot of Florida, in the 1950s. It was years before air-conditioning. . . . The swamps of the Florida panhandle. . . . That was really terra incognita in those days. . . .* So it was a glimpse of *wild America*, but not the picture postcard, Reader's Digest, *wild America.*

What if Roger and James had visited many of the famous national monuments or parks, such as Yellowstone or the Grand Tetons? *Wild America* might have had less impact, Weidensaul thinks, and served more as a tourist guide. "I think it would have been just a little bit flatter."

Neither was *Wild America* just about the grand spectacle, nor the birds Roger and James could see, despite their Big Year achievement. "Obviously, they were going to places where the bird life would be interesting, but they also took in all this other stuff—the cypress gardens, knowing . . . that there would be a lot of swallowtails around the flowers at that time," says author-naturalist Kenn Kaufman, adding,

> *Going through the Great Smoky Mountains, which, . . . in the fourth week of April, is decent for birds. It's probably more interesting just in terms of the botany there—really excellent plant life. . . . They went to one of the habitat dioramas at the American Museum of Natural History, and then went to the exact spot that it had been based on. Just the fact that they took the time to go look at geological features like Crater Lake and made a point of going to look at redwoods and so on. . . . Theirs was really more of a natural history trip.*

A conservationist thread ran throughout the book. Almost every page was a celebration of what America still possessed and needed to preserve. "The whole thing is about asking the general member of the public in America to look after their birds," Clem Fisher posits. Roger and James looked in vain for the ivory-billed woodpecker. They admired the whooping cranes, scarce in number, and the negligible population of California condors.

At the end of the book, James Fisher praised Americans for making their country a "garden," for being steps ahead of England with their national parks system. But Roger was dismayed by the condition of the Jersey Shore since war's end: "The sandy coast, the dunes, and the estuaries are now one continuous line of flimsy beach dwellings, bathhouses, billboards, and hot dog stands. Even Barnegat and Brigantine, wild beaches that resounded to the calls of plovers and curlew when I knew them, are now almost completely built up."

Wild America has been an inspiration for many of today's naturalists. It inspired Kenn Kaufman's own early 1970s, lone jaunt across North America, which he chronicled in *Kingbird Highway*. Kaufman was (and is) an unabashed fan of Roger Tory Peterson: "I had read and memorized *Wild America*." He and his friends who knew *Wild America* so well would try to stump each other on trivia from the book. (Kaufman says one question was, "What was the date when [Roger and James] saw their only rusty blackbirds of the trip?" The answer: April 19, 1953.)

Kaufman was tantalized by Roger's Big Year number for 1953. "By the time I went on my trip, the birdwatching community had developed up to the point where there was so much information available," he explains. "The American Birding Association had just started. Suddenly, you could get precise directions to things that Roger had gone to search for . . . by just knowing that somewhere in the Chisos Mountains there's going to be a Colima warbler."

In 1973 the teenaged Kaufman knew that Roger's Big Year record of 572 species had been beaten two years later by Englishman Stuart Keith who got 598, and that record still stood. Kaufman aimed to break the 600 mark and hold the new Big Year total. While he did break 600—actually reaching 666—another birder saw 669 species that same year. But it was the thrill of the chase that made for fun reading in *Kingbird Highway,* Kaufman's *Wild America* tribute.

Wild America is also that rare book that engendered two sequels. The first was *Looking for the Wild,* written by Lyn Hancock, a Canadian by way of Australia. Hancock wrote:

*"Dearly beloved, as we are gathered together in the bus," Gus intoned
facetiously from the wheel of his rented van as we left St. John's and
turned southwest across the Avalon Peninsula, "let's start reading
Wild America." Although we had read and reread Peterson and
Fisher's book before, we were to read it again daily on the trip.*

*April 12, the first day of our expedition, set the routine for the
next one hundred days. Bird walk before breakfast. Read what
Peterson and Fisher did on the same day thirty years before. Explore
their destinations and add more of our own. . . . Reread Peterson
and Fisher at night to compare and contrast our experiences.*

Gus was Gus Yaki, the Canadian owner of Nature Travel Service, founded in 1973. The trip that became *Looking for the Wild*
was his brainchild. "I have been a naturalist all my life, born in
1932," says Yaki.

*As soon as I could afford it, I bought a copy of RTP's first bird
book and I have, ever since he was on the staff of the National
Audubon Society, followed his role in the development of conservation awareness and ethics. Soon after the publication of . . .*
Wild America *in 1955, I obtained a copy and read it. . . . About
1980, I again picked up and reread* Wild America. *At this time,
I realized that I had been to many of the sites that Peterson and
Fisher had visited on their epic 1953 journey. I had also met many
of the folks they had encountered. Accordingly, I decided to offer
a repeat of their journey, attempting to visit the same sites, on the
same dates, that they did.*

Yaki figured it would be best to offer the trip in 1983, exactly
thirty years after the first one. He invited author-teacher-adventurer
Lyn Hancock to come along and write about it.

Yaki had hoped that Roger Tory Peterson would join them.
"Unfortunately, he was much too busy, until the end," recalls
Yaki. "I believe that Peterson made about eight flights overseas

for speaking engagements during the ninety days of this trip. He was able to join us on the final days of the tour in the Pribilofs."

To Hancock, a trip in search of wild America was immediately appealing. She and her husband, David, had sailed between Alaska and California in a rubber raft, partly to get the "general public involved in protection of the Arctic, long before it became a cause célèbre." She raised puffins, seals, and other wild animals at home to learn and write about them, and brought them into school to teach about them. Like many tourists she had traveled through the United States with her parents, but it wasn't satisfying. It wasn't Peterson and Fisher's America. "I really didn't want to go around anymore, but with Gus, it was entirely different," she says. "I would go to wild America—not concrete America, which I had done before."

She arrived in Canada from Australia as a college student in 1962. Her husband-to-be was studying ornithology at the University of British Columbia. "I had to learn in a hurry," she laughs. "I was given the Peterson field guides and told to get with it. That's where I first learned the name of Roger Tory Peterson."

Hancock was well prepared for Gus's 1983 trip. But it wouldn't involve just *two* explorers. She remembers: "We were a small group because that's the way Gus likes it. But there were new people each week.... Otherwise, it would have been very expensive. There were a lot more in the Alaska session. . . . At least a dozen. At other times, we were six or seven."

Gus Yaki started the daily *Wild America* readings. He says the group thus reminded itself of

> *what Peterson and Fisher had seen on the corresponding day thirty years earlier. . . . It would be one way that we might measure the impact of environmental changes that had occurred during the intervening years. We never did see the variety or number of individuals that they did. Were the numbers down because of habitat loss or environmental degradation? In the end, we really couldn't*

make a valid comparison. One major reason was that 1983 was a
big El Niño year. The spring season was particularly late.

Some of the Canadians and Australians on this commemorative trip, including Lyn Hancock, began affectionately referring
to Roger and James as "the boys," as they considered the men's
journey and what had changed since.

The boys? "That's quite British, actually," Clem Fisher remarks.
"It is a kind of endearing thing, that—people over here always refer
to their children as the boys or the girls . . . , even when they're
sixty-four!"

The boys would have been saddened to see some of what Yaki,
Hancock, and the others noticed. In the decade when Roger and
James passed through, wildlife refuges were opened up to hunting, fishing, and trapping. By the 1980s oil and gas exploration,
timber harvesting, and (sometimes) too many human visitors
had degraded a number of the refuges. The Pine Barrens near
New Bedford, Massachusetts, "once an almost continuous forest of pitch pine with stands of southern white cedar rising from
swamps," wrote Hancock, were now crisscrossed by highways.

Hancock saw hope too and pointed out positives. "One of my
purposes in writing *Looking for the Wild*," she asserts, "was to be a
little bit different than the words of doom and gloom that were
surrounding me in that time." People making a positive difference are often overlooked. Thus, *Looking for the Wild* highlights
the Jamaica Bay National Wildlife Refuge, established in 1972.
What was this area in New York Harbor like when *the boys* came
through? In her book Hancock wrote: "Park Ranger David Avrin
told me that in 1953 the air was polluted, the waters were almost
dead, many species had disappeared." It could have been developed commercially, but wise commitment transformed the area
into a haven for 315 resident or migratory bird species.

In 1953 Big Bend National Park in Texas was nine years old,
but still suffering the aftereffects of decades of abuse by ranch-

ing, mining, and various forms of lawlessness that had left the area eroded and with little vegetation. By 1983 Hancock wrote, it was a "good example of Wild America Reclaimed." It had been improved for people, with trails and information centers, and wildlife. A park naturalist informed her, "Vegetation has made a remarkable recovery. . . . Predators have increased. We have panthers back. . . . Peregrine falcons are increasing, too."

In *Wild America,* Roger had written of the terrible Tillamook Burn, which in 1933 destroyed five hundred square miles of virgin forest near Portland, Oregon. Twenty years after the fire, he sadly reported, the place still was more notable for its "great tree skeletons" than new growth. By 1983 the Tillamook Burn had become, Hancock announced, the Tillamook *Forest.* The "great tree skeletons" were reduced to the occasional dead snag. The forest was home to deer, elks, and bears.

Roger joined the Yaki-Hancock group on its flight from Anchorage to the Pribilof Islands. "Of course, it was a great joy to see him again," says Yaki, who had first met him in Trinidad in 1969, "especially since we had been so intimately following in his footsteps."

"He seemed to be a very quiet man," says Lyn Hancock of Roger, then nearly seventy-five. "He talked in a kind of gentle, quiet voice."

Yaki recalls,

All the participants were thrilled. . . . to be in his presence. He was genuine. There was nothing highfalutin or anything like that. He was just one of the crowd. We would all be rubbing shoulders with him at one time or another as we got into better position to photograph some bird on a cliff nearby. . . . It was in the evening that he really shone. He was able to relate his experiences and answer questions.

Roger reacted well to what was, essentially, *Wild America, Part Deux.* "He was not a person who had any airs or graces," remembers Hancock. But he was flattered. "He enjoyed the attention.

Don't we all? We'd been talking about it [the trip] for so long. . . .
We were looking forward to it and I think he was, too."

Canadian artist-naturalist Robert Bateman, a great friend of
Roger's, was there for the Alaska portion of the trip. "It was terribly exciting," says Bateman. "It was partly that it was Roger and
partly that he and James Fisher carved out this brilliant idea. . . .
I wish more people did it. In fact, I wish kids had competitions
in it and that sort of thing. Trying to go around America and
see as many different things as you can see I think was a brilliant
concept."

Twenty years later would be an even bigger *Wild America* anniversary. Another book would chronicle the adventure anew.

Scott Weidensaul was already the author of several noteworthy
books about wildlife before he decided to reexamine the wilds of
North America on the golden anniversary of *Wild America*. Since
reading the book as a boy, he had been attracted to the notion of
having a similar adventure. "It just lit this fire to get out and see
these places," he says. But he didn't try to retrace the steps of *the
boys* until around 2002, when he realized that the historic trip's
fiftieth anniversary was coming up fast.

"It seemed like such a perfect opportunity," he reflects, adding:

> *Fifty years is a nice, round period of time, and the previous fifty
> years, from '55 [when* Wild America *was published] until 2005,
> have been nothing short of tectonic for conservation. We went from
> there being this kind of tiny, fledgling, . . . conservation movement
> that had been . . . focusing on preventing the direct extermination
> of wildlife, to clean air, clean water, endangered species, wilder-*

*ness system, wild-and-scenic river system, . . . just on and on—all
these bedrock environmental protections—the 1970s explosion of
the environmental movement. And now, in the last five years, and
to a large extent perhaps in the last ten, [there has been] a pretty
significant erosion of a lot of those gains. So it seemed like a good
opportunity. It was a handy framework to look at the changes
over the last half century.*

First, Scott Weidensaul asked Kenn Kaufman—a walking,
talking Peterson apostle—if he wouldn't mind Weidensaul's tackling such a commemorative project. (Wasn't Kaufman the ideal
person for this venture, after all?) But Kenn gave his blessing, and
Weidensaul embarked on his adventure.

Weidensaul reflects:

*What always struck me is the degree of hubris in titling the book
Wild America when you hug the coast and manage to miss the
whole of the upper Great Lakes, the Canadian boreal forest, and
the Rockies, Hudson Bay—just huge areas that they missed. . . . Yet,
for my purposes, the route they plotted out, I almost couldn't have
done better if I'd planned it myself. . . . So many of the places that
they visited were just perfect spotlights on subjects that I wanted to
talk about, whether it was sprawl development, wetlands protection, landscape or ecological restoration, water policy, fire policy,
. . . climate change, and on and on.*

But Weidensaul's trip did not operate at the breakneck speed
of his predecessors. As he wrote in the preface to *Return to Wild
America*:

*Where they sprinted, I would ramble. Peterson and Fisher pushed
themselves relentlessly for three and a half brutal months, taking
just two days off in all that time, often driving through the night
to keep to Roger's meticulously plotted schedule. The breathless*

quality that comes from this perpetual motion is one of Wild America*'s charms, but I needed time to dig deeper, to look more contemplatively at a continent that has changed dramatically in fifty years. And so I would make most of the journey over the space of about nine months, gaining in insight, I hoped, what I lost in perfect replication.*

Many times, as he followed the original route, Weidensaul felt as if he were standing on hallowed ground:

When we were out in the midst of the tern colony on Garden Key and Bush Key [in the Dry Tortugas]. When I was in Mexico, down in Xilitla, to stand in the same big sinkhole cavern where they stood, and hear the same squawking green parakeets that they described. The two places, I guess, where I really felt that connection—one was in southern California, up at Hopper Mountain National Wildlife Refuge looking for condors, because I was there exactly 50 years to the day they were. . . . But particularly up in Yukon Delta National Wildlife Refuge at Old Chevak [Alaska] in that old field station that used to be the Catholic church in the Eskimo village, literally treading the same floorboards that Peterson and Fisher did, looking at the photographs they'd taken up there. . . . There's such a sense of timelessness.

As the Yaki-Hancock group had concluded in 1983, Weidensaul determined in 2003 that the wilds of America evidenced victories as well as defeats for conservation. But *the boys* would have been pleased to know that largely because of the vigilance of conservationists, including the many whom they inspired, Weidensaul could report: "[the] land, the rugged heart of natural America, retains an essential timelessness, which on my own journey I discovered again and again. Ours is still, at its core, a wild country."

For *the boys, Wild America* was just the beginning of their passionate mind-melding.

Roger always had a multitude of projects going on simultaneously. For him the 1950s was a decade filled with writings, paintings, and drawings in various stages of completion. Some involved James Fisher; some did not. A digest of bird-related literature edited by Roger appeared in 1957. He wanted *The Bird Watcher's Anthology* to showcase some of the writings he had most enjoyed over thirty years and sought input from a couple of British friends: "One evening at the Savile Club in London, Julian Huxley became very enthusiastic when I told him of my project. He immediately jotted down a dozen titles for me to think about. James Fisher . . . spent half an evening at my home systematically recalling from memory significant items out of his many years' reading."

The result was a flavorful volume of essays spanning the gamut of avian-oriented literature featuring words by luminaries of natural history, including early commentators—Audubon, Seton, Gilbert White, Alexander Wilson, Thoreau, and Alfred Russel Wallace—as well as more contemporary authors, many of whom Roger knew well. Work by Peterson, Fisher, and Huxley also crept in.

Roger didn't just select the pieces, but edited them, authored introductions to them, organized them by theme to show the "classic progress of the bird watcher from the first spark of his interest through the discovery and listing stages to the thoughtful observations of the mature student," provided an original frontispiece for each section of essays, and otherwise scattered lovely black-and-white illustrations throughout. Between these artistic pieces, and the profusion of line drawings in *Wild America,* he was breaking free of the schematic shackles of his field guides.

In 1961 Roger was working with Paul Brooks as editor of a new natural history series published by Houghton Mifflin, *The Naturalist's America,* patterned after James Fisher's *New Naturalist* series. The first entry in the series was to be a book about the Appalachians by West Virginia University professor Maurice Brooks, whom Roger had personally recruited. At first, Roger kept atop his responsibilities as editor. By August 1963, things had unraveled.

Barbara wrote to an exasperated Brooks:

> *Unfortunately your letter of August 28th did not reach us until Roger had left for England (on the 27th). He had to return there to do the final checking of color proofs and text with James Fisher. As you know they have been collaborating on a book on bird biology. . . . It has taken far longer to do than anyone had anticipated . . . [with hours and] hours more work for Roger and consequently everything has fallen behind.*

By 1964 Roger was back at the helm as editor for Maurice Brooks's *The Appalachians.* But what was this irksome collaboration with James Fisher?

It was called *The World of Birds* and took five years to finish. The work presents an overview of the history and fundamentals of birdlife, as well as a discussion of the manner in which birds have been studied and the nature of Homo sapiens' troubled relationship with birds. Roger and James's partnership this time wasn't quite like it had been for *Wild America.* As usual Roger did all the artwork—dozens of color and black-and-white paintings and other illustrations of living birds and species long extinct.

The ambitious centerpiece of maps showed the range of every bird family ever known to the world, above which Roger placed a silhouette of a typical member of each family. As one couldn't observe extinct species in the field, nor could one check museum skins for the precise field marks of most of them, Roger consulted with, among others, Professor Pierce Brodkorb of the University of Florida, discoverer of bird fossils in Florida, plus old friend Alexander Wetmore of the Smithsonian, for feedback on his bird shapes, as well as illustrations he was doing for his 1963 Life Nature Library volume, *The Birds*. "It is quite a problem visualizing some of these birds, but it's fun," confided Roger.

James wrote the first draft of *The World of Birds*. Then he and Roger wrestled over its details. One point of contention was the cause of species' extinction since 1680 when the dodo vanished. Roger gently protested in an aside to Brodkorb about James's opinion: "He . . . states that only half of the 78 species that have become extinct in the last 3 centuries became extinct because of man. I think practically all of them did, except for several puzzlers like the Labrador duck."

Roger and James both got their way regarding human-caused extinctions. Instead of concluding in their book that all extinctions were due to man, as Roger argued, or only half the extinctions, as James contended, the authors compromised. They did this by pointing to definite causes for half the number and suggesting that at least some of the remainder "may . . . have been driven to rarity and extinction by the competition of better-adapted species introduced into their habitat from elsewhere."

Disagreements between the two were always friendly. Heavy discussions are what bonded them. They talked about birds from morning till night, wherever they were. A typical site was the Old Rectory, the Fishers' first family home, later converted into a studio when mother, father, and kids moved down the path to what they dubbed Ashton Manor.

"Perhaps they would discuss something very intently, but it would be in a very positive way," says Clem Fisher. "They would be feeding ideas off each other, rather than saying, 'Oh no, don't be so stupid. That's wrong.' I never remember any of that, really."

It was hard to attract the attention of *the boys* when together they intensely engaged their cerebra. "They would work down there [at the Old Rectory] and then come up for meals," Clem recalls. "I remember my mother used to have to ring them up about ten times to pry them out of there. . . . You'd see them walking up . . . [the path] very slowly, gesticulating—and still talking. And they'd come in and sit down and still talk. Have food, and still talk. And then leave, still talking."

When *the boys* joined forces, they were an infuriating pair. Says Clem,

There was no going down the pub and drinking or anything like that. I don't remember them ever going out, actually! . . . The only time I remember . . . is when my mother made them go to a concert. She was in with the local bar choir in Northampton. She made them go to a concert she was singing at. And she got really cross because when she got in the car afterwards my father just started off back to our house, and he and Roger started talking about birds. They never even mentioned the concert! My mother was fuming that they hadn't even said, "Oh, well done," or "That was good." . . . She was really cross. That kind of went into family folklore.

Said a review in *The Auk* about *The World of Birds:* "If anyone still doubts that James Fisher and Roger Tory Peterson are more addicted to birds, as a total way of life, than anyone else in our times, with this book these two—with the happy and rarely equalled abandon of a pair of drunken sailors on shore leave—seem now to have proved it for all time."

Part Three:

PARADOXICAL HOMO SAPIENS

Chapter Six

A Super Pair and Their Habitat, Nest, and Brood

Roger and Barbara Peterson made a formidable pair. During their nearly thirty-three-year marriage, which ended in 1976, they knew their respective roles and—usually—performed them harmoniously.

Better stated, Roger was going to do what he was going to do anyway—that is, write, paint, read, ponder, travel, speak, and be collegial. But the reason he was able to do these things, prodigiously, was because Barbara took care of all household matters; raised the boys; acted as her husband's secretary, manager, gatekeeper, and chauffeur; and cheerily hosted his colleagues and friends from around the world.

"I think early on in their marriage they slipped into roles where Mom took care of the kids and made sure that the nuts and bolts of the business functioned. . . . and Dad camped out in the studio when he was at home and cranked out work," says son Lee.

Although she approached her life in a distinctly nonfeminist manner, Barbara believed in what she did, shared Roger's views on nature, and was outgoing, proactive, and articulate. She had to be highly intelligent to provide chief support to a brilliant man who was always working on overdrive. In another era, and given her own talents, she might have made a name for herself; still, she was proud of her status as "Mrs. Roger Tory Peterson," which was how she signed letters that she wrote on his behalf.

Peterson observer Roland Clement thinks Roger was a "sort of laid-back, big Swede" who needed the structure Barbara provided. "Roger would not have become the guru if she had not bucked him up. She made a man out of him, you might say." Peterson protégé Fleur Ng'weno puts it another way: "I think Barbara was crucial to Roger's success. She took care of all the mundane things that had to be done, allowing him to be a genius."

The Petersons announced at the end of 1954 that they had moved to Old Lyme, Connecticut, in October. "We are on a slope overlooking the Connecticut River," they wrote. "We hope that before too long you will find your way to our door. . . . Remember, we are on Neck Road, the first Road, up-river after crossing the Connecticut River Bridge going East."

Old Lyme was the ideal location for Roger Tory Peterson. It put him midway between New York, with its museums and the National Audubon Society, and Boston, home of Houghton Mifflin, both easily reached by train. "He took a look around, and saw what was there at the mouth of the Connecticut River. He had it exactly right," says Peterson protégé Paul Spitzer, who grew up in Old Lyme. "There was a railway station in Saybrook, one in New London, and the Connecticut River Valley is awesome. It's very beautiful and has tremendous biodiversity in a limited area."

Roger and Barbara were "very glad to be operating in a rural setting," continues Spitzer. "Old Lyme, when they moved there, was still rural. The Connecticut Turnpike just went through in the mid-'50s. . . . It was paradise."

There was a strange detail about the Petersons' new home. It made them neighbors of a direct descendant of John James Audubon.

Belton and Genie Copp lived down Neck Road from the Petersons. Genie was descended from Audubon. "It went John James Audubon, Victor Audubon, Delia Audubon, Victor Tyler—Delia Audubon married Morris Tyler—so then it went Victor Tyler, Morris Tyler, and Morris Tyler was my father."

"Well, I think it was just a coincidence," she says of the fact that Roger Tory Peterson, who was being hailed as the twentieth-century Audubon, moved in next door.* "He was looking for a place to live up in this area. Somebody referred him to my husband for legal and real estate information. Belton was his lawyer for many years."

Was Roger impressed with this coincidence? "He was aware of it," says Genie Copp. "But I don't think it made a bit of difference. He was really very focused on himself and on his deadlines"—she laughs—"I would say *harassed* by his deadlines."

The Copps's property had been in Belton's family since 1681 and opened onto the Lieutenant River, which merged into the lower Connecticut River estuary, a couple of miles from the Long Island Sound. Nearby was the Great Island marsh, home of numerous pairs of nesting ospreys, a huge attraction for Roger.

For Lee Peterson, the Peterson property of seventy-odd acres was an idyllic place. "It was a nice childhood," he reflects. Lee was a loner and enjoyed natural history pursuits. Of the property he says:

---

* Roger often said he preferred to think of himself as the "first Peterson."

It was a wonderful mix of things. The house was on one side of a ridge. On the other side of the ridge, it was just woods going down to a salt marsh. It wasn't that I hung out in the salt marsh, but there was a wonderful little stream on the back side of the property that went down into the salt marsh. . . . There were rocky outcrops where you would find owl pellets. When we first moved in there, there was an open field behind my father's studio that was rapidly going to cedars, and so forth, that whippoorwill would do their courtship displays on. . . . There were deer coming through all the time. My parents would feed [them] table scraps, they'd put them out at night, so you'd have all sorts of raccoons, skunks, and opossums coming in at night. You were there, right in the middle of everything. It was pretty magical for a kid who was pretty adept at entertaining himself. . . . This is a time when kids could pedal their bicycle all over. . . . I had friends who were anywhere within two, three miles of me. We'd get together and do things out in the woods. . . . I fished, which again was a sort of individual pursuit. All of that was fairly near at hand too.

Was Lee influenced by his father's example? "In very subtle ways. It wasn't like my father would put his arm around my shoulder and steer me into things. . . . If I was interested in something that required some assistance, he was always available for assistance." At one point, Lee "dabbled in watercolors"; Roger advised him on illustrating a luna moth. One grade school project required making a map of Brazil "in relief. . . . with plaster of Paris and things like that. . . . I remember him showing me how to get the effect of forested areas in mountains and so forth using a sponge in the paints. We were dabbing with the sponge to get this mottled look."

Lee went through a bird nest phase also. Barbara noted in the January 1961 "New Year's Letter from the Petersons": "Last year Lee's great passion was collecting old bird nests so we now have a combination rock and bird nest museum on the second floor."

"There was nothing out there, no books, that specifically dealt with birds' nests," says Lee. "I would bring the birds' nests to Dad and he'd identify them. I'd just tell him what kind of vegetation was in the area and how high up it was. . . . I had three or four dozen different birds' nests at one time that were all identified."

If Dad was home, he was in the studio. "I never thought about it at the time," says Lee, "but he never showed any impatience with me interrupting."

Like the children of other well-to-do families in the affluent Connecticut suburbs, Tory and Lee were in boarding school by the fifth grade. Barbara bore the brunt of everyday pressures whether the boys were home or not. In friend Katie Lewin's estimation, Roger was not a good husband.

"He was a wonderful guy," Lewin says. But "he was not there." And just where was he? *Away.* As the inside flap of 1957's *The Bird Watcher's Anthology* revealed: "In a typical year . . . he spends about half of his time away from his home in Old Lyme, Connecticut." When one is a world-renowned naturalist, one's central duties are exploring continents and meeting and conferring with conservationists and fellow naturalists around the globe. Such duties are deathly for family life.

According to Lee's wife, Courtney, Christmas Day in the Peterson household went thusly: "Roger would wake up, I guess they'd do presents, and then he'd go to the studio and they'd call him when they were ready to sit down for dinner. Period."

Even if Roger was willing to provide insight and assistance, Barbara plainly declares that she was both "mother and father . . . . Roger had nothing to do with his children." She remembers one instance where the weight of parenthood relaxed a little: "Lee had been in the living room and he and Roger had been talking. When Lee went on upstairs again, Roger very proudly swore, as he sat on the sofa and I sat beside him, 'Lee understands me.'"

While Roger never shared this with his son, Lee speculates about its meaning: "The way we approach work is very similar. I tend to procrastinate and then work very intensely. That was my father's pattern his entire life—to go through periods where he would procrastinate about doing a task but then . . . get single-mindedly focused about it and work around the clock to complete the task." There was their mutual interest in the outdoors. "I think our values were similar," he says. "Our tendency in the debate between the economy versus preservation—we were always falling on the side of preservation." Lee adds, "What would you rather do with your free time? Go to a car race, or go out in a salt marsh and slog around in the mud? Well, we chose the mud."

There was no mutual understanding between elder son Tory and Roger. While Tory was interested in natural history, he was at least as interested in many other activities. "It's just that we had different views on what was important," says Tory, today a financial adviser. "It's sort of like his relationship with his father . . . , because I'm not sure he was really encouraged hugely either."

When Tory said no to birding, he was very small: "Apparently, the last time I ever went with him was when I was five. I refused to walk several miles and my mother said that was the last time he and I had much to do with each other in terms of bird walks."

"Tory was an exceptional athlete growing up, and that's where he focused things," comments Lee. "Tory . . . was an exceptional team sport player. Dad never really understood my brother. He didn't understand that aspect of Tory. Me, on the other hand, . . . while I was a decent team sport player, I really excelled at individual pursuits." Individual pursuits fit his father's frame of reference. They dictated his entire life.

In some ways both boys were brought up to be like Dad. Roger and Barbara sent them to Camp Chewonki every summer, to Tory's chagrin. "It was some place, frankly, that I went to, not totally willingly at the beginning," admits Tory, "because I was always involved in little league baseball . . . , and I had to get out right in the middle of it every summer. When I got there

[Chewonki], I loved it. So it was not a place that I did not like. It was just that it was sort of, 'Oops, there goes little league again.'"

If there were family vacations, they tended to be without Roger, who was usually away during the summer.

"Basically, the way things worked, when I was out of school, those tended to be the times of year that Dad was also doing fieldwork of one sort or another," says Lee. "For the most part, unless he was going to South America, his trips were spring to fall." He remembers being at camp with his brother while both parents spent an entire summer in Europe so that Roger and James Fisher could work on *The World of Birds*. At other times, there were cross-country trips with Barbara to see her parents in Seattle.

Occasionally the family vacationed together. Tory recalls being in Canada with his father when Roger was using a "camera that looked like a rifle. It was set up on top of a rifle stock." Roger let him photograph a moose from ten feet away until Dad thought better of being so proximate to the animal. A trip to Yellowstone was special. "I remember a blue and white Ford station wagon," says Tory.

> *He might have been doing the flower guide, but . . . one of the things that he did have access to was all these park rangers. . . . I remember we got taken out at night to go look at the grizzly bears at the park dump where nobody was supposed to go, and seeing hundreds of bears. That was sort of exciting. So there were a lot of things that I got to actually do, from a natural history standpoint, that I wouldn't have, ordinarily.*

Another treat was entering an ostrich cage at the Bronx Zoo so his father could study the bird.

In the summer of 1963 Lee accompanied his father on a drive to Michigan, partly to honor the rare Kirtland's warbler. It was mainly a botany trip, since Roger was still trying to finish the wildflower guide. Lee was his "assistant" traveling northward to Michigan to the small town of Mio where local conservationist Les Line had engaged an artist to carve what Line now describes as a "pretty ugly fiberglass model of a gigantic Kirtland's warbler, probably about a thousand times the size of the real bird." Roger spoke at the monument's dedication. Lee remembers the perks of the journey—such as picking up a new, complimentary Oldsmobile at a dealership to use for the drive. "Presumably he was supposed to say nice things about it afterwards, or maybe it was just a fellow birder," Lee says.

Tory enjoyed the benefits of being Roger's son in the summer of 1964 when he used the Fishers' Ashton Manor as a base of operations to attend the Henley Regatta, in which some schoolmates were competing, and take a train to the south of France where he bicycled there and on through parts of Italy. Lee was also the beneficiary of a summer of '64 perk, joining Roger's friend, ornithologist Finnur Gudmundsson, north of the Arctic Circle in Iceland as Gudmundsson's assistant in studying the rock ptarmigan. "I was of minor assistance," remembers Lee. "It was 'tote this bag for me' kind of assistance. Much of the time he was just sort of sitting in the middle of the heath, watching [bird] behavior, so a lot of the time on the study I was on my own." He revived an interest in geology, finding and admiring "wonderful crystal structures, either cubes on cubes or things that looked like little pin cushions, millions of needlelike crystals."

The Icelandic trip was educational in another way, demonstrating the diversity of individuals Roger was friendly with. Gudmundsson "was just a wild character," Lee marvels. "He was about six-eight. . . . He was not really slender, either, with a receding chin and pale, reddish hair. . . . A chain smoker, he'd go through three packs of cigarettes a day. . . . In Iceland at that time . . . , it was just gravel roads, and he'd be driving like a bat out of hell. . . . He'd be talking and smoking at the same time. It was just unbelievable!"

Gudmundsson was one of many naturalists who might be guests in the Peterson home at any time of year. Barbara noted in January 1961, "Late in the summer, just before the A.O.U. meetings in Ann Arbor, Francois Bourliere of Paris visited us for several days. He is an almost annual guest—as is James Fisher of England, also virtually a commuter." By 1962, the house on Neck Road was essentially an international naturalists' hostel. With meetings of the World Wildlife Fund, the International Council for Bird Preservation, the International Ornithological Congress, and a first international meeting concerning national parks, the Peterson household saw, as Barbara reported, a "succession of guests such as Max Nicholson, Eric and Dorothy Hosking, James Fisher, Peter and Philippa Scott, Desmond Hawkins, and Francois Bourliere."

With house guests like these, Lee realized quite young that his father was an important man. Rosario Mazzeo, a first clarinetist for the Boston Symphony Orchestra, was also a birdwatcher and a family friend. When the Petersons visited him in Boston, "I spent most of my time riding up and down the elevator in their apartment house," says Lee.

From age eight or nine, Lee attended some of his father's lectures on the Audubon Screen Tours circuit. "He's up there doing the lecture and all these people are saying, 'Aren't you proud to be his son,' and clustering around him." Was Lee proud? "Oh, sure," he says. "Who wouldn't be?" But being asked that could be embarrassing. As a child, he thought the question was pointless. The answer was obvious.

Roger's studio, about one hundred yards up a hill from the main house, fit his fame, talents, and ambitions. "It was a spectacle," says Les Line, who assumed editorship of *Audubon* magazine in 1966, becoming Roger's sometime editor. "It was absolutely, totally organized. Every colored slide that he ever took was organized into drawers with detailed information, dates, and stuff. There was certainly no chaos at all. Quite amazing. Paintings were filed carefully in big map drawers. . . . There were works in progress around his studio."

Virginia Cadbury's daughter Peggy, an aspiring watercolorist, was dazzled by a visit with her family to the studio in the early 1960s. They had just returned Tory from a school dance date with Peggy's older sister, Betsy. "I was impressed that he had this wonderful space, separate from the house, where he could retreat and paint," Peggy remembers.

> The light was marvelous, [the studio had] big windows, and large drafting tables with tons of pencils, paints, brushes, et cetera. It seemed to a young teenager like a dream studio. He also had an impressive collection of bird specimens, carefully preserved and logged in drawers, as well as eggs. It was like a miniature natural history museum. . . . I just remember thinking how fortunate he was to be able to spend hours doing exactly what he loved, in a space designed just for that, full of every possible resource.

Roger Tory Peterson had come a long way from the modest streets of Jamestown.

All the while, Barbara Peterson "kept everything humming," as family friend Rob Hernandez says. She "did an enormous amount of correspondence, probably thousands of letters a year that came in." A large proportion of the letters were from wide-eyed fans. Those Barbara usually answered herself. "I have a great admiration for her and her role in Roger's greatness," says Hernandez, "that she allowed him to do nothing more than focus on the things that were important to him."

Barbara answered the letters of children who said they wanted to be a bird artist, or wondered how they could begin watching birds. "She got very good at forging Dad's signature, too," says Lee Peterson. "That was impressive to me as a kid, that she could do that."

Garden clubs hoping to snag Roger for a talk sometimes got Barbara instead. "It was a bit of peace for Roger," explains Barbara. "Of course, he'd been lecturing for quite a while by this time. I was seeing how it was done and I was managing him." It proved an invaluable experience for her, even if her audiences "tended to be a little on the fluttery side," she says, laughing. *Fluttery?* "That's just my description of the ladies who used to wear bonnets. When they would have a meeting, the ladies were always dressed." In the days when gender roles were well defined, knowledge of natural history was less a province of women than of men. Barbara helped "those ladies who wanted to learn a bit, at least, of what their husbands were talking about." If there were questions she couldn't answer, she consulted her husband. In so many ways, they had a marriage of cooperation.

In November 1962 Barbara accompanied Roger to the Audubon convention in Corpus Christi, Texas, where he was the keynote speaker. There was plenty to do. As inclined as her husband to be outdoors, she would write: "We had the privilege of visiting the fabulous King Ranch, and it was exciting to see some of their fine quarter horses and their methods of range management. On another all-day field trip we took a boat up the inland waterway into the Aransas Refuge to see the newly arrived whooping cranes."

Virginia Cadbury recalls a private moment with Barbara during the convention: "She was practically on the verge of tears.

"I said, 'What's the matter?'

"Finally, she said, 'It's Roger. He's just a beast.' So they were having marriage troubles then."

Whatever her private thoughts, Barbara was as busy and dedicated as ever. Given her duties as spouse, mother, secretary, manager, and "palace guard," "I think she was frazzled at times," says Les Line, adding that she nevertheless had a fairly steady temperament. She must have, to have lasted.

Through the years, Barbara maintained close ties with Roger's side of the family. When his stepfather, Lewis Saxton, died in December 1962 (Roger's father had died some fifteen years earlier), she welcomed his mother to Old Lyme for an extended stay. The following year, en route to her parents in Seattle, she drove cross-country to assist her mother-in-law's move to live with Roger's sister, Margaret, in Ventura, California: "When I had the boys in school and Roger safely in Africa we closed her little house near Jamestown and headed West." It was a wonderful trip, full of adventure. They saw longhorn cattle in the Wichita Mountains

National Wildlife Refuge and were happily surrounded by 135 buffalo while remaining in the car. Next were Arizona's Painted Desert, Petrified Forest, and Grand Canyon. Last was the scorching Mojave Desert.

"It was good to see Roger's family," Barbara wrote, "and we had an all-too-brief reunion before I headed up the coast."

Strong and assertive by nature, Barbara was in her element when she could be proactive. When her eighty-four-year-old mother-in-law and nineteen-year-old niece, Rosalinda, showed up on the Petersons' doorstep in 1964 announcing their intention of traveling to Europe by boat, Barbara stepped in to make sure it went smoothly: "They had booked passage on a boat without the remotest idea of what they were going to do when they got to the other side. No hotel reservations, no travel plans, etc. Babes in the woods, both of them. So after seeing them off I decided to fly over and give a helping hand. A good thing too. . . . Without someone who knew the ropes their travels might have been difficult." She met them in London, traveling with them through Holland before returning to the United States to "see the boys safely out of school." She then flew to Iceland with Tory and Lee, where she left Lee with Finnur Gudmundsson and Tory began his trip through Europe, its center at the Fishers' Northampton, England, home for the Henley Regatta. Thereafter, she rejoined her mother-in-law and niece in Sweden. In a "leisurely fashion we motored southward through Denmark and Germany," the last stop being Paris and the French countryside. "When Rosalinda and her Grandmother were safely emplaned for the U.S.," Barbara felt free to sightsee in England.

Sometimes Barbara had time to indulge her passion for horseback riding and raising show horses. In the summer of 1960 she formed, with the help of a friend, a "horseman's club for the horse enthusiasts of Old Lyme." They taught about thirty young people the "basic rules of horsemanship" and were pleased to see them "doing quite well with their riding." In between, she showed horses. "As a result of our showing the horses and teaching the youngsters I have probably done more handling of horses, but less riding this year than last," she wrote. "Nevertheless we sneak in a mile or two now and then."

In other years, Barbara may not have ridden as much as she would have liked, but still helped with horse shows at her nearby place of respite, the Whippoorwill Horseman's Club. In 1963 she "had charge of the obstacles and decorations and managed to create some real trials for the suburban jumpers."

Barbara Peterson had her credentials in natural history and conservation, not just because she shared her husband's views and managed his career, but also because she could on occasion thrust herself into the faces of environmental malefactors. Indiscriminate spraying of insecticides became an increasingly urgent issue facing communities around the United States. She would not sit back quietly:

> I jumped into the fight against spraying indiscriminately for "bugs." I won that one. No aerial spraying has been done in Old Lyme—although they still fog for mosquitos [sic] along the road edges and each year I go out and throw myself in front of the trucks and say, "NO," not on our property. They say: "All right, lady, if you want the bugs!" I do.

While Barbara had helped her young sons collect butterflies and moths, their efforts winning first prize at a local fair, once such highly toxic pesticides as DDT took their toll there were "few of either butterflies or moths."

The Women's Committee of the New York Zoological Society honored her on January 27, 1976, with the Vera Award, named for a captive female, concave-casqued hornbill to which a benefactor of the Bronx Zoo had taken a liking. In response to an invitation submitted to Roger in secret the previous year, he informed the Women's Committee that Barbara would be "delighted to give her own short lecture, rather than ride on my coattails for she would like to do it on her own merit."

Roger accompanied his wife to the award ceremony. She wrote a friend who had congratulated her on the award:

> The Vera Award was truly a high point in a 32½ [-year] career as wife of. It and you give me great courage to be my own woman. I quote you my remarks in my acceptance speech—not that I have been gung-ho for women's lib. . . : I have long felt that every time an award was given to the husband a small replica should be made to the wife for her charm bracelet. More often than not the behind the scenes efforts are a shared endeavor and we, as wives, more often than not just bask in reflected glory.

It was a shock to all of Roger and Barbara's friends when the early 1976 installment of their annual letter concluded with the following news:

> At the close of the year Roger and I arrived at a decision that we had pondered for some time—that it would be best for each of us to go our own way. Therefore this will be the last letter that will be signed jointly by us.
>
> At this juncture I am driving west and will live in Seattle where I shall be able to keep tabs on my mother, now in her 97th year. Roger, because of his work base, his studio facilities and library will stay in Old Lyme.

We will remain as friends and continue to face the future with optimism.

"I remember when Roger told everybody," says Katie Lewin. "It was at an art show in Montreal that we all went to, big Canadian show, and he told everybody, all of his close buddies. They were shocked! . . . They tried to argue him out of it, but of course it was too late. It was just because they knew how wonderful Barbara was. They knew how Ginny had probably done this."

"Ginny" was Virginia Westervelt, an Old Lyme neighbor who, Peterson friends and family members believe, insinuated herself into Roger's life at a time when he and Barbara were not getting along and he was particularly receptive to some very positive attention from someone of the opposite sex. Tory says his mother didn't know how to "stroke" his father well. Or, perhaps, after decades of allowing her feelings and ego to be subservient, she lost interest in perpetuating the status quo. However warm, friendly, and collegial Roger was, he had an overwhelming sense of mission and his ability to fulfill it. He was not one to submit to the needs of others, even of loved ones.

Katie Lewin recalls a boat trip where Roger's self-centeredness had infuriated Barbara:

I remember Barbara complaining, as anybody would, that she really needed a cabin to herself. This wasn't just a complaint. This was for real. She needed a cabin because, evidently, he spread all his camera gear all over the bed. Probably the floor and the closet as well. She said something about the "Great Man," meaning that his ego was so huge and he had to have everything. . . . So, eventually, she did get a separate cabin.

Another factor in the breakup, from Roger's perspective, may have been that Barbara had actually played her supporting role too well, that he began seeing her not as his wife who acted as his manager but simply as his manager. "One of the difficulties between them," remarks Genie Copp, "was that since he would work all night, he would say to Barbara, 'I want to get up at such and such,' you know, to do such and such, maybe seven, let's say. He would put that on her and she would wake him and it would make him increasingly angry because he was so short of sleep. He was angry with her.

"She was a good manager. It's just that she couldn't make managing really fun! Who can? . . . I admire her very much. But that's not an easy role to play, to have to be the manager. Eventually, you resent your manager."

Given the awkward position Barbara found herself in as her own needs rapidly surfaced against Roger's incessantly strong desire for positive feedback, one might say that their marriage couldn't have lasted, but that it was invaluable to both of them for a long time. "I think they did have some really good times in their relationship," says Tory. "I just think that it wasn't so good for longer than she really would own up to [today]." His mother "really, really was becoming a lot of her own person," he adds. "She was always a very practical, curious, really capable person. She could do anything."

It isn't clear whether Ginny Westervelt knew what was happening between Roger and Barbara. But Katie Lewin observed that Ginny "manipulated things so that she bumped into Roger. This was premeditated. She went in and grabbed him. . . . She probably gave him all kinds of praise which he would have adored."

While both Barbara and Roger had their grievances, Roger asked for the divorce. And this was because of Ginny. "I think certainly she was a catalyst for change," says Lee. "She provided a reason to make moves rather than to just let things be."

One of the most important partnerships in natural history had come to an end. And Ginny had big shoes to fill. In the opinion of friends and family alike, her feet were too small for those shoes. "I didn't care for Ginny very much, frankly," Katie Lewin divulges. "Barbara was very practical. She was very bright. Extremely bright. Ginny was a bunch of fluff, and unsubstantive."

Before long, Roger's never ideal relationship with his sons became further attenuated. Lee's wife, Courtney, compares what happened next to the "cowbird throwing out the two children and putting her kids in the nest." Ginny, now divorced from her first husband and with two daughters of her own, built a wall between Roger and his original family. It became a challenge to see or contact him. Why would Ginny do this? Tory's wife, Janet, offers that Ginny "probably felt insecure. She knew that she really did not measure up to the man."

Chapter Seven

A Natural Obsession

Roger Tory Peterson's enormous intellect couldn't protect him from a certain shortsightedness in dealing with people close to him. "I just really feel that when you're dealing with someone on the level of Roger and the genius level that he had in terms of what he did," says Courtney Peterson, "the normal things that people have front and center in their lives just kind of drop out."

Some believed he was shortsighted about the entire world; that he was obsessed with birds to the exclusion of all else. Admittedly, birds were his favorite subject. If he was with companions and the topic drifted from birds, at the first conversational lull he would announce something he had just figured out about the avian world. When he was with James Fisher, the topic was always birds.

"He was a monomaniac," says neighbor Belton Copp of Roger.

> He was the kind of person who was dedicated to one thing, . . . seulement—only—birds! . . . Everybody had that impression. My wife was very impressed about the fact that all he could talk about was birds when he came here. We have a big, plate glass window in the front of our house and it's about twelve feet high by sixteen feet wide and he was at that window looking out. . . . No matter what you were talking about, if he saw something, he didn't pay attention to what you had to say. He would look at the bird! That tells you something about him.

Roland Clement agrees: "There was no end to Roger's talk. All he could talk about were birds. If you were together with four or five people, and you got tired of hearing his lecture on birds, you took off on another topic. He'd be watching you, and the minute you let down your guard, he would go back to birds! Birds, birds, birds! He was a bit boring that way."

"Let me give you one example of Roger's utter dedication to nothing but birds, birds and birds," offers William Sladen, with whom Roger first traveled to Antarctica in 1965. When they were camped at Cape Crozier on Ross Island at the Adélie penguin colony, Roger "had a nightmare. And you know what his nightmare was . . . when with the penguins? He dreamt of a grackle that he couldn't identify." Roger was so firmly taken with the entire world of birds that being surrounded by icy desolation teeming with flightless birds could not deter neurotic fears involving even a comparatively dull land bird as the grackle.

Actually, this wasn't evidence of an unrelenting obsession with birds. Instead, it demonstrated an extraordinary ability to concentrate on a subject (or an object), regardless of what was happening around him. His focus could be so strong, it threatened his physical well-being.

Veteran cameraman Rudi Kovanic filmed seventy-year-old Roger for Canadian television doing one of the things he did best—ignoring his health and safety as he focused on the task at hand. "He was so dedicated to getting a shot he wanted that he was completely unaware of anything else that was going on," says Kovanic. "I saw him trying to film an eider duck. . . . It was molting on a lake. He couldn't get it in focus and he . . . waded in right up to his waist in ice-cold water over the top of his boots . . . , with his camera, trying to get the shot he wanted. He apparently didn't notice that he was that far into the water. That was the kind of dedication he had."

Roger's intensity of mind once forced a friend, acclaimed sculptor Kent Ullberg, to literally bail him out. Ullberg, a Swedish immigrant, lived on Padre Island near Corpus Christi, Texas. In the early 1980s, Roger "stopped by for a couple of days," says Ullberg. "He was specifically working on peeps. He wanted to get some pictures of different sandpipers. . . . I live right on the National Seashore, so we have hundreds of miles of beach. . . . You can go to some pretty remote beach places. . . . That day he was supposed to fly to Austin, I believe. There he was going to be honored." Roger was to meet British royalty.

"I had something to do," Ullberg notes, "and Roger said, 'Drop me off at the beach here and pick me up. . . .' [so he could] catch his flight. . . . Then I decided to stay, because he was getting older, and I was a little worried."

At Roger's request, Kent drove the sandpipers toward him for photographing.

I was a couple of miles up beach, walking slowly down. All of a sudden, I'm looking, and here is bloody Roger standing, probably almost up to his waist in water, on the bloody beach, and the wave had come in, and he is completely absorbed in photographing these peeps. I'm thinking, "God—now we have an hour before he's going to catch his plane and he's in his travel clothes!" And he's completely unperturbed! He is so absolutely focused on what he is doing! I feel responsible. I'm here with a world-famous birder and he is going to go and meet royalty.

I said, "What are you doing, man?" He said, "Oh, I've got some great pictures here!"

I said, "Roger—we have to go! We have to go to the airport!"

So I took him home, quickly. Off with the pants and his shoes and into the dryer, banging around. They got kind of crackly with the saltwater. I put him on the plane, and his feet were still squishing. He was completely unperturbed. That was not something that was important to him. The peeps were far more important—to get one expert picture! In my mind, that was how Roger was. Com-

pletely focused! He had his priorities. He couldn't have done what he did if he hadn't.

Nearly twenty years earlier, cameraman Rolph Blakstad had witnessed starker examples of Roger's ability to focus. It was animalistic and immovable. "He had the eyes of a bird of prey," Blakstad remembers. "He would get a fixed look in his eye and it would be needle sharp and his head wouldn't move. He'd just stare intently at what he was looking at."

Blakstad adds, "The thing I noted about Roger. . . . [about] his ability to concentrate with great intensity on what he was looking at—to do that, you need to be able to concentrate your thought, and not be bothered by stray thought." He remembers once Roger was intently looking through binoculars and, feeling the urge to urinate, peed where he was standing rather than miss any of the action.

Although birds were Roger's favorite subject, they weren't all that he considered with his bird-of-prey eyes and active mind, no matter what it may have seemed to some. Victor Emanuel, founder and owner of Victor Emanuel Nature Tours (VENT) and one of Roger's progeny, disputes his mentor's supposed avian monomania. "Anyone who thinks that he was single-minded about birds didn't really know him very well," argues Emanuel. "People might think that about me, but I'm interested in many, many other things. So was Roger. We'd talk about politics, we could talk about conservation, we could talk about other things besides birds—wildflowers and butterflies. He was very interested in butterflies." Political conversations centered on which politicians were best for conservation.

Ornithologist and author Susan Roney Drennan, who first met Roger in the 1960s, agrees that birds were his favorite subject and he would take any opportunity to talk about them. However, she found that there was much more to Roger than birds. "In the years I knew him, we covered an enormous amount of topics," she says. "Way beyond birds. We'd often discuss personal things. But we also would discuss the latest articles that came out, . . . and they often tended to politics, although I was more interested in politics than he was. Although he was pretty darned well informed."

Naturalist-writer Clay Sutton, along with his wife, Pat, the program director at the Cape May Bird Observatory, hosted Roger in Cape May twice in his later years. Clay thinks that Roger may have made people think he was single-minded about birds because of his polite and deferential nature. "He was such a gracious man, very engaging," says Clay. "If he was with Pete Dunne, I'm sure he'd talk about birds. I think, probably, the people he met to some degree would guide the conversation." This may not explain why Roger would continue to ponder birdlife—and try to insert an avian consideration at his first chance—while his companions talked of World War II diplomacy or military strategy. On the other hand, Sutton's theory does support the notion that Roger sought commonality with people. Birds more readily than other topics provided that commonality.

Roger could not have been a natural history teacher as he was at Camp Chewonki and the Rivers School, or the author of educational Audubon pamphlets on a wide range of nature topics, nor could he have written the all-encompassing *Wildlife in Color* if his knowledge or passion was limited to birds. As Kenn Kaufman noted, Roger couldn't have planned the *Wild America* trip without knowledge of flora, fauna, habitats, seasons, and life zones. Emanuel and Drennan urge, however, that Roger's curiosity went beyond natural history. There is more than anecdotal evidence for that. "If you look at the text for *Birds Over America* you'll see somebody who's sampled deeply of the culture," says Peterson protégé

Paul Spitzer. "He's writing about birds in relation to America. There's a sophistication and depth there with regard to the whole country and the culture. A monomaniac would be incapable of writing such a book."

A quick glance at *Birds Over America* yields evidence supporting Spitzer's assertion. Roger examined centuries-old literature for his history of falconry and told of its glamorous embrace by royalty and its significance to European and Asian warfare, before describing its development in the United States and the societal forces that might influence its spread.

Had he been a monomaniac, Roger couldn't have been editor of a whole series of field guides on different natural history subjects. He wouldn't have written and illustrated a field guide to wildflowers.

Since boyhood Roger had loved wildflowers, spending much time as a teen identifying and listing them. Doing a flower guide would have seemed perfectly natural. For this project, begun in 1941 with writer Margaret McKenny, Roger assumed artistic responsibilities. He soon realized that the 650 species he and McKenny had agreed upon were not nearly enough when a botanist "might dispute with his colleagues whether there are 4,660 species of flowering plants and ferns in the Northeastern quarter of the continent . . . , or 5,520 species . . . , or even more." To address this problem and ensure the book's portability, he omitted trees, shrubs, ferns, grasses, sedges, and certain other plants but still drew 1,300 species. Roger wrote the additional 650 wildflower descriptions too.

But while he had first conceived of the wildflower field guide idea at age thirty-three, it wasn't published till he was sixty. Other work kept intervening; *The World of Birds* was one such culprit. Another was his affliction with an incurable genetic condition. As Barbara wrote in the January 1963 New Year's letter: "Usually the main news is about the travels of Roger who seems to have an insatiable streak of Viking wanderlust."

Some of Roger's travels were devoted to his wildflowers. He recounted: "I covered thousands of miles by car in the Eastern and Midland states, trying to catch the brief period of bloom of various species. My station wagon crawled at its slowest speed along back country roads while I kept one eye on the road and the other on the flowers; indeed, I became slightly walleyed." He made an unusual tourist, placing samples in his "vasculum" (botanist's specimen case), unless the plants were rare, in which case he drew them "while lying flat on the ground." He drew the ones collected in his vasculum in cabins and motels, replacing the typical room's forty- or sixty-watt bulb with his own two-hundred-watt "daylight" bulb.

The Peterson *Field Guide to Wildflowers* was not the first to group wildflowers by color, but it was the first to order the species in each color category according to "general shape and structure and then to distinctions between similar species," rather than ordering them phylogenetically (the traditional method, which follows the evolutionary relationship between species). Roger liked the idea of teaching wildflowers through, essentially, a "pictorial key . . . based on readily noticed visual impressions rather than on technical features."

"I had many arguments with him about that," says William Sladen, Roger's Antarctic companion. "That he arranged it in color order, a bit of an insult to anybody trying to learn botany. . . . I'm an amateur botanist and I learnt my botany . . . by looking up keys."

A plant key is a manual that takes the reader through as few as a couple or as many as dozens of steps, in the form of one cross-reference after another, to identify a plant species. Using a key requires patience and knowledge of a "bewildering terminology," as Roger wrote. He noted that there were "at least 60 ways to say that a plant is not smooth, that it has fuzz, hair, prickles, or roughness of some sort." Few of these weird words (such as *bullate, hirtellous, pilosulous,* and *rugose*) were familiar to the average person.

Roger the teacher responded to Bill Sladen's criticisms by say-ing that he was "trying to help people learn botany a simple way."

In the 1960s Rick Radis's first bird guide was a Peterson. As a budding amateur botanist by the 1970s, he picked up another Peterson, *A Field Guide to Ferns and Their Related Families* (written by Boughton Cobb); then, Roger's wildflower guide. In May 1993 botany-obsessed New Jerseyan Rick was asked by Pete Dunne to pick up eighty-four-year-old Roger and wife Ginny in Old Lyme and transport them to Cape May, a six- or seven-hour trip, for the Cape May Bird Observatory's annual World Series of Bird-ing. Rick had met Roger before, once at the American Museum of Natural History in the 1970s while researching shorebird and pelagic bird skins, and once in the 1980s while studying snipe eggs. He remembers: "He wasn't what you would call outgoing, but he was . . . sharp as hell."

Chatting with Roger for a while in a museum was different from spending twelve to fourteen hours round-trip with him and his wife on a Friday morning traveling congested New Jersey high-ways. "I said, 'Oh, my God, I'm going to make a complete idiot out of myself,'" says Rick. "I was very worried that I wouldn't be able to hold up my end of the conversation. Even though I was just a glorified chauffeur." The Petersons had him park at their home and drive their Lexus.

Why was Rick worried? "I'm a very good birder," he explains, "but I'm not a world-class birder." His knowledge of plant life was a different story. "In botany I can hold my own with anybody, pretty much." Rick needn't have worried. He and Roger talked botany the whole way. They engaged in plant name dropping:

[Roger] mentioned a fairly obscure plant like Gray's lily, which only occurs in the Appalachians, or swamp pink, which is mostly only in the Pine Barrens in New Jersey. Gorgeous plants, but quite rare. You pretty much have to know somebody to see them. . . . He knew spots in Newfoundland that I had actually just been to. . . . There's an orchid called small world begonia on which I had actually done some work . . . that was listed as an endangered species about fifteen years ago. . . . But Roger had found a population of that orchid in Virginia. . . . [which was a] very closely guarded . . . secret. . . . Peterson somehow wormed that information out of . . . [someone] so he could go and draw or paint this orchid from life.

To Rick, now editor of *New Jersey Audubon* magazine, Roger was a true descendant of the early naturalists: "It's just that he had a certain special knowledge of special plants and special places that he had to get from these people, these old field botanists, who were handing down lore that comes down from Audubon's time, practically."

In May 1987 Pat and Clay Sutton enjoyed a similar revelation hosting Roger in Cape May. They took him to Kimbles Beach, Reeds Beach, and other "shorebird spots" for his photography. In the evening, they had him over for dinner. "We probably had fresh seafood and fresh South Jersey vegetables," reminisces Pat.

Just kind of a low-key, casual evening. At the time, I was raising one of the silk moths, called a royal walnut moth. They were in the caterpillar stage, which is called hickory-horned devil, because they're really scary looking. Roger loved silk moths. As a young

man, he had been very familiar with them. With a lot of the spray-
ing in Connecticut, it had been years since he had seen royal wal-
nut moths or a lot of the other silk moths. He practically begged
me to give him some of these caterpillars to take back, which I was
delighted to do. I had a great, big, mesh enclosure just full of them,
and sent him home with some hickory-horned devils. . . . He was
just thrilled.

In May 1994 the Suttons hosted Roger again for the Cape May Century Run, a sort of laid-back, noncompetitive arm of the World Series of Birding. "He confided that he was just as excited to be seeing butterflies here as well as birds," Pat recalls. "He's certainly so well known for his bird field guides, but he loved butterflies and the large silk moths as well." Roger was a "true naturalist," says Clay, "Not just a birder. That's an important point to emphasize."

The late Charles Remington, who began his career at Yale University in 1948 teaching biology and went on to found Zero Population Growth with Paul Ehrlich, used to take Roger to lunch at Yale's Pierson College. "We would go sit around, shooting the breeze of ardent naturalists over lunch," said Remington in 2006. They talked about far more than birds. "I would take him to the Lepidoptera hall, and he essentially salivated," Remington remembered.

Ever collegial, Roger often raised new field guide ideas with Remington: "He came to me for advice on possible authors on insects and plants." Moths were another concern. "I'm hearing a great enthusiasm for doing a good moth book," Roger mentioned to Remington, who said, "Butterflies had already been done by Alexander Klots, so it wasn't needed in Roger's series. But moths were badly needed. I found a very good moth guy in Kentucky named Charles Kovell. He did a superb job with the moths. . . . The moth guide is one of the most interesting of all in the Peterson series."

Remington was a mentor to a young fellow who would make a huge name for himself in butterfly study and nonfiction, natural history works. This young fellow, Robert Michael Pyle, also loved birds and got his first Peterson in 1966. Pyle couldn't have predicted how he would meet the series' namesake. There was nothing ordinary about how they hit it off. And it might not have happened when it did if Pyle hadn't been a student radical at the University of Washington.

In 1970 twenty-three-year-old Pyle was an activist in the Conservation Education and Action Council at the University of Washington. The council's big issue was an area known as the Montlake Dump, composed of Union Bay Marsh and the Montlake lowlands, which had been leased by the university to the city of Seattle and turned into a landfill. "We were taking over that dump," says Pyle. "Other people were charging into the administration building, and taking over the administration building and taking . . . the president prisoner, and demanding peace and justice. We took over the dump and demanded topsoil and trees. . . . Because that was one of our causes célèbres, the [Montlake Dump] became the name of the lefty, hippy, environmental, antiwar coalition that started to take over the student government as well." Eventually, the movement known as the Montlake Dump assumed control of the Association of Students at the university.

"They had some money left over in the budget and decided to send a whole delegation of student conservationists and activists to the National Audubon convention [in Milwaukee] to bring up issues of the war and sexism and gay rights and all kinds of things that Audubon had no interest in hearing about," Pyle muses. What a scene it must have been. The Audubon president was Elvis Stahr, a former secretary of the army—the first head of Audubon to be recruited via corporate headhunters—and he wasn't "interested in having a bunch of longhairs come and talk about these issues, although he was polite to us. Condescending, but polite."

At the convention Pyle purchased a Peterson eastern bird guide; when he saw Roger alone for a moment, he moved in. "I just happened to see for the first time that he wasn't thronged with people, which is why I descended on him and thronged him myself. By the way, I was pretty singular in appearance at that time. I had long hair, but I also had an extremely long, ZZ Top sort of a beard."

Was Roger, then nearly sixty-two, repulsed by the approach of an excessively hirsute person? The elder naturalist didn't recoil. "I do remember that he was interested in young people," Pyle continues.

> He was definitely interested in the fact that we were all there. Why were all these young, hairy, hippy, conservationists there? . . . I can't imagine that I didn't tell him the history [of the Montlake Dump]. . . . Because the Montlake Dump was not only the place we took over to try to restore, it's eventually been restored, not fully as a marsh, of course, but as a marvelous habitat. But it was . . . [then] our primary birding place on campus.

When Pyle presented his field guide for Roger to sign, the usual autograph-seeking encounter didn't quite transpire.

"I went up and asked him to sign it for me, which he did. Then he said, 'Oh, yes, what are you interested in?'"

"I said, 'Well, actually, I'm a keen birder, but mostly butterflies.'"

"He had the usual beleaguered—I mean, I've signed a great many books, not anything on the scale that he has, but certainly many thousands, and there's a certain—you know, it's a funny thing," Pyle stops and reflects.

> You're always honored and delighted that anyone would want your book and pleased and honored that they'd want you to sign

*it, but it can become a little bit repetitive. For Roger at an Audu-
bon convention you can imagine the tedium that could set in with
that activity. . . . There was a real change in his demeanor when I
said that I was involved in seeing butterflies. He said, "Butterflies!
Let's go have a milkshake. Get away from these bird people." . . .
So we went out onto the street and there was a drugstore or something, or . . . it might have been the café in the hotel. Anyway, he
loved milkshakes. Loved chocolate milkshakes. . . . That was a real
fave of his. . . . And we talked butterflies. It became very apparent
that he, too, loved butterflies. That he was just delighted to have a
moment to talk about butterflies instead of birds. . . . It was funny
for me because, here we were, sipping milkshakes out of straws,
which are basically—butterfly tongues are drinking straws, you
know. It was fun that we were duplicating the activity of butterflies and talking about butterflies.*

A decades-long association ensued between the young man
of long hair and endless beard and the older, beleaguered man
of pale mane—a lover of not just birds but also butterflies and
milkshakes.

Chapter Eight

Hidden Roger

In the years before publication of Roger's first field guide, like other respectable ornithologists of the era, he "collected," or shot, birds for scientific study. When asked in the 1970s whether he collected or otherwise hunted birds, he remarked, dispassionately, "No. Well, I've got a collecting permit, but I don't use it. I had collected years ago, but there's no need to, really." For hands-on study, there were museum skins. For hands-free study, there were rapidly improving optics, Roger's still sharp eye, his incessant picture taking with state-of-the-art equipment, and the field guides he had authored.

Roger was never a hunter. He wasn't comfortable with it. He wasn't preachy, but at times couldn't hold his feelings in. Some of his unhappiness with hunting came to the fore in the early 1960s when hunting interests were lobbying for permission to hunt additional species—plovers in Hawaii, sandhill cranes in Texas, and tundra swans (then called whistling swans) in Utah. As he railed in a letter to Carl Buchheister, John Baker's successor as president of the National Audubon Society:

> I think that before long we have got to take a stand against all hunting except a few selected sorts. We should not underestimate our numbers. We are growing and in fact it is quite possible that the hunting group may well be a minority group in the not-too-distant future. Don't we have a say as taxpayers and shouldn't the Fish and Wildlife Service now angle its efforts more in the direction of

enjoyment of wildlife in other ways than just harvesting it? Some forms of hunting and fishing, of course, can be perpetuated indefinitely, but I question, for one, whether waterfowl hunting can be, but to put cranes on the hunting list, or shore birds, birds with a low reproductive potential to me is an evil thing.

Excuse this outpour.

Days later, Roger wrote to Buchheister again, relaying complaints from people in California and Connecticut concerning an apparently uncritical Audubon statement about shooting doves. Audubon's position, the opponents of dove hunting contended, had "'cut out the ground from under us,'" reported Roger. He sided with the opponents:

I do think the opponents of dove shooting have a point. As for Connecticut I think it is completely wrong to have a dove shooting season—a bird that lays but two eggs and is enjoyed by the vast majority of people who are non-hunters. I think we have got to stiffen our backbone on this general disintegration of restrictions on many species that seems to be exploding now in all parts of the country. We are going to find that before long everything but passerine birds will be regarded as legal game. As I grow older, and I am not a sentimentalist, merely civilized, I feel more and more strongly that the day of blood sports should be ended.

Rob Hernandez, who in the mid-1970s lived in a cottage on the Peterson property while he assisted Roger in the studio and attended college, enjoyed hunting and took Lee Peterson along one day. "Roger knew I hunted. I didn't flaunt it in front of him, but he knew that I hunted and he didn't give me any grief about it," remembers Hernandez.

> One day Lee and I went out and he shot a duck and brought it back and we ate it. . . . Roger would come down very often in the evening to the cottage where I was because I was in my last year of college in those days, and I was always active—a lot of young people around and stuff. He found it fun to have a little bit of a break because he wasn't a monk, but he didn't lead an active social life in Old Lyme. One day around dinnertime there were a couple of ducks in the oven and it smelled wonderful, and he came in with Carl Buchheister. He said, "Oh, Rob, smells really good. What are you cooking?" . . . I was absolutely aghast. I'd never met this other great man, who had led National Audubon for years, and I said, "Oh, some chicken."
>
> Roger quickly opened the oven door, peeked in, closed it again, looked up, and said, [Rob mimics Roger's incredulous voice] "Funny-looking chicken." . . . He wasn't going to let Carl know. . . . It was typical Roger too. Roger was not a man of confrontation. Ever.

Roger didn't confront—at least he didn't go toe to toe with people, as Rob Hernandez expresses it—but he could set an example. His good friend Belton Copp was a duck hunter until Roger stopped him.

"He didn't convert me by saying I shouldn't do it," says Copp. "He just converted me by his example. . . . He was quite tolerant of what I was doing. . . . Roger taught me, among other things, that it wasn't any fun to shoot a duck. It's much more fun to see it. I gave up shooting ducks after being at it—God—for many, many years."

If he could do it over, Copp says, he wouldn't have been a hunter. "I now resent anybody hunting! A real switch," he acknowledges. "I became involved with the fish and game department of the state of Connecticut. I was one of the trustees . . . , appointed by the governor. . . . I was trying to do everything I could to shorten seasons and all that sort of thing."

A real confirmation that Roger had arrived socially came when Copp sponsored him for membership in the Ariston Club. "Ariston," says Copp, is Greek for "best." He disarmingly describes the club as a "pretty haughty group" of over twenty men. "Every month, we would get dressed in black tie and so forth and go and meet at a dinner that one of the members in turn would give," he explains. "The meals were very, very good. They were fancy, nice meals. . . . [The members] were leaders of the community." Copp obtained his membership, before he had established himself as a community leader, through his uncle Christopher L. Avery, once a justice on the Connecticut Supreme Court of Errors and descended from the settlers of Groton.

"Then I got Roger in," says Copp. "I remember Roger had a paper—we called it a paper—early on, and he gave his paper to the club. Everybody was quite impressed. . . . I think it was about birds! . . . I was pleased that he did this and everybody else was too."

It was curious that Roger wanted to be a member of a club completely unrelated to natural history, even if he could give a paper on birds. His acceptance by the Nuttall Ornithological Club notwithstanding, one would assume that associating with a bunch of socially rarefied men would have been awkward for the son of working-class immigrants. As Paul Spitzer points out, Roger was not one to ascribe to old class structures: "He was enough up from the land himself, if you will, that it just wasn't the way he operated."

However, when he became an Ariston member, he was branching out in the world, establishing links with people of varying backgrounds including impressively educated and privileged ones. He could work with a Spanish nobleman, like Mauricio González; explore natural history with Lord Alanbrooke, a British aristocrat and chief of Britain's Imperial General Staff during World War II; confer about birds with Peter Scott, an athlete descended from an adventurer; thoroughly embrace a brainy ornithologist, James Fisher, educated at a couple of Britain's best schools; or show Prince Philip, a real live royal, a few birds.

The social status of others neither impressed nor intimidated Roger. "He'd talk to prime ministers and kings in the same way that he spoke to schoolchildren when he was explaining the marvels of nature as he saw and experienced them," says cameraman Rudi Kovanic, "which was quite refreshing, because status of individuals seemed to have no effect on Roger from what I could see, which I found an endearing trait."

This unflappability may have applied whether or not the subject was birds so long as he received respect. "I think Roger liked the attention," reflects Copp. "He liked to be recognized as somebody. If you were a member of this club you were supposed to be one of twenty or twenty-four—I can't remember the number now—'somebodies' in the area. Most of the people were, of course, chairman of the board of the biggest bank in New London and the president of the biggest company in New London and all that sort of stuff."

Depending on whom you asked, the Roger Tory Peterson at home in Old Lyme was not the man he was on the road. He could be reclusive, almost shut off from others. Photographer Bill Burt, a teen when he first visited Roger in his studio, saw him as a "quiet, withdrawn man," and assumed he was always that way.

Lee Peterson explains that his father was reserved at home.

Dad was happy to be interrupted on occasion by friends. . . . But he was quick to go back to the studio. Once he got that momentum going of producing in the studio, he was not social in nature. He'd be good for a little while but within a half an hour or an hour he'd want to be back up there. . . . One of the things that made Dad successful was that ability to focus for extended periods of time, the ability to flip that switch and go full tilt. . . . He became much more of a social animal on the road.

Jimmy and Dolores Zaccaro, who lived in the neighboring town of Lyme, can attest to a side of Roger people rarely saw. They met him through mutual friends, but never met Barbara, "so Roger felt quite comfortable dropping in on us. With Virginia [Westervelt]," says Dolores. "'Cause we were the only ones who were in kind of la-la land, so to speak."

Although they were not birdwatchers, the Zaccaros knew of Roger. "I have to tell you, everybody in that area knew who he was," Dolores confirms. "He was a big guy. . . . We'd see him at the store and say, 'Oh, there's Roger.' Every town has its famous people. And we had ours."

Roger introduced birds to Jimmy, a photographer and producer of commercials, and Dolores, a costumer for print and television commercials. "He used to sit on our screen porch and just listen and say, 'Oh, you've got this, you've got that, you've got this, you've got that,'" Dolores remembers. "He identified all the birds we had!" If the Zaccaros couldn't identify a bird in the yard, they would call him and he'd come over and identify it. When they decided to put up bird feeders, Dolores says, "He told us to feed the birds in the summer as well . . . 'cause a lot of people say, 'Don't feed them if you're not there every day.' And he said, 'That's not true! Feed them whatever you can, because whatever they can get is *more!*'" Roger also explained how hills and wind direction affect bird flight, the importance of thick shrubs for small birds trying to avoid predation, and the pigeon's habitat, highway underpasses.

When the Zaccaros had Roger to their dinner parties it didn't matter that none of the other guests were birdwatchers or that most had only a passing interest in natural history. This marked a change from his youth when he avoided socializing. "Roger was very, very social," Dolores remembers, adding,

> He did . . . hold court a bit. He'd usually sit on the sofa, and everybody would come around and then one group would leave and another group would come. He wasn't the one who moved about. He kind of plopped himself down and everybody would come to him. . . . I don't think he did it purposely. Maybe he liked to sit down. But that's the way it was.

As Jimmy points out, birds can comfortably lead to talk of other subjects: "The thing about birdwatching is it's sort of all-encompassing, in a way. It's not . . . like a golfer who is interested in golfing and that's it. The interest in birds makes you talk about . . . the South Pole, the Arctic, the Antarctic, and this and that."

Another topic Roger liked and wasn't shy about commenting on was the opposite sex. "If we were sitting in a car waiting for someone we were picking up at the train station," says Jimmy, "and an attractive woman passed by, he'd see it, notice it, and comment on it. . . . It was funny. I was impressed that the old guy was still looking at things."

Greg Lasley, a birding and photography companion during the last ten years of Roger's life, was also privy to this side of a man not known for frivolity or, frankly, lasciviousness. "Roger appreciated attractive-looking young women. He would enjoy looking at them and he sometimes would make . . . jokes that were not for publication. Let's put it that way," Lasley chuckles, elaborating only that Roger "enjoyed looking at females, and he appreciated the physicalness of the female form."

Roger's appreciation of young women's bodies may have been a weapon against aging. He hated getting older but had a wizened appearance before he was even fifty, perhaps because of all that time in the sun, or because of the way he naturally aged. Although his sons believe Roger's face-lifts in the 1960s and 1970s were meant to correct facial injuries suffered in a 1964 car accident, a 1973 letter from Barbara to her mother suggests otherwise: "It seems to me RTP has a case of accellerating [*sic*] aging. After all he is only 64—but looks 74 to me—with all his face lifts! . . . I know no one who fears age as much as he. It is sad. James F. once said RTP shd. read more philosophy."

Roger's fear of aging sometimes made him attack close friends. "I remember him being critical of Peter Scott over his attitude," says Keith Shackleton.

> *It's the time that Roger was beginning to feel that he was getting old. He would say, "God damn it! People like you just make me sick," he said to Peter, "because you don't give a damn about getting old! And you ought to. There's lots of things we've all got to do. But you just accept it!"*
>
> *"Then he turned on me and said, 'And you're just as bad!'"*
>
> *I said, "Well, look—what the hell can you do, Roger? Time goes on and you get older. And there it is."... He was terribly worried. But he was so worried about it that he used to take it out on*

*us for not being worried about it, if you see what I mean. He was
not prepared to let things unfold in a normal sort of way. He had
a grudge against fate for making him old. You can't get anywhere
with that philosophy, can you, really?*

Bob Bateman had to prevent Lyn Hancock from suggesting
aloud that Roger might not have time to write a *Wild America*
sequel. The nearly seventy-eight-year-old Roger ended up wist-
fully hoping in his foreword to Hancock's 1986 book, *Looking for
the Wild:* "After a suitable lapse, . . . Ginny and I will put the finishing touches on our own book, *Wild America Revisited.* By then there
will have been other things to tell, other changes, other insights."
He broached this desire in Alaska while Gus Yaki's group chatted
awhile after a day's exploring.

Says Hancock, "He wouldn't have done it. . . . It was something
he would have liked to have done. But I don't think his heart was
in it. Certainly, his schedule was not in it. I remember Bob Bateman said, 'If you're going to tell him he's not going to be able to,
it would be like saying he's not immortal.' Because Roger was very
interested in his health. . . . He had an emphasis on that. Because
there were so many things he wanted to do, and he believed that
he still could always do them."*

Bateman doesn't remember the exchange—"Oh, did I say
that?"—but corroborates Roger's openly expressed fear. "He
talked about death a fair amount. . . . Most people don't talk
about it at all."

In his later years, Roger was often quoted saying he planned to
live to 110 because of all the books he had to write and all the painting he wanted to do. Belton and Genie Copp's son Allyn, a photography enthusiast, visited Roger in his studio in the 1960s to use

---

* Roger's dream of writing a *Wild America* sequel was the reason Hancock called her
book *Looking for the Wild* rather than her proposed *Looking for Wild America.* Hancock believes that her book, a best seller in Canada, would have done better in the
United States if she could have kept her original title.

the dark room. Allyn was surprised at Roger's interest in discussing health issues with him, a high school kid. "He was something of a hypochondriac, which was kind of amusing," says Allyn.

> *He was always asking me about what I ate and what I thought people should eat. . . . I think he wanted to live a long, healthy life. . . . I had a great uncle who lived to be 104, and . . . had two eggs and bacon for breakfast with some orange juice. Then he'd have a big lunch of meat and potatoes and vegetables. Then he'd have the same thing for dinner. He did that every day of his life for 104 years. At the time, when people were talking about all the things that ail you, that would not have been a recipe for longevity.*

Roger was taken with Allyn's great uncle's ability to "buck the trend."

Lee Peterson agrees that his father was a hypochondriac. "And worried about his mortality," he says. "He had an awful lot of time by himself in the studio to think about stuff like that."

Part Four:

CONSERVATION STORIES

Chapter Nine

Embryonic Conservationism

As Roger Tory Peterson fought his aging, he always retained a youthful optimism about the fate of birds. Were he alive today, Cape May Bird Observatory director Pete Dunne says, Roger would be hopeful where others might despair of the future of the *rufa* subspecies of the red knot, the bird that has prompted conservationists to protect its diet of horseshoe crab eggs in Delaware Bay. The knot, which winters in Patagonia and Tierra del Fuego and stops on Cape May area beaches to fatten up on the eggs before flying northward to its Arctic nesting grounds, numbered approximately 95,000 in the early 1980s. Then certain entrepreneurs found horseshoe crabs excellent bait for conch. They harvested the crabs at increasingly aggressive levels, severely depleting the eggs' abundance. The food supply of the knots and three other shorebird species was decimated. By 2003 the knots' numbers had plummeted to 16,000. In 2007, only 12,375 came through Delaware Bay. Encouragingly, in efforts to replenish the birds' food supply, New Jersey imposed a two-year moratorium on crab harvests in 2006. (A similar moratorium in Delaware has been challenged.)

Pete Dunne says,

> *I think Roger would probably . . . be more confident than many that the bird . . . will make a comeback. . . . He had the well of his experience to draw from. He was in New York, he told me, when the first Forster's tern returned. . . . He saw North America . . . when its natural dowry was pauperized. And he saw a lot of birds*

*come back. . . . We're far better off as birders now, there are far
more species, species diversity is greater now, than when Roger
was learning his birds. . . . We would talk about the doom and
gloom and Roger would point out, "You know, . . . there was a
time when things looked pretty bleak."*

The good sense of people banding together to fight for animals
others were destroying was the reason for this turnaround in fortune. Roger understood this as a very young man. Herbert Job's
Wild Wings did more than provide the fledgling photographer with
hints and tips. It also passionately pleaded for the preservation of
the birds Job obsessively photographed. Roger learned of the Audubon warden Guy Bradley, who, two years before he was murdered
by plume hunters, had been a guide for Job in the Everglades.

A boy so wedded to birds who read Job's passionate attacks
on those who used nature at a breakneck pace until it was used
up was likely deeply touched by Job's outlook:

*This whole business of the slaughter of . . . birds . . . for their plumes
for millinery purposes is one that every lover of nature and every
person of humane feeling who understands the case will regard
no less than infamous. This is one of the moral questions—to be
classed with the opium traffic and the slave trade—to which there
is but one side.*

*In these days there is arising a many-sided and tremendous prob-
lem in regard to saving the natural world from ignorant, shortsighted, commercial vandalism. Every tree must be cut down,
every plant pulled up, every wild thing slaughtered, every beautiful scene disfigured, if only there is money to be made from it.*

In *The Passenger Pigeon,* the late-1920s quarterly newsletter of
the Nature Correspondent Association, eighteen-year-old Roger
wrote in a Job-ish way of ignorant people prejudiced against

predators, killing snowy owls during the previous winter, with its "marked influx of boreal species: Throughout the northeast, the newspapers have told of Snowy Owls having been killed here and there, told in a manner indicative of praise and prowess in sportsmanship. Such misguided fools! Such slaughter shall put our race to shame in time to come."

Roger's Junior Audubon membership and his study of Job's *Wild Wings* lit a fire in his psyche. By the time he joined the Bronx County Bird Club and been tantalized—although intimidated—by the confrontations of Rosalie Edge, the youth was more than a willing vessel for Edge's educational writings. He was already a teacher, spreading the word in camp and school and as he prepared his first field guide. He had surrendered his life to conservation.

While still working on that field guide, he offered a glimpse of it in an illustrated article about gull identification for *Nature* magazine. His writing was matter-of-fact—strictly informational—but a conservationist message emerged amid practical pointers on distinguishing between the plumage of glaucous and Iceland gulls:

All of the gulls are increasing because of the protection they have been accorded during the past few years. With the growth in the numbers of individuals has come a corresponding increase in visits by the rarer species. This is unquestionable evidence of the success of organized conservation, to which wild life is always quick to respond. We might assume that the future of these, among the most graceful feathered creatures, is now secure.

Modern society and its propensity for devising ever more spectacular destructiveness introduced new challenges to the conservationist. True, a growing patchwork of enlightened laws existed, as did a federal government, particularly under the New Deal, which increasingly dedicated resources to conservation. But the war against Hitler, Mussolini, and Tojo, with oil the chief propellant of the killing machines, caused the deaths of—at minimum—thousands of birds off U.S. shores in the months following Pearl Harbor. Writing about this for *Audubon* magazine, Roger carefully presented the facts without passing judgment, which would have been unwise when the entire nation was consumed with winning a global war.

The phenomenon of birds dying because of oil slicks—their feathers losing buoyancy and insulating properties—was nothing new, Roger said. A ship destroyed on a rocky coastline will leak its fuel. A vessel stuck on a reef may need to dump oil over the side to break free. It had been a violation of U.S. law since 1924 for a boat to discharge its oil within three miles of land or in a harbor, but no international agreement could be reached to prohibit the release of oil farther out to sea.

By late February 1942 reports were coming in of thousands of wintering ducks along the northeast coastline harmed by oil slicks. Roger quoted from a Ludlow Griscom letter: "Just last Sunday I discovered the greatest disaster of oiled birds at Monomoy [Massachusetts]. We estimated that 25 per cent out of approximately 20,000 wintering birds were more or less badly affected. The sight was pathetic and extraordinary and was immeasurably worse than anything previously recorded in the waters of the state." Before long, similar stories arrived from all along the Atlantic coast of thousands of birds succumbing to oil. A respite occurred when surviving birds flew north and inland to breed in spring. Soberly Roger commented, "No humane-minded person can see oiled birds along the beach without being saddened. . . . If birds are badly affected, it is kinder to put them out of their misery as quickly as possible." He noted that it was becoming difficult for birders to monitor the incidences of oiled birds on beaches; because of their binoculars, birders were suspected of spying.*

Roger related several tips for treating oiled birds, from the Royal Society for the Protection of Birds, individual U.S. coastal residents, and cosmetics manufacturers. He acknowledged: "While the war lasts, it seems totally improbable that we can prevent oil pollution at sea. When, however, the conflict is over, not only should public opinion force strict enforcement of existing laws against pollution within the three-mile limit, but every effort should be made to gain international agreement to ban oil pollution on the high seas." He also urged that even during the war a civilian ship's discharge of "oil-contaminated ballast water" be controlled.

World War II did more than kill untold millions of people in the most brutal and efficient ways or usher in the Cold War or introduce the nuclear age. It also led to reliance on the use of chemicals as the avenue to a better life.

Eradicating insect pests seemed a realizable goal. A category of organic but synthetically created chlorinated hydrocarbons

---

* In July 1942 John Baker recounted in a letter an encounter Roger had had with law enforcement. "Roger Peterson went out to photograph some European goldfinches in their nests on Long Island last Sunday. No sooner was he comfortably or uncomfortably . . . ensconced in a big tree with his camera, when numerous persons nearby reported him to the police as a suspicious character." Upon being questioned by the responding officer, Roger explained he was birding. The officer mentioned that earlier he had spoken with a couple of birdwatchers who were viewing the same goldfinches and they showed him a book by a "Mr. Peterson." Continued Baker in his letter, "When Roger timidly announced that he was the Mr. Peterson a fast friendship was established." The officer became a birder.

was formulated in European laboratories during the war. One would become the most notorious of the bunch—DDT. During the war, only the military used DDT, in powdered form, applied directly on soldiers' bodies as an insect repellant. Writing in 1972 Audubon biologist Roland Clement indicated that such applications of DDT during the war "undoubtedly saved millions of lives from typhus, malaria, and other insect-borne diseases." However, after the war DDT was approved by the U.S. Department of Agriculture for domestic use and typically was mixed with oil or other solvents, "mostly to facilitate aerial application over large areas." Applying the chemical in this way, Clement pointed out, rendered the substance fat soluble and, as he was able to say after over two decades of activism by conservationists and environmentalists, "Our troubles began here."

At the tail end of the war, Sergeant Roger Tory Peterson was assigned to conduct a DDT study with fellow ornithologist and artist George Miksch Sutton. Roger reported that the purpose of the study was to "determine whether birds are killed or adversely affected by aerial spraying of DDT." The concentrations used on the two spray dates were three-tenths of a pound per acre on August 7, 1945, and six-tenths of a pound on September 1. Roger censused bird populations on two test plots in Lake County, Florida, over a forty-four-day period between July 23 and September 21 with assistance from Sutton.

The one-square-mile test plots were selected for their diverse habitats. As Roger divulged, the test had some inherent limitations. The two control areas were not directly comparable to the test areas, and with just one other person to count birds there was little time to regularly survey the control areas. Also, censusing had to be done early—7:30 to 10:30 a.m.—while birdsong was still evident and birds were most active; both test plots could not be censused on the same day. Additionally, the Peterson/Sutton team could not thoroughly cover one entire test plot on a given morning because of its size.

Furthermore, much birdsong had ceased by late summer. Many breeding pairs had departed. Accordingly, Roger reported that the timing of the test sprays was less than optimal:

> *Suffice it to say there are distortions in our present picture. We have such factors as cessation of song; secretiveness because of molt; wandering of families; departure of some breeders, such as Redwings [red-winged blackbirds] and Mourning Doves from the area as soon as their nesting was over; arrival and departure of migrants from the north; departure of Hummingbirds because of the termination of the flowering period of their local food plants, etc.*

Roger found only one dead bird, close to the time of the first test spray, but could not conclusively state it died from the spraying. At the end of the study period, he was able to report, while being candid about the study's limitations, that he and Sutton "could find no evidence of a diminution in bird life resulting from the aerial spraying of DDT. Actually there were more birds present at the end of the two months period. . . . than earlier. This, however, can be ascribed principally to two causes: . . . young on the wing and the presence of migrants from the North."

There was reason for disquiet, as a detached Roger disclosed, because of "(1) the heavy scent of kerosene in the air; and (2) the thin, irridescent [*sic*] scum on the river in which dying Gyrinid water beetles were seen floating downstream."

As an aside, Roger noted that a test in Pennsylvania involving aerial spraying of *five pounds* of DDT per acre did not result in any bird deaths until after forty-eight hours, but that the mosquitoes "were far less bothersome." Presumably, he did not go into further detail about the Pennsylvania test because it was not directly comparable to their efforts in Lake County, Florida, where the military was using far less than a pound per acre for each spray.

But what happened in Pennsylvania was horrible. As Dick Pough disclosed in a report to the National Audubon Society, the two forty-acre test plots were situated near Wilkes-Barre and Scranton, Pennsylvania. Aerial spraying was done at the height of the nesting season by a local agency concerned with controlling pests including the gypsy moth. Pough wrote that at the "end of 48 hours the woods went 'dead', without a sign of bird life or song," adding later in his report, "certainly, the results of this experiment, in which I estimate some 4000 old and young birds were poisoned, proves false the oft-repeated statement that D.D.T. is harmless to all warm-blooded organisms."

Three years later in *Birds Over America* Roger acknowledged the dreadfulness of the Wilkes-Barre/Scranton experiment, noting that the DDT concentrations used in his 1945 study were "light," sparing most insects except mosquitoes and a few other sensitive, invertebrate species. However, in the "Pennsylvania experiment nearly every bird in the woods died when five pounds per acre were used." Although Roger allowed for the possible usefulness of DDT as an alternative to draining marshes in efforts to thwart mosquitoes, he warned, "by using this dangerous poison widely, before we know more about its properties, we run the risk of turning our world into a biological desert." It remained to be seen whether *any* concentration of DDT was safe.

Roger couldn't have known then, but postwar use of DDT would have a deleterious effect on one of the chief attractions of his Old Lyme home—the nearby nesting of 150 osprey pairs. As early as the summer of 1957, about three years after moving to Connecticut, he noticed that few young ospreys were fledging. Thence began a search for answers and embroilment in a fight against a man-made scourge that would reach crisis proportions within the decade.

Chapter Ten
Adventuresome Flights of Conservation

In the 1950s and 1960s, Roger Tory Peterson had his finger in a multitude of pies. Not only was he always revising or working on a field guide, editing his field guide series, writing books, painting birds, and lecturing widely, but he was also active in numerous scholarly, scientific, social, artistic, and conservation organizations. Besides the National Audubon Society for which he served varyingly as a board member, secretary, and consultant in the years after World War II, and the National Wildlife Federation, for which he served as art director for nearly thirty years, he eventually ascended from Audubon delegate of the International Council for Bird Preservation to chair of the U.S. Section, attended conferences of the International Union for the Conservation of Nature, served as president of the Wilson Ornithological Society and the American Nature Study Society, and after about three decades in the American Ornithologists' Union was elected first vice president.

From the first days of the fight against the plume trade, the American Ornithologists' Union expended some resources in monitoring conservation issues, although it was primarily a scientific body. Roger could be useful as either scientist or conservationist. As scientist he might do something as seemingly routine as lead an AOU session on a topic of avian physiology, but what he did had meaning for others. Ornithologist Philip Humphrey remembers an AOU conference in Salt Lake City where a paper on molts and plumages that introduced a new nomenclature he had coauthored with Ken Parkes of the Carnegie Museum subjected them to near condemnation. "The top ornithologists in the world were all upset about this," says Humphrey, who recalls Roger onstage leading a session when Humphrey and Parkes were in the audience, and the first speaker was quite critical of their work.

Humphrey said, "When he was finished, Roger said, 'Before I ask for general questions from the audience, I want Phil or Ken to respond.' Kenny nudged me, and I got up. I was the senior author. I responded to this extraordinary talk, . . . [and] summarized Kenny's and my beliefs and sat down. . . . Roger was very thoughtful to ask us to respond first."

Concomitant with Roger's scientific bent was his hunger for learning. He must have gobbled up every last word at sessions like the one Humphrey relates. Peterson protégé Noble Proctor believes Roger was involved in these organizations because he "enjoyed the interaction with the people, . . . [and] also to . . . sort of keep a monitor level on what was happening."

In turn Roger became a valued information source. In 1962, years before enactment of the Endangered Species Act, U.S. Fish and Wildlife official John Aldrich knew he could go to Roger with questions about endangered or threatened species of birds:

> *Roger, if you were to list the species of North American birds which are endangered because of known numbers and environmental conditions, which would you include? If you were to plan a series of research projects to find the causes of the scarcity or decline of these species which ones would you select as being chiefly in need of study because of current lack of information? I know you get around a lot and talk with a great many people and that you are interested in this particular subject, so you probably have some ideas on it.*

Roger quickly listed twenty species that were "endangered because of low numbers or restrictive or demanding environmental conditions." He maintained hope in the ivory-billed woodpecker, which he included on the list: "any left? What about recent reports from east Texas?" He also warned of the neglected swallow-tailed kite: "it is a very much reduced species and could be on its way out in North America."*

"Roger was one of those people whom everybody looked up to," says Peter Ames, one of several ornithology students who worked with Roger and Barbara Peterson on tracking breeding ospreys at Old Lyme in the 1960s. "We respected him as a conservationist, as a person who got things done, who got land dedicated, who got things on and off the Endangered Species Act. . . . He was influential in a lot of these things."

Peterson was a behind-the-scenes player in conservation rather than a table pounder like Rosalie Edge. His reputation attracted Francis Kellogg during formative meetings of the World Wildlife Fund, held in New York somewhat concurrently with Peter Scott's efforts in England. As Lady Philippa Scott recalls, the idea of the World Wildlife Fund arose in the wake of a meeting of the International Union for the Conservation of Nature. "Peter was horrified that here were these people doing wonderful work with scientists going all over the world but they hadn't enough money. The people they were employing on these projects never knew whether they were going to be paid at the end of it all," she says. "And so they reckoned that, because . . . this organization [the IUCN] consisted of scientists, . . . it needed somebody who was not a scientist to raise the money because scientists are not necessarily very good at raising money."

Francis Kellogg, in 1961 president of the International Mining Corporation and a friend of Peter Scott's ("an old friend of mine from the days when we used to go upland shooting") spoke in 2006 about the seminal World Wildlife Fund meetings on New

---

* According to the Cornell Laboratory of Ornithology, the swallow-tailed kite's U.S. population today "appears stable."

York's Park Avenue, site of his company's offices. "Roger Tory Peterson and Russell Train and several others—maybe two—called me on the telephone and asked, 'Could we use your office for a meeting?' . . . I said, 'Sure.' . . . They came with the idea of starting the World Wildlife Fund. I sat in on and listened to the conversation and became involved. You suddenly find yourself a party to a new venture. And this was exciting."

Kellogg was energized by these meetings. Although the organization's scope wasn't immediately clear, it soon became evident that the fund's mission would be broad, not limited by species or geography. What was Roger's role in this? "He was a very senior voice in the conservation world even before the World Wildlife Fund," said Kellogg. "I was interested to see how he was going to proceed and how he could use the organization that seemed to be in the offing, how he could use that to accomplish what he wanted, which was the preservation of, particularly, birds."

Added Kellogg, "He was very valuable because he was such a stellar figure in his field that he gave credibility to our organization." Roger was both influential and a font of information: "His knowledge was so universal and so detailed. . . . He was the voice on the board representing the world of flight."

Remembering that Roger's books were kept in the "minute [small]" library of the organization, Kellogg fondly recalled: "Every once in a while Roger would reach up and take one down and read a paragraph that was pertinent to our discussion. . . . So he referred to his own works!" The author of these guides and other books acted as a teacher in this conservation-oriented milieu. Kellogg got a "father/son feeling" from the naturalist. "He would put his arm around me, pat me on the shoulder," Kellogg reminisced, "and say, 'Now we're going to do' this or that. It would be very exciting."

Russell Train, a man of impressive credentials, having served in posts ranging from U.S. Tax Court judge to head of the Environmental Protection Agency, agrees with Kellogg's assessment of

Roger's importance to the nascent World Wildlife Fund. "Most of the board members were businessmen," says Train. "He brought a background in professional conservation, obviously ornithology and that sort of thing, that most of the members didn't have. He spoke with considerable authority. People listened to him."

Roger loyally attended board meetings and, as Kellogg noted, was "there to be called on and welcomed any questions on matters that required his knowledge." When he assumed the presidency of the fund's U.S. branch, Kellogg eagerly anticipated talking with Roger before board meetings. These informal chats were often a window into the flip side of Roger's notoriety in which he preferred to bring up contentious issues while staying in the background. Kellogg said,

> He would arrive, let's say, a half an hour before a meeting and we would sit in a corner and discuss projects. . . . I always looked forward to those fairly brief moments because they were so instructive. . . . He'd give me his point of view. . . . He would depend on me, if he had an objection, to lay it on the table. He would . . . [mention] the project about such and such and say, "I don't agree with the conclusion that your project committee has come to," and why this particular project requires a diversion from other things. . . . He didn't want to [broach the issue] at the meeting, so I would.

Given Roger's stature, this self-effacing approach to tackling difficult matters was a curious one. But it got results. The board would act to fund a project that Roger considered meritorious or reduce funding for a project he didn't.

Among the earliest initiatives of the fund was the protection of the Coto Doñana in southwestern Spain. The first international meeting of the World Wildlife Fund was held in this remote place where, "if you don't have the proper clothes, say, rubber [boots] . . . that cover up beyond your knees," Kellogg recalled, "you're in trouble, sinking in the mud all the time as you walk around."

We did a lot of walking. It was so remote that you couldn't get a car there, so we would walk two miles to get to the meeting. . . . If I happened to be lucky enough to be with Roger Tory Peterson, he would make it well worthwhile. . . . To walk along with him, you got a lecture every step of the way. . . . You'd come across some birds and there would be a lecture on that species. The next second, you'd be talking about another species. . . . It was very intense.

The Coto Doñana, Spain

Initially the Coto Doñana was simply the destination in 1952 for a nature artist who needed to round out his European bird list for the sake of a field guide in development, although he did travel with a few companions—Guy Mountfort and several French scientists, the most celebrated of whom was François Bourlière. A large chunk of the sixty-seven-thousand-acre coto was owned by the family of Mauricio González, the Spanish nobleman who would soon author the Spanish translation of the Peterson-Mountfort-Hollom field guide. The coto also served as an abbreviated name for a region of biodiversity containing a huge area of swampland known as Las Marismas. Roger later wrote of Las Marismas and its environs:

> *On a detailed map you will find, southwest of Sevilla, a great, roadless triangle—450 square miles of grass, mud, and water. Flooded by winter rains, dried out by mid-summer, these vast marshes are hemmed on the seaward side by a belt of dunes, scrub, and pastureland from one to eight miles wide and about 40 miles long.*
>
> *Between the swampy wilderness and the sea lies the Coto de Donana, a game preserve of Spanish aristocracy made famous half a century ago by the writings of the naturalist Abel Chapman.*

The first brief trip there was also a reconnaissance mission to examine about one-quarter of the terrain and establish the basis for future explorations. Before reaching the coto and the hospitality of Mauricio González, the party traveled by auto southward from Madrid, a distance of more than three hundred miles, birding all the way. If anyone hadn't yet experienced some of Roger's distinguishing characteristics—his memory, powers of concentration, and absentmindedness—now was their chance.

Roger had never seen little bustards before, but "it was he who beat us all by a split second in identifying them," marveled Guy Mountfort. Evidently, the one non-European had already learned the bird's field marks through means other than field study. Within a few minutes, he recognized something else—that he had left his Leica camera on a stone wall earlier that day while captivated by the spectacle of a Bonelli's eagle taking flight. Roger was "inconsolable" at the camera's loss. (It was stolen from where he left it.) Mountfort wanted Roger's photographic skills for the rest of the expedition so he lent him his own Leica. Upon reaching the coto, Roger took his absentmindedness to new heights, losing Mountfort's Leica too! "Fortunately we found it again," reported Mountfort, "and nobody can possibly be cross with Roger for long."

One day, after reaching the coto and with the explorers riding side by side on horses, Roger again demonstrated his extraordinary "powers of concentration on ornithology," as Mountfort put it. "Deep in a dissertation on the dimorphism of certain herons," Mountfort recalled, their respective horses sloshed through shallow water when, upon reaching dry sand, Roger's horse "suddenly decided to roll in it . . . in a flurry of flying hooves." The American did not appear to notice the mishap, "stepping neatly off sideways," watching, somewhat dazed, as the horse righted itself, mounting it once again, and continuing his discussion as if nothing had happened.

Mountfort carefully planned a second, more substantial, expedition to the coto. In selecting participants, his two main eligibility criteria were professional qualifications and good companionship. Thus, among the crew of the spring 1956 journey, besides Roger, were James Fisher, Fisher's protégé James Ferguson-Lees (then the young editor of *British Birds*), photographers Eric Hosking and George Shannon, and Lord Alanbrooke.

The flight from London to Gibraltar, from where they would eventually arrive in the coto, proved expensive for Roger. Although nearly everyone brought camera equipment, James Ferguson-Lees says Roger had so much paraphernalia that his "excess baggage charge" cost more than his return fare! (Here was another inkling of the comfortable living he was making; the 1920s Jamestown teen, living mainly hand to mouth, would have been shocked to know with what nonchalance he could spend money in the future.)

Besides being an observer, Roger was one of the few performing filmmaking and photographic tasks. Everyone who had a camera used the blinds at one time or another to photograph birds. James Fisher had introduced Eric Hosking to Roger, who "felt an immediate rapport with this open, friendly man," a bird photographer who had lost an eye to an angry tawny owl. Roger liked to tease him about the blinds (called "hides" in England) that Hosking liked using on the hot, steamy coto: "Eric Hosking, one of England's top bird photographers, had brought with him nine of his fine gabardine photographic 'hides' . . . , but I felt that my own blind of burlap was better suited to the Spanish heat. I must admit that Eric's were fancier; they had everything but hot and cold running water." Rather than take offense at Roger's mild mockery, Hosking quoted from it in his autobiography in a discussion on the usefulness of a good blind or hide to achieving the best bird pictures.

What did Roger actually mean about Eric's hides? "I don't know," muses James Ferguson-Lees. "Eric, he did have very nice hides. . . . He would have things like thermoses of hot water and tea and food. . . . Roger, I think, . . . if he went into a hide, he was only concerned with photographing or filming what he was looking at. I don't suppose he really bothered very much about creature comforts."

Fellow coto explorer-photographer George Shannon, another of several Englishmen, was surprised at how roughly Roger treated his cameras:

The mental picture of Roger, which I retain, was him with, at least, two Leica cameras draped around his neck, [which were] swinging wildly as he dashed about, with a 16 mm Cine, which horrified me, [as I was] treating my vintage Leica with overanxious care. But, then I consoled myself with the thought that they were probably provided by National Geographic. *I cite this not as an indication of carelessness, but of his total concentration on the task in hand. I recollect that he had some adaptation of a gunsight on his 16 mm Cine, which was a huge advantage in shooting sequences of flying birds.*

Evenings at the *palacio*, a medieval castle where the González family hosted the explorers, were spent reviewing the day's findings. Shannon recalls that even if Roger was not the most loquacious person there, he contributed important observations to the accumulated wisdom, usually prefacing his remarks with, "Now, here's a thing." Then, all ears were his. Adds Shannon:

At the end of a hard day in the field on the Coto, *when we sat at the long dining table in the ancient* palacio, *well-provisioned with the liquid products of the Gonzalez bodegas, conversation continued late into the night with Roger the centre of attention.*

My remark that Roger "was the centre of attention" should not be interpreted as implying that he dominated the conversation, but that anything he had to say was of significance, and worthy of close attention. . . . [Roger's] transatlantic angle gleaned from long experience was heard with interest & with profit to the hearer. . . . No, Roger did not seek to dominate. He could be described best as "Primus inter pares" [first among equals].

Days on the coto were illuminating—the explorers recorded all manner of life there—and a bit dangerous. Members of the party never knew when they might come upon a couple of bulls fighting over territory or perhaps about to knock over one of the blinds someone was sitting in. Another hazard was the leeches concealed in the marsh.

Roger had a close call in a blind forty feet off the ground and twelve feet from a red kite's nest situated in a cork oak. The entire party had shared in the task of building the pylon with blind on top, and Eric Hosking called first dibs. The red kite was extremely rare in Great Britain and he had his heart set on photographing it. Roger was next. Like Hosking, he stayed all day watching, among other things, the mother kite feed a small rabbit to her two nestlings. All was well until "late afternoon [when] the wind had become so strong that," Roger wrote, "I feared the guy ropes would not hold. I had visions of myself crashing from the treetop perch, cameras and all." But he stayed put, as the filming of the birds was the thing, and did not descend from the blind, "now leaning at a crazy angle," until 6:30 p.m. Thankfully, Roger had recorded the images he wanted.

During the 1952, 1956, and 1957 expeditions (Roger didn't participate in the last), the explorers recorded a prodigious amount of wildlife on the coto—193 species of birds, 29 species of mammals, 22 species of amphibians and reptiles, and 300 species of insects. They did not collect spiders but did harvest samples of 240 plant species. As Max Nicholson wrote in a postscript to Mountfort's *Portrait of a Wilderness,* the expeditions solidified knowledge of the region's ecological importance and the need to protect the area from encroachment:

> *The different habitats, as has been seen, have their characteristic species, yet all are interlocked, and it is the broad series of differing opportunities for existence which make this delta so remarkable*

for its fauna and flora.... It has also ... been shielded by vigilance and care over many generations from the damage inflicted almost universally in Europe by modern economic exploitation. It therefore forms a natural monument of outstanding importance and scientific interest.

Guy Mountfort was among the expeditions' participants who published papers in Britain about the coto. His book, *Portrait of a Wilderness,* Nicholson's coda, and Roger's account of his two adventures in the coto published in *National Geographic* sounded a clarion call for preservation that became increasingly urgent in ensuing years. Roger's conversationally intimate writing slyly flagged a conservationist message while he emphasized the birds of the region:

Above all we saw birds—squacco herons and rare masked shrikes; black vultures, the largest birds of prey in Europe; breath-taking flights of rosy-winged flamingoes; red kites, which etched the skies of Elizabethan England but now barely hold their own against the egg collectors in mountain valleys of Wales; and the Spanish imperial eagle, of which heart-rendingly few individuals still exist. On the near-by hills ranged great bustards, the last of these turkey-sized fowl in southern Europe.

Then came the film *Wild Spain,* to which several of the explorers including Roger contributed. It was used in immediately succeeding years in lectures by Mountfort, Hosking, and George Shannon. The film's uses became ever more urgent, Shannon says, as outside pressures against the coto intensified:

Briefly, the whole area was coming under increasingly adverse pressures, not least by the Spanish government. Injudicious tree and crop planting posed a threat. Inevitably there was illegal hunting from without, and foreign consortia were seeing opportunities

Photographing birds: Roger Tory Peterson
in his early twenties. *(Courtesy U.S. Trust Company)*

Clarence Allen, shown here in
1938, gave a boy of "potentially
great genius" the opportunity to
teach natural history.
(Courtesy Douglas Allen)

William Vogt as a young man: he urged Roger to expand his diagrammatic field
sketches into the first field guide to birds. *(Courtesy Denver Public Library)*

One of a series of photographs taken by Edwin Way Teale of Roger for *Audubon* magazine in 1942. Roger is seen sketching snow geese in the field for an *Audubon* cover. *(Courtesy University of Connecticut)*

Teale shows Roger back at the drawing board as he studies a snow goose skin for reference. *(Courtesy University of Connecticut)*

A fuller view of Roger's early 1940s no-frills studio.
(Courtesy University of Connecticut)

"The boys," Roger and James Fisher (right), on their *Wild America* trip, exploring Great Smoky Mountains National Park, Gatlinburg, Tennessee, 1953. *(Courtesy the family of S. Glidden Baldwin)*

Barbara Peterson with chipmunks, Mount Rainier, Washington, July 1953, at the end of the *Wild America* trip. *(Courtesy the Estate of James Fisher)*

Roger filming in the Coto Doñana, Spain, 1956.
(Courtesy the Eric Hosking Charitable Trust)

Guy Mountfort (left) with Roger in Spain, 1956.
(Courtesy the Eric Hosking Charitable Trust)

A super pair: Roger and Barbara Peterson with dog Dusky in
their front yard, Old Lyme, Connecticut, 1958.
(Courtesy Lee and Courtney Peterson)

With a Galapagos tortoise on Isla Santa Cruz, January 1964.
(Courtesy William A. Weber)

Roger and James Fisher were "like brothers," said one observer. They are seen here in mid-1960s Slimbridge, Gloucestershire, England, site of what is now called the Wildfowl and Wetlands Trust, brainchild of Sir Peter Scott. *(Courtesy Lady Philippa Scott)*

Roger with Eric Hosking (left) and H. E. Axel (right) at Minsmere, Suffolk, England, 1966. *(Courtesy the Eric Hosking Charitable Trust)*

Eco-tourism visionary Lars-Eric Lindblad, shown here in Antarctica, circa late 1960s, "loosened" Roger up in his later years. *(Courtesy Lindblad Expeditions)*

Roger in search of the brown-capped rosy finch, July 1970, Rocky Mountain National Park, Estes Park, Colorado. *(Courtesy Kent Dannen)*

Aboard the MS *Lindblad Explorer,* early 1970s. *(Courtesy Lady Philippa Scott)*

Roger with Olin Sewall Pettingill (left), Keith Shackleton (right), and gentoo penguins, Antarctic Peninsula, December 1974/January 1975.
(Courtesy Robert W. Hernandez)

The King Penguin with king penguins, South Georgia Island,
December 1974/January 1975.
(Courtesy Robert W. Hernandez)

Roger and Virginia Peterson with a nesting albatross in the sub-Antarctic, circa late 1970s. *(Courtesy Lydia Lazi)*

Roger with fellow bird artist Owen Gromme (right), 1978. Behind is Roger's first Mill Pond Press painting of snowy owls. *(Courtesy Leigh Yawkey Woodson Art Museum)*

Photographing birds at Shamrock Island, Texas, 1991. *(Courtesy Greg Lasley)*

With Greg Lasley (right) at Hato El Cedral, Venezuela, April 1992.
(Courtesy Greg Lasley)

At the grand opening of the Great Texas Coastal Birding Trail, September 1995.
(Courtesy Greg Lasley)

In deep thought at a Woodson Art Museum event, 1983.
(Courtesy Leigh Yawkey Woodson Art Museum)

The Great Man.
(Courtesy Susan Roney Drennan)

*to move in and exploit the potential for hunting and tourism. . . .
In the UK the media, TV in particular, were stimulating public
interest and concerns, and there was a demand for wildlife film. It
is in this climate that the contribution of our film should be viewed
. . . . So bit by bit the gospel of conservation was spread here and
beyond our shores, and the* Coto Donana *was saved, to become
the reserve of world importance that it remains. . . . I have to say
how I look around now, envyingly, at the range of magnificent
camera and sound recording equipment, beside which our equipment was terribly basic. We even envied Roger's adapted gunsight
which was of such help as a viewfinder for flight shots. Nevertheless
I think our field craft does not suffer unduly by comparison [to that
of today], and remember how much that owed to Roger's contributions to identification in the* Field Guide.

The founding in 1961 of the World Wildlife Fund heralded
the raising of necessary monies to protect the Coto Doñana
from development and despoliation. Through international
fund-raising pleas, the World Wildlife Fund was able to secure
enough, with some loans added to the mix, to purchase most
of the coto, except for marshlands and a small portion of land
toward the south retained by the González family. As for Las
Marismas, although development was making inroads, the fund
was able to purchase twenty-two square miles of the marshes,
dubbed Marismas de las Nuevas. A research station was established in the coto, with headquarters at the *palacio* where Mountfort, Peterson, and the others had stayed. All property purchased
by the World Wildlife Fund was then turned over to the Spanish
government, which would manage the land.

Today, says conservationist Trevor Gunton, preserving the
ecosystem of the coto remains a challenge. "We've already beaten
off attempts to make a holiday village immediately bordering on
the park, and a couple of golf courses," he says. Nevertheless, the
coto remains a showcase of the fund's early successes.

Lake Nakuru, Kenya

In the spring of 1957 Roger visited Kenya, then a British colony. Within mere months he would create the necessary public awareness for conservation of one of Kenya's most beautiful bird magnets.

Roger had been tempted to go to East Africa several years earlier when he met a fellow named John G. Williams at the British Museum in London. "He urged me to see for myself the bird wonders of East Africa," Roger later wrote.

The place in Kenya that made the greatest impression on Roger—in fact, the greatest impression he had had of any place up till then, was Lake Nakuru. Fleur Ng'weno says:

> *Lake Nakuru is an alkaline lake near the town of Nakuru in the Great Rift Valley. Tiny blue-green algae grow in the lake's shallow, nutrient-rich waters, and thousands—sometimes up to a million—Lesser Flamingos come to feed on the algae. . . . It is the most popular national park in Kenya after Nairobi National Park. Various species of wild mammals can be seen as well as birds. Fish were introduced into the lake in the 1950s, and now magnificent flocks of fish-eating white pelicans feed there as well as flocks of pink algae-eating flamingos. In times of drought the lake shrinks and the flamingos go elsewhere for a while, but overall it remains "the world's greatest ornithological spectacle."*

Roger has long been credited with calling Lake Nakuru "the world's greatest ornithological spectacle." "This past August, in Africa," he wrote late in 1957, "I witnessed the most staggering bird spectacle in my 38 years of bird watching." His column in *Audubon* magazine that commenced with this proclamation led to the designation of the lake as a bird sanctuary less than three years later and as a full-fledged national park by 1968. In 1957 Lake Nakuru was even more spectacular, particularly from a flamingo admirer's point of view, than it is today.

Leslie Brown, the "eagle and flamingo authority" of Kenya, Roger said, had counted no fewer than 1 million flamingos, and likely as many as over 1.2 million. Roger struggled to believe this figure, even if he did defer to Brown's expertise:

Beyond [the plain] lay the lake, its 30-square-mile expanse literally covered with flamingos. How one would estimate their numbers I had no idea. Birds were everywhere on the water, many of them swimming, but the densest concentrations were along the shore where they formed a wide band of pink. . . . When dealing with such astronomical numbers I am frankly baffled. As far as I was concerned there might have been 2,000,000 or even more.

Most of them were lesser flamingos; a few were greaters. Amid the sea of pink were marabou storks, sacred ibis, blacksmith plovers, and various ducks, among other species. Captivated, Roger erected his ten-minute burlap blind and began snapping away. He and companions watched the lake for nearly a week. Every evening, more flamingos arrived at Nakuru from elsewhere.

Roger emotionally remarked: "We agreed that Lake Nakuru was one of the most beautiful lakes we had ever seen and that if it was not already a sanctuary for birds it should be one. I wonder if the residents of the favored town of Nakuru realize what a gem is theirs? . . . Do they realize that it is not only a local showplace, but almost unique in the world, a magnet for visitors from distant lands?"

This column was reprinted in the local press; in response, Nakuru's municipal government designated the lake a bird sanctuary. But even after Lake Nakuru became a national park, it faced serious challenges. As Roger wrote in a 1970 article for *Massachusetts Audubon,* the lake was being polluted at an alarming rate. Over "200 chemical compounds are available for putting onto agricultural land in Kenya" and the lake's "watershed catchment basin . . . drains some of these farmlands." The town of Nakuru, with its "fertilizer plant, a battery factory, railway workshops" and more, contributed to the lake's pollutants. Roger hoped that the just launched Baharini Wildlife Sanctuary, whose board he served on, could raise sufficient funds to conduct research on the extent of the lake's pollution, as well as plan research and education centers to be built at the head of the lake. He pleaded to readers with uncharacteristic bluntness: "I feel it is my duty as a conservationist and a world citizen to alert people to this very real need [to raise funds]. We cannot let this go by default." The World Wildlife Fund, he said, had given priority to the problem.

Today lesser flamingos and other birds still flock to Lake Nakuru, although Fleur Ng'weno acknowledges that it is "threatened by silting." This is because the lake is shallow and "without an outlet," she says. "Outside the park, the slopes of the catchment are intensively cultivated, and forests have been cut down to make way for farms on the highest slopes. The rivers have become seasonal, and arrive laden with silt and plastic bags. There is currently a major effort underway, spearheaded by the Kenya Wildlife Service and local support groups, to clean up the plastic waste and plant trees on the catchment slopes."

Birding and ecotourism in East Africa still raise awareness about what can be and is being lost. Hope for the future rests, to an extent, with those who use field guides. Roger Tory Peterson had a positive impact on places like Lake Nakuru. He was also the father of East African field guides, which help populate the area with watchful citizens. He encouraged John Williams, who had urged him to visit East Africa, to write a field guide himself. When Roger arrived there in May 1957, reporters meeting him as he exited the plane inquired about his plans for producing a field guide to the region's birds. As Roger later wrote:

> I replied, "Oh no! But the man who should do such a book is standing here beside me—John Williams." Whether that was the moment when John Williams first conceived the idea of an East and Central African Field Guide I do not know, but we soon

talked earnestly of such a book. I urged him to feel free to use my well-known Field Guide system which had proved so practical in both Europe and North America, but I regretted that I could not paint the colour plates because of the overwhelming pressure of other commitments.

Williams, curator of birds at the Coryndon Museum in Nairobi and with admirable field skills, seemed the perfect choice to Roger for field guide authorship. The format Williams used in his 1963 publication was similar to that of Roger's 1947 eastern guide, with a mixture of black-and-white and color plates, birds on the same page usually facing the same direction for easy comparison, and little arrows drawing the reader's attention to the salient field marks. Williams's compact descriptions too were Petersonesque. Fleur Ng'weno says:

For thirty years Williams' Field Guide was the field guide for the region, the start for countless local and foreign bird-watchers. It is a direct descendant of the Peterson field guides. Although it is not as good as a Peterson guide (it does not include all the birds, . . . and the artists lacked Roger's genius) it was a field guide, accessible to the general public, opening doors to enjoyment of the outdoors and awareness of the environment.

Today Williams' field guide has been supplanted by better books, but its work has already been done: awakening a generation to the wonder of birds, the richness of the region's birdlife, and the joy of participating in the sport of birdwatching. People often complained about the book, but no one else wrote one for thirty years—and for those thirty years we were the beneficiaries of Roger's inspiration.

Since 1971 Ng'weno has been leading weekly bird walks in Nairobi on behalf of Nature Kenya; all birders have used the Williams book for most of the years since. "There is now a generation of bright young African birdwatchers and tour guides, who learned with that book, although they now carry others," she remarks. "The excellent books that we have today are still fundamentally based on the Peterson field guide format."

Don Turner is coauthor of one such guide. Growing up in Britain, the first guide he used was the 1954 *Field Guide to the Birds of Britain and Europe,* which he took with him when traveling the continent as a teen. He arrived in Kenya in the late 1950s as a member of the colonial police force. Remaining after independence, he went into tourism and writing. Turner first met Roger in 1963 when the IUCN met in Nairobi. In ensuing decades, they went on safari together. Turner paid partial homage to Roger in 1996 when he coauthored *Birds of Kenya and Northern Tanzania,* a "cross between a field guide and a handbook," with its seven hundred plus pages devoted to over one thousand species. In 1999 the book was trimmed to a "field guide edition," closer to the size of a Peterson. Like the Petersons, its language is succinct; words referring to the most important field marks are italicized. Also like the Petersons, similar species are pictured on the same page, although perhaps 10 percent of the species are pictured more animatedly and less for comparison's sake.

In 2002 BirdLife International's John Fanshawe coauthored with Terry Stevenson the field guide *Birds of East Africa: Kenya, Tanzania, Uganda, Rwanda, and Burundi,* which covers most of the territory Williams had addressed while depicting and describing 1,388 species, about 900 more than Williams included. Descriptions are brief, and for the most part similar species on the same page face the same way. Fanshawe explains:

> Terry and I, . . . we both belong to that similar generation of influence of the Peterson field guide in the UK. But, of course, when we started working on our own field guide, we were replacing a book that had been published in Kenya by John Williams. . . . Our book is a sort of new generation Williams, and it draws down a lot of

the influence from, well, the early Peterson guide. . . . It's like an evolved version of the Peterson guide. . . . Almost the longest period of time was spent deciding how to lay out the plates . . . , something which I'm sure he must have [done] himself. . . . But that early decision of how to organize the book and what pictures to put on what plates and how to group the birds is critical. So his influence is right there.

Roger Tory Peterson wanted field guides to spur conservationism in third world countries too. Don Turner remembers talking with Roger about this in the early 1990s during one of the latter's last trips to Africa. "I think he realized that his field guides had . . . [made] a lot of people . . . pretty aware of conservation issues," Turner says. "He was a strong believer that if people carried his books with them, that basically took them on the first step toward conservation. . . . Later in his life he became very conscious of the effect that bird tourism or eco-tourism [had] and its benefits for, particularly, third world countries."

The Bolivian Andes and the James's Flamingo

The year Roger urged John Williams to author an East African guide and proclaimed Lake Nakuru the site of the greatest bird spectacle starring a million or more flamingos, he was close to photographing all of the world's flamingo species. Thus, in 1957 he endeavored to capture on film the rarest, most elusive, flamingo on Earth—the James's—in the Bolivian Andes. He would call this expedition "one of the toughest field trips I have ever made anywhere, and certainly my most difficult photography assignment."

Facing daunting obstacles in a wild place, Roger persevered with little consideration for the consequences—whether it was 1957 or 1927. This was partly thanks to his famous ability to focus but also to confidence in his physical prowess. His self-regard, which bordered on foolhardiness, was evident from his youngest days and didn't abate with time.

Before and after his nineteenth birthday, he wrote to Joe Hickey of his explorations of Chautauqua Gorge near Jamestown, whence he kept returning despite falling off a precipice several times. In early August he announced: "About a week or 2 ago Clare[nce Beal] & I covered the fearsome . . . Chautauqua Gorge at night—in inky blackness—guiding ourselves along the faces of the cliffs by the light of the moon. I fell over the edge 3 times, but sustained only minor cuts & bruises." He masochistically returned to the Gorge in December, reporting another accident to his Bronx friend: "By the way on Dec. 4 I had a nice little experience at the conclusion of the day—I tried to climb a 15-foot cliff at Chaut. Gorge & 10 feet from the top I lost my hold and down I went!—Ow! . . . My pants were all cut up as was my coat & underwear (me too)—I broke my fingernails all up grabbing onto the rocks on the way down. Such is life with us boys from the rugged west."

In 1935 a nearly twenty-seven-year-old Roger suffered a different kind of fall while scouting the site for the Audubon Camp in Maine. His goal was to film great blue herons nesting in spruce trees on a small island in Boothbay Harbor. He recounted some forty years later:

> I wanted to get a nice clean shot, but there was a small spruce tree in the way . . . of one of the nests. So I thought I would treat it like a birch tree . . . you just climb the tree and then lean back until it bends to the ground. It didn't [work] with the spruce tree. It snapped and I went to the ground, striking my shoulder blades on the granite rocks. I had a horrible back for some time because of this. . . . I was in extreme pain for the next two or three weeks. However, I did get some great blue heron pictures.

Getting those pictures was all that mattered. Peterson protégé Paul Spitzer met him not long after the 1957 ordeal in the Bolivian Andes. In his fifties, the elder naturalist was still, Spitzer said, "physically a robust guy." The James's flamingo trek, which punished Roger with headaches, nosebleeds, and shortness of breath as he advanced in the altitudinous mud, might have defeated a less-vigorous man. Reflecting on the trip years later, Roger offered no more than a detached acknowledgment that the hike at almost fourteen thousand feet above sea level toward Laguna Colorada, home of the James's flamingo, was a "month-long stint in endurance" and a "most trying physical ordeal." He left the anxiety to his Chilean guide, Luis Peña:

> One morning my Chilean guide told me of a bad dream he had about the awful mud. He dreamed that I had disappeared somewhere out toward the flamingo colony. He called out, "Doctor . . . Doctor." No answer. Then he noticed my red cap far out on the lake. Crossing the treacherous mud, he gingerly lifted the cap— "But no Doctor!" [Peña called Roger "Doctor" because in 1952, Franklin and Marshall College in Pennsylvania presented him with the first of his twenty-three honorary doctorates. Hence, he was known as "Dr. Peterson" in certain circles.]

A couple of years after Roger's Andean adventure, he advised William Conway, the young curator of birds at the New York Zoological Society, on searching for the James's flamingo. St. Louis native Conway had grown up with the Peterson guides. "My interests in biology and ecology . . . really were enormously stimulated by Roger's field guides," he says. Although they met briefly in 1948 after a talk Roger gave in St. Louis, it wasn't until 1956 when Conway joined the staff of the New York Zoological Society that they became friends.

"He's the one who stimulated me to become more interested in flamingos," Conway remarks.

Part of the inspiration came from Roger's film of all six species of flamingos, which he showed at the 1958 International Ornithological Congress in Helsinki. Conway recalls:

James Fisher introduced Roger. He went on at great length, while Roger was standing there, uncomfortably, at the podium, . . . about Roger being the only man, the only scientist, the only ornithologist, who had ever seen and photographed all six species of flamingos in the world. Then, he stepped away from the podium a foot, and suddenly turned back just as Roger was trying to take the microphone and said, "Of course, when you've seen one flamingo, you've seen 'em all." . . . He brought down the house. The place was in an uproar! Poor Roger couldn't get a word in or get going at all. . . . It was absolutely hilarious.

By 1959 Conway had decided to try to capture the James's and Andean flamingos. Roger further fueled the fire when he invited Conway to Old Lyme Thanksgiving weekend to talk more about it and view his slides from the trip.

"Roger had slides that just went from *A* to *Z*. We sat down and went through them, one after the other," says Conway. "He had a screen there that he could throw them up on, so that I could understand what I was getting into. And we talked about how I was going to handle it." He adds, "We went through his slides and maps . . . for a couple of days solid. When I left, he said, 'You better take my boots!' So I took his waders. I wore them in Bolivia."

Conway also used the same guide Roger had, and the same truck, literally following in Roger's footsteps: "Although people go there in numbers now, in those days, when I went in 1960, so few people had been there that there were no one else's tracks. I could follow Roger's tracks. I was with his guide, Luis Peña, and Peña would point them out to me. There were no others."

The Conway group—including Peña, Peña's two assistants, and *National Geographic* photographer Bates Littlehales—was composed of comparatively youthful men. Conway himself was twenty years Roger's junior. Yet they had as much trouble as Roger had had at age forty-eight dealing with the severity of the elements. Peña often told Conway—somewhat unhelpfully—as they neared

Laguna Colorada and the nesting James's flamingos, that his trek with Roger had been the "worst experience" of his life. And now he was repeating it with another American scientist!

Writing for *National Geographic*, Conway recounted the harrowing experience of having to take their boots off to avoid being mired down:

> *Blundering into seemingly bottomless holes caused by subterranean springs, we stayed close together to assist each other. The gummy mud became knee-deep, in places even hip-deep. . . . Layers of sharp salt crystals cut our feet mercilessly, causing them to bleed. Progress became a series of short struggles punctuated by long gasps for breath in the rarefied air.*
>
> *Even talking was an effort, but Gerardo felt compelled to announce: "Here Doctor [Peterson] crawl on knees."*

Besides capturing several James's and Andean flamingos for the Bronx Zoo, the expedition led to conservation of the birds whose eggs were being stolen by native people—a remarkable situation considering the inhospitable terrain. Conway says, "I got reserves set up for the flamingos in the area where Roger and I went," a consequence of Roger's expedition and his mentoring of Conway.

Despite the reserves, the flamingos today are threatened by industrialization, tourism, and once again, egging by natives. Conway's organization, now called the Wildlife Conservation Society, is monitoring the situation. Society representatives are hopeful that its research efforts and those of a consortium of South American scientists and conservationists, the Grupo de Conservación de Flamencos Altoandinos, will yield strategies for protecting the birds based on their breeding and migrating habits.

Midway Atoll and the Laysan Albatross, Pacific Ocean

Sometimes the conservation challenge wasn't in a remote, virtually inaccessible place where civilian populations barely made a living but still encroached on the habitat of wild birds and other animals. Sometimes the conservation challenge was a Cold War controversy, triggered when the U.S. military sought the use of public lands. To conservationists' dismay, public lands were often coveted and secretly or nearly secretly secured by military officials; or animals living around military bases were condemned by the creatures' mere presence.

Even members of the normally staid American Ornithologists' Union became upset over such things, aided by the success of the organization's Committee on Bird Protection in unearthing plans of some branch of the American armed forces that interfered with birds doing what they do best—living. In 1955 Roger and his fellow committee members, including Ludlow Griscom, announced several military efforts to interfere with the wildness of wildlife. The committee complained: "One of the most critical current problems presented to conservationists is the apparent unending enthusiasm of the Armed Services for invading and taking over wildlife refuges. There have been so many moves to take over wildlife areas that it appears to be a concerted effort by the services to get all they can while the getting is good."

The committee reported several moves by the military, some surreptitious, some not quite so: the army winning congressional approval of a $1,000 appropriation for the administrative costs of transferring 10,700 acres of the Wichita National Wildlife Refuge, an important range for turkeys, bison, and long-horned cattle, from the Department of the Interior to the army without Interior's input or consent; the expansion of the Matagorda Island Air Field to the edge of the Aransas National Wildlife Refuge for "photoflash bombing," which could further threaten the continued existence of the almost extinct whooping crane; and preliminary moves to acquire large portions of other refuges and national forests, home to a wide variety of mammal and bird life. The angry conclusion of the committee was that "with the huge funds now at the disposal of the Armed Forces, they are all attempting to acquire great areas of land." The committee urged AOU members to pressure relevant agencies to stop these military incursions.

Then came the U.S. Navy's plan to eliminate a huge proportion of the world's population of a majestic, seafaring bird with a silly nickname. The dastardly "gooney bird" was deemed a national security threat. The area of concern was Sand Island, Midway Atoll.

Midway is in the leeward chain of the Hawaiian Islands. When Theodore Roosevelt established the Hawaiian Islands National Wildlife Refuge in 1909, Midway was excluded; it had been designated an American naval base several years earlier. In 1935 airplanes were introduced when the U.S. Navy permitted Pan Am to set up operations. National Audubon Society sanctuary director Bob Allen expressed the hope that the navy would prevent the molestation of birds. Allen warned that a commercial airline might also inadvertently introduce pests (i.e., cats and dogs) that could harm or eliminate the birds entirely.

Roger Tory Peterson observed that the Laysan albatross, otherwise known as the "gooney bird," was "beloved of servicemen who have been stationed at Midway." The atoll is most famous for being the locus of a key early battle of World War II. It couldn't have been too pleasant for the birds then, and the unpleasantness continued into the Cold War when the navy instituted the Distant Early Warning radar system. "They were running patrol flights between Midway and Adak, Alaska, one of the islands out in the Aleutians," explains Chandler Robbins, then a scientist with the U.S. Fish and Wildlife Service. "There was an ongoing thing 24 hours a day . . . monitoring aircraft movement across the Pacific in relation to Japan and the Soviet Union." The birds got in the way of this sensitive operation. Says Robbins, "Birds were nesting not only alongside the runways, but soaring along the dunes that were parallel to the runways, and these soaring birds would wheel over the runways." Collisions with propeller-driven aircraft were the result.

A report prepared by the U.S. Fish and Wildlife Service regarding Midway's Sand Island noted aircraft-albatross strikes between October 30, 1957, and April 17, 1958, numbering 310, or 17 percent of all airplane landings and takeoffs, with the Laysan species responsible for 286 of these, and the less-numerous black-footed, only 24. Seven percent of all strikes, or a total of eighteen instances, caused damage to aircraft, most of it minor, and none of it serious enough to "endanger the plane during landing operations." No people were hurt, although the birds died.

The plane strikes occurred chiefly because of updrafts that created conditions favorable to soaring. The updrafts were caused by physical features, adjacent to one runway in particular, of "high trees, dunes, and revetments." Remove these features, and most updrafts over the runway could be eliminated. In fact, one "major soaring area" had been eliminated as a hazard by clearing and leveling the features causing updrafts; albatross soaring from that location was "greatly reduced." But instead of further "terrain modification," the navy was fixated on killing the Laysan albatrosses nesting adjacent to the runways. Therefore, the navy instituted a "small-scale experimental killing program" in 1957. It did not yield positive results. The navy then decided to institute a slightly larger experiment the following year, killing about thirty thousand birds, mainly Laysan albatrosses.

The killings of the tame, docile birds, which occurred over a two-month period beginning in mid-January 1958, were effected by fifteen "enlisted men" assigned the task full-time. They used "heavy wooden clubs, the birds being dispatched instantly by a strong blow at the base of the skull." (Were the birds really "dispatched instantly"? The U.S. Fish and Wildlife report revealed that only 8.2 birds were killed per "man-hour.") The men expended 3,697 man-hours "killing, pick-up, hauling, burying, etc." Inexplicably, the Bureau of Sport Fisheries and Wildlife of the U.S. Fish and Wildlife Service was consulted on the plan and agreed to it, but apparently didn't inform outside conservationists. (Admittedly, the bureau also recommended terrain modification to best address albatross-aircraft collisions.)

The whole business came to light the next year as the navy readied plans to rid Sand Island of *all* Laysan albatrosses, which could take five to seven years because an annual crop of formerly young, nonbreeding birds matured after several years into breeding birds and returned to land for nesting. The person who brought this to light was Roger Tory Peterson.

"That's a beautiful story, let me tell you," says Roland Clement, an Audubon staffer then. Roger and several others, including Eugene Eisenmann, a research associate at the American Museum of Natural History, attended the International Ornithological Congress in Tokyo, returning to mainland United States via Hawaii. "They land on Hawaii and they find a way of taking a look at Midway. . . . So there they learned about the problem, the threat." Roger shifted to behind-the-scenes-activist mode.

"When Roger came back," says Clement, "he came to my office and he said, 'Roland, I'm very concerned! The navy wants to eradicate the Laysan albatross from Midway!'

"He said, 'We've got to find a way of doing something about that!'"

Clement consulted Eisenmann and a joint conference was called for October 20 of the Audubon Society, the American Museum, the International Council for Bird Preservation, and the Linnaean Society to confront the navy about its plans.

"I almost got fired over that," asserts Clement,

because Roger is a talkative guy. Roger . . . told Harold Coolidge, who was a big shot in the conservation field in Washington, that we were going to confront the navy, and Coolidge, not being very discreet, told some military people about it. . . . So, naturally, it got back to navy headquarters that the "Audubon Society is going to confront you on this." [John] Baker . . . walks into some admiral's office in Washington to tell them what Audubon is planning and they said, "Oh, we already know about you. That young man Clement of yours is setting up a trap for us." That didn't please Baker very much. . . . Naturally, Baker told [Carl] Buchheister, and Buchheister calls me in and says, 'You are in hot water. . . . What happened?' I said, "The only thing I can think of is that I told Roger about this. And Roger's a great talker! He tells all his friends about . . . [these things], you know." He said, "Oh, obviously that's the problem. . . . I know Roger!" Buchheister covered for me. He told Baker, "Look, it's not Roland's fault this got out."

It was that troublemaker Peterson, an independently operating superstar—and untouchable.

The fact that it got out meant the death of the navy's killing program *before* the October 20 meeting. Three days beforehand, the *New York Times* reported the cancellation of the plan. The confrontation with the navy thus turned into an informational session. And, on October 22, the Department of Defense issued a statement: "A conservation project has been ordered by the Navy in an effort to encourage gooney birds to leave Midway Island." A budget of $110,000 was allotted to "contour modification . . . to remove dunes along runways."

Roger's column protesting the plan was gravy by the time it appeared in *Audubon*'s November/December 1959 issue. He wrote:

It was recommended that dunes that create updrafts be leveled so that "unemployed" soaring birds would not be concentrated at certain spots.

This could be done at a cost considerably less than that of one of the planes which the Navy wishes [to] protect from the birds. This has not yet been done. . . . Now the Navy announces that they will proceed to kill all the albatrosses, starting this November when the birds return from the sea. . . . One-fourth of the world's population of a species will be wiped out in the name of national defense. It is argued that we cannot jeopardize the super-constellations which are used in our "Distant Early Warning" radar network. But what about the recent Navy announcement that they have a 5,000 mile radar system now in experimental use? Will not that eliminate the need for the tremendously expensive radar plane patrol? Will not that make Midway just another way station instead of a national defense outpost?

Still, the navy wished to keep its killing plan in reserve. In its view, the albatross population still presented a problem. Hence, a February 1964 Audubon press release had new Audubon president Carl Buchheister acquiescing to a navy "bird-control project" gassing about 20,000 of 150,000 nesting albatrosses on Midway (a method he adjudged "humane") to allow for paving of the area and to prevent the "site-tenacious" birds from returning to the vicinity of the runways.

But in 1965 use of the super-constellation radar aircraft the birds were colliding with was discontinued. Over time, the navy's activities on Midway Atoll shrank to nothing. Today the site is known as Midway Atoll National Wildlife Refuge. Laysan and black-footed albatrosses still breed there.

Patagonia and Tierra del Fuego, Argentina

The adventures of Roger Tory Peterson took him from Pacific islands to the near-bottom of the world. In the fall of 1960 he joined his young friend and neighbor Philip Humphrey, a Yale University ornithologist, in an exploration of the bird life of Patagonia and Tierra del Fuego, Argentina.

Phil Humphrey first discovered Roger when, as a boy growing up in New England, he luckily acquired a Peterson guide. "That opened up my whole attitude toward birds," Humphrey reflects. "I knew what they were all of a sudden. Prior to that time, bird books were really hard to use. Roger was revolutionary in his contributions in that regard. I loved that book."

Humphrey remembers their first meeting during the war, not long before Roger was drafted. A friend took him, still a high schooler, on a trip to the National Audubon Society headquarters. Says Humphrey: "Roger was working on a painting of three snow geese for a cover of *Audubon* magazine. . . . [H]e had cutouts of each of the three snow geese and he was busy moving these around on the background."

They had more substantive encounters once Humphrey became an ornithologist, joining Yale's faculty. "Roger frequently borrowed bird specimens from the Peabody Museum of Natural History," Humphrey recalls. "He and I became good friends early on, because I was in charge of the collection."

In the spring of 1960 Humphrey was awarded a Guggenheim Fellowship to study the birds of Patagonia and Tierra del Fuego. Additional funds from Yale allowed him to bring his family. (But they would not accompany him south through Patagonia and beyond.) When the subject came up with Roger, they agreed he could come too if he paid his way. In return, the Humphrey family dog, a standard poodle named Cindy, got free room and board at the Petersons' Old Lyme home, along with training in the ancient canine art of running after whatever horse Barbara Peterson was riding.

Roger joined the Humphreys in September at a *pensión* where they were staying outside Buenos Aires. Dinner was at a long, communal table with simultaneous conversations in Spanish and English. In October the trip south began. Humphrey hired two youths as field assistants. José Franco was an immigrant from Paraguay, Atilio Kovács a refugee from Hungary. Roger's job was to engage his eyes and ears, take copious field notes (which he shared with Humphrey), and shoot roll after roll of film to feed his photography addiction.

Camera equipment had to be looked after—putting a tarp over it if they were surveying surf-soaked rocks, ensuring that nothing fell apart if they hit a bad section of road. "In those days a long lens was really long. We didn't have the reflexes we do now," says Humphrey. "You can get a major multiplication of an image, forty times or so, without any length at all. But in those days, a long lens might be two feet long! And they were heavy. Roger would be on the front seat beside me. . . . We went over a bump, and his camera broke in two! The long lens became separated because of the bounce. Fortunately, Roger was able to get it back together again. He got some beautiful pictures."

They drove from town to town, stayed in $3-a-night hotels, and made contact with local dignitaries and oil company representatives when necessary to gain access to an area, borrow a boat, or further international diplomacy. Roger had letters of introduction to officials of the Chilean company Empresa Nacional del Petróleo, which meant a sanctioned crossing from the Chilean coast across the Straits of Magellan into the Chilean half of Tierra del Fuego.

While Humphrey, José, and Atilio collected bird specimens for shipment back to the United States, Roger admired and recorded the interesting avifauna, harvesting botanical samples on the side. Among his more enjoyable efforts was secretly watching and photographing the colonial nests of monk parakeets.

East of Ushuaia, the southernmost city in the world, Roger observed the habits of the flightless steamer duck, which swam rapidly in a "steaming" manner. He witnessed a display between two of the birds: "One bird, presumably the male, at least it was the larger bird, elevated the tail to a vertical position, exposing the fluffed-out white under tail coverts, and held the neck quite erect and stiff, while the other bird raised the head and pointed the bill in a skyward gesture."

Roger's ears were the real organs of service, identifying calls and songs of birds from passerines to waterfowl. Humphrey remembers: "He'd say, 'Oh, boy! Listen to that! That's a "whatever" bird.'

"I said, 'How do you know?'

"He said, 'Well, I just know!'

"He did know bird songs unbelievably. This is true in the United States, and he learned them quickly in Argentina. He was a wizard from the standpoint of his ability to recognize birds without seeing them."

Humphrey recalls that Roger worked a bit during the long trip on the art for the second edition of his *Field Guide to Western Birds,* due out in 1961. Often lacking fresh water, he "dipped his paintbrush in the toilet."

More than once the Humphrey-Peterson team ran out of gas. There were also tire blowouts or oil leaks or their truck got stuck in the mud until someone came along to help them. "[We were] going up this old road over the mountains that had been plowed up and muddied by oil trucks," Humphrey recalls. "Sometimes we felt that we were just going to go over the side. And then we were totally stuck."

Their fortune was superb crossing a river in their truck en route to the Argentinian side of Tierra del Fuego. "We crossed uneventfully, much to the astonishment of the [watching] soldier who had fully expected us to bog down in the middle," Humphrey later wrote. Bogging down would have been disastrous; some men who had arrived with horses just as the Humphrey-Peterson truck dipped into the river declared the heavy vehicle untowable.

While camping, exotic food replaced conventional fare. One night, it was rhea, a relative of the ostrich, marinated in red wine. Other evenings were tamer. Humphrey remembers stopping for a night at a hotel in Santa Cruz Province where the restaurant served a gigantic basket of steamed mussels. "We had two large pots of melted butter. One for Roger and one for me. We polished off all the mussels. They were big ones. . . . It was just fabulous. Roger and I got along well where we were devoting our minds to food instead of birds."

But an incident involving a rowboat, a burly oarsman, and a "white" island populated by cormorants, various sandpipers, steamer ducks, penguins, oystercatchers, sheathbills, and skuas, proved life threatening. The destination on November 7, 1960, was Isla Blanca, off Camarones in Argentina. There wasn't room in the boat for José and Atilio, so they stayed behind with instructions to pick up the ornithologists in the afternoon. The oarsman assumed rowing duties on the way out. With the wind at their backs, the three-mile boat ride was short and nice. Enchanting, even.

"Giant petrels—*Macronectes*—large as albatrosses, flew by on stiff, flat wings. One came close enough for us to see the tubed nostrils on its huge beak," Roger later reported. "Skuas hawked over the water like heavy-set falcons. . . . A platoon of Magellanic penguins stood like a welcoming committee on the shelving rocks as we approached."

Roger was uncharitable in describing the same penguin species he more fully observed after landing: "At close range there is nothing endearing in those fishy, watery-looking, bloodshot eyes as the bird wags its head from side to side as though to focus more clearly on the 'super penguins' invading their island." Likewise, he had little good to say about the sheathbill, a species of unappealing gastronomic preferences (sea lion excrement). To him, they were "dumpy, white, [and] ptarmigan-like, . . . aberrant shorebirds" of "snow-white" plumage, with "rather ugly faces and waddling walk."

Perhaps what happened within a couple of hours of meeting these birds colored his memory of them. The wind rose and the oarsman told Humphrey and Peterson they should all head back. This time the ornithologists were enlisted as supplementary oarsmen. The wind strengthened and waves washed over the men as they pushed, pushed, pushed their oars for a backbreaking return trip of three hours. Roger's long legs were a liability—he had little room to move his oar without hitting his knee each time. The pressure to keep rowing, through pain and exhaustion, was palpable. Had anyone missed just one or two strokes, the boat might have capsized in the tumultuous waters. Even so, the rolling waves filled and refilled the boat. "We would actually be sitting in icy water," Roger recounted.

"The whole angry sea was moving upon us from the agonizing coast that seemed to remain forever distant," he wrote. "The spray that splashed our faces dried to form white patches of salt crystals." Those mean penguins mocked them, braying like donkeys as they swam effortlessly through the surf. From the mainland, José and Atilio agonizingly watched through a telescope as the boat disappeared from view for minutes on end.

Finally, after interminable, desperate labor on the part of the tired men, their boat reached shore. José and Atilio ran up, helping to pull the boat onto the sand. Roger just collapsed in it; that night leg cramps set in.

A month later they were chatting with a man in the guano business who owned the now infamous Isla Blanca. He said they were fortunate they survived, relating the tragedy of two of his employees who attempted the same trip a month before Humphrey and Peterson under similar conditions but succumbed to the freezing water. "There was nothing we could do about it," he told them. "You were lucky!"

In looking back at those nightmarish hours from the safety of a full year, Roger wrote: "I realize that this experience, one of the most grueling in my life, and unpleasant at the time, was one that I wouldn't want to have missed. To take a chance once in a while and to get away with it is to feel alive."

It wasn't the last time he'd look at such a frightening experience this way.

Roger left Argentina on New Year's Eve, a month ahead of his companions. The day before, Roger, Phil, José, and Atilio went to dinner and a movie. Prior to the movie, his companions presented

Roger with a Christmas gift inspired by his penchant for traveling with bulky photographic gear.

"I got a couple of bricks, gift wrapped them in a box, and gave them to Roger while we were at dinner in Río Gallegos," says Humphrey. "He had to take them with him as carry-on luggage on the airplane. And he had all his camera equipment. He was absolutely flabbergasted. . . . We finally broke down and told him what the deal was. He was fortunately amused. We had a good time."

Humphrey used their findings on Patagonian and Fuegian avifauna in his university teaching; Roger gave lectures about the trip. Two publications emerged belatedly. First was a book, *Birds of Isla Grande (Tierra del Fuego),* a hefty manual published by the Smithsonian in 1970. Roger received coauthor billing along with Humphrey, researcher David Bridge, and the late Percival Reynolds whose papers on the region's birdlife the Reynolds family presented to Humphrey and Peterson in Argentina.

In 1978 Humphrey and Peterson conferred further on the monk parakeets they had observed in 1960. The result was a paper in the *Wilson Bulletin* on the birds' nesting behavior in southern Buenos Aires Province.

Scholarship by Humphrey and Peterson concerning the birds and terrain of the places they visited in 1960 may have brought the birds and other animals a step closer to wise stewardship.

The Galapagos

The Galápagos Islands, a volcanic archipelago of unique flora and fauna and a province of Ecuador, lies about six hundred miles west of the mainland. Roger first visited this birthplace of Charles Darwin's theory of evolution in January 1964. He was among a team of fifty scientists participating in the six-week-long Galápagos International Scientific Project, supported by the University of California and the Ecuadorian government.

"I had been privileged to join the fifty participants who attended the dedication of the Charles Darwin Research Station,"

Roger later wrote, "and who remained to study the birds, the tortoises, the tide pools, forests, lava flows, and volcanic peaks."

Wherever he went, Roger knew people. In the Galápagos, he camped and explored with Dean Amadon, chair of the ornithology department at the American Museum of Natural History. Individuals from Roger's past were on the islands too—Robert L. Pyle, the young meteorologist/birder who joined Roger's DC Audubon field trips during the war, and Bill Weber of the old Sialis Club of the Bronx and witness to the "Dovekie Deception" of the 1937 Christmas Bird Count. Weber, there to study the islands' mosses, wrote decades later:

> In 1964, Roger Peterson joined us for a day on Isla Santa Cruz in the Galapagos, following the dedication of the Darwin Station. Roger started out loaded with cameras, especially with a little camera that had a wire frame that helped him center images. There were so many of his devotees in the group that, before many minutes had gone by, everybody was carrying Roger's gear. . . . We camped in an open meadow surrounded by Scalesia trees. Several tortoises were coaxed out of the brush, and I have a photograph of Roger . . . seated on one of them.

Riding Galápagos tortoises, massive beasts weighing hundreds of pounds, was only a diversion in a period of intense study. Roger summarized the exploits of the scientists, writing of his explorations and those of his compatriots in the third person:

> The Government of Ecuador provided patrol boats, and the United States lent ships and helicopters. From dawn to dusk the scientists pondered the ways of sea lions and sea birds, hammered at rocks, dived for marine life, collected plants. They examined not only the insects but also the smallest parasites of the insects. Nothing was too obscure to escape their scrutiny. And wherever

they went, Darwin's finches sang their coarse songs to remind them of the genius who found his greatest inspiration in these islands.

The finches, perhaps the most famous animals in the Galápagos, prompted Darwin's theory. He posited that the thirteen finch species each evolved in isolation from the others from a common ancestor, developing radically different bills, adapted to the way each species made its living. Some had massive bills for crushing seeds; others, tiny bills for catching insects; still others, bills sturdy enough for handling a twig to dig grubs out of rotting wood. The bill of one scary finch was adapted for lightly puncturing the flesh of large, unsuspecting seafaring birds to drink their blood. Roger said Darwin's finches were made of "particularly tough, plastic stock—evolutionary potter's clay."

There were dangers. Roger checked his shoes every morning for scorpions. On his first night camping on Point Espinoza, Fernandina Island, he sensed a visitor of immense proportions by his sleeping bag: "I spoke but received no reply. Fumbling with my flashlight, I shot a beam of brilliant light into the glaring eyes and bristling whiskers of a huge bull sea lion. It had mistaken my sea-lion-size silhouette for an invading rival. Whooping and howling, I sent him off down the beach with half a dozen of his cows lumbering behind."

Roger had heard of an "outpost" flamingo colony, descended from the West Indian species, on Santa Maria Island and hired a fishing boat to go there. He found just forty birds, and proclaimed them in his 1967 *National Geographic* article about the Galápagos the "most endangered birds in the archipelago."

Studying life on the islands, conservation was always in Roger's thoughts. He estimated hundreds of thousands of tortoises had been slaughtered over the last couple of centuries for their fat and meat. He charged, "The pitiful remnant surviving today—estimated at 8,000—is a rebuke to human ruthlessness." He worried about the flightless cormorants, with a population of less than one thousand, which were drowning in lobster traps. He noted that introduced mammals—cats, dogs, pigs, and rats— had wreaked havoc on the tortoises and land iguanas. He warned against introducing foreign birds.

After six weeks in the Galápagos, Roger and other leaders of the scientific expedition boated to Guayaquil to review their findings at a three-day symposium. According to Pyle, Roger focused on conservation issues in his speech, talking of the "status" of the birds he observed and recommending areas to be included in the proposed national park, established the following year by the Ecuadorian government.

In the spring of 1965 Roger was back in the Galápagos with a Canadian Broadcasting Company team filming the wildlife for John Livingston's television series, *The Nature of Things.*

Livingston had grown up on the eastern Peterson guide. "He would have had the book from the very beginning," says Livingston's son, Zeke. "It would have been new when my Dad was first setting out."

Like Roger, John Livingston did not have formal scientific training, but his avocation of bird and nature study eventually became his vocation, and by the 1950s he had assumed the presidency of the Audubon Society of Canada (now called Nature Canada). Inevitably, John's path crossed Roger's; they became close.

Zeke remembers Roger frequently visiting the Livingston home outside Toronto, either for birding purposes, business related to *The Nature of Things,* or while attending a convention of naturalists. "I think they both had admiration for each other," says Zeke. "Perhaps [it was] a little more my Dad having admiration—because Roger was older—having a lot of admiration for Roger and his work . . . in his field guides and his painting . . . . They were also very, very bright. The two of them would talk about all kinds of things," including environmental philosophy, which John eventually taught at York University.

The men complemented each other. "I think my Dad was probably more outgoing," Zeke reflects. "My Dad was a little . . . rough around the edges, maybe. . . . He had a tendency to rub people the wrong way and he certainly wouldn't pull any punches. . . . So I think they were very different in that respect." Zeke thinks Roger was more tactful, which comports with Roger's reluctance to be a table pounder like Rosalie Edge.

Rolph Blakstad, a cameraman on *The Nature of Things,* watched John and Roger interact: "My impression was that Roger was an infinite encyclopedia, much more so than John." The unit manager for *The Nature of Things,* George McAfee, recalls filming in the Galápagos and East Africa, wherein Roger worked as a lowly, additional cameraman. ("I don't think Roger cared, as long as he was there in the field and finding new birds and shooting new stuff.") If John or anyone else brought up something about the natural world, McAfee laughingly recalls, "Roger would immediately give a whole history of it. . . . Somebody pointed out a particular bird and Roger knew all about it. He didn't like to be one-upped in any way. But I think that's common with people who've made their mark in the world. . . . They're always very up, I guess. But he was up in a nice way, in a very soft-spoken way."

But, as Roger was behind the camera on his Galápagos trip with Livingston, he surrendered any claim to notoriety that would come with being in front. He was just one of the guys in the crew, shooting, in McAfee's estimation, about 40 percent of the footage. Yet, as Roger was a famous man, there were perks to be had by having him on your crew. On the Galápagos trip this meant, for the whole entourage, dinner in Quito with the British consul, an avid birdwatcher.

(Perks abounded when the crew filmed in East Africa two years later. "He knew everybody there," says Blakstad. "He knew Louis Leakey and Joy Adamson. We had dinner with all the main naturalists there. Because he was one of the founders of the World Wildlife Fund we were able to stay in the Ngorongoro Crater all day and all night, and filmed for the first time a hyena kill. We were up all night with Dr. Gunn [the sound recordist] and a parabolic microphone listening for hyena calls. So we had a lot of adventures because of Roger's fame.")

But Blakstad and McAfee noticed a less-glamorous aspect of being Roger Tory Peterson. In day-to-day matters, Roger was the child, and Barbara, his nerve-wracked mother. She fussed over him at the airport, entrusting important documents like airplane tickets to McAfee lest the brilliant naturalist lose them. McAfee also was supposed to remind Roger, the man with the steel-trap mind, of the contents of each vest pocket: "He might be a little forgetful, you know."

To reach the Galápagos for *The Nature of Things,* Blakstad recalls, "We had to arrange transportation, because in those days there was no transportation. . . . The occasional freighters went. So we had to arrange with the Ecuadorian air force the rental of an air force plane to take us. Then we had a meeting with Beagle the Second to get us on an island which had an air strip for landing."

Beagle the Second was *Beagle II,* a ship of the Darwin Research Station named for the vessel Darwin sailed to the archipelago in 1835. *Beagle II* was overseen by Carl Angermeyer, a one-time German refugee who in 1937 had settled on the islands. The ship took the crew from island to island.

Blakstad recalls the magic of nights on *Beagle II:* "Standing on the bow in the middle of the night with stars shining in the sky and phosphorescent movements in the sea reflected in the stars . . . . Sitting, anchored in a tropical cove, under full moon, . . . with

Carl Angermeyer playing on the accordion Hamburg sailor songs and huge manta rays leaping out of the sea at sunset, slapping the parasites off their backs." The crew took such images back north, where Canadians learned of the wonders of the lava-based islands that changed the course of science.

"Ecuador, proud of her famous islands, encourages the new breed of traveler who comes to see, to marvel, and not to destroy," Roger wrote in 1967, adding hopefully: "Here, the tortoises, the iguanas, and the rare sea birds will always have a haven."

The Antarctic

The flower guide and the Mexican bird guide would both be closer to completion were it not for the tempting expeditions which Roger at his rapidly advancing age believes he should make. It had been his cherished ambition to bird on all seven continents and this objective finally was realized when he was given the opportunity to join Bill Sladen in the Antarctic.

So wrote Barbara Peterson in March 1966 in a belated New Year's letter. Johns Hopkins University professor of environmental health and ecology William Sladen, a British transplant and Antarctic veteran, had invited Roger to Antarctica to spotlight the need for protection of the Earth's most desolate (but beautiful) region. Sladen wrote: "A person of RTP's stature could help create a needed awareness in the USA, indeed the world."

The Antarctic wasn't a place where people could pop in. If the Galápagos were remote, Antarctica might have been the moon. Sladen got Roger there by persuading the National Science Foundation, which was sponsoring long-term Adélie penguin studies, to hire him as Sladen's "assistant." The latter still chuckles at the unlikely arrangement. "That was sort of funny!" he says. "The great Roger Tory" reporting to another ornithologist was a strange thought.

In November 1965 Roger flew from California to New Zealand. It was his first time there, and as he wrote to Barbara ("Darling," the letter began), Christchurch was "more like England than England. The same neat gardens & hedges, lots of lilacs, rhododendrons & wallflowers—lots of girls & boys in the uniforms of their schools, little tea shop[s] like those in London, etc. and to top it off no native songbirds in the town but instead, ever so many British blackbirds, chaffinches, yellowhammers, greenfinches, dunnocks, European goldfinches, redpolls, starlings, skylarks, etc."

His celebrity followed him: "Apparently the local birders learned of my presence so I was taken around (saw a lake with 100,000 black swans) & was feted at an evening buffet." From New Zealand, Roger told Barbara he flew to the U.S. base at McMurdo on the Ross Sea, where he was given a crash course in Antarctic survival by New Zealand "mountaineers." "Tried it myself—such as learning to use an ice axe, climbing slopes, negotiating crevasses, building a snow cave, an igloo, etc."

Roger later admitted that at fifty-seven he wasn't the most promising student: "The New Zealand instructors showed us how to stop ourselves with an axe if we slipped on an icy slope. You grasped the axe just so and rolled with it. I found myself on line, axe in hand. The instructor, noticing I was a rather super-annuated type, said solicitously, 'You don't have to do it.'" Roger insisted on trying, sliding down the slope "a mile a minute" until he halted his descent with the axe faster than the other students had done. "Apparently I was so terrified that I did it right," he said.

The next destination was Cape Crozier, where Roger joined Bill Sladen and his graduate students. Cape Crozier was possessed of considerable notoriety, having been the starting point of what was dubbed the "worst journey in the world" in a book of the same name about the 1911 expedition of three Brits in search of emperor penguin eggs. The problem was that these penguins laid their eggs during the Antarctic winter. Roger summarized: "For nineteen days the three men pulled their sledges over the rugged terrain in the endless darkness with temperatures that dropped to 40 degrees below zero and once to 77 degrees below. On the return trip conditions were even worse. . . . They only hoped to die without much pain." Living in a hut at Crozier, Roger felt "guilty" that, unlike the three men who struggled so but survived to tell the tale, the modernity of 1965 meant that he could be rescued at any time by a navy helicopter. (Also, it was now Antarctic summer.) "The rocks that . . . [the 1911 explorers] had piled up to afford shelter were still there on a headland, a reminder that these men were not a myth," he marveled. "Never before had I experienced such complete isolation."

Everyone on the Johns Hopkins University expedition had a turn at the stove. "So I gave Roger a can of baked beans to warm," Sladen laughs. "He was helpless. With Barbara looking after him hand and foot she probably . . . packed his luggage and did everything for him."

The self-described "super-annuated" naturalist had a wonderful time. "Temperatures at camp ranged from about 5 below to about 25 above. It is getting warmer," Roger told Barbara. "But the thermal clothes are terrific. . . . The 3 weeks at the Adelie penguin colony were terrific (took 4800 feet of film, 2000 still shots). Also took film for 3 days for [Marlin] . . . Perkins when he was with us for his 'Wild Kingdom' show—It will be shown in April—The Adelies (300,000 of them) were terrific (3 terrifics—I must stop that)—It is very dramatic watching their attempts to avoid and outwit the leopard seals."

Roger had been looking forward to a genuine Antarctic blizzard. One kept them in their hut for two days; winds rose to sixty miles per hour. He ventured out for a short while to sample it. "Yeah, he came in with drift all over his face and his beard," Sladen recalls. "You can't go to the Antarctic without that. It's like going to Alaska. You can't go to Alaska without coming back with your bear story. . . . No, it wasn't a serious storm. Just a lot of drift, et cetera. It wasn't as bad as some of the ones we usually had, of a hundred miles an hour or more. But it was good enough. Roger went out and got all drifted up."

Although Roger had seen penguins before, in Patagonia and in the Galápagos, he had never seen the cute (but tough) little Adélies with their expressive flippers and buttonlike eyes. "The Adelie is the most penguiny of the penguins," Roger would later write, "the stereotype that most people have in mind when they think of those appealing birds—'The little chap in the tuxedo.'" Nor until now had he ever seen the biggest penguin of all, the emperor, just a short helicopter ride away on the "sea ice below the great Ross Ice Shelf," as Bill Sladen later explained. More important was a third penguin species that Roger finally witnessed on the sub-Antarctic Macquarie Island, between Antarctica and the southern shores of New Zealand and Australia. It was then that his life changed.

Macquarie wasn't the most inviting place for a life-changing experience. For one thing, it wasn't a pleasant day when Roger set eyes on his first king penguin rookery. "It was a most miserable, miserable day," says Sladen. "It was raining, dull, and windy. It was really miserable."

The island also had a horrible legacy. While by 1965 the Antarctic Treaty protected the sub-Antarctic islands from wanton exploitation, Roger knew that the key was to ensure enforcement of the treaty's provisions, as enforcement had been central to the success of conservation legislation in America and the establishment of national parks in places as diverse as Spain and Kenya. Calling the history of Macquarie a "conservation shocker," he would later describe the abuse that wildlife sustained, in some cases to the point of extirpation at the hands of greedy early-nineteenth-century whalers. Hundreds of thousands of fur seals were butchered until none were left. Within another decade, the elephant seal was nearly gone, slaughtered for its blubber and "waiting to be rendered for oil to light the lamps of the pre-Edisonian world," Roger wrote. The rampaging humans next turned on the king penguins, the second largest penguin species after the emperor, and boiled them alive for *their* blubber. Although the kings were not completely wiped out, when they had dwindled to a very few, the next victims became the royal penguins, more resilient than the other animals because they numbered in the millions. Roger noted that the bloodbath ended only when profitability did, and was pleased to say that the Australian government had since adopted "enlightened conservation policies." The respective populations of elephant seals and king penguins had recovered; fur seals were reappearing on Macquarie from elsewhere.

By the time he set foot on Macquarie, the penguins as a family had already gripped Roger's emotions as well as his brain. "They are highly specialized birds dedicated to penguinism," he instructed, "a life molded by the cold impersonal sea, harsh climate, and the crowded colonies in which they reproduce." But seeing the king penguins was love at first sight. "Few other sights in the bird world are as spectacular as a wall-to-wall carpet of Kings," he stated. Eventually, they provided him an alter ego. "When I was asked to choose a bird name as my pseudonym," he said, "I hesitated. Should it be Wandering Albatross or King Penguin? I finally decided on King Penguin, my favorite species in my favorite family of birds."

King Penguin, devoid of feathers but of human height and form, was born.

In 1966, at Bill Sladen's behest, Roger gave a talk at a meeting of the Antarctica Society. Roger's speech concentrated on conservation—the depredations wildlife had suffered on sub-Antarctic islands, the value of scientific research there and on the continent, and the dangers posed by man and his habit of introducing harmful, nonnative animals:

> Antarctica fits my definition of Eden—a harsh Eden. But like the Galapagos Islands which for a long time screened man out as an inhabitant, technological advancement and modern transport have opened up the continent to occupancy. A century of exploration of the most grueling kinds is now being followed up by permanent human settlements of several nations. The communities they have established will have an inevitable effect on the ecosystem—if there are no controls. In fact, even a few people with no biological background or judgment in any area can damage the natural values.

The annual meeting of the American Association of Zoological Parks and Aquariums in October 1976 held a symposium on penguins in captivity. The symposium's purpose, Bill Sladen wrote in the *International Zoo Yearbook,* was to highlight the tendency of zoos to "concentrate on exhibiting a few individuals of several species of penguin, rather than a substantial colony of one or two species. The importance to penguins of social behavior has been stressed for some years by observers of wild birds."

By then Roger had seen and photographed all seventeen species of penguin and been to Antarctica a dozen times. Bill urged him to chair the symposium, which he did, as well as offer a paper on the world's penguins, the conservation issues facing them, and how zoos could help. Roger wrote of the two endangered penguins, the Humboldt's and the African (then called the black-footed): "It may seem anomalous that the two most endangered penguins are the ones most frequently kept in captivity. The question may well be asked: have zoos contributed to the decline?"

Roger's answer was no. Oil spills and careless fishing kill more penguins than are ever exhibited in a zoo. "Actually, there can be a very positive side to zoological exhibits," he continued. "They make it possible for people to know animals that they may never see in the wild, and, they may also act as a holding reservoir for endangered species—if they can be consistently bred in sufficient numbers."

Sladen believes that the symposium directly resulted from his initiative of bringing Roger to Antarctica in 1965 and piquing his interest in the birds that would become his favorite, penguins. The symposium in turn led to zoos changing their penguin exhibition and breeding practices. "Roger's participation in this helped so much," Sladen wrote. "Now, of course, there are many zoos raising penguins and there is no need to catch them in the wild any more."

However, a chilling finding in Antarctica fueled conservationists in a 1960s struggle against U.S. chemical companies.

Chapter Eleven

DDT, the Osprey, and the Old Lyme Offspring

"Spring is a tremendous time for a field biologist," says Paul Spitzer, a Peterson protégé.

> *The ospreys come early. Among the neotropical migrants, they're the first to come back, along with the turkey vulture. Some turkey vultures are here all winter, so it's different. Ospreys aren't here all winter. And they're a harbinger. Everybody sees them that way. They're very visible and noisy. People love to watch them court and they love to watch them build the nest. . . . Connecticut was changing [in the 1960s] and people somehow saw the ospreys as part of what they loved about Connecticut. . . . There are some great things about ospreys. First of all, they operate at a pace that human beings can relate to. Kind of one thing after another, and not too fast. Second of all, their breeding season plays out over four months. . . . April, May, June, and well into July. You can live it. It's not ephemeral. . . . There's predictability. The nests are there from year to year. So you can build your life around them. You can show them to people.*

Roger Tory Peterson greatly valued having 150 osprey nests nearby. One was in an oak on a ridge behind his studio. His neighbors also viewed osprey nests on their property as a status symbol and built nest platforms out of poles with cartwheels lying flat on top to encourage the birds, which had no problem with encroaching civilization. Roger wrote: "Some [ospreys] were living in wild, undisturbed areas; others were right in town, even on telegraph and private poles. In fact the attitude toward the osprey was very much like that of Europeans toward their storks; no persecution whatsoever."

The ospreys were a wonder to watch. Roger described an osprey eyeing the mouth of the Connecticut River estuary:

Cruising over its fishing grounds, it checked itself 40 or 50 feet above the water and hovered on laboring wings in one spot. Scanning the riffles below, it took a bead on its quarry, then plummeted, its needle-sharp talons thrown far forward and its head in line with them. This falconlike thrust plunged the big bird completely out of sight in a splash of spray, but a moment later it reappeared to flap off with a fish. As it almost invariably does, it carried its prey nose forward like a silvery torpedo.

Of ospreys at the nest, Roger commented:

I never tire of watching them as I canoe the quiet backwaters of the Connecticut. High over Great Island one fish-laden osprey after another wings its way homeward. . . . From my canoe on the Connecticut I have often watched the male enter the eyrie with his catch. After he eats the head, his mate takes the remainder from him and feeds the young the choice center part, bit by bit, saving the tail for herself.

But Roger and Barbara noticed a disturbing phenomenon in 1957. By summer, when the osprey nests of Great Island should have been active with young birds, they were not. "I looked over the marsh and wondered why there were no young on the nests," Roger noted. "The nesting season had been a failure. So was the next year. We found that some of the birds incubated to no avail for 60 and 70 days. The normal incubation of osprey eggs is 30 to 32 days."

Peter Ames discovered the ospreys of Great Island at age twenty-one from an unlikely vantage point—the window of a train on the New York-New Haven-Hartford line—some years before the Petersons moved to Old Lyme. (Ames lived in Cambridge, Massachusetts, and began birding as an adolescent, using the Peterson guides from the first.) He says, "I was aware that when you got to the Connecticut River . . . there were all these ospreys there. You could look down on Great Island and see the birds in the nests. You could see them in the oak trees. Dead oaks, particularly. There were poles in people's yards. . . . The place was alive with ospreys. It impressed me."

By 1959 when Ames began graduate studies at Yale University's Division of Birds, he was observing the ospreys to learn why they were having problems breeding. He would continue to do so through the 1965 nesting season, when he earned his doctorate.

Ames believes Belton Copp introduced him to the Petersons and the possibility of together tackling the ospreys' nesting failures. "From Belton's property—he had a wonderful house up there—. . . . you look right across this flat, marshy island known as Great Island, and there were all the ospreys," Ames says.

But there were fewer and fewer to admire. Roger knew from the ornithological literature that there had been a high of 200 nests in 1938, reduced to 150 by 1954. Six years later, there were just 71 nests with only seven young raised; the numbers kept decreasing so that by 1965 Roger noted only 13 nests and two young.

Why the ospreys' numbers were in free fall was a puzzlement. Roger considered whether a lack of food, poor parenting, predators, or habitat loss could be the culprit, but suspected early on something more sinister.

America was awash in chemicals. Lots of them, in high doses, sprayed over wide areas across the land to keep crops, trees, the air, bug-free. And not just any chemicals. Chlorinated hydrocarbon chemicals, like DDT and its even deadlier cousins heptachlor and dieldrin. Chemicals to kill the spruce budworm. Fungus-bearing bark beetles. Gnats. Mosquitoes. Chemicals to kill, in effect, harmless and beneficial insects, plus mammals, fish, and birds living downwind, downstream, or down on their luck.*

Roger related in *The World of Birds,* his second book with James Fisher, that the use of chlorinated hydrocarbons had resulted in some spectacular wildlife disasters. In Canada, an attempt to eradicate the spruce budworm with DDT "ruined the salmon population" of New Brunswick's Miramichi River. DDT was applied in Clear Lake, California, over eight years to eliminate gnats, which it did. Roger explained: "It was also eaten and concentrated 250 times by the water plankton. . . . It was found in 500 times concentration in the small fishes that ate the plankton. It killed most of the western grebes that ate the fishes, and they died with an 80,000 times concentration."

In the Midwest, Roger noted, Dutch elm disease, caused by the bark beetle and its accessory, fungus, was battled with DDT—sometimes in concentrations of twenty-four, and in one instance, one hundred, pounds to the acre—but failed to defeat elm disease. However, in places it killed 90 percent of breeding passerines. People looked on helplessly as robins died, wracked with muscular tremors, on the greenery of college campuses.

On learning of these disasters, Roger reflected that the number of birds evidently affected constituted a fraction of those that died in the area where they were found. As he noted on another occasion, "Dying birds try to hide."

---

* *Chlorinated hydrocarbons* was the term generally used in the 1950s and 1960s for the new line of insecticides exemplified by DDT. This group of chemicals is also often called *organochlorines.* For purposes of consistency, chlorinated hydrocarbons is the only term used here for this line of insecticides.

Perhaps the most infamous instance of wildlife mortality from the application of chlorinated hydrocarbons occurred in the late 1950s with the fire ant eradication program instituted in the Southeast. Roger stated in 1964:

The ... [fire ant] campaign, for the chemical industry, was, by the admission of their own trade journals, a "sales bonanza." ... At the start ..., heptachlor and dieldrin, hydrocarbons respectively 10 and 60 times stronger than DDT in their toxicity, were broadcast at two pounds to the acre. Fortunately the campaign never soaked the 27 million acres it aimed at; but it started in 1958 with a million, and killed almost every sort of domestic poultry and mammal, many wild mammals, in places at least half the birds, including nearly all the ground birds, meadowlarks, quail and turkeys. The U.S. Department of Agriculture (responsible for the campaign) gave an imitation of an ostrich, burying its head in the sand. It took the birds a full three years to recover. The fire ants survived. So did the pesticide companies.

The fire ant campaign was based on three-way funding—one-third by the federal government, one-third by the state involved, and one-third by affected property owners. A 1959 National Audubon Society report disclosed that property owners like farmers and "cattlemen" became wary of the program once its impact on domestic and wild animals became known. States began stalling their appropriations. The report opined that the impact of this chemical broadcast over what was by then 1.25 million acres could have consequences beyond the easily documentable deaths of animals. It asked whether residues of chlorinated hydrocarbons would accrue in soils over time, accumulating in "insect larvae, the worms, the reptiles and amphibians, the rodents and other life in the soil which form important food-chains that are essential to the ecology of the Southeast."

Old Lyme's most famous resident knew that the impact on wildlife was not always going to be obvious to the naked eye in the form of large numbers of dead and dying birds and other animals following a spray campaign. He was certain, long before most, that chlorinated hydrocarbons were behind the disappearance of the osprey in his backyard and elsewhere, as well as the bald eagle and the peregrine falcon.

"Roger became convinced that it was DDT from fragmentary evidence, which was the genius of Rachel Carson [too]," says Paul Spitzer. "That's real courage in science, to get out in front. Connect the dots, if you will, and take partial evidence. . . . The more you live and the more you think about it, you realize every day you act with incomplete knowledge—about your own health, about all kinds of things. It's fundamental to the human condition. So Roger . . . was pretty convinced that it was DDT."

One reason Roger was convinced was that he could find no other empirical cause for the disappearance of some of America's most beloved birds. He had a rebuttal for any other cause his colleagues suggested. While it wasn't his way to have face-to-face confrontations, he knew his facts and wasn't afraid to express them. Barbara Peterson says people didn't tend to confront Roger, either, but if they did, "he would talk them to death. He . . . used the English language very well. People just backed off. He was far more intelligent than they were."

But Roger preferred to stay in the backgrond and work quietly. Belton Copp says Roger was behind an anti-DDT campaign in Old Lyme. "They, of course, [wanted to] spray because the mosquitoes were at that time rather thick down here because we're really close to the saltwater," Copp says. "Roger persuaded me to work with the town on seeing if we could get them [not to spray]. I did. . . . He changed a lot of people's minds on DDT in the town. They gave up on it."

To say that Roger was annoyed with some of his best friends over their reluctance to blame DDT for the decline of birds of prey would be an understatement. When in 1962 he learned that the National Audubon Society had secured U.S. Fish and Wildlife funding for a project to study bald eagles, he complained that one part of the project was to study healthy bald eagle nest sites. "We are dealing with three areas where the eagles are doing well," he wrote to Carl Buchheister. "We are not going to find out what is wrong with the bald eagle by concentrating on these three areas."

He was also upset about the skepticism of Sandy Sprunt* and even his old friend Allan Cruickshank regarding the late Florida "eagle man" Charles Broley's "hunch on pesticides" affecting the bald eagles Broley had banded and studiously observed. Persuasively marshalling his facts, Roger asked for a heart-to-heart talk with Buchheister, arguing:

> *The fact remains that Broley's birds were about all the usual eyries [aeries] but not raising young for several years before he died. It was not just a matter of loss of nesting sites. These eagles were willing to put up with almost anything and had been for some years, as I saw when I went around the eyries in 1946. They managed to raise their young in the hearts of towns, in the backyards of schools, on golf courses. The big predators being at the peak of the food chain are going to be the ones that get the really lethal dose or sublethal dose of residual pesticides.*

In 1964 Buchheister relayed to Roger news of the peregrine falcon resulting from a study overseen by Joe Hickey: "It would appear that the Peregrine Falcon has disappeared as a nesting species in the Eastern United States." Roger responded, "The shocking news does not surprise me but I had hoped that the situation was not quite as complete a blank." Again persuasively marshalling his facts, he continued:

---

* "Sandy" was Alexander Sprunt IV, the son of Alexander Sprunt Jr., the South Carolinian naturalist-cum-Audubon stalwart with whom Roger, as a teen, birded off the Carolina coast in 1927.

I do not know what conclusions the Hickey researchers came to—whether they felt that pesticides were involved. Of course we cannot prove it now that there are no Peregrines to work with, but what other inferences can be drawn? To assume that it was disturbance . . . would be complete nonsense because how could you disturb every last eyrie, even the remote ones? And this all happened, mind you, in a period of 5 to 7 years in the early fifties. Yet these same birds had long withstood the depredations of falconers who took their young, eggers who in the old days took their eggs and, of course, gunners. These birds had their rapid disappearance when egging was no longer practiced, when the falconer was almost non-existent and when the Peregrine itself was protected in many states. Even the pair on the Sun Life Building in . . . Montreal which raised young year after year while being watched from the windows and the roof of the building (certainly disturbance) . . . raised young successfully. But during the early fifties that pair suddenly disappeared with all the others.

For a long time the chemical companies dominated the debate about DDT and its deadly brethren. No one knew this better than Rachel Carson, Roger's friend from DC Audubon days. Being on the Burroughs Medal Committee since receiving his award, he was instrumental in her receipt of the honor for 1951's *The Sea Around Us.*

In 1959 Roger told his editor Paul Brooks, also Carson's editor at Houghton Mifflin, "Our present use of poisons is the greatest threat to wildlife since time began," and that the book Carson was writing, later named *Silent Spring,* "could do more than anything else to apprise the public of that fact." Brooks mentioned this to Carson, who welcomed this viewpoint considering what she was learning herself. By the time *Silent Spring* was excerpted in *The New Yorker,* a few months before the book's fall 1962 publication, a rush of vilification braced to surge her way. And it did.

Velsicol Chemical Company, manufacturer of heptachlor and the related chemical chlordane, tried intimidating *The New Yorker* and Houghton Mifflin into not publishing Carson's writings. Then the company orchestrated a meeting with Audubon officers to suggest they quit questioning the safety of these pesticides if they knew what was good for them. This was only the beginning.

Upon the publication of *Silent Spring,* the National Agricultural Chemicals Association (NACA) spent over a quarter of a million dollars to discredit Carson. The Manufacturing Chemists' Association also expended considerable resources toward the same end. She was called a spinster, a Communist, an emotional woman, a science fiction writer—and a nonscientist since she only had a master's degree. NACA hired a public relations firm to do maximum damage. This led to the persistent anti-Carson exclamations of an executive of American Cyanamid, Robert White-Stevens, and a former American Cyanamid employee, Thomas Jukes. While Carson had allies who spoke publicly in her defense, among them Audubon's Roland Clement, noted anthropologist Loren Eiseley, and Nobel Prize-winning geneticist Hermann J. Muller, neither she nor the Audubon Society had the resources for a real counterattack.

(In a speech to the Women's National Press Club at the end of 1962, Rachel Carson pointed to chemical industry support of scientists' research appearing in academic journals and asked, "Whose voice do we hear, that of science or of the sustaining industry?")

One of White-Stevens's arguments, which particularly incensed Roger, was that Audubon's own Christmas Bird Count numbers refuted the notion that the robin's population was plummeting because of pesticide use. Roger spoke about this before Congress. Legislators in Washington had become increasingly interested in the pesticide controversy, even as the U.S. Department of Agriculture resisted it. On April 22, 1964, just eight days after Rachel Carson's death, Roger spoke at a U.S. Senate subcommittee hearing called by Connecticut senator Abraham Ribicoff regarding pesticides. In leading up to his recommendation that "all compounds of the chlorinated hydrocarbon complex be banned," he spoke of his innocent experience with DDT in 1945:

[Birds] seemed to be able to withstand small percentages of the poison but larger poundages per acre would kill them. It seemed, then, just a matter of prudent application. But in those days we did not suspect the residual effects—that a bird slightly poisoned might add to the ingested stable [of] poisons till a lethal threshold was reached. . . . These residual effects are much more subtle and sinister than the immediate results of spraying. Earthworms ingesting leaf mold months after elms have been sprayed with DDT against the Dutch elm disease accumulate the poisons. Ten such infected worms may be enough to kill a robin, but the mass dying may not occur until the spring after the spraying.

Regarding White-Stevens's contention that the Christmas Bird Counts show there is nothing to worry about, Roger said:

These public relations men use statistics to their own advantage and not being biologists . . . fail to interpret their meaning. True, more birds are recorded in the U.S. on the Christmas Count because there are now ten times as many . . . [observers] participating in these counts. Due to long experience and streamlined bird guides such as my own field guides, bird watchers are now ten times as efficient. And inasmuch as the count is really a game they go where the birds are; they skip the birdless areas.

He explained the reason insects at the bottom of the food chain were often able to develop resistance to pesticides, while birds could not:

Insects such as . . . [mosquitoes] or flies, near the base of the life pyramid, have an enormous reproductive potential. And if one in millions has a mutation that enables it to live with the poison, that stock can breed back rapidly to fill the vacuum. . . . The predacious insects on the other hand are less numerous. . . . Insect-eating birds, which exist in still smaller numbers therefore have but an infinitesimal chance of such mutations. The end result is that we find the pest still with us while most of the natural controls have been eliminated.

No one, including Roger, knew yet *how* accumulated pesticides in a bird of prey's flesh led to nesting failures, but he was certain pesticides were the problem. He revealed that less-harmful chemicals were being developed by companies like Dow but were more expensive to produce than the chlorinated hydrocarbons; if the government banned the latter, however, all companies would compete on equal footing. In the meantime, Roger said:

We are in a sad way if we always think in terms of profit regardless of the general good. . . . We must think seriously about these things and not allow the tyranny of special interests to ruin America. These interests will insist they are dedicated to public service. That was the original idea but some of them have lost their vision.

Roger was frequently frustrated in the early 1960s. Frustrated because it seemed to him that people who meant a lot to him, like Joe Hickey, appeared slow to acknowledge the harm that chlorinated hydrocarbons were causing birds of prey. Frustrated because there was nothing but bad news about ospreys, peregrines, bald eagles, even the gentle brown pelican.

He told Senator Ribicoff's subcommittee: "The fish kills at the mouth of the Mississippi have received a lot of attention, and I cannot but suspect that there may be a connection with the disappearance of the brown pelican as a breeding bird in Louisiana. Although the brown pelican is the State bird of Louisiana, last year they even removed it from . . . automobile license plates."

Roger was also frustrated about Peter Ames's doctoral dissertation. Ames was dissuaded by, among others, two people whom Roger respected, Dillon Ripley and Phil Humphrey, from using the ospreys' Connecticut River nesting failure as his topic. Roger bitterly wrote to Bill Vogt:

> When Peter Ames, whom I know very well and admire, went to his professors at Yale—Dillon Ripley, Phil Humphrey, et al., he asked to do this [osprey study] for his doctorate. They said that the project was not worth a doctorate, and . . . told him that he was to work instead on the syrinxes of thrushes. This sort of thing makes me very irritated and critical. The fact that the [osprey] study was done at all is because Ames went ahead and did it on his own.*

Ames explains that Ripley and Humphrey suggested a different topic because they "felt that the biology faculty would view this as a conservation study involving wildlife management . . . [which] had] a separate department . . . at Yale. Therefore, my advisers felt that the faculty might reject this as a thesis topic. . . . But I did continue every spring from the time I entered in 1959, spring of '60, say, through 1965, to document the fledgling production, to band the young birds and, in this, Barbara Peterson was a major player."

Of Barbara, Ames continues, "She was certainly a driving force in many aspects of the osprey study. She kept a lot of the records. She made sure we always had the boat . . . , which slipped at the

---

* Ames says his dissertation topic was the syrinxes of flycatchers, manakins, cotingas, antbirds, and ovenbirds.

Copps's.'" Then-elementary school student Allyn Copp, operating a twelve-foot, six-horsepower outboard motorboat, "ferried them around and helped them with some of the trapping and banding." Copp adds, "We set up a big blind next to one of the nests, . . . quite a large contraption, where we could actually look down into the nest from the blind and so forth."

Before long Roger got them funding from the National Geographic Society so they could set up nearly two dozen platform nests on Great Island. "Roger had an awful lot of clout," says Ames. "That is, if he pushed the National Geographic Society or the National Audubon Society or someone like that a little bit they'd cough up funds to support a graduate student, or anybody." The platforms provided the ospreys with optimal conditions for raising young. The birds were safe from predators as well as floodwaters.

Peter Ames remembers being pleased with the ospreys' cooperative nature. "Great Island suddenly started sprouting these poles, with platforms at the top, and just about as fast as we put them up, the birds would be on the top of them."

Ames recalls a typical day checking the osprey nests:

I would get out there at eight o'clock in the morning . . . , we'd shove the boat in the water, and I had printed maps that showed Great Island and all the nests were marked on it and numbered . . . . So we'd take a clipboard and we'd visit each nest on the island and then we had certain nests on the mainland, in oak trees, mostly. . . . We did that probably once a week from May 1 until about the first of July when the birds started to fledge. We'd get out there and try and find the fledged young, make sure they were flying well and so forth. . . . But it was pretty evident that very early on nestling production was down. We weren't getting the hatching rates that the literature said we should be getting. The adults seemed to be doing fine. They seemed to be bringing in lots of fish.

So it wasn't predators, a shortage of food, or other physical characteristics of the habitat that prevented the birds from raising young. In fact, raising young once they hatched was easy. "The main factor contributing to the decrease of this population has been failure of a high percentage of the eggs to hatch," Roger wrote.

Says Ames: "I discussed it [the osprey study] with Roger a good deal. . . He made suggestions frequently." One of Roger's suggestions was to have some of the unhatched eggs analyzed for pesticides. The result confirmed that the eggs contained nearly triple the DDT residues of eggs from the healthy osprey colonies of the Chesapeake Bay.

Roger wasn't happy that Ames wouldn't blame DDT for the osprey egg dilemma. In his letter to Bill Vogt, he complained that Ames "will not state unequivocally that the lack of reproduction is because of DDT, DDE and other metabolites found in the eggs. He admits the presence of these chemicals in the eggs (and in 30 fish recovered from the nests) but will not say that they have inhibited reproduction. In taking this hypercautious view he is avoiding the economical hypothesis."

At the University of Wisconsin, Joe Hickey worried about the peregrine falcon. Ironically, as an academic in a setting where one assumes raising questions would be encouraged, he faced an atmosphere hostile to examining a possible link between DDT and the bird's disappearance from the eastern United States. Even by the late 1960s, "Hickey was kind of standoffish about it [his DDT work]," says Frank Graham, who was then working on *Since Silent Spring*, a follow-up to Rachel Carson's *Silent Spring*.

When I was working on my book I got in touch with Hickey and asked him a number of questions and he preferred not to answer them. I got kind of a chilly reception from him. Later on, after my book came out, I happened to be at an event . . . at Hickey's place. He came up to me, in fact in the kitchen, and he kind of apologized in an indirect way for not having been more cooperative. He said he had a lot of pressures at that time from people at the university. There was so much influence by the agriculture departments and so on at the Big Ten universities and the big land-grant universities that he just hadn't done as much as he'd hoped to be able to do at that time.

It was even bad for writers contracted by the University of Wisconsin Press. Robert Rudd, a zoology instructor at the University of California at Davis, finished writing *Pesticides and the Living Landscape* in 1962. However, as Rachel Carson biographer Linda Lear recounted, its publication was delayed "while the entire [Wisconsin] entomology department and then the president's office reviewed it." Wisconsin finally published the book in 1964.* Because of his writings on pesticides, Lear says, Rudd lost his position with UC Davis. Thus, Joe Hickey had agitators like Roger coming at him from one end and the tentacles of the agricultural and chemical industries coming at him from the other.

A crash of the peregrine population in Great Britain, documented by 1963, was more perplexing. In typical quiet fashion, Roger plotted a rescue. Reflected Hickey nearly twenty years later upon receiving the Audubon Medal:

We were indeed in trouble. That same spring I visited a half dozen raptor-research scientists all over western Europe. Their peregrine populations were crashing too from Switzerland north to Finland.

It therefore seemed absolutely imperative that we call an international symposium to bring all these population stories into

---

* As Frank Graham has noted, a University of Wisconsin colleague of Hickey's, I. L. Baldwin, an agricultural bacteriology professor, in 1962 wrote a negative review of *Silent Spring* in *Science*, the journal of the American Association for the Advancement of Science, which parroted the chemical and agricultural industries' criticisms of Carson. (According to Graham, the AAAS later indirectly rebuked Baldwin in siding with Carson's position.)

focus and plan the research that was needed to explain exactly what was taking place. I did get immediate encouragement from the U.S. Public Health Service, but the U.S. Departments of Agriculture and Interior turned me down cold. It was at this point, when I was becoming very discouraged, that Audubon's Pres. Buchheister phoned me, right out of the blue, to say that his Board of Directors had just voted me some $8,500 to help make the Madison Peregrine Conference a reality. I never had communicated with Audubon about such a symposium, and I never did learn how they reached a figure like $8,500. I was told the whole idea was the brain-child of board member Roger Tory Peterson. It seems to be absolutely certain that this was the critical decision that brought scientists and naturalists together from seven countries and led to the extraordinary discovery that on two continents parent peregrine falcons were breaking and eating their own eggs.

Usually, Joe was a fun guy. His graduate student during this period, Dan Anderson, first met Roger at some of Joe's hotel room parties during various ornithological conferences. "RTP and a heck of a lot of other people would . . . go to Joe and Peggy Hickey's room for their famous Manhattans and bird discussions," says Anderson. "Hickey . . . always brought along a box with two bottles of whiskey and one bottle of vermouth and he'd mix up Manhattans in his room."

There was an air of gravity, though, at the fall Peregrine Conference of 1965 in Madison, Wisconsin. Tom Cade, then a young ornithologist whose boyhood interest in birds was boosted by Roger's field guides, remembers Roger leading "one of the paper discussions. We all sat in on all of the discussions that followed those papers. We had a lot of private discussions late into the evening, up to ten or even eleven o'clock. It was a pretty intense meeting. In fact, I think it was the most intense one I've ever been to."

Anderson recalls Roger speaking, quite predictably, about the plight of the osprey. "He had a little graph. . . . He plotted the line down . . . , just extended the line down and predicted there would be an extinction if things went the way they . . . [were going]. He made everybody scared. It was effective."

Hickey would later say that the purpose of the Peregrine Conference had been to "crystallize hypotheses that we could test" and that it succeeded in this mission. Work proceeded apace.

The monitoring of the osprey nests at Great Island continued after Peter Ames left in 1965 for an academic position in California. His replacement was Tom Lovejoy, another Yale graduate student, who witnessed the ospreys continuing their decline. Osprey breeding, Lovejoy recalls, was "headed straight down the tubes."

Once Lovejoy had the opportunity to continue his academic work in Brazil, Paul Spitzer, a premed student at Wesleyan University, stepped in. "I went out with Lovejoy [to the osprey nests] in '67 and I was really getting a taste for it. . . . I thought, 'Oh, man. This is going to be perfect.' Because I lived right there. It was happening on my doorstep." Spitzer earned course credit for the osprey work. He was "getting royally sick of taking courses without an obvious purpose."

He continues: "The great projects as a field person, as an ecologist, you live them. And I saw right away, I'm going to be able to live this. . . . That's what you look for. A project through which your life flows. . . . Tom invited me along [to Brazil]. . . . I initially agreed to do it. Then I took a long look at the osprey stuff and I realized I . . . wanted to stay at home and work on the ospreys. So I did."

The ospreys weren't in decline just in Connecticut but also in other places where they previously had flourished—such as Gardiner's Island off Long Island and the Cape May peninsula in

New Jersey. Roger Tory Peterson and Joe Hickey conferred closely on their respective quests to learn why the eggs weren't hatching.

Then in 1966 came alarming word from the Antarctic. DDT had been found there too. Bill Sladen had published a paper in the journal *Nature* regarding tests done in 1964 on six adult Adélie penguins and one young male crabeater seal on the one hand, and on the other, a fifty-year-old, frozen emperor penguin collected during the infamous 1911 "worst journey in the world." To keep warm, Sladen says, the earlier explorers had burned emperor penguin blubber inside a stone igloo. "I collected a little wedge of blubber—the penguins were still frozen at the base of the igloo—as my control," Sladen says, since the bird providing the sample had died decades before DDT had first been used.

Shockingly, the Adélies and the seal tested positive for "minute traces of DDT," while the decades-dead emperor tested negative. How could this be? Sladen theorized that pesticides were concentrated in migrating shrimp and plankton that traveled between the "Antarctic surface water" and the "warm deep current" and that the Adélies and crabeater fed on. As Roger commented some time later, "DDT anywhere is DDT everywhere. Even the one 'pristine' continent in the world is not immune."

In 1967 came more startling news. British ornithologist Derek Ratcliffe published a paper on his discovery that DDT and related pesticides inhibited calcium production in the British peregrine falcon. This meant extremely fragile eggs.

Peter Ames explains: "Calcium dehydrogenase . . . , the enzyme which controls the deposition of calcium in the shell . . . is an enzyme that the mother bird produces that regulates the production of calcium into the eggshell. . . . What happens, of course, when they get a certain amount of DDT residues in the system, the calcium dehydrogenase is blocked, the shells come out thin, the mother puts her foot on them or moves them around against each other, and they crack. Fluid is lost and the embryo desiccates and is lost."

The key was to document this in the eastern U.S. osprey. Paul Spitzer decided to switch eggs between healthy osprey colonies in the Chesapeake Bay area and ones with little recent breeding success in Connecticut. He says that Roger was "very supportive" of the idea. Comments Rob Hernandez, who, as an enthusiastic high school student, assisted Spitzer:

> [It was] really remarkable for its time. . . . He was trying to quantify in nature what had been seen and proven just then in laboratory experiments and scientific analysis of the thin egg shell phenomenon. . . . I think Paul's genius, really, was that he put together a very small but neat experiment that . . . demonstrated that thin egg shells . . . weren't just an environmental consequence of the behavior of parents or other environmental elements. . . . [Paul] developed the techniques for the eggs and young transplants, which had never really been done in the wild.

Paul Spitzer's experiments proved that osprey eggs from an unaffected area like the Chesapeake had about the same hatching success in Connecticut as they would have had at home; likewise, eggs from Connecticut had about the same lack of hatching success in Maryland as they would have had at home. Barbara Peterson reported on Paul's efforts in the January 1969 New Year's letter, noting an egg exchange of twenty-one from Connecticut with twenty-two from Maryland. She wrote:

> Nine of the Maryland eggs hatched in Connecticut (41%), about the same percentage of success that the Maryland colony has been enjoying all along. Only one of the Connecticut eggs hatched in Maryland, tending to confirm our belief that the trouble is intrinsic in the eggs (chemical pollutants, apparently affecting calcium deposition) and not due to extrinsic factors such as disturbance, inadequate food supply, etc. To test further the matter of food supply, a batch of young ospreys about 2 weeks old was flown from

Maryland to fill each of our local nests with a full brood of three.
In the weeks that followed all the babies, save one, grew fat, fledged
and flew.

Suddenly vestiges of the bad old days of man's abuse of wildlife showed value. Spitzer says that around the time of his experiments, Dan Anderson, under Joe Hickey's direction, "went around
to all the museums measuring these eggs. There was this wonderful irony, because there was this preposterous old activity of ool-
ogy, egg collecting. . . . So the museums were full of these dusty,
old cases of blown-out eggs. . . . Fresh clutches of osprey eggs are
beautiful. They just glow with these colors of cinnamon and lav-
ender. . . . And peregrine eggs are beautiful, too. That's why both
species were extensively collected, and items of trade. . . . But, of
practical value? Practically none. Except that here, out of the blue,
comes this eggshell-thinning phenomenon and all of sudden,
these [old eggs] are wonderful things to have." Hickey and Anderson were able to demonstrate eggshell thinning in North America
by comparing modern eggs of the peregrine and other birds with
antique, but properly thick, eggs of the nineteenth and early twen-
tieth centuries.

What did Roger think of all this? "He was gratified," says
Spitzer. Roger had been right all along.

Yet DDT would not be banned by the federal government until
December 1972.* The ban of the other chlorinated hydrocarbons

---

* The banning process was an arduous one. It wouldn't have happened had President Richard M. Nixon not ordered an executive branch reorganization in which
matters of the cancellation and suspension of pesticides and herbicides, as well as
most other environmental programs, were allocated to the Environmental Protection Agency. Prior to this, the use of DDT and other pesticides was regulated
by the U.S. Department of Agriculture, which sided with agricultural interests.
The agriculture secretary at the time, Clifford M. Hardin, had been reluctant
to act in response to petitions by environmental groups; EPA head William D.
Ruckelshaus took over the process under the new authority he had been granted
and finally issued the order that ended the use of DDT in the United States.

came later. All American uses of heptachlor and chlordane were prohibited in 1988, closely on the heels of dieldrin, aldrin, and endrin.

For some time Roger noticed negative aftereffects of DDT on other creatures important to him in Old Lyme. In 1974 he dejectedly remarked:

> *About 8 or 9 years ago when there was a gypsy moth outbreak, aerial spraying eliminated several species of butterflies that I haven't seen since, and all the large Saturnid moths. I used to see Luna Moths two or three times a week at my studio windows at night. I haven't seen one now for at least 8 years—and with the big moths gone—the whip-poor-wills also went from the ridge.*

In ensuing years, the ospreys began a resurgence. Wrote Roger in 1988: "At its low point, our local population of ospreys dipped to a mere nine pairs; but now that DDT has been eliminated from the wetland environment they are recovering, and it is but a matter of time before this population may again reach full strength." He predicted that the ospreys could become more populous than they were before their decline "because so many people are putting up platforms."

The peregrine falcon has been reintroduced to the eastern United States thanks to the Peregrine Fund, an organization founded in 1970 by Tom Cade, one of the 1965 Peregrine Conference attendees. The fund was able to raise peregrines and then introduce them in promising places, a process called "hacking." Roger wrote approvingly in 1988 that the "seed stock of wild breeding Peregrines is now doubling its numbers every year or two in eastern North America, and the species is making a strong recovery in other parts of its range as well."

And America's symbol, the bald eagle, declared endangered in 1967 and six years later falling under the new Endangered Species Act, was removed from the endangered list on June 28, 2007. From an all-time low in the continental United States of just 417 breeding pairs in 1963, today there are 10,000 pairs.

Chapter Twelve

The Wilds
of Lindblad

In the late 1960s Roger Tory Peterson had the chance to promote environmentalism, socialize with admirers, and have loads of fun at the same time. He did this by lecturing for the pioneering eco-tourism trips of Lars-Eric Lindblad.

Barbara Peterson, modestly portraying her proactive role, illustrated in her 1972 New Year's letter the challenges the average Lindblad tourist faced in the subantarctic:

> *When we landed at Campbell Island it was completely socked in with drizzle and fog, but there were several thousand royal albatrosses up there in the mountain mist, so everyone gamely started out. This meant an uphill scramble of at least an hour for a teenager; two hours for a senior citizen (and some took six hours up and back). . . . While Roger forged ahead with George Holton and the other obsessive photographers, I stayed with the laggards, cheering them on as they slithered through the pockets of mud between tussock grass and rock.*

Barbara was the den mother on these voyages. "If anybody had a problem I was supposed to look it over . . . and come up with a solution," she says, recalling Lindblad's typical appeal: "*Do something, Barbara!*"

In his autobiography, *Passport to Anywhere,* Lindblad recounted a grim example of the real dangers his passengers faced. On an excursion to the Galápagos, a woman named Mrs. Green was thrown from her horse, suffering multiple broken bones and temporary paralysis. Following a full recovery and a return to further Lindblad trips, she wrote to Lars thanking him for the wonderful experiences she had had and specially commending the "tender loving care" she received on the boat from three fellow passengers, including Barbara.

"I think Barbara . . . [took] her position as a staff member's wife . . . very seriously," remembers Keith Shackleton, who, like Roger, worked on the MS *Lindblad Explorer.* "She was great to have around. . . . If you saw her on the ladder with a helping hand and all, you were very happy to see it."

Roger said he first met Lars at an Audubon banquet after giving a talk on the Galápagos. But Roland Clement claims credit for actually putting them together. "Roger was sort of a [travel] model for a lot of us. He did it first, because he had the connections, because he was a celebrity," says Clement. "Everybody offered him opportunities of traveling. We said, 'God, what a lucky guy. How can we do that, too?'" Following Roger's example, full-time Audubon scientist Clement moonlighted as a tour leader in East Africa. Acquiring a reputation for his tour leading, Clement says, Lars eventually snatched him for Lindblad's first tour to the Galápagos. Afterward Lars requested that Clement recommend his ecotours, asking, "Do you know Roger Peterson?" Clement said yes. Lindblad said, "Invite him on my behalf, and we'll talk."

"So I called Roger," Clement says, "and he wasn't the least bit interested. I said, 'Roger! This is made for you. It's a ship tour. You go ashore to bird all morning. You have lunch on the beach. At three o'clock you come back on board the ship, you take a shower, you have before-dinner drinks and you socialize. Nothing easier!'

"He went on . . . [a] trip on my recommendation and he loved it, because he and Lindblad became buddies. Lindblad said to him, 'Anything we find interesting I can sell, so let's go and explore the world together and that will build [new] tours.'"

Why did Roger and Lars hit it off? Lars's son, Sven-Olof, suggests that "their heritage, love of nature, [and] love of wild places" drew them together. Sven adds: "My father very much appreciated art. There was just every reason on earth that they would gravitate to each other."

Roger and Lars also shared an interest in thrill seeking, even if Roger never expressed their relationship in this way. Lars had gotten into some precarious situations in the process of finding another great spot to take tourists where few had ever been.

Lindblad, of towering stature (he was several inches taller than the vertically privileged Roger and nearly twenty years younger), nurtured an interest in travel from his youth. He was especially fascinated with exotic places far from Western civilization, and discovered he loved animals too. After graduating from college in the late 1940s, he began work at a Stockholm travel agency. In the early 1950s, searching for better opportunities, he moved to the United States with his wife, Sonja, and son, Sven. He made a name for himself as a travel agent for Lissone-Lindeman in New York as the one who could arrange and book unconventional vacations to places in India. Lars became so well known in the travel industry by 1958 that he was able to open Lindblad Travel in New York that September.

In bringing tourists to Africa for Lindblad Travel's Wing Safaris, Lars, and sometimes his customers, narrowly escaped death. Lars had booked a resort in "rugged territory" near Lake Rudolph in Kenya. Over time many Lindblad tourists would come through with happy results. Once while Lars was on the Kenyan coast, a group had just left the resort when the owner, Guy Poole, and a visiting priest were shot to death by Somali rebels. The rebels then kidnapped an Italian truck driver who had stopped to deliver supplies and skinned him alive. In another close call, Lars was scouting an area of the Congo that he thought was politically stable when he, an associate, and his Ugandan driver were menaced by a group of Congolese. The foreigners only escaped after Lars, at the Ugandan's suggestion, posed as a Catholic bishop on an "inspection trip."

A slow ride up the Amazon on Lars's recently launched cruise ship, the *Lindblad Explorer,* had been cleared by Brazilian federal government officials. This didn't matter to local police who arrested Lars and Moacir, his Indian guide, when they came ashore. Lars and Moacir were imprisoned in adjoining cells; the Indian was beaten. Freed after some hours, they returned to the boat where they had to pretend that nothing untoward had happened.

Roger had close calls as a Lindblad scout, although they didn't involve corrupt government officials or internecine violence. "On some trips," says Esperanza Rivaud, Lars's French-Argentinian assistant, "it was Roger, Lars, and the photographer. Roger was there to pay attention to what animal life was there, Lars was doing the planning of all the logistics, and the other one was taking pictures."

Roger later wrote of some of his reconnaissance missions:

I have many memories of dicey incidents while scouting for Lars—such as the time my tent collapsed under an unexpected snowfall in the high Himalayas, or like the situation I faced in the mountains of Ethiopia, when my mule walked onto a ledge, much too narrow, stranding me on a 1,000-foot precipice. Later that same day, while trying to film a large troop of gelada baboons, I was charged by a big, saber-toothed male, but instinctively I stood my ground and turned him away.

Another involved a trying but rewarding exploration of the Seychelles, a picturesque island-chain nation, then a British colony, off Africa's east coast in the Indian Ocean.

"Recently Roger wrote a piece in defense of Aldabra atoll in the Indian Ocean," Barbara reported in the January 1969 New Year's letter. "Not having been there, he felt a bit presumptuous, so when Lars-Eric Lindblad invited him on an exploratory expedition (with a view toward full-fledged tours next year) he couldn't say no." (In response to a 1967 call for help from the British Ornithologists' Union, Roger had written a passionate *Audubon* article opposing a naval base planned for the ecologically rich atoll in the Seychelles. The protest campaign torpedoed the proposal.)

Getting to Aldabra in November 1968 was a roundabout affair beginning with a flight to Kenya and then a voyage on the British India line's MS *Kampala* from Mombasa to the island of Mahé in the Seychelles. In Port Victoria, Mahé, the group boarded a forty-year-old, thirty-ton copra schooner called the *Iron Duke*. The deck was crowded with a ladder, a fuel drum, and a barrel of drinking water, leaving the men with a "sun and promenade deck" of about six feet by eight. Quarters for the explorers, plus the captain and a cabin boy, were minimal, with cabin dimensions about twelve feet by six. The space contained four bunk beds but no place for clothing or anything else.

"We were so cramped," Roger wrote decades later, "that I had to sleep (with my cameras) in a bunk so short that my feet were soddened from the rain that dribbled through the porthole." All were confined to the tiny cabin for three days during a storm that sent waves twenty to thirty feet high washing over the boat; after it subsided and they emerged for fresh air, photographer George Holton and the cabin boy were briefly washed overboard by a surprise comber.

"Even so," Roger would remember, "it was a month of idyllic island hopping, with frigatebirds hanging under tropic skies and porpoises leaping in jade seas."

Idyllic except for two instances of murder. They visited the small, lovely island of Astove, occupied by a British family and their employees, one of whom had smashed the skull of another employee with a coconut. When the *Iron Duke* reached Aldabra, they learned that the chief cook for the eight scientists stationed there had been fatally poisoned by his assistant. In both cases the explorers were asked to take the murderer back with them to civilization so justice could be dispensed. But there was simply no room on the schooner for additional people.

Lars Lindblad's prized vessel, the *Lindblad Explorer,* was launched in 1969. It took mainly monied, curious Americans to remote places on virtually every continent. (Tourists from elsewhere, like Europe and Japan, became more common later.) Besides Roger and Keith Shackleton, other famous artist-naturalists who regularly lectured were Peter Scott and Bob Bateman; ornithologist Olin Sewall Pettingill was another prominent onboard lecturer.

"The clientele was very wealthy," says Jim Snyder, who spent many years on Lindblad's staff.

It cost a lot of money, especially for those days, to be on board ship. It was a very informal place. So people would not be coming to live in the lap of luxury. They'd be very comfortable, but it certainly wasn't a ship that was designed for . . . tuxedos, . . . grand balls, and that kind of thing. And it wasn't a casino-discotheque. That narrowed the focus on just who would be interested to come on board ship. . . . To a large extent, they were wonderful shipmates . . . . Many people stayed on for several cruises or would come back several times a year just to see different places in the world. . . . It was like a little family that came back. So we'd always know these people. It was just wonderful.

Lars's son, Sven, recalls the importance of these wealthy travelers to conservation:

One of the things it did . . . was to bring people into contact with areas and, as a consequence, with issues that were brought up. You had a . . . rarefied clientele . . . [whose interest] would often result in financial support and involvement in any number of conservation projects in one form or another. . . . A lot of them were developed organically aboard. . . . What happened was you'd get this community of people who had this great shared experience and then decided that they wanted to give something back in one form or another. . . . Roger might auction off a drawing of his, or Bateman [might]. . . . At times, quite a lot of money was raised. . . . Most of the monies that were raised aboard supported research or some project that was going on.

(Roger once described how the Lindblad expeditions raised tens of thousands of dollars for the preservation of Cousin Island in the Seychelles and in support of the Darwin Research Station in the Galápagos; one well-off passenger actually bought an island in the Falklands off Argentina that was home to innumerable black-browed albatrosses and rockhopper penguins.)

Sven describes a typical day on the *Explorer:*

You might . . . navigate a beautiful channel in the morning, arrive somewhere and then land, go ashore and explore a penguin rookery . . . , learn about that, and then spend the afternoon at a scientific base and learn about the activities of the scientists. . . . You'd be ashore on a regular basis. People would come back in the evening and talk about . . . [their day] and maybe you'd have a [lecture] . . . , have dinner, and usually go to bed fairly early because you were exhausted from all this activity.

The *Explorer*'s auditorium was named the Penguin Room, because it sported a Keith Shackleton mural of Adélies. This couldn't have displeased Roger, who was becoming known as "King Penguin" and whose favorite Lindblad destination would remain Antarctica. "He was just really consumed with the photography of penguins," recalls Rob Hernandez, who, through Roger, got a job on the *Explorer* as an expedition leader.

Aboard ship, it was possible to see Roger and Peter Scott play a game of ornithological trash talk. Hernandez remembers,

Roger was very competitive with Peter about everything from "how many birds have you seen" to "what have you seen today" or "what's your life list" or "what are your accomplishments" or "who is more famous." It was very much one-upmanship. It was humorous, but there was a real steely resolve on the side of two extraordinarily competent and accomplished men in their own right who wanted to beat each other. I think I saw that probably between them more than anybody else.

This atmosphere could spill over into lectures. "My own procedure as lecturer-leader on the . . . Explorer has been to hold forth in the evening in the Penguin Room," Roger innocently wrote in the early 1970s. "I recount the day's adventures, give my personal impressions and an interpretation of what we have seen."

Keith Shackleton saw two sides of Roger then—the Educator and the Competitor. Usually it was the Educator in his element, passengers crowding around him trying to get a little time with the Great Man, as he was increasingly becoming known. "He was very definitely the great draw because . . . everybody knew him," Shackleton observes. "The fact that Roger was going to be on board—everybody wanted to go. He must have been a great shot in the arm for Lindblad Travel, . . . for people not just to be able to say they'd been to the Antarctic with Roger, but for what they got out of it, because there he was, a sort of captive to answer all their questions and help them. It was a huge experience for everybody, and certainly was for me. . . . He was the great guru."

What was Roger's lecturing style like? "He had a good rapport. One of my recollections in a general way is that he really wasn't particularly academic," recalls conservationist Nigel Sitwell, who along with Roger served on the second Lindblad-Galápagos trip, among many others.

> He had the knowledge, but he didn't come over in any way as an academic type of person. He just told you the sort of cool information that you might want and [that] might attract people. . . . He was a very engaging lecturer. . . . On these trips, there were . . . passengers who were, some of them, pretty expert, but a lot of them were not at all, and he was able to talk to them—everybody—in a way that they profited from. The academics thought it was good. They probably knew much of the stuff. But they could never tire of listening to him. The ones who didn't know much really enjoyed his easygoing style of putting across the information. . . . He was a really wonderful guy.

Then there was Roger the Competitor. "People just hung on his words," says Shackleton.

> We used to have these things called recaps. . . . It was a very valuable form of lecturing. . . . At the end of every day, when people

were having highballs and things around the bar and sitting in the lounge, we'd have a recap. They would take turns to talk about what we'd all seen, and invite the passengers to share what they'd seen. . . . Roger, being what we used to call "senior naturalist," used to set the ball rolling. He would get it together. He would come round and say, "Look, what do you think you'll talk about?"

I remember one time saying, "Well, I don't know, Roger. I thought I'd talk about genetic diversity at high latitudes because it's very pertinent to Antarctica. . . . The higher the latitude north or south, the fewer species there are, and the bigger the populations are of those species." I was explaining that . . . if you climb up very high mountains, you find exactly the same thing applying. . . . Roger got up to start the recap. He said, "Well, I thought I'd tell you something about genetic diversity."

Lars was standing next to me. He said, "There. Now you've learnt your first lesson, Keith. Don't ever tell Roger what you're going to recap about."

Roger pulled the rug completely out. [When it was his turn Keith said,] "I was going to tell you what Roger just told you about. And I've just learnt something. . . . You never tell Roger what you're going to recap about."

The great thing about Roger was that he didn't mind a joke against himself at all. He laughed with everybody.

But real revenge came in the Antarctic. "I was just clearing up when everybody had been ashore on a penguin colony," says Keith, "and I found all Roger's camera gear standing on a rock.

I thought, "Well, that's extraordinary." I wandered round again, and there was no sign of Roger. So I put it all in the boat and went back to the ship and when I went up to the larboard [port side] and dumped this stuff aboard, I said, "Is Roger aboard?" [Someone] . . . said, "Oh, yes, he's in the bar having a good old chat about birds with people."

So I put my boat away, took all his gear into the cabin, and stuffed it under his bunk to the back. It was a terrible thing to have done to him. . . . Suddenly, at breakfast he looked sort of ashen and said, "Oh, my God!"

We said, "What's the matter, Roger?" knowing exactly what the matter was. He'd suddenly remembered all his camera gear. We'd already told the captain of this. I'm afraid we were like children. We were pulling Roger's leg terribly. [I was sure that Roger was] going to come up to the bridge and say he needs to go back to Lockroy and fetch all his gear. And, sure enough, he did. . . . Roger arrived in a state of near collapse [at the feet of Swedish captain Nilsson], and said, "Gotta go back."

Nilsson said, "This is more than my job's worth! I can't turn this ship around. It's all right—we'll be down next year. . . . The penguins will have walked over your gear a little bit, but . . . nobody's going to see it or touch it or anything."

Roger came back to the breakfast table. Finally we could bear it no longer. I felt I'd been so unkind. I said, "Roger, go into your cabin and look under the bunk." And there it all was.

I felt awful about this since then, but . . . one sort of felt every now and then you had to keep your end up a little bit with Roger.

As much as Roger may have loved conveying what he knew to Lindblad passengers, he got more than that from being on the *Explorer.* "I would say that Roger was at his happiest on board the *Lindblad Explorer*," says Rob Hernandez. "He was surrounded by kindred spirits, he was in extraordinary places around the world, in his element, he was appreciated by those around him, yet he was in a protected world too. Because he was a bit of a recluse. I want to emphasize that he was naturally a gregarious person when you put him in a social setting. But he wasn't of his own volition that way. When he was alone, he was a recluse."

Just spending time with Lars broadened Roger's horizons. Roger was a knowledgeable, erudite man. But before meeting Lars, he didn't have the insatiable fascination with other lands and peoples that blossomed once he'd spent some time with his Swedish friend.

"Lars in some respects was the very opposite of Roger in that Lars's interests were quite extraordinarily wide," Keith Shackleton points out. "He was enormously interested in art and in cultures and in languages and everything to do with the world—customs and habits, anthropology and the lot. . . . I think that Roger loosened up a lot towards the end."

In his book, *Passport to Anywhere,* Lars expressed his credo of "freedom, creativity, and conversation. . . . I believe in complete individual freedom—freedom in literature, the arts, film, theater. I believe in freedom of clothing—in bikinis, topless dresses, or no dresses at all, if you like."

Being conservative in his habits and dress, Roger slowly changed with Lars's influence, shaking off his inhibitions. By 1969 he jokingly called himself a "crypto-hippy." Barbara included his naturalist's definition of the term in their 1969 New Year's letter: "a dropout who assumes the concealing coloration of a normal citizen."

"Certainly, his dress sense [changed]. . . . He wore what, a year or two before, he would have regarded as being extraordinarily outlandish clothes," Shackleton says. "We used to pull his leg about it. . . . Every now and again he would come out in some wild sort of Palm Beach hat or something like that to our great amusement. He'd laugh at himself. He knew he was doing it, that it was all a lot of fun, which I don't think he would have done a few years before."

It helped, Shackleton remembers, that "most of the staff on the ship were a good deal younger than Roger. I think he . . . thought, 'Well, they seem to be having a lot of fun. Why don't I join in?'"

Roger also loved being on the *Explorer* because there were few tedious obligations—except for the ship's log. "All the scientists who came on board, we had the logs on the ship, and they would take turns recording the day by day," remarks Esperanza Rivaud. Then she laughs. "He would make some drawings, and things like that, which he always left unfinished. He was a procrastinator, like Lars was too. He saved it for later on, leaving the empty space for another moment. I remember we had to press him to sit down and do it."

Although Roger soaked up the adulation he got on board ship, he never let it affect him. Despite his world fame, he didn't see himself as better than or apart from other staff on the ship. He enjoyed the camaraderie. Jim Snyder, who served as naturalist-lecturer, expedition leader, and Zodiac inflatable boat driver, values a memory he has of Roger demonstrating this point.

During the 1978–79 season Roger disembarked the *Explorer* after an Antarctic trip and was waiting for a flight home in Ushuaia's small airport when Snyder arrived in Ushuaia to board ship for another Antarctic voyage. This was before they had met. "What struck me was that he waved to me!" says Snyder. "I was coming, he was going, in this little hole-in-the-wall, one-room lobby at the airport in Ushuaia, which is basically just a strip of asphalt.

"So I walked up to him. I said, 'Roger, I always wanted to meet you! Sorry I missed you on this cruise.'

"He said, 'Jim Snyder, right?'"

Roger apparently knew him from pictures of the staff that decorated the ship's walls. Snyder says,

My impression was, one, how friendly he was to me, and two, how inspiring the guy was. Because here we have the great big picture

window in this hole-in-the-wall waiting area at the airport, and there's nothing but the wilderness of Tierra del Fuego outside that window. . . . And he had about ten people with binoculars looking out through the glass. They couldn't stop birding, even as they were about to board a plane. It was just wonderful. . . . They obviously were interested, but just by virtue of the fact that he had such a passion for it. . . . They were just inspired! . . . [They figured] maybe they'll catch a glimpse of something else that's rare that Roger knows all about. . . . I'd always heard great things about Roger. We had many well-known figures come on as staff, specializing in one given area—whether it was Alaska or Polynesia or someplace else—and, oftentimes, these people were not only very full of themselves, but they had an air about them that made them very difficult to deal with. Clearly Roger was not that way. He was one of us.

As much as Roger loved exploring, he would forsake it to be with his best friend. James Fisher went on one Lindblad excursion in 1969 to the Galápagos. His daughter, Clem, was there too and says: "I remember when I was with both of them in the Galápagos and they just really enjoyed being together. They would talk to other people, but somehow they would always rather talk to each other. By that time, my father was very lame. He later had his hips replaced. . . . He couldn't do a lot of things. Roger was obviously rushing about photographing everything. But . . . they would always meet up again . . . to compare notes on what Roger, in particular, had seen, and all that."

Although the Lindblad staffers tried to make James as mobile as possible, there was one horseback ride in the mountains he couldn't make. "There was no other way of getting him up there," Clem says. "Roger decided not to do that either so he could stay with my father and look more at the seabirds, which was OK, because they could watch those from the ship or go off in the Zodiac."

Part Five:

INSPIRING
FLIGHTS

Chapter Thirteen

Worldwide Progeny

Local Hatchlings
Paul Spitzer

Years before Paul Spitzer worked with the ospreys, before he lived in Old Lyme, he was a young boy after the model of Roger Tory Peterson. Unlike young Roger, who had little to work with to identify local birds, Paul, living on Long Island, had his Peterson.

In the late 1950s eleven-year-old Paul moved with his family to Old Lyme, and immediately learned who lived nearby: "I got a big buildup from people that Roger Peterson lived up the road." It was like a fairy tale, especially when he participated in a Christmas Bird Count, accompanying Roger to his favorite Connecticut River haunts.

"When he found a pair of receptive eyes and ears and mind, he liked nothing better," says Paul, now an ecologist specializing in bird studies. "Some of it, you might say, is parlor tricks, like calling in an owl with a screech owl call, but it's not parlor tricks too because there's a whole world out there, and as you go through life, these things become familiars for you and can root you very deeply in love of life. . . . Roger, probably more than anyone else, showed me that."

On the count they found owls, rough-legged hawks, even a few bald eagles despite the toll DDT had taken. Roger joyfully praised Paul when he found a bird no one else did: "I spotted a yellow-bellied sapsucker, a good winter bird in Connecticut. Roger made a big fuss over it. You can imagine how that made me feel." At dusk they stood in a cattail marsh, listening to the *wak-wak-wak-wak-wak* chorus of Virginia rails. "Roger was cool as a cucumber. . . . He wasn't full of himself. . . . It was just like it is in the out of doors when you're with good friends. . . . He was very good company in the field."

As he grew older, Paul made use of Petersonia. "Barbara made it all possible because she opened the house to young naturalists," he recalls. "Within limits, she let me read correspondence that was coming in. In those days . . . there would be an incoming file. There would be a stack of correspondence. That, for me, was pure gold." Barbara also let him peruse the amazing Peterson library. Because of Roger's involvement with Audubon and other organizations, and his editorship of the Peterson series, "every book on the environment got sent to the Peterson household. . . . They were all there on the shelves. European books too."

As a teen Paul collected night insects and moths. Late at night he would sneak over to Roger's studio and show off what he'd found. "Then he was in his element," Paul says. "You could actually watch him paint. Within limits. You never imposed. And you felt your way along. . . . Some of my best visits with Roger were between 10:00 p.m. and 1:00 a.m. . . . I had a little collection of what I'd found, and he often would tell me things about those moths. He'd give me a little exposition on this or that species. Because he loved moths too."

Roger also provided Paul with concrete assistance. Just mentioning the youth's name in the 1969 *National Geographic* article about ospreys opened up doors; also, Roger wrote a letter of recommendation for Paul to Cornell for his doctoral studies. But the intellectual and spiritual inspiration was invaluable. "Roger was an object of awe, partly because of the way he lived," observes Paul. "He had the world pretty much on his own terms. That was very seductive stuff! . . . You knew that simply by being around him you were going to absorb information. And the people who came through the household—James Fisher, Peter Scott—if you had a chance to wangle an invitation to be around when naturalists visited, by all means, you did that."

Perhaps most significant for young Spitzer was how Roger validated his desires: "Roger said it was OK to look at those leaves and smell that breeze. He legitimized a lot of things that a young person wants to do."

Thomas Lovejoy

Tom Lovejoy, who spent a season or two studying the ospreys' decline on Great Island, had started birding in high school and used the Peterson eastern bird guide. "Roger was a godlike figure to me," says Lovejoy. He met Roger in 1961 as a Yale sophomore through a mutual friend, nature illustrator Rudolf Freund, who spent time at the Peabody Museum, as did Lovejoy. When Freund and his wife were invited to dinner at the Petersons', they brought Tom along.

"Even when I was a sophomore, Roger didn't talk down," Tom says. "If you were interested in birds, that's all Roger cared about. You were in." He considers Roger a mentor: "Yes, indeed. He was always very helpful, and inspiring! Just because he was who he was."

When considering career options after earning his PhD, Lovejoy received an offer in 1973 from Francis Kellogg to work for the World Wildlife Fund. Roger played a "significant role" in Lovejoy's saying yes. "He said to me . . . , 'You should take it, because you will worry about the kagu,' which is a very unusual bird that lives only on New Caledonia. He knew I worried about things like that."

Lovejoy eventually became executive vice president of the fund's U.S. branch. He and Roger became colleagues; he could query Roger on any issue that might be of interest at a board meeting. "Dear Roger," Tom once wrote. "Hope this gets to you in time. I would be most grateful if you would be prepared to comment in particular on (1) Xerces Society (2) Macaw survey (3) Conservation of plants."

Why pick Roger's brain? "That would have been the logical thing to do," says Lovejoy, today president of the Heinz Center for Science, Economics and the Environment in Washington, DC. "He would know what the answers were! . . . He knew so much."

William Burt

Author-photographer Bill Burt first met Roger in the 1960s at 15. Burt's grandfather lived in Old Lyme and knew Barbara, who got him a choice few moments, tattered Peterson guide in hand, with her husband in the studio. "Peterson said he liked to see them that way because that meant they had been used," says Burt.

The following year Burt visited Roger again; this time, the youth broached the subject of an annotated list of area birds he was compiling. Would Dr. Peterson contribute his own records? "His tone was one of pure collegiality," Burt later wrote, "as if he were speaking not to a young boy but an equal." Reflecting on this now, Burt comments, "I'm sure he saw in me someone who was very sincere, and the great thing was that we shared that. . . . I'm sure he got beseeched by a great number of people." A year after that encounter, they compared notes—"Which birds were where. Why this bird or that used to be here and isn't anymore."

Thus began a long friendship. Burt's eventual immersion in bird photography meant comparing images: "I'd show him photographs that I was able to get after long struggles. . . . I also looked at a number of his slides. He'd come back from Africa, say, and he'd have boxes of slides on his viewer. We'd go through them."

Burt was touched and encouraged by Roger's praise at a showing of the younger man's photographs some years later. "That was a heart melter," declares Bill. "As I recall, he made sure he was back from a trip expressly to be able to attend and speak at it, which meant a whole heck of a lot to me, I will tell you. . . . He lent an aura of celebration to the thing. He was a celebrity giving it his blessing."

Afterward, Roger took Bill Burt aside and said, "We need to make you more ambitious."

Noble Proctor

Connecticut native Noble Proctor has been watching birds since age eight; two years later his parents bought him a Peterson. Proctor first met the author in 1960 at the Petersons' residence where local birders had gathered after the Christmas Bird Count. But their earliest meaningful meeting occurred a couple of years later at an Audubon convention. Then twenty, Proctor was interested in all aspects of natural history, not just birds. "Natural history, of course, was one of the key things about Roger," says professor-naturalist Proctor. "He didn't just have an interest in birds, he had an interest in everything. Butterflies. Insects. Plants."

It was refreshing for Proctor to have broad discussions with Roger about the natural world. "Back in . . . earlier days," Proctor notes, "I didn't know that many people who had the same broad-scale interest, so it was great being able to visit with Roger."

Between his bachelor's degree and postgraduate studies, Proctor led nature tours, which allowed him the flexibility to frequently visit Roger. Proctor succeeded in prying him out of the studio to bird. "He was very relaxed," Proctor remembers. "He enjoyed everything immensely." A bird would sing, a butterfly alight, an interesting flower come into view. "The immediacy of the moment was the wonderful aspect of that," he explains. "To enjoy what you were looking at in that given space. And totally enjoy it, rather than being in anticipation of what's coming next."

Roger made these walks an educational experience. Proctor remarks: "Roger acted as a teacher in almost everything he did. He was acting as a teacher when he was writing his field guides; when he was doing his painting,; when he was talking about things, he always pointed out things that were important for that species."

Robert Hernandez

Rob Hernandez's entry into Roger Tory Peterson's world happened the way it had for Paul Spitzer. "I grew up from age eleven right across the Connecticut River from Roger," says Rob. "I became a nature enthusiast and birdwatcher. The field guide was the book that I used, as everyone around me did. Then I became aware that the Great Man lived just a few miles away from me. That intrigued me, in the sense that, 'Oh, my gosh, maybe someday I'll be able to meet him.'"

The pinch-me moment came at a Christmas Bird Count in the mid-1960s when Rob was fourteen. "[Everyone] would get together and sit in somebody's living room and regale each other with stories of what they saw, and the numbers would be read out," he remembers. "They were wonderful gatherings. That's my first recollection of going to Roger's house and meeting him and meeting Barbara and being surrounded by, probably, between twenty and thirty-five similar birdwatching enthusiasts, most of them adults, who were just as awestruck as I was to be there."

Hernandez met Paul Spitzer at one of these gatherings, which led to his assisting Spitzer on the osprey work and, in turn, a friendship with the Petersons. Soon Rob became a "gofer assistant to Roger in his studio, and to Barbara, to a lesser extent."

The work was important but not glamorous. Among Rob's typical tasks were organizing Roger's slides by bird species, location, and image quality; filing visual and substantive clippings from magazines and newspapers that Roger used for reference; and generally keeping things orderly.

Most important was the example Roger set: "He quietly knew his stuff, he recognized the values that were important in wildlife, he had an enormous intellect, he had a great work ethic, and all of those things are impactful on one when you're young."

Rob extracted concrete lessons from observing Roger's habits. "He was an enormously disciplined worker," Hernandez notes admiringly.

He always had a great big white board, like a foam board, . . . four or five feet wide and two feet high, that he would prop on an easel or prop up on the floor against the wall and on it was a spreadsheet . . . he'd drawn lines [on], . . . like a calendar, of two or three months ahead, at least, where he'd fill in his deadlines and what he wanted to do and what he was going to do. Essentially like a diary schedule. You and I would keep an appointment book. He did it on these big boards. . . . "Eat lunch twelve to one" and then "two to four, write Audubon *story," and then "three to six draw* bah-bah-bah-bah," *whatever. He did that for months on end on the same board, so he knew instantly what he was supposed to be doing. I was pretty impressed with that as a young teenager first, and then a young man in his twenties who was, like most young men, mostly undisciplined. I remember being very, very awed by that type of discipline.*

What came next was the stuff that dreams are made of. Hernandez had still only completed a couple of years of college when one morning, while he was asleep on a cot in Roger's studio, "Roger came running up . . . and said that Lars Lindblad . . . is looking for a young naturalist-lecturer to be on board the ship in the Amazon in twenty-four hours! 'Are you interested?'

"I said, 'Are you kidding me? Of *course,* I'm interested!'

"And so twenty-four hours later, I was on the deck of the *Lindblad Explorer* as she slid out of New York Harbor and headed for the Amazon!"

Rob, who likens working on the *Explorer* to being "a Grateful Dead groupie who's invited to be on the band's tour bus," served on the ship for two years before finishing college, although he did return as a staffer on future expeditions. He went to some of the world's most exciting places. Besides the Amazon Rob visited the Arctic, New Guinea, Indonesia, and the Antarctic. Of course, Roger was on several of the latter voyages.

"I will always be extremely beholden to Roger," Rob says. "He must have seen something in me. . . . He was very encouraging with me. He always helped me. . . . He didn't know where his student was going, but he realized that his student could be of value to the things he felt were most dear. . . . I was thankful for that encouragement."

The Lindblad job opened doors for Rob. "It gave me broad, international experience. . . . I went into filmmaking, I went into writing, I went into photography, photojournalism, which eventually led to *National Geographic*." He is now senior vice president of international publishing for the National Geographic Society.

"There's no doubt," Rob reflects, "that without Roger's encouragement, Roger's friendship, Roger as a role model, I wouldn't be who I am."

Fleur Ng'weno

Fleur Ng'weno began life as Fleur Grandjouan, a daughter of French diplomats. Growing up in New York, she was obsessed with natural history. Before entering Connecticut College in 1955, at the end of her first summer at the Audubon Camp in Maine, she met the Petersons. They always stopped there en route home from Camp Chewonki where they'd collected Tory and Lee. Says Fleur: "At the Audubon Camp, the Peterson field guide was *the* field guide. Roger Tory Peterson was viewed with awe and admiration. The young student assistants would spend hours, day after day, leafing through the field guide and discussing the finer points. The Petersons' arrival at the camp was a red-letter day for all the birdwatchers."

"Everyone was so excited," she adds. "That was just their wildest dream fulfilled to get to meet Roger, have him autograph their book, and speak to him in person."

Roger was surrounded by admirers, so Fleur approached Barbara and struck up a conversation. This led to Barbara inviting Fleur to stay with the Petersons during school breaks in the fall.

"This was so wonderful," Fleur says, not just because she could spend time at the home of a great naturalist, but because she didn't feel comfortable at Connecticut College with its homogeneous student body. "It was getting away from all those girls who looked like peas in a pod"—she laughs—"and being with a family and being with people I could talk to about nature. . . . It was just so nice, being in a family atmosphere. We would go out and play with the kids." They birded the nearby marshes in the aftermath of the Connecticut floods, which meant Roger could easily show Fleur her first least bittern, usually reclusive but washed out of its normal abode by the rising waters.

Although Fleur was much closer to Barbara than to Roger, he played a key role in her collegiate success. "I was having a terrible time with math and chemistry," she recalls. "My experiments kept going wrong, and the chemistry was really getting me down."

She continues: "One day, when I was bemoaning how difficult chemistry was, how I would rather study nature than be in class, Roger said, 'Birds and flowers have chemistry too.'"

This simple statement is what kept her in school. "Because he said it," notes Fleur, "it had more impact than if a teacher had said it, or a friend. Because he was not only a friend, but he was also sort of a mentor, a role model and an important person. . . . In the end, I did OK in chemistry. Once I changed my attitude."

Roger has been an inspiration to her since. While still a young woman, "[If I] felt low and scared by the future, I could look at the beautiful illustrations of beautiful birds, calm down and find new hope. Later, as a writer and educator, I hoped that I could reach people as he did." Living in Kenya since the 1960s, she married a native Kenyan, Hilary Ng'weno. For many years they published a children's magazine featuring environmental and news content. She has also written several children's books about nature and ecology.

Today, Fleur Ng'weno is a mentor to East African naturalists. She is following in Roger's footsteps.

Lee Allen Peterson

Roger's son Lee seemed poised to follow in his father's footsteps, but in the end went his own way.

Upon graduating from Johns Hopkins University, Lee wasn't sure what to do with himself. While his father's fans went to Roger for advice or inspiration, Lee went to Belton Copp. "I wanted someone outside my normal sphere," says Lee. "I just knew Belton in a very casual sort of way." He admired Belton for being a thoughtful person and liked Belton and Genie's practice of taking a morning walk to plan their day.

Lee talked to Belton for two or three hours about life in general. Copp reassured him, "It's OK not to be focused right now," and invited him to visit with the Copps that summer on their ranch in Alberta, Canada.

This allowed Lee time to think, and work on a serious hobby— the study of edible wild plants. The project was an outgrowth of his time at Camp Chewonki. His father's wildflower guide had just come out. Then someone handed him Euell Gibbons's *Stalking the Wild Asparagus.* He used both books to teach campers about plant identification, as well as the fundamentals of living in the wild. Soon he pondered developing a possible guide to edible wild plants. Even before joining the Copps in Alberta, he had researched the subject as it pertained to Connecticut. Genie recalls that in Alberta: "Lee would pick this stuff and he would give it to me and my daughter, Lucy, who was interested in it and we would chew away on it. It just tasted terrible! We had to spit it out over the cliff. It was wild licorice or something like that. It was abominable. We wouldn't be his guinea pigs anymore." (Allyn Copp has a more charitable memory of mountain climbing with Lee and enjoying the taste of sorrel.)

Back home, Lee casually mentioned to Dad his interest in self-publishing a book on edible wild plants of Connecticut. Serendipitously, Houghton Mifflin had just asked Roger about adding an edible wild plants guide to the Peterson series. Roger put his publisher and his son together, resulting in the only Peterson authored by a different Peterson.

"Even though I hadn't really been doing anything like that, I felt that I could do—he made it so easy. I grew up with the format, so I was very comfortable with the whole concept of trying to paint word pictures and tailoring the length of things to fit within the format." Lee did most of the illustrations, with some pulled from his father's wildflower guide when necessary.

What did Roger think of the book? "I think he was proud of it," Lee remarks. "I think he was happy with the results." He adds: "I think he felt I took too long to do it." Published in 1977, the book, limited to edible plants of the east, took Lee six years to complete. Even if he was comfortable with the format of the Peterson series, "I had no idea how to do an extended project like this. Up to this point, I'd done term papers. . . . Books are a different thing altogether."

For a time, Lee thought authoring field guides was his destiny. He was ready to do a companion western volume. Then a southeastern flower guide. "And take over the editorship of the field guide series. . . . I had this whole plan!" Lee says. "Then at some point I realized that, no, I didn't really want to follow in my father's footsteps in that way. A lot of the reason was because I couldn't. There's always a first. The people who follow are always seen as followers. I think that, subconsciously, that entered into the decision. . . . That was a dream derived from what my father did, kind of like inheriting the kingdom." Once Lee proved to himself he could do it once, there wasn't much need to do it again. He noticed also that his father always seemed hamstrung by the field guides, always having to update them, always being asked to do a new one in the series that perhaps no one else could do.

"I just let it go," Lee continues. He chose not to go through the doors that opened for him. For over two decades now, Lee has used the creativity he inherited from his father to handcraft jewelry from various metals alongside his wife, Courtney, for their business, Courtney Design. They live peacefully on a two-hundred-year-old farm in the Philadelphia area, also home to sheep, llamas, turkeys, and ducks. Occasionally, local groups ask Lee to lead nature walks or give presentations.

Hatchlings from Far and Wide
Edward O. Wilson

E. O. Wilson is probably the most celebrated, if unexpected, of Roger Tory Peterson's progeny.

"As a sixteen-year-old in Decatur, Alabama, having . . . reaffirmed what I'd already decided when I was only nine or ten years old, to become a professional outdoor field biologist," says Wilson, "I bought a copy of the original Roger Tory Peterson *Field Guide to the Birds* with my earnings as a paperboy. And went out with binoculars to watch birds. And that's when the story ended. Because I see out of only one eye. . . . I wanted to be an entomologist, anyway. I was just broadening my scope by including birds as all real Americans do"—Wilson chuckles—"They have some contact with birdwatching if they have any interest in nature."

Roger's field guides inspired Wilson and many others to become scientists even if ornithology was not their interest. "Although I was not drawn into birdwatching, . . . nonetheless the entire idea of field guides encouraged studying nature in the United States," Wilson notes. "The easy portal that they provided in making that kind of study and bringing it even to a professional level was the inspiration that I'm certain affected not only me, but most of my generation. . . . When I was at the University of Alabama, we all had field guides. . . . What this did was make a clear and strong invitation to young people like myself to come on in to natural history."

The Peterson system emphasizing field marks directly inspired an ambitious monograph Wilson wrote and illustrated in 2003 on the ant genus *Pheidole,* called *Pheidole in the New World: A Dominant, Hyper-Diverse Ant Genus,* which covers 624 species, or 19 percent of all known ant species in the western hemisphere.

This book has over five thousand drawings by me, which are done in not quite the Peterson style, but nonetheless with a lot of the

qualities of Peterson's style. I drew ten or so views of each ant spe-
cies, . . . and then I drew in some features of the sculpturing of the
exoskeleton, the tightness of the ant and the hairs and the shapes of
all the various parts, and then I used the Peterson-style field marks,
the lines coming down, pointing to each trait. . . . Obviously, this
is for professionals, because your average ant watcher, if there are
any such people, is not going to master 624 ant species. But it's
proven very successful. Many entomologists who have used this
have expressed appreciation for making it so accessible. . . . I was
able to communicate . . . [this knowledge] in part because of the
style and methods that I had picked up from Roger Tory Peterson.

Wilson met Peterson only once, in 1995. "The only contact . . .
I had with Roger Tory Peterson—amazing—was when I got an honorary degree at the University of Connecticut," Wilson recalls. "It
never occurred to me to get in touch with the Great Man. You're
like that with people you looked way up to when you were younger.
But he showed up just to meet me! That really made it very special
for me. We had a wonderful conversation."

There was one topic that stands out for Wilson who says he
wishes he'd recorded their conversation. "I asked him, 'What is
your considered judgment concerning the status of the ivory-
billed woodpecker?'

"He used one word: 'Gone.' I wish he'd lived long enough to
hear about the possible rediscovery in Arkansas."

E. O. Wilson gave the first Roger Tory Peterson Memorial
Lecture at Harvard University in 1997. Since then the lecture has
become an institution, attracting, among others, such conservationist stars as Bruce Babbitt, Paul Ehrlich, and Jane Goodall. In
recent years, speakers have received a medal in Roger's name.

David Allen Sibley

David Sibley, whose field guides to birds of North America are
today the most popular American field guides, got an early push

from Roger Tory Peterson. It was the early 1970s. Sibley was a twelve-year-old aspiring bird artist. After an Old Lyme Christmas Bird Count, Noble Proctor arranged for Sibley to meet Roger in the studio.

Sibley was "encouraged a lot by meeting Roger and seeing his house there in Connecticut and knowing that he was there, and knowing that you could actually make a living doing bird guides. I had a father who was an ornithologist who didn't think that was crazy. But I actually had an example right there. Roger was the example for all of the professional birdwatchers today."

They met again in May 1984 at the World Series of Birding in Cape May, where he and Roger were on a team with New Jersey birding heavyweights Pete Dunne, Pete Bacinski, and Bill Boyle. "I remember when we did the World Series," says Sibley, "I was working on drawings of hawks that eventually were published in the book *Hawks in Flight*. . . . [Roger] was very supportive of what I was trying to do. . . . [He said] that he was impressed with how well I was capturing the shapes of the birds, which obviously meant a lot to me at that time. I was twenty-two years old or so. To have him saying that he was really impressed with those drawings, it was just so encouraging."

When Sibley started planning his own field guide, he found the Peterson influence impossible to shake.

Once I started working on the field guide more seriously, really trying to map it out, kind of figuring out what worked and what didn't work and how I wanted to do the illustrations and how I wanted to show each species. . . . I ended up in the end, I think, going back to something very similar to Roger's first field guide, with the birds all in very similar poses, all facing the same direction, all the images lined up on the page, so that the differences really stand out, the illustrations themselves kind of simplified and more patternistic, . . . less artistic and more diagrammatic, so that the differences that I want people to notice stand out more. . . . I started out thinking that I wanted to do a field guide that I wanted to be artistic, birds in lots of different poses, and lots of detail in all the paintings, and I ended up, after six years of working on it, . . . going back to some of the basic principles that Roger had started with in the 1930s. He really had it right from the very beginning.

Peter Alden

The Roger Tory Peterson growing up in Jamestown with little except his dreams for fuel couldn't have imagined he would become an idol to succeeding generations. Says Peter Alden: "As a kid, [if you're asked] who do you want to grow up to be? Do you want to be Ted Williams? Do you want to be Mickey Mantle? Do you want to be a fireman? Do you want to be president of the United States? Or do you want to be Roger Tory Peterson? Well, to me, it was obviously a no-brainer. I wanted to be Roger Tory Peterson."

For the young Alden in Massachusetts, *Wild America, Birds Over America,* the yearly National Wildlife Federation stamp program, and Roger's column in *Audubon* magazine were windows into a world he couldn't wait to explore.

Alden had met Roger at an Audubon Screen Tour event. He noticed what all Peterson admirers quickly learned, that the naturalist liked seeing them carrying a beat-up copy of his book: "If he came to some kid or adult with a totally tattered, dirty Peterson, worn edges, covered with mud, and twelve dead mosquitoes squished into the pages, that guy got ten or twenty minutes."

But in 1960 the teenage Alden made an indelible impression on Roger by carrying with him, on a train going south from Boston, a mud-free copy of the just published *A Field Guide to the Birds of Texas,* the only Peterson devoted to the birds of one state. Roger was returning home from an editorial meeting; Alden, a high school sophomore, was meeting birders in Providence. He had already annotated the Texas guide on which birds he expected to see, and where, on a planned summer trip to the southwest. Alden approached Roger, book in hand, and introduced himself.

Roger said, "Oh, that's my *Birds of Texas!*"

Replied Peter: "Yes! I'm going down to Texas and Arizona over the summer to look at birds! All these places you were telling us to go!"

Would Peter like to be quizzed on the birds?

"So I got the Great Master, and I was a pimple-faced, buck-toothed kid. . . . He went through . . . [the book] for the forty-four miles to Providence on the train. . . . He covered up all the facing page text . . . and tried me out on a hundred different birds. Page after page. *What's this—what's this—what's this?* I only messed up on two birds—the Cassin's and the Botteri's sparrows. Otherwise, I got like a ninety-nine on it. He remembered me ever since."

Birds Over America was such a pivotal book for Alden he took a recommendation in it to heart. "One passage caught my eye—he said, 'If I had to choose one place to live in the United States with the greatest variety of breeding birds and the greatest variety of habitats and elevations and the most number of interesting-to-see things, I would choose to live in Tucson, Arizona.'"* Thus, Alden, who believed he'd seen enough of New England birds, decided on the University of Arizona at Tucson for his higher education. Being in Tucson meant proximity to Mexico; he became a leader of bird tours to Mexico. His *Finding the Birds in Western Mexico* was published by the University of Arizona Press in 1969.

As he and Roger had kept in touch, Peter was invited in the early 1970s to Old Lyme in connection with Mexican birds. Roger was painting plates for his twenty-years-in-the-making *A Field Guide to Mexican Birds,* cowritten with Edward L. Chalif and finally published in 1973. "He wanted to show me all his paintings, and critique his paintings and see if there were things he should add

---

* Roger wrote: "If I were to pick a place in the Southwest to live, a place that is paint-able, where every landscape composes and has color, where I could always have my fill of birds and of plants, mammals, reptiles, insects and all the things that make an artist-naturalist happy I should choose Tucson. From there I could have most anything within a day's reach—the low desert and the high mountains, too."

or subtract or whatever," says Alden. "He was the first one to paint most of the birds of Mexico."

Alden has led tours all over the world and authored over a dozen books on birds and other wildlife, including coloring books about birds and mammals in a Houghton Mifflin Peterson series for children. But birding with Roger was never less than a thrilling experience for him:

> *If he looks left, you look left. If he looks right, you look right. If he lifts his binoculars up slowly, you lift your binoculars up slowly. If he puts his binoculars up fast to the top of a dead tree, you put yours up real fast. . . . You learn skills. Then he'd cup his ears and point out the various calls. . . . But whenever you went with him on a nature walk, and I did nature walks with him in Tucson, Texas, Missouri, and it was like people following Jesus. Because they were already birders, or at least botanists, or [into] butterflies or something like that, but he had this very enormous presence.*

Pete Dunne

When Pete Dunne was ten, he waited eagerly by the mailbox for delivery of the usual manila envelope from the National Audubon Society. In it would be Junior Audubon educational leaflets. The grown-up Dunne wrote in his book, *Feather Quest:* "I read those leaflets, and reread them, and reread them again, until there was no reason to read them anymore—because I'd memorized them. The leaflets were written by a man named Roger T. Peterson."

Then a favorite uncle died and left him Peterson's *A Field Guide to the Birds.* The deal was sealed. Dunne said: "For as long as I have been a birder . . . there has been a man named Peterson whose guidance has figured every step of the way."

Pete settled on the road to friendship with one of America's most accessible celebrity mentors when, as the young director of the Cape May Bird Observatory, he penned a chatty letter to Roger. "I probably initiated our relationship by sending a T-shirt and *Peregrine Observer* newsletter one day," says Pete. "This was probably . . . the early '80s. I just said, 'Look. You don't know me, but you've been an inspiration to me my whole life. I want to do something to thank you. I'm making you a life member of the bird observatory. And, by the way, here's our T-shirt.' He wrote this wonderful, cordial letter back."

It wasn't that farfetched then for Pete to call Roger up and invite him to compete in Cape May's first World Series of Birding in May 1984. "I guess I must have made a pretty good case, because . . . [Roger exclaimed] 'Whose team can I be on? Can I be on yours? We should start at the Great Swamp at midnight—don't you think? Then go to the hills above Boonton.' He was already way ahead of me. He was already falling back on Big Days that he'd done in New Jersey. He was already deep in plotting a route."

While Dunne doesn't remember feeling nervous about birding on the same team (the Guerrilla Birding Team) with Roger, it was an exciting way to meet the elder naturalist. "Roger's addition was a wonderful asset," Dunne reflects. "First of all, I got to see the human side of a person whom I'd revered almost as a god. And I recognized that I liked the human Roger Tory Peterson as well. . . . His participating brought standing and stature to the event. And . . . he was, of course, a very skilled, a very talented, birder."

Roger was available, not standoffish, to birders. "Roger was very conscious of the community," says Dunne. "It was a little bit like—I remember during the war protests in the '60s, Dr. Spock was out there with the kids protesting. They were his kids! We were Roger's kids. He sired us."

George H. Harrison

In 1976 Roger reminisced:

> It must have been at least 35 years ago that Hal Harrison . . .
> wrote me that he was leaving his newspaper job in Tarentum,

Pennsylvania, to free-lance as a naturalist. My own career, he said, had inspired him to make the move. He rationalized that if a man could free himself to do the things he loved most, why subject himself to the monotony of a 9-to-5 job? Why submit to a subtle form of slavery? Since making that decision, Hal Harrison has distinguished himself as a wildlife photographer, writer and lecturer. He is perhaps best known to the ornithological fraternity for his recently published [Peterson] Field Guide to Birds' Nests, *the finest treatise on North American birds' nests ever published.*

In 1949 Hal Harrison brought his twelve-year-old son, George, and younger daughter, Gretchen, to a gathering of the Brooks Bird Club in West Virginia. "Everybody at the camp knew [Roger] was going to be there that day, so when he arrived, of course, all the adults were gathered around him most of the time," George remembers. "As a child, and also being shy, I didn't see that I was going to have any opportunity to talk to him." The boy continued trying to photograph an eastern phoebe with what he calls his "primitive" Speed-Graphic (4 x 5) press camera.

George didn't know that seeing a child engrossed in a nature activity would pique Roger's interest: "Roger happened to notice what I was doing over there, so he came over and struck up a conversation." How did the boy react? "I was a bit frightened by it, being timid and so forth, at that age, but I was pleased," says George. "He was easy to talk to. He asked some questions, and I was able to answer them. So we got into the photography aspect of it." George estimates they spent about fifteen to twenty minutes talking during Roger's visit with the Brooks Bird Club, quite a chunk of time.

The boy grew up to be an accomplished photographer and nature journalist, following in the footsteps of his father, whose own path had been inspired by Peterson. When George became managing editor at *National Wildlife* magazine, he and Roger visited regularly to brainstorm articles or confer, as Roger was a magazine contributor. "I sat with him, and we talked, explored ideas," Harrison says. "I looked at his pictures and then I'd have to ride him for weeks or months to write the text. He was always overbooked."

One such session transformed into George Harrison's first book, *Roger Tory Peterson's Dozen Birding Hotspots*. "I went to Old Lyme to do a story for *National Wildlife* magazine on birding hot spots and it evolved in his living room," says Harrison. "I asked him if he could name twelve places in North America that he would consider birding hot spots, and when they were hot. . . . It didn't become a magazine story for *National Wildlife* but it did become my first book for Simon & Schuster.

"I think he was very pleased about the book," says George, who prefaced each chapter with a quote from Roger. "He wrote the introduction."

The book recounted the travels of George and his wife, Kit, who spent a good part of 1974 visiting all twelve hot spots when they were "hot," driving thirty-eight thousand miles and flying a bit too. At one site, Horicon National Wildlife Refuge in Wisconsin, George and Kit joined Joe and Peggy Hickey who were hosting old friends Roger and Barbara Peterson for a few days.

"I wanted to have Roger at one of those [hot spot] places while I was there," says Harrison.

As a good friend of Roger's, but not being responsible for his comings and goings, George gained a dispassionate insight into the challenges of being his "minder." Harrison says Roger was the "kind of person who, if he was walking down the street, and a stranger walked up to him and said, 'Are you Roger Tory Peterson?' he'd say yes, and he would stand there and talk to the person as long as they wanted to talk to him. In that way, he was a very nice person. It drove people who were trying to get him to do things crazy. . . . His wife would be driven batty by it."

Then again, if Roger had not been generous in his fame, he might not have broken from the gawking adult members of the

Brooks Bird Club to talk with a timid boy named George about photographing an eastern phoebe.

Victor Emanuel

Like so many growing up in the decades following publication of Roger's first field guide, Victor Emanuel of Texas used a Peterson. His father gave him *Birds Over America* when he was ten; he grew to love *Wild America* also. "I think he had a very nice writing style," says Emanuel. "A very clear style." Although Emanuel shook his idol's hand at the 1962 National Audubon Society convention in Corpus Christi, it wasn't until April 1978 that they became friends.

Emanuel was president of the Texas Ornithological Society and hoped to entice Roger down to McAllen, Texas, to receive an honorary membership, never before bestowed on a non-Texan. If Roger came, Emanuel hoped he would also agree to colead a two-week trip with Emanuel's tour company, VENT, down the Texas coast in time for spring migration and flowers.

"I wrote him about ten months before the meeting and told him about the honor, and [asked] would he come to the meeting, and would he lead this trip," says Emanuel. "I didn't have a reply . . . . I was leaving in November to go to the fall meeting to make the final plans for the spring meeting, thinking he wasn't going to accept. We had to make some other plans."

Then something happened worthy of a *Twilight Zone* episode. "I'd left my house for the airport, and as I was driving away, I saw the postman walking toward my house. For the only time in my life, I stopped and said, 'Do you have any mail for me?' Not even thinking about Roger. . . . I'd given up hope. He had a letter for me from Roger . . . accepting both offers. It was very strange."

If the Texas Ornithological Society meeting was a success, the VENT trip was even better and boosted Emanuel's young company. "Roger had a very good time," Victor remembers. "And it was one of those wonderful springs. We had the right kind of rain. We had great wildflower shows and great fallouts of warblers that were migrating across the gulf. The weather and the birds and everything cooperated beautifully. It was one of the best trips I've ever had. . . . People on the trip, of course, felt it was very special, being with him."

Since the Texas trip had gone so well, Emanuel figured a trip to Mexico led by Roger should do at least as well. "We promoted it in our very small, little newsletter we had then. People signed up right away and that filled it up and that helped give us a boost." He chose a top hotel for his customers and reserved the necessary rooms, paying in advance. One month before the trip, he received a call from the hotel informing him that the resort had overbooked and, in fact, he had no rooms. Emanuel was petrified of telling Roger the bad news.

> *I had a little bit of anxiety about doing that, that he would get irritated or upset. . . . I said he had to know what was going on. He, I think, sensed [my anxiety] . . . and right away, he said, "Don't worry about it. If we don't get any rooms, we'll just go owling all night." Which, of course, was not very practical, but it was a way to relieve my anxiety. Then he said, which amazed me even more, because it was something that was more likely to be the case, "Well, Victor, if you don't get enough rooms, and Virginia and I have to share a room with another couple, we'll be happy to." In India or Japan, that wouldn't be a big deal, but in America— Americans are like, "We want our own space.". . . . That was just the kind of kindness and sensitivity he had.*

Fortunately, Emanuel found another suitable hotel with enough rooms. The revelation, however, was Roger's accommodating character. Actually, Roger was so pleased with VENT that he declared the trips "some of the best birding experiences of his life," notes Victor. "Because he did feel this way, I asked him if he would make a quote about our tours that we could use in advertising. . . . That was enormously helpful."

Was Roger a mentor?

"Very much so," says Victor. "Particularly at that stage of my life when I was starting my business. He was always concerned about how we were doing, how things were working out. . . . He'd had his own career of doing books and paintings and he knew what it was like to be in business."

Through the years Roger led a number of VENT trips. A special thrill came twice for Victor Emanuel when he received two different awards named after his mentor. The first, the Roger Tory Peterson Excellence in Birding Award, was from the Houston Audubon Society. As long as Roger was alive, he traveled down to present the award, so Victor got his from Roger personally. The second, the Roger Tory Peterson Award, came in 2004 from the American Birding Association. (Pete Dunne and David Sibley also received the Peterson ABA award.)

Kenn Kaufman

The fledgling American Birding Association first convened in Kenmare, North Dakota, in 1973. Nineteen-year-old Kenn Kaufman, in the middle of his *Kingbird Highway* survey of America, reached Kenmare in time. He saw a familiar face there, as he later wrote:

> *It was my hero, Roger Tory Peterson.*
>
> *I admired Peterson intensely for both his accomplishments and his approach. He had come into his world eminence in birding via his own route, without going through channels. . . . He had been just the kid from Jamestown, New York, many years ago—the kid who would not become a professional ornithologist, and who was told that he could not make a living as a bird painter . . . until in 1934 he . . . launched a legendary career. In the years since then he had been acclaimed as the great painter, great writer, great photographer, great fieldman, great man; he was, without a doubt, the world's best-known ornithologist.*
>
> *At a distance, Peterson looked his age, about sixty-five. . . . But at closer range I noticed his eyes. Those eyes blazed with a*

fiery blue intensity. The eyes had the same burning gaze they must have had fifty years before, when he had first sought birds in the hills of western New York. His eyes had never lost their youthful keenness for birds.

Kenn Kaufman heard Roger speak, commenting in his book that "he could hold a room full of birders spellbound simply by reminiscing, by improvising." Roger rambled a bit, but "was quite articulate in whatever he had to say. . . . He had a very crisp, clear speaking voice." The association members were so starstruck that Roger could have "read the phone book" and they would have loved it.

Toward the end of the convention, after most birders had left, Kaufman and about twenty others birded with Roger, who showed he still had the ears of a young man. Roger also couldn't help but teach. "There were veeries there," Kaufman says.

There were little groves of trees out in the prairie, and veeries. I always thought of a veery as being an eastern forest bird. . . . [Peterson remarked that] the veeries were doing well here and that's [interesting] because . . . the brown-headed cowbird really parasitized their nests in other areas of the continent. He said, "I wonder if the nesting birds here are better adapted to deal with cowbird parasitism because this is the plains, and there always have been a lot of cowbirds here. Whereas, in the northeast, the cowbird is more of a recent invader and [veeries] haven't adjusted to them as well yet." . . . I'd never thought of anything like that. It seemed really interesting. He wasn't just out there trying to identify birds before anyone else. He was thinking about relations between birds.

By age six Kaufman was learning the birds of his neighborhood; a sympathetic stepuncle noticed his interest and sent him a box of bird-related books, magazines, and newspaper clippings.

The books included *Birds Over America* and the 1941 edition of *A Field Guide to Western Birds,* which didn't apply to eastern Kansas where Kenn lived. The magazines were old *Audubon* issues from the late 1940s and early 1950s, some of which contained "Roger Peterson's Bird's-Eye View." Kaufman used the western guide as well as he could until he could purchase the latest (1947) eastern. Meanwhile, he read Roger's *Audubon* columns over and over, memorized whole chapters of *Birds Over America.* Then he learned that the local library carried *Wild America;* he bicycled the five or six miles into town forty or fifty times just to borrow the book. "Eventually," says Kaufman, "my parents took the hint and bought me a copy a couple of years later."

As a new Audubon member at ten, Kaufman was disappointed that the magazine no longer featured Roger's column. However, one issue of *Audubon* contained a flyer advertising *The World of Birds.* "It was expensive," Kenn remembers. "But I was so wanting this magical book, that . . . [although] we weren't that well-off . . . my parents bought that book for me for Christmas."

Kaufman has had time to ponder the quality of Roger's writing that he studied so assiduously as a boy. "His meaning is always really clear," Kaufman says. "It's not obscure at all, and he . . . uses colorful descriptions of things without falling into clichés. . . . I could pull out certain paragraphs where the pacing is really good. The length of sentences and the variation and the timing of the sentences. They're paragraphs that hold together, that would sound good even if you didn't know what the words meant."

Roger's writing was Kenn's model. "Later on, when I got to know him," Kenn reveals, "he actually said I was a very good writer."

One of the more recent volumes in the Peterson series is Kaufman's *Advanced Birding.* Kenn proposed it to Houghton Mifflin as a stand-alone book, but Roger wanted it in the series. "Whenever I finished a section and sent it to my editors at Houghton, I would send a copy to Roger," recalls Kenn, "and he would write back, often with just a few little comments, suggestions, sometimes with questions. He wrote to me a couple of times with questions about things relating to southwestern birds when he was revising the western [1990] guide."

Kenn appreciated Roger's collegiality: "He was always interested in other people's opinions. I never saw anything that looked like arrogance from him. "

The younger naturalist had dreamed of having his own field guide series. Roger was his role model after all. Kenn proposed a bird guide to Houghton Mifflin only because the publisher had the right of first refusal on his books. To his surprise, Houghton Mifflin exercised its option. By the late 1990s Kenn was hard at work on the first volume in his own series (Focus Guides). His *Field Guide to Birds of North America,* published in 2000, differed from Roger's by employing photographs instead of art (Kaufman used computer technology so the images showed the field characters of each species), but to make it as user friendly as possible, he followed Roger's lead in other ways.

For example, Kenn grouped similar-looking birds: "large long-tailed birds" (ring-necked pheasant, greater roadrunner, wild turkey) and "mockingbirds and shrikes." A new twist, but Petersonesque in its simple logic, was the grouping of birds of common habitat: "birds of rocky shores" (ruddy turnstone, purple sandpiper), and "woodland hawks" (broad-winged hawk, hook-billed kite). Then there were the "stickpins." Harry Foster, Roger's editor in his last years, and now Kenn's, informed Kaufman that Roger's method of using arrows pointing to salient field marks wasn't copyrighted. However, the designers went with stickpins instead.

Don't the stickpins—close enough in appearance to those famous arrows—make Kaufman's guide a direct Peterson descendant? "I can't really break it down to say that I was influenced in this way because it's such an influence that goes so far back that everything I've done with natural history has been influenced by Peterson's work one way or another," Kenn answers. "It's more of an attitude thing, trying to make it usable . . . and [considering] the primary audience as people who haven't seen the bird before and don't know what it is."

Kenn knew Roger's books so well that, when they were in the field, he recognized some of his mentor's anecdotes from the printed page. "He told stories about things that he had described in one of his books," Kaufman recounts. "One of those times I told him that I remembered reading that. He looked kind of irritated and said that I knew his books better than he did."

Swedish Hatchlings

A Field Guide to the Birds of Britain and Europe opened up new vistas for countless Europeans, winning Roger innumerable admirers and disciples. But he had a particular impact on two young men from the country of his ancestors, Sweden.

Lars Jonsson

Lars Jonsson had been interested in birds since he was four or five. Somewhere between ages ten and twelve, when Jonsson had already had considerable experience with local birds, he acquired the Peterson-Mountfort-Hollom guide. "It was a revelation for me," he says. "All of a sudden you saw that there was not only one wheatear. There were four or five more species. So I remember it was like a new door that opened me to another field. . . . A continent opened. . . . I was just pleased with what I saw. The textures of the birds, the way he put them side by side."

As a young teen with artistic talent, he began feeling the urge to supplement Roger's artwork: "Some of the birds were not done in color," Jonsson points out. "There were some birds . . . that were not depicted in a sitting image, like the osprey. There was only a head, flying bird, or something like that. So I actually painted small images that I folded into my Peterson guide. I was already trying to improve it," he laughs. Improve it, he admits, because the Peterson guide was an "absolute inspiration" for him.

Jonsson experimented with the Peterson approach: "I also remember that I did some plates of some longspurs, which I still have. I did the male in one way, the female slightly hidden like he had in his book. . . . I was hooked on this field guide thing." When he traveled the continent in his late teens, he brought the Peterson guide along.

It would be some time before Jonsson published his own European guide. By then he had established a reputation as one of the world's leading young bird artists. As such, he traveled to Wausau, Wisconsin, throughout the 1980s for Birds in Art at the Leigh Yawkey Woodson Art Museum, where some of his paintings were being shown. There he met Roger, an early patron of the Birds in Art program.

"He was an easygoing guy," Jonsson remembers. "Somebody who was on his level, or talked his language, there's no barrier. . . . He spoke to every birder as if it was his brother."

Lars acknowledges that when he finally produced his European field guide (*Birds of Europe*) in 1992, he "broke with the Peterson field guide system." Jonsson's book is radically different. It concentrates more on the intrinsic beauty of each bird than on field marks that aid in identification. Birds are often shown against a full-color backdrop of their respective habitats, and rarely in similar poses facing the same direction. Written descriptions are much wordier than Guy Mountfort's Peterson-imposed terseness. For example, Lars writes at length about juvenile plumages of birds of sea and shore. His paragraph on the Arctic skua is over half a page long, with a precise narrative of the juvenile bird's axillaries and underwing coverts, among other things. While Jonsson's guide is breathtaking to look at, it is not the same kind of educational tool a Peterson is.

"My generation . . . was the first generation . . . who started to use telescopes," says Jonsson. "What happens with the telescope is that you come closer to the bird again. You can see more details. You can see there are different plumages. There are juveniles. There are adults. . . . So what I did was sort of switching, not backwards, but another step forward, all of a sudden . . . aging [determining the age of] birds." It was like the bird-in-hand identification of old, except the bird was safely not in hand.

"But I was raised on it," Lars says of the Peterson guide. "I was shaped by him. And certainly, . . . if you want to take a step forward, you need something to step on. On someone's shoulders. I'm standing on his shoulders."

Kent Ullberg

Growing up in a Swedish fishing village where his grandfather had a trawler, Kent Ullberg worked on trawlers in the summertime and developed a fascination for marine life, including birds. His father, a landscape artist, would take Kent around the countryside to paint scenery and set up a little easel for the boy, but Kent was more interested in the ravens nesting below the sea cliffs. Ullberg pored over bird books by "local Swedish writers." At twelve he discovered the Swedish translation of *A Field Guide to the Birds of Britain and Europe.* He saved up money from his paper route to buy it, and couldn't have asked for anything better.

As Kent had a relative named Roger Peterson, he figured that the Roger Peterson of the field guide was just somebody who lived down the road. This supposedly local fellow made Kent want to see the continent, as the field guide "showed all these interesting birds, from southern Europe, exotic locales, even North Africa— some of the European accidentals from North Africa."

In art school during the 1960s, Kent was scolded by his teachers for realistically sculpting subjects, such as bears, from nature. (Realism was a no-no). He switched to science and earned professional accreditation in the museum exhibits field. "Part of the exam, ironically, was being able to identify most of Europe's birds from study skins," says Ullberg. "There again, Roger was with me! I learned about all this stuff, basically, from Roger's guide." Working in museums in Germany, Botswana, then Denver, he used his sculpting talents to adorn the natural history exhibits he curated. Remaining in America, his sculptures drew attention and awards. He was able to leave museum work and sculpt full-time.

Ullberg met Roger in 1976 at Fred King's New York art gallery, the Sportsman's Edge, which was showing an exhibit of the works of members of the Society of Animal Artists. "Here's this tall guy pointed out to me," says Kent. "I don't think I even knew what he looked like. . . . You can imagine I was really quaking knees when I approached him." He needn't have been nervous. "I found out what kind of open and friendly and kind man he really was. He put me at ease." Thus commenced a friendship that lasted the rest of Roger's life.

"Roger took a great interest in all young naturalists," Ullberg notes. "I think he was very, very keen on carrying on his legacy. He knew his legacy. He knew his importance as a naturalist and a conservationist and he wanted people to follow him. He was very encouraging, very kind, to young artists."

Kent remembers how Roger supported the artists whose work was shown at the Birds in Art exhibit at Woodson Art Museum. Roger interacted with all of them. "Normally, we drank wine together and got to sit in the bar with him and listen to his stories. He was just one of us, even though he was our hero."

Roger, the third recipient of the Master Wildlife Artist Award at the Birds in Art exhibit, was Kent's choice to present him with his own medal in 1987. "When you receive the award you can ask for a person to represent you and hand you the award," Ullberg explains. "I wanted Roger to do it. It was a high point in my life to receive that medal from Roger's hand."

The elder artist admired Kent too, writing in a foreword to *Kent Ullberg: Monuments to Nature:* "No one during the latter half of this century has celebrated the animal form with greater enthusiasm and virtuosity."

A favorite memory Ullberg has of Roger happened along the Texas coast one of the times Roger visited the sculptor at his home.

"We went out on my boat, and there's a high bridge . . . from the mainland in Corpus Christi, out to my island where I live. We were going under the bridge in the boat, . . . slowly, slowly, gliding under the bridge.

Roger said, "You know what—there should be some peregrines roosting here."

It was the winter, and they migrate down there. I knew there was a peregrine out there, because I'd been out before, and sometimes they did roost under there, but Roger hadn't [seen this]. As we glide under the bridge—this is absolute truth—down comes a feather, you know how a feather sort of floats down on the air, and settled on the boat.

And Roger said, 'Whoa! That's a marbled godwit!' He looks up, and there's a peregrine sitting way up under the bridge plucking a marbled godwit. . . . I mean, here is a greeting from a peregrine to the greatest birder, you know? . . . Every time I'd see Roger, he'd say, "Hey—what's the peregrine eating now?"

I'd say, "Oh, laughing gulls."

It was kind of a neat experience. I mean, (a) he predicted that it would be a peregrine sitting under there, and (b) he knew immediately, from one feather, what the bird was [that the peregrine was eating].

Chapter Fourteen

Offerings

To some, Roger Tory Peterson was not a generous man. Virginia Cadbury, widow of one-time Audubon Camp director Bart Cadbury, remembers Roger's reluctance to make a large donation to a fund named for Carl Buchheister, a mutual friend and the camp's first director, who died in July 1986. The fund was Bart's idea. He figured people he knew with money, like Roger, would provide the fund with a strong foundation.

"When he wrote to Roger about it," says Virginia, "Roger wrote back . . . and said, 'Well, here's a check for a thousand dollars.' He said, 'I'm sorry I can't do more. I'd like to, but I have to think of my children. And their inheritance.' When Bart got that letter, . . . he was so upset. He said, 'How could Roger be such an idiot?' He thought Roger should have been more generous. He thought a thousand dollars was pretty pathetic from somebody like Roger Peterson who really cared about Carl."

Arthur Klebanoff, who represented Roger in the licensing of his artwork from the 1980s onward, remembers Roger being pleased to earn money without having to work for it. "What he did understand was that the work he had already done could be licensed to somebody else, and they sent money," says Klebanoff. "The money that came from licensing, for him, was his play money. . . . It was actually his 'personal fun' kitty. Not that he was exactly short money, anyway, but . . . my impression is that he was pretty cheap. And tight with money."

Roger liked money. He came from a working-class background, scrimped and saved for things as a boy, and grew into a man at the height of the Depression. Unemployed after his second summer session at Camp Chewonki ended in 1931, Clarence

Allen came to the rescue with the Rivers School job offer. Income from the field guide was modest at first. The National Audubon Society offered a steady paycheck, which he didn't give up until he had to—when he was drafted.

In 1966 Golden Press published *Birds of North America,* coauthored by Chandler Robbins, Bertel Bruun, and Herbert Zim, with illustrations by Arthur Singer. It was the first book to give the Peterson guide real competition.

One volume covered all North American birds. Unlike the third edition of Roger's eastern guide (1947) and the second edition of *A Field Guide to Western Birds* (1961), all illustrations were in color. Most of the nonpasserines were shown in flight on the same page where they were depicted standing or perching. Range maps were featured rather than the mere range discussions found in the Petersons. Robbins's brainchild, the birdsong sonogram, accompanied almost every avian entry.

The *Golden Guide* (as Robbins's book was nicknamed) also lifted some Peterson techniques. Most birds were shown in similar positions facing the same direction. Bird silhouettes were found throughout. Bird descriptions were short and punchy.

Robbins, a Boston-area native, who as a teen in 1933 had first met Roger and been floored by the latter's sharp birding eye, held great affection for the elder naturalist. He had been reluctant to do a competing guide. "In the first place, I told Zim I wasn't going to have anything to do with the *Golden Guide* because Roger and I were good friends and I didn't see the need for another field guide," says Robbins. "When he finally talked me into it, I said, 'Well, OK, but on a few conditions, that it would be completely different so that it would add to what Roger's had rather than compete with it."

While the *Golden Guide* wasn't completely different, it was different enough and colorful enough that it became the one to beat.

Penguin authority Bill Sladen remembers a book signing where Roger was seated at one table with his field guides and Chandler Robbins at another with the *Golden Guide*. Of Roger, Sladen says, "He was extremely competitive and very jealous of anybody who might be competing with him. . . . Roger was always [saying] . . . , 'Oh, my God, is he going to sell more books than me?'. . . It was such a contrast to Robbins, who couldn't really care less."

(Roger's livelihood, his name, his reputation, were synonymous with his field guides. A dampening of their primacy was a dampening of Roger's legacy. Conversely, Robbins's main career was that of an innovative research biologist at the Patuxent Wildlife Research Center in Laurel, Maryland, where he made a name for himself by, among other things, instituting the Breeding Bird Survey, now an essential measure of bird populations.)

Roland Clement thinks Roger took his celebrity as evidence of his intrinsic worth, making him believe he was something he wasn't. "Now celebrities are not ordinary people," says Clement. "The world treats them differently and, therefore, they react differently. So Roger, after the field guide and after *Life* took him on—very different person. He talked like a celebrity. He expected adulation. He wore his heart on his sleeve all the time. He was insulted if somebody neglected him. . . . He was a great guy. Very substantive. He learned as he went along but, nevertheless, being a celebrity, he expected to be treated like one."

However Roger saw himself, however possessive he was with money, however fearful he was of being upstaged, he was generous. He loved to share information. He adored being with those who shared his passions. He gave credit where it was due. He mentored young nature enthusiasts and artists. He donated artwork to raise money, or just because.

Roger hadn't liked the orchard oriole he'd given to the Georgia Ornithological Society back in 1936 for the cover of its journal, *The Oriole,* calling his effort a "rather poor scratchboard." He added in a 1987 letter to friend Bob Lewin, "It was so bad that recently I did a new cover—one in color." This appeared first on the front of the *Oriole* issue commemorating the society's fiftieth anniversary. Roger gave the society permission to use the handsome painting for fund-raising; it became a signed, limited-edition print.

If the Georgia Ornithological Society was dear to Roger's heart, Camp Chewonki was more so. From the beginning of his association with Chewonki, he designed, then redesigned, the camp's logo depicting an osprey in flight. "There's a variety of different ospreys that Roger drew from the thirties on," says current camp director Don Hudson. "Just because his art, his style, changed a little bit, so too did the logo."

Lending his name to an organization he sympathized with was never a concern to Roger—so long as it didn't add to his burgeoning workload. By the 1950s, it seemed everyone wanted his involvement in one conservation organization or another. His name was golden. But by 1957 he had to draw the line somewhere. Responding to a friend's request to place his name on the Advisory Committee to the Conservationists United for Long Island (a group opposed to rampant development), he hedged: "If my name . . . simply means my name, I should be most willing. But . . . I am in danger of becoming a casualty of intersecting deadlines and have not been able to handle all my correspondence for weeks in addition to my normal work load. . . . Recently I have allowed the use of my name on two committees thinking that no work would be involved, and I was flooded with letters which demanded answers. In many cases I simply was not able to answer." Roger asked that his name be used for "window-dressing" only. His friend Grace Murphy guaranteed it.

Without more, Roger's name on a letterhead was hugely valuable. George Archibald, founder of the International Crane Foundation in Wisconsin, notes the Peterson name had been on the foundation's letterhead since its 1973 inception. "This gave us credibility," he says.

Arthur Klebanoff noticed that Roger "gave generously of his own time. He also . . . would be happy to let nature nonprofits use his name and likeness to make money for themselves. . . . His position was, 'It's for the cause.'"

Sometimes neither time nor money was an issue. Foolhardiness took over and Roger would crave sharing his joy of discovery with someone else, regardless of the circumstances. Gus Yaki, who had his most treasured time with Roger during the trip across North America on the thirtieth anniversary of *Wild America,* recalls the favor the elder naturalist wanted to do for him upon meeting in Trinidad in 1969 on the occasion of a conservation assembly. Following the event, Roger and Barbara invited Yaki to join them for a day's birding:

> *At day's end (about 4:30 p.m.), Peterson discovered that I had not yet seen the unique oilbirds that nest in a grotto deep in the valley below. He was fully prepared to lead my companion and me down to see these birds. Fortunately for him, our ride arrived about this time. Had he taken us down to the site, we would have had to return in total darkness over trails that were difficult to negotiate even in daylight. At this latitude in the tropics, the sun sets at about 6:00 p.m., and there is no twilight. Nor was there any artificial lighting. I have never forgotten his unselfish willingness to allow us to share that experience.*

Jealousy was part of Roger's life, but it was not necessarily jealousy on his part. Says National Audubon Society historian Frank Graham:

> There were . . . bird-watchers and other ornithologists who were sincerely jealous of Roger and his success. They would always make snide remarks about Roger's success. Whatever he did made money. These people were writing books and hardly selling two thousand copies or so. Roger was selling thousands and always outshining everybody. Outshining them just because of his name, his reputation, and so on.
>
> There was a man named Sewall Pettingill who was head of the Cornell Lab of Ornithology and he was part of the Audubon [Screen] Tours. . . . He would always make some kind of snide remark: "Roger will capitalize on that." He told me once he was really taken aback when he was giving a lecture somewhere . . . in the Midwest and somebody was introducing him at a kind of ornithological club and they were giving him a big buildup as a leading person and then introduced him as Roger Tory Peterson! He was kind of shocked about it.

Steve Kress, who teaches ornithology at Cornell and is ornithology program director at Hog Island Audubon Camp in Maine, remembers Pettingill expressing resentment concerning Roger's celebrity status at the fiftieth anniversary celebration of Hog Island. "Roger was about the last of the original staff who was still alive," says Kress. "He was in good form. [But] he seemed to have some tension with Sewall Pettingill. . . . I think Pettingill left early. He said, 'This is Roger's party.' So I always thought there was some tension there. . . . I never heard any of that coming from Roger in the other direction. Never a negative word about anybody else."

Indeed, perusing Roger's correspondence and Barbara's New Year's letters, one finds expressions of affection and respect for Sewall Pettingill and his wife, Eleanor. Similarly, Roger had had much collegial contact with Kenneth C. Parkes, an ornithologist at the Carnegie Museum and one-time associate of Philip Humphrey. "Parkes was quite anti-Peterson," notes Kenn Kaufman. "He just thought that the guy got way too much attention and credit." Of this, Roger became aware, often commenting in his latter years that he preferred not hearing more carping from Parkes.

Bob Bateman remembers an act of petulance: "There was one occasion on a ship, probably a Lindblad trip, where, I think it was an older gentleman, maybe closer to Roger's age, [who] saw a great rarity and pointedly didn't tell Roger about it until it was gone. That hurt Roger, obviously! It's just meanness and selfishness."

"If you've got a rock star in your midst and you've got a bunch of aspiring musicians," says Roger's son Lee, "you're going to resent the fact—'Why am I not him? I'm just as good.' Either it's a matter of people not seeing their shortcomings, or it's a matter of pure luck. Being in the right place at the right time. . . . A lot of it is having the right combination of skills and abilities. Or personality traits. And Dad had 'em."

One personality trait—a passion for natural history—led Roger Tory Peterson to pen well over one hundred forewords, introductions, and prefaces to the books of others, even books that could compete with his field guides or prose works. He wrote encouraging words, in the hundreds or the thousands, for publications as diverse as a volume of ruminative essays about nature, a children's book about bald eagles, a manual of birdwatching, a birding memoir, an encyclopedia of world birdlife, and guides to birding in one state or another.

Requests for introductions and the like really began piling up during Roger's last three decades. However, even by 1962 his munificence had begun to haunt him—and annoyed Houghton Mifflin. This was evident in a letter he wrote to Herbert Zim, who was then starting work on the *Golden Guide*. Zim had asked Roger whether he would agree, for a small honorarium, to be among those vetting the manuscript for accuracy. Roger replied that he would be happy to help "unofficially"; therefore, he could not accept the honorarium. "My publisher . . . is getting very sticky about my doing work for other publishers and this includes writing forewords, etc. It seems that [the author of] every bird book that comes out nowadays wants me to write the foreword."

In 1981 Roger delighted friend Susan Roney Drennan, then editor of the Audubon publication *American Birds,* with his foreword to her book *Where to Find Birds in New York State: The Top 500 Sites.* But he was just as delighted as she was. Drennan remembers: "I said, 'You know, Roger, it would be very nice if you could write something for the beginning of the book.'

"He said,"—Drennan imitates his gasp—"'I would just be thrilled!'. . . And that was such a nice thing. . . . It's not like he didn't have anything to do. He had millions of things to do. But he was very excited about the book because at the time there weren't many . . . state bird books that said, 'OK, go to this place, during this season, and look for these birds.' So he was quite excited about it. . . . I've never known him to write anything so fast. It was very nice."

Tom Cade was also happy with Roger's willingness to write the foreword for the follow-up volume to Joe Hickey's tome *Peregrine Falcon Populations: Their Biology and Decline,* called *Peregrine Falcon Populations: Their Management and Recovery.* "We had a second international conference about the peregrine falcon after it had started to get better. . . . We had a twenty-year kind of repeat of that conference that Joe Hickey had called in 1965. This is in 1985. . . . It was attended by even more people than the first one. Unfortunately, Roger himself wasn't there, but . . . he wrote a very nice preface to the book for us, in which he said something to the effect that, 'Well, if we can do this for the peregrine, maybe we can also do it for the condor.' And, of course, now we're heavily involved with work on the condor. He was a little prescient on that particular subject."*

Roger wrote the foreword for one of Robert Michael Pyle's first books, 1974's *Watching Washington Butterflies*. He helped Pyle in another butterfly-related endeavor also. In 1971 while still a graduate student, Pyle founded the Xerces Society, the invertebrate conservation organization; Roger enthusiastically agreed to become a Xerces counselor. While he couldn't make the first annual meeting of Xerces at Yale in spring 1974, he made sure to attend the second one the following year, when it was held at Cornell, even though he was suffering from jet lag.

"I remember him saying that he was one of the very first westerners who was allowed in to Bhutan," says Pyle. "They had a good birding trip and it was very successful and he saw life birds and he was exhausted. . . . We were all so honored and delighted he would come."

Xerces attendees were surprised by Roger's unassuming demeanor. At one point, Pyle recounts, "Roger lay down in the back of the room, this academic building at Cornell, on a concrete floor, put something under his head and took a nap, because he was so tired from the jet lag. He had come directly there from Bhutan. Everybody thought that was very cool, that this king of the birders, who was such a famous person, would just lie down

---

* Roger wrote in his foreword: "This new book, based on the Sacramento conference, . . . shows that avicultural methods can be a very effective tool in saving a species on the brink of extinction. Will it also work for the California Condor? We hope so."

on the concrete floor in the meeting and take a nap. . . . Nobody was offended that he fell asleep instead of just nodding at the desk as most people would do. . . . Everyone thought that was very, very cool."

Once refreshed, Roger was actively engaged in the goings-on. Remembers Pyle:

He just came to observe, to watch, to see what was happening, and, I think, to lend his support, but also, he was just plain curious, [and] . . . he really liked butterflies. At that time Xerces was mostly butterflies. . . . Roger had a particular bee in his bonnet about Lepidoptera conservation—the giant silk moths, the lunas, and the cecropias, and things like that, which he felt took a real beating with the DDT spraying. They never were as abundant at Old Lyme as they had been prior to that. He was always eager to talk about that. . . . He gave a very nice pep talk at one point. And he certainly took part in the discussion . . . , the questions and answers after the meeting. He took part in a nice, unobtrusive [way]. . . . I never saw Roger be pushy or supercilious or in any way pushing his stature. Or taking advantage of it.

Wrote Kent Dannen for *Backpacker* magazine about a chilly July day with Roger twelve thousand feet above sea level: "He had seen so many birds that a new species was a great event for him. The brown-capped rosy finch was now on his life list." That day in 1970 Dannen helped Roger. Roger in turn helped Dannen.

This happened at the first National Wildlife Federation Conservation Summit in Estes Park, Colorado. Roger was proclaimed dean. ("I suppose [this] made me a sort of Den Mother," Barbara mused in her early 1971 New Year's letter.) The summit served as a crash course in natural history and outdoor living with classes on subjects ranging from birds, flowers, and geology to outdoor photography, hiking, backpacking, and conservation activism. Besides being the main attraction, Roger was among three people leading early-morning birdwalks. The others were Kent Dannen, then a struggling wildlife photographer, and Ron Ryder, who taught ornithology at Colorado State University. The three conferred before the summit to apportion birding territory. It was then that Roger asked Dannen if he could show him a brown-capped rosy finch, one of three birds in North America that had eluded him. Dannen said yes.

"There was nothing particularly remarkable about being able to find one," Dannen, who today concentrates on dog photography, says. "It was just a matter of going where they were and looking for them."

The finch search occurred one afternoon after the end of classes. Initially, Roger and Kent were followed by a small contingent of birders, including Barbara. After awhile, the followers stopped climbing and returned to the parking lot along Trail Ridge Road, where they worriedly watched the two men continue their ascent. Apparently many were fearful of Roger's ability to keep up—after all, he was nearly *sixty-two*—yet Dannen, then a young man, worked hard to keep up with Roger. On the group's apprehension over Roger's well-being, Dannen reflects: "Here's a really important person, and although he got much older after that, he wasn't a young man at the time. He had this great shock of white hair and I think that everybody was trying to be real protective of him."

Dannen adds, "They were, perhaps, a bit nervous about him tramping along the top of a cliff." The finches appeared on what are now called the Lava Cliffs, flying to and fro, feeding on seeds, and allowing the men within four or five feet of them. "He did sort of sit on the edge of a cliff and watch the birds flying up and down with his feet hanging over the edge." That really made the birders below anxious. Unafraid of heights, however, Roger was perfectly comfortable up there.

People back at the conservation summit had been rooting for Roger to see the bird. When he announced that he had, he also made sure to tell everyone that *Kent Dannen* had shown him the bird. "I was just getting started as a wildlife photographer then," Kent says. "It really helped boost my career! . . . It seems odd to say that, but I did have that fifteen minutes of glory that . . . made my name known in places as somebody who showed Roger Tory Peterson a new bird. . . . It was, of course, strictly a coincidence. Certainly, there are zillions of people who know more about birds than I do. But it was one of those classic 'right place at the right time' sort of things. . . . He was very vocal in his praise for me there at the conservation summit."

Roger wanted him to share the limelight.

Chapter Fifteen

Maturing with National Audubon

Long after he left the National Audubon Society staff, Audubon remained close to Roger's heart. He was grateful to Audubon for giving him a position teaching natural history on a national level and enamored of its storied life in battling commercial forces bent on destroying the natural world.

Thus, Roger remained an Audubon insider. He served on its board of directors from the late 1950s through the 1960s, and as secretary during the first half of the 1960s. "Roger Peterson's Bird's-Eye View" commenced with *Audubon* magazine's September/October 1952 issue. Editor John Terres announced that summer: "Mr. Peterson . . . will tell of his experiences during his travels, and share with us his ideas and opinions on a variety of subjects. The feature will be illustrated with some of Mr. Peterson's sketches, which will be made especially for *Audubon* magazine."

After the column ended, Roger still frequently contributed to *Audubon*. For issues involving Audubon policy, Roland Clement was his mole. "He wanted to know what was going on all the time," says Clement. "When he wrote those columns for *Audubon* magazine he wanted to be sure that he had covered his bases properly. . . . I was on the inside. He needed that contact. . . . In other words, he would say, 'You agree this is a real problem? Can we get Audubon involved?'"

Les Line was Roger's editor at *Audubon* beginning in 1966. Line remembers: "He was a fine writer. . . . When he was doing things for us it was the kind of story that an editor likes to get because you change a semi-colon into a comma, cross the t's and dot the i's, and send it off to the printer."

On one of those red-letter days when the Peterson family visited the Audubon Camp, Roger's arrival was a markedly important occasion for Peter Mott, a Trenton, New Jersey, native who had had the eastern Peterson since the second edition's publication in 1939 and swears by his Peterson to this day.

Meeting Roger, Mott "was overwhelmed and probably almost unable to speak, even as a young man, even as an adult. He was just a wonderful, wonderful figure."

(In 1958, Mott took over as bird instructor after Allan Cruick-shank's departure—a tough act to follow. "If they saw a new bird, Allan would stand on his head," Mott says. "Everyone was pleased to tell me about that. I had to figure out what I could do. Unfortunately, the best I could manage was to smoke a cigar.")

The camp regulars—the Petersons included—were like family. Says Virginia Cadbury's daughter, Betsy: "Joe [Cadbury] and Lu were my real aunt and uncle, so I called them Uncle Joe and Auntie Lu, but all the rest of them on the staff when we were children, we were told to call them all Uncle Carl [Buchheister], Uncle Allan and Aunt Helen Cruickshank, and Uncle Don and Aunt Elizabeth Borror. When [the Petersons were there] . . . , we were told to call them Uncle Roger and Aunt Barbara. Barbara just took exception to that right away. She said, 'Nobody calls me aunt. I don't want to be aunt. Call me Barbara.' So it was Uncle Roger and Barbara."

Art Borror, son of "Uncle Don and Aunt Elizabeth," and now married to Betsy Cadbury, says that around 1950 or 1951, Roger was at the camp a good part of the summer: "He was at work on the paintings he was preparing for his field guide to wildflowers. He had a studio in one of the rooms up there."

After the war Audubon's offices at 1006 Fifth Avenue were still home to Roger, but as an independent contractor hired to revise and update the Junior Audubon leaflets, he could come and go as he pleased. "He proudly claimed an office down in the cellar," remembered the late Jane Kinne in 2006. She met Roger in March 1950 as a new Audubon employee. All the Junior Audubon leaflets were kept in the cellar, she noted. "You'd find him on his little move-around stool down there if you wanted to talk to him, nine times out of ten."

John Baker assigned Kinne to transform the Photo and Film Department, once Barbara Peterson's domain, into a functioning photo agency. Until that time, the photos Audubon kept were nothing more than a reference file of images taken by Roger, Allan Cruickshank, Karl Maslowski, and others. However, to ensure a steady flow of new images into Audubon's files meant that photographers would have to receive compensation for their work. "One of my assignments was to hightail it downtown to all the photo agencies and try to find out how you ran one, how much money they made, what kind of contracts they had, the whole basic principle," said Kinne. "Roger had a vested interest in this. He understood that John Baker was absolutely right. Unless the guys producing this material could at least make a small amount of money, they were going to have to abandon it. And everybody wanted the photographers to continue."

Among her other duties, Kinne was responsible for lending 35 mm slides to local civic, nature, and garden clubs for a small fee. "You could write in and say, 'I'm going to give a lecture on the birds of southern Ohio. Please send me an appropriate set of twenty slides.' Here I was, brand new, had been taught a fair amount of just regional, basic, natural history growing up in Wisconsin. . . . Roger would appear each day knowing that I would address these mail requests. He'd stand behind me, and as I was about to put a cardinal in southern Ohio, he said, 'I wouldn't do that.' Then he'd explain to me about the range of a cardinal. Of course, today it would be a different story. . . .* So, anyway, this is how our friendship started. He mentored me through all of that."

Working in the cellar was exhilarating, Kinne found. She was surrounded by former (Dick Pough) and current (Bob Allen) Audubon staffers, as well as artists like Don Eckelberry, Arthur Singer, and Roger. "Roger loved to come, because I had the big table wherein the Don Eckelberrys of the world would come, look through files, and do some sketching. They would sit around my table and talk. . . . It was very much a time of exchanging ideas and challenges. . . . I first had to keep moving and do what I was supposed to do. But my background music was not the radio. It was what was going on."

Kinne and other Audubon staffers also assisted Roger and Barbara with the nuts and bolts of his Audubon Screen Tour lectures.

---

* Since 1950, the northern cardinal has dramatically expanded its range northward to include all of Ohio and parts north, such as most of Wisconsin, Minnesota, and Michigan, as well as Maine and beyond.

Local Audubon Screen Tour sponsors around the United States received this eager message in 1957 from Wayne Short, the tour's architect and organizer for Audubon since the 1940s:

> *Audubon Screen Tours are without question the major leagues in the nature lecture field. It's competitive. Only the best players are selected to do the batting and the fielding. . . . Where have you ever heard of such a team before? A Ph.D. doing the pitching—Arthur A. Allen [Cornell Laboratory of Ornithology founder] himself. And the Dean of Women of the Audubon Camp of Maine giving him the signs—Allan Cruickshank catching even the wild pitches. And the shortstop! Roger Tory Peterson stopping every hit that comes his way. And then there's Alex Sprunt at first base, arguing with the umpire.*

Along with Alexander Sprunt Jr., Roger had been among Audubon's first Screen Tour lecturers. The new program started off shakily because not everyone had film footage to use. Roger hadn't yet thrown himself full bore into filmmaking and disdainfully remembered making do with rejects from other people's bird movies.

Roger's debut on January 2, 1948, was in Corpus Christi, Texas. The film was *The Riddle of Migration,* dominated by second-hand footage that gave him trouble during his cross-country travels. It was, he said, "much too full of splices which would very often break apart during the course of my lecture. In fact, this happened 11 times during the course of one lecture." He was downright embarrassed in Corpus Christi—"I suspect my debut was a near-disaster"—but legendary Texas birder Connie Hagar loved his talk. Wrote her biographer, Karen Harden McCracken: "Connie sat entranced . . . , and she was tempted to stand and cheer when he asserted, 'You on the Gulf Coast are inclined to take the brown pelican casually, but those from the north coming here probably want to see this bird more than any other fowl.'" As fishermen viewed the brown pelican as a competitor for fish and sometimes persecuted the bird, although it was legally protected, Hagar "wished all fishermen on the coast could have heard that."

Things improved when Roger bought his own filmmaking equipment and began religiously recording birdlife with moving pictures. "The screen tours did two things, basically," he commented in the 1970s. "First, they entertained. . . . But at the same time, . . . [local communities] also got educated as to what conservation was, what ecology was, and the environment. So the lectures educated while they entertained. But beyond that, the lecture films gave a solid activity which attracted members who would then do important conservation things in the community."

Roger tried footage out on his family before taking his films on the road. "We'd sit in the living room and he'd put on the film and do a lecture," Lee Peterson remembers. "It was fine-tuning to see what worked, what didn't work, and how it all felt."

Lee and Tory enjoyed seeing rough versions of these films, accentuated by such souvenirs as a Masai spear or a shield. "They were very exotic kinds of things," Tory says. "Even the films were exotic."

"I don't remember having to be dragged kicking and screaming to watch one of Dad's films," Lee reveals, "because what I was watching was Africa and South America. It was incredible stuff. Dad was really into flamingos at one point. So there were some really incredible shots of the Andes and incredible numbers of birds and the same thing in Africa, . . . seeing secretary birds stalking along the African veldt."

Roger was a self-taught filmmaker. "He was not a cinematographer," says Lee. "He was not doing big production stuff at all.

He was not doing a soundtrack to go with this, other than the sounds of the creatures, and he was talking over it. You had the sounds of the birds, but the narration was always extemporaneous, off the cuff, at the lecture."

In the days before Marlin Perkins's *Wild Kingdom,* let alone the Discovery Channel and Animal Planet, the films by Roger and other Audubon Screen Tour lecturers were all many Americans might see of faraway places and unfamiliar animal life.

In January 1963 Barbara summarized their screen tour adventures:

> *The Audubon lecture tour comes up each year as irrevocably as the income tax. Planned far ahead there is nothing to do when the fateful date arrives but go. This year the tour extended for a full month from mid-March to mid-April—the mud season. Showing his film* Wild Europe, *Roger covered the Northeast from Providence, Rhode Island, west to Madison, Wisconsin, and north to Quebec City. He had a number of too-close connections and near misses in Wisconsin and Michigan because of snowed-in airfields and round-about routings, but his record remains intact; he has never missed a scheduled lecture. The last two weeks I joined him with the car. He insists it is the only way he will do his lecture traveling in the future.*

Barbara was a frequent assistant, loading up the station wagon and, at the various whistle-stops, operating the projector.

"I remember talking with Barbara afterwards," says Betsy Cadbury of a lecture in the midsixties at Cornell. "She did all the work, setting it up, making sure the slides were in order, and all that. . . . She was extremely competent and organized. And very, very socially adept."

Another 1960s stop, the annual New Hampshire Audubon Society meeting, stands out for Art Borror: "I remember Barbara making a comment to the effect that people expect a very highly professional presentation by Roger, and therefore she . . . always took special care to make sure things were set up right. The audio-visuals, the screens, the projectors, and so on."

A small cadre of Audubon staffers, including Jane Kinne, were often present to help. "Barbara was there, but you need extra arms and legs," said Kinne. "You can't leave the projector, and the light switch is how far away?"

Kinne loved Roger's talks. "Of course, after you've heard *Wild America* a few times, and *Wild Europe* a few times, . . . you're more into 'How is he doing it this time?' 'Is it different?'. . . We used to clean and mend those films in between lectures."

Roger was deft at handling the audience during the postfilm question-and-answer session. "He tended not to be repetitive, even if you asked the same question," Kinne recalled. "You would get a slightly different . . . response. No, he was busy making sure he didn't sound rote. He was a very savvy show person."

As Roger said, his mission was to create new conservationists. "I always liked to have dinner with the officers or the sponsors before my lecture," he noted, continuing,

> Sometimes these dinners . . . might involve only half a dozen peo-ple; at other times we might have 50 or more of the important club members there. And very often I would have a few words to say at the dinner and it might be that I had heard about some local conservation problem. Often I would hear about it at the dinner. Then when I was on the lecture platform I held forth a little about that, how important it was to save that marsh at the edge of town, how I hope you will do something about this, et cetera. I may have learned that there was to be a spraying next week. I would ask them to monitor this and see what effect it might have on the local mockingbirds and cardinals. The lecture was always a vehicle by which you could . . . get local projects underway.

If Roger was coming to town, "people turned out for him," says Susan Roney Drennan. "Of course, in the big birding centers up and down the East Coast, there was standing room only most nights when Roger would speak. He took those opportunities to really talk about conservation of birds. In the public mind, not only was he the leading birder, but the leading spokesman for birds."

Drennan once wrote that Roger "learned how to marshal his tremendous vitality into a one-man conservation dynamo, galvanizing others to act on behalf of birds." What did she mean by this?

These local land trusts, these local conservation organizations, who were . . . stewards of the land, were very heartened by Roger, and many people joined them because of Roger. He would say, "Blah-blah-blah-blah-blah, *now here's what you can do. This is an effort that's going on in your area. X-Y-Z is the president of the organization. What they need are some people to go out and monitor the upland forest,* or something-something-something. *Make sure to go to your town meetings." . . . There was always that urgency of "Get out and do something. I want you to look at the birds, and there's nothing better than enjoying these birds, but let these birds be a pathway for you to take some local action." It was really quite wonderful because . . . he didn't have to do that! He could have just stood there and showed slides or his own movies—* "OK, this is where I've been lately. Look at these birds." *But he didn't. He worked hard on "What can I bring to these people."*

In September 1964 Roger was finally victimized by his scary driving. Barbara wrote months later:

Shortly after the A.O.U. meetings in Lawrence, Kansas, . . . Roger came very close to writing finis to his career. He was driving alone to Ithaca, New York, to attend a council meeting of the Laboratory of Ornithology. Just before reaching Ithaca at dusk he misjudged a curve, reacted too quickly with the brakes, and sent the car out of control. He took off three guard posts, plunged over an 18 foot embankment and went through the windshield. Fortunately, a farmer fixing his roof saw the accident and help was on its way within minutes. Otherwise Roger may well have bled to death unobserved. 210 stitches were required to piece together his face.

Roger informed a friend: "I am taking a somewhat more benign view of the world now that I am living on borrowed time. After looking at the car I don't see how I survived. . . . I still have a nasty lump on the chin and if it doesn't go down I may have a bit of plastic surgery. Fortunately, my eyes and my hands were OK and my skull was intact. I did break my wrist but with a light cast on it I find that I can write and paint without too much extra effort.

"I had always thought that accidents happened to other people. From now on I will fasten my seat belt," he said.

Shortly after the accident, Lee Peterson accompanied his mother to Ithaca to see Dad in the hospital. Barbara was quite anxious but arriving in his room and finding him there was a relief. "I just remember him being in the hospital bed with bandages and stuff like that," says Lee. "By that time, he was obviously not going to die and his nose was in place, or had been put back in place."

Given the countless potential distractions Roger faced everywhere, it's surprising he didn't have a major accident before this. Lee thinks his father was deep in thought just before it happened: "Dad had a really good capacity to focus in on things. Unfortunately, that was an instance where he focused in on the wrong thing."

Paul Spitzer, a family friend for some years by then, regards the accident as a harrowingly close call. "He wasn't totally himself for a whole year after that," Spitzer remembers. "He's damn lucky he didn't die in that one."

Yet Roger quickly returned to the Audubon Screen Tours circuit—just three days after being discharged from the hospital. Barbara reported to friend Bea Wetmore: "This was probably the best thing he could have done for though it did tax his strength somewhat I feel that it was built up more rapidly than it might have been otherwise." But Barbara did the driving and, according to Lee, Roger never again drove himself "if he could avoid it."

Chapter Sixteen

Shooting Birds

At 1:00 a.m., Jane Kinne and her husband, Russ, were sleeping when their ringing telephone shook them awake. Russ groped for the phone, barely uttering: "My God—who's dead?"

Through the receiver came a startled voice: "No, no, no! It's Roger!" The middle of the night was the middle of Roger's work-day. As such, it was prime time for him to think of a technical camera question. When Russ realized it was just one of Roger's routine, dead-of-night calls, he relaxed and good-naturedly answered his friend's query.

"Roger was not a technical, mechanically minded person," says Russ, a longtime wildlife photographer. "He was an artist. His second wife once called him a 'destroyer of cameras.' I didn't see that. He treated them pretty decently the times I was with him. But I was in the testing lab of *Popular Photography* magazine. I knew my stuff, and I guess I am mechanically inclined." So Russ was an ideal candidate for camera-related brain-picking—at any hour.

Connecticut neighbor Jimmy Zaccaro, another professional photographer, also noticed Roger's technical deficiencies, which could be quite basic. "He'd come to me and ask why the lights and the meters weren't functioning," says Zaccaro. "I said, 'Well, Roger, at the end of the day when you put your equipment away, you've got to turn the buttons off so that they are ready and fully charged the next morning.' He didn't get that."

Photography was a form of therapy for him—Roger said constantly—after he'd been stuck painting field guide plates and he could finally be set free to do one of the things he loved best—

watch birds through the lens of the latest photographic equipment and snap away.

"Roger was always behind his camera," Lady Philippa Scott says. "We used to deplore the fact that he was so busy photographing. . . . Everything had to be photographed to the exclusion of sort of actually looking at things."

George Harrison agrees: "It's difficult, we've all found, to watch birds and take pictures of birds at the same time because the only birdwatching you do is through the lens of a camera. You miss something by doing that."

But Roger really did see the birds through the camera lens as well as through every other avenue possible. "Dad was always looking at birds," says son Lee. "He was always seeing and keeping track of them. He was always coming to the dinner table and saying such and such a bird was singing outside the studio. . . . It's one of the ways that he kept track of his world, kept order in his world. Somebody would take a look at a watch; Dad would watch what warbler was migrating through to know the time of season."

Keith Shackleton remembers Roger's habit of engaging in "saturation photography." While he might have taken many more images than necessary, he was apt to get that ideal one he sought amid the prodigious dross. Shackleton explains: "If you are running with a motor drive through a whole sequence of an albatross circling the ship, you're going to find one where everything is absolutely right. You've got the albatross and an iceberg and everything in the right juxtaposition . . . , and the others are probably hopeless, because you've got somebody's left ear in it, or something."

"I am a compulsive photographer who shoots an appalling amount of film but sells relatively little of it for actual reproduction," Roger revealed in his introduction to Russ Kinne's *The Complete Book of Photographing Birds.* He said he needed these images for his frequent talks, and also as a reference for his art to make sure he accurately represented any bird he painted.

Russ comments: "He did some beautiful, beautiful photography. And what was not absolutely superb photography he used as . . . reference for his own paintings. . . . It was very valuable to him, even if the sun wasn't quite right or the shutter speed . . . , [or] it was too dark. . . . He'd get the information out of his own photographs. In the behavior, for instance. How does the wing look when it's about to take off? Even if it's a lousy picture, he would get information out of it."

Roger didn't keep all of his pictures. Jane Kinne, who served as Roger's photo editor almost from the time they met in 1950, discarded a lot of it. "I would appear at his request," she said, "or if there was a project, I would be on whatever schedule had been arranged and go up to Old Lyme and sit there over the light box with my loupe and decide what we were going to present or what was the best of a group. Roger was reasonably good about doing his own preliminary edit, which got rid of, you know, when the camera goes off when you didn't need it to."

Ultimately Jane Kinne edited over one million photos taken by Roger Tory Peterson; by the time he died, the number of images stored in his studio had been whittled down to 516,000. With such a plethora of pictures, one would assume Roger didn't mind people perusing them. But one would be wrong.

"For years, he had these half million photographs," says Roger's agent, Arthur Klebanoff. "He had selected fifty or seventy that, from his point of view, were OK pictures. Anybody asked the question, 'I want to use a picture,' they could pick from the fifty or seventy. Anybody asked the question, 'I gather you have more than these.' 'Yes.' 'Can I pick from any of those?' 'No.' 'Can I see them?' 'No.'"

Virtually everyone was "limited, literally, to a handful of shots Roger had picked out years before," Klebanoff adds. "He said, 'Take it or leave it. I don't care.'"

Roger's stubbornness may have harmed his photographic legacy. People have seen few of his pictures, so as a body of work they are discounted. Jane Kinne asserted that, actually, his achievements as a photographer are *not* underappreciated precisely *because* "he never pushed it." Presumably if Roger had touted his photos and approved their wide distribution but saw them dismissed, *then* they could be considered underappreciated. She said: "Things would appear with articles, but very few people had any idea of the depth behind. I was one of the photo editors on . . . [Roger's book *Penguins*]. You have no idea what was behind those few photographs! . . . He made seventeen trips to the Antarctic! Penguins figured in all of them! . . .You'd look at . . . [the photo files] and say, 'How can I possibly get through all this?'"

Besides Jane Kinne, George Harrison was one of the few whom Roger permitted to "rifle through his files," as Harrison put it. Harrison had his pick of pictures for *National Wildlife* magazine articles.

Wherever Roger went, he had cameras and lenses hanging from his neck and often someone trailing behind toting the rest of his equipment. The lucky toter could be Barbara, a young protégé, even Arthur Klebanoff.

Although Roger was notorious for constantly depressing the camera shutter, crowding his studio with the spoils of his shooting sprees, he sometimes patiently labored over a scene to secure the best possible image. Kenn Kaufman recalls an early-1990s trip to Arizona. Stopping at some ponds in Wilcox, Kaufman amused himself by exploring the area's avifauna while Roger struggled for at least two hours in extreme heat to obtain that flawless shot of avocets feeding among flooded grasses. "He didn't take a huge number of photos," says Kaufman. "But he was really concentrating and focusing that whole time on getting just the right artistic photo of the avocets with this grass in the water. . . . He was pretty single-minded in his focus on that."

As with his interest in getting that perfect shot, Roger also concerned himself with the impact of nature photography on nature appreciation.

In 1957 Jane Kinne married Russ and left Audubon; the following year she joined Photo Researchers, a photo licensing agency, first as the head of the natural history department, then as vice president until her 1993 retirement. "One of the first people who arrived on my doorstep was Roger. He said, 'I want you to tell me how this works, what's going on.'" Soon, he moved his images from Audubon to Photo Researchers. Although he was not a huge promoter of his photography, if he wanted something seen, said Kinne, Photo Researchers was "reaching a much wider audience" than Audubon ever could. Eventually, Audubon followed, asking Kinne to manage their files under contract.

Said Kinne: "Roger mentored me, but it was a two-way street. He kept me abreast of everything I needed to know natural historywise, made sure I read or had certain reference books at hand. . . . I in turn would answer questions for him about what the standards were in photography, what was happening, how do we properly archive things, what information should be with the photo." Kinne went on to be active in numerous professional photography organizations, acted as appraiser of photographic collections, and served varyingly as a consultant or an expert witness in hundreds of state and federal court cases pertaining to professional photography. It wasn't surprising that Roger hired her as his photo editor.

Kinne's impressive curriculum vitae didn't keep Roger from teasing her, though. In fact, it provided the perfect fodder for many mischievous, verbal go-rounds. "It would get intense enough at times that Ginny Peterson never, ever adjusted to the idea that he would get on my case and tease and tease and tease. She would become uncomfortable." Roger and Ginny invited Jane and Russ down to the Antarctic in December 1993. On Christmas Eve, the Kinnes shared a bottle of champagne with the Petersons and others on board ship.

"We broke out the champagne and were wishing everybody a Merry Christmas and Roger got started," said Jane. "He was teasing me to death—'What are you going to do this year?' 'Who are you going to sue?' 'Which photographer's in trouble?' I would keep answering, and he would keep going. Finally, Ginny was so uncomfortable, she said, 'Roger, finish your drink. We're going to our cabin.' As he stood up and was leaving, he turned and wished us both a Merry Christmas. He put his finger on the end of my nose, as he had done for forty-odd years. He looked me straight in the eye, and said, 'You know I didn't mean a word of it.'"

Jane said she never felt awkward when Roger teased. On the other hand, she wasn't afraid to retaliate: "I was once guilty of telling him to shut up! Everybody stopped and looked at me. He didn't say a word. He knew he'd asked for it."

Kinne's expertise presented an educational opportunity for the Roger Tory Peterson Institute of Natural History, founded in Jamestown in 1985. Understandably excited about the institute's promise, Roger assigned Jane and a woman named Ann Guilfoyle the task of planning the first wildlife photographer forum, to be held at Jamestown Community College under the institute's auspices. One hundred and forty of the "busiest and most well-known wildlife photographers" attended the three-day session, said Kinne. At its conclusion, "What Roger had hoped for happened. Frans Lanting got up and said, 'This has been so great. We are not going to let this be the only one.'" About seventeen people, including

Jane and Roger, stayed on to talk about a possible wildlife photography association. After awhile, Roger "famously stood up and
said, 'I think it's time I go home. Jane will see that this happens."

"Hence, I got stuck," Kinne remembered. But it was a good
kind of stuck. As a result of Roger's command, the North American Nature Photography Association was born. NANPA, three
thousand members strong, holds annual summits and regional
forums and brings in high school and college students to mingle
with prominent wildlife photographers and go on field trips with
them. The organization's mission is to promote nature photography, establish professional standards for creating the material
and handling it commercially, nurture its artistic side, and further the environmental cause.

"The most telling mentoring picture in my mind that involves
Roger was at the first of these meetings which occurred in Fort
Myers in [January] 1995," Jane recalled. "He was the one who
said, 'We all of us professional photographers want to talk to one
another.' I kept looking up and finding him seated on a wicker sofa,
with all these students all around! And great discussions going on!
I would just stand there and sort of say, 'I can't believe this!'"

Chapter Seventeen

Painterly Birds

In May 1971 following a trip on the *Lindblad Explorer* with Keith Shackleton, Roger wrote to remind him of a conversation they had had on board about painting. Admitting that he had done only two oil paintings in the last decade, Roger surmised: "Now that I have put a new wing on the studio I can sling paint around more freely." He hoped that Keith could share with him trade secrets he had forgotten or lost track of, such as whether Shackleton painted on canvas, canvasboard, or some other surface; and the brand of oil paints and kinds of brushes he preferred. "I frankly don't know what is currently available or preferable," Roger confided.

"It says a lot about Roger's feeling of being artistically shackled by demand for his guide book illustrations—and longing to get out and paint 'pictures,'" writes Shackleton now. "He was always pressing me on these sorts of issues—and Peter Scott too."

The older he got the more Roger openly fretted that he hadn't devoted enough time to "painterly painting" of birds. It wasn't that he hadn't done a lot of bird painting in his life prior to writing Keith that letter. He hadn't just done field guide plates. Besides the numerous illustrations he drew or painted for other books, magazine features, and charitable or educational purposes, he had contracts with various companies to sell his bird art. In the 1940s it was Quaker State. In the 1950s, there were meat manufacturer John Morrell & Company and printing and greeting card company Barton-Cotton Inc. Roger painted bird vignettes for mass-produced prints, calendars, bird games (such as "Bird-O,"

a bird-related, bingoish, educational game for children), and collectible tea cards.

Over the years Roger had done few bird portraits or, better
yet, paintings with a full background—"painterly painting," as he
called it. He also craved the respect he believed he deserved as an
artist. The idea of being regarded as a mere illustrator of birds
bothered him immensely. After all, he reasoned, he was trained
and had the talent to be an artist.

But why did Roger care whether he was regarded as an artist?
He had an adoring public—those who loved birds loved him, not
just in North America but in many parts of the world. He lacked
a college degree but was regarded as a scientist by the most educated scientists. He was friend to some of the most brilliant, talented, accomplished, and fascinating people in the world. Every
year he visited exotic places around the globe. He had made a positive impact on thousands, perhaps millions, of people's lives, and
on the lives of the plants, animals, and ecosystems being admired
and saved as a result of his work. His field guides and other books
were best sellers. He was raking in money by doing what he loved.
(Paul Spitzer calls Roger a human oxymoron—a "millionaire naturalist.") So what was the problem?

Rob Hernandez may have the answer. "He was a very simple
man in many ways," he says. "Unostentatious. Certainly, he had
an ego . . . [which evidenced itself] through his pride in his work.
He was horribly competitive. . . . He was always driving himself.
He was, in a sense, . . . somewhat insecure in his own abilities. He
never believed in his own greatness."

For Roland Clement, Roger's quest for respect as an artist was
misplaced:

> *He was not an artist. . . . He became a good illustrator, not an art-*
> *ist. An illustrator and an artist are very different animals. . . . He*
> *was a competent illustrator of birds and he got promoted to heaven,*
> *you might say, because the general public became interested in*

birds and they took him as their guru. I didn't expect him to be an artist, but you must not claim what you are not. He constantly [said], "I want to go back to paint the kind of pictures that I was trained to paint in art school," which he never did. And I could see that he never would.

It's hard not to peruse, say, *The World of Birds* and keep your mouth from hanging open. The colors, the variety of animated bird scenes, all of which seem as based in reality and clothed in the essence of life as anything in Roger's field guides, without the static nature of his field guide portraiture, make one wonder why these couldn't be considered painterly painting. The montage on page nineteen of bird feathers of species found around the world would look gorgeous in someone's living room.

Wild America isn't primarily known for Roger's black-and-white drawings. Yet it's impossible not to appreciate them while reading of Roger and James's adventures across the continent. Despite the fact that the drawings are by definition illustrations, not conceived in some part of the brain freed from the dictates of the text, they can exist independently of it. Individual birds, butterflies, mammals, and plants, plus cliff, forest, and jungle scenes beg for enlargement and wall space. "He had [wildlife artist Francis Lee] Jaques there as a model," says Paul Spitzer, "and nobody could better sketch halftones than Francis Jaques." But Spitzer says the competitive side of Roger set out to at least equal Jaques—and bettered him.

A sampling of Jaques's black-and-white drawings—deft and pretty—can be seen in Louis Halle's *Spring in Washington*. By comparison, Roger's drawings in *Wild America* are extremely rich, offering up the natural world whole, stimulating the senses.

But this wasn't painterly painting. What was holding Roger back? "Dad, I think, if he had been a fine artist in the traditional sense," says Lee Peterson, "always would have had an eye on his audience. That was his makeup to be so. It was in his personality, as opposed to somebody who didn't give a damn what people thought, who lived in poverty and painted whatever he wanted and was discovered after he was dead. Dad wanted to be discovered when he was alive."

That audience motivated Roger to return to the drawing board and paint something he hoped would be more lasting than his book illustrations. He apparently just needed someone to come along and say that if he painted birds, the images would be sold. And not sold any old way but as limited-edition, signed and numbered prints. Not sold by, for example, a meat manufacturer but by a new firm dedicated to promoting wildlife art as legitimate unto itself, as a bias still existed against viewing wildlife art as worthy of the automatic respect that human-related art had historically been given. The aim of the new firm would be to gain exposure for a variety of wildlife artists.

Roger's old friend Bob Lewin had an epiphany in the early 1970s as a new retiree. Lewin had served as Roger's informal career adviser since the late 1940s when he was a salesman for Brett Litho and Roger was haplessly trying to administer the National Wildlife Federation's art program. Now that Lewin was retired and had moved to Florida, after living for decades in Rye, New York, he needed something to keep him busy. For a time, he had a puzzle company, Spring Bok. Roger's painting of penguins was a Spring Bok best seller. Then Lewin had another idea. What about becoming a publisher of wildlife art?

"You paint it," Lewin told Roger. "I'll publish it."

Katie Lewin says: "Roger was the foremost bird artist in the country, who wanted to do what he called easel painting. He'd been doing his books for so long, . . . that he wanted to make a statement by showing that he could do the—put quotes around it—easel painting."

In 1973 at age sixty-five, Roger became the first artist, along with fellow bird artist Maynard Reece, in the Mill Pond Press roster of painters. Mill Pond, based in Venice, Florida, quickly became a major art publisher, not just a hobby to keep Bob Lewin from boredom. The relationship between Mill Pond on the one hand and Peterson and Reece on the other was a symbiotic one. "It was good for Mill Pond," says the Lewins' daughter, Laurie Lewin Simms, "because when you begin a company you want to lead with your best possible choices. . . . As soon as we began to publish Roger and Maynard, . . . their reputations then increased even more, because Mill Pond really, really worked hard at creating a market." Eventually, such great talents as Brits Keith Shackleton and Peter Scott and Canadian Robert Bateman became Mill Pond artists.

Roger was responsible for bringing Bob Bateman to Mill Pond. It happened in 1975 at an exhibition of Animals in Art at the Royal Ontario Museum in Toronto. It happened because, in the mid-1960s, Roger had admired a wildebeest painting by Bateman hanging in the Nairobi home of a mutual acquaintance. Ten years later at the Toronto art exhibit, "Roger singled me out to . . . Bob Lewin . . . [who had] asked Roger . . . , 'Here we have a gathering of the clans of the supposed top animal artists. I want to increase my stable. Who should I go for?' Without hesitation, . . . Roger said, 'Oh—try to get Bateman.' . . . [That was] the most important event in my career. Without the [Mill Pond] prints, I doubt there would have been [Bateman] books out, because prints gave me that fame and got my name spread around and then the books came, et cetera."

To Bateman's surprise, Roger approached him and gave him a personalized tour of the exhibit. "Here I was with this legend who was more or less taking me by the arm and saying, 'Come on over here and look at this.' He was critiquing other people's art, whose names I guess I won't mention, . . . and saying how hopeless his elephant painting was. And then I had a pair of elephants, and contrasting that. I mean, you can imagine. I was a youngish guy then, and here I am going around with this legend, and here he is candidly knocking other people's work and praising me. It was pretty heady stuff. He was always very candid and very frank. I think he was this way with everybody. He wasn't a . . . smooth operator. He was a straight shooter."

Although Roger began his affiliation with Mill Pond by painting vignettes—that is, portraits of birds perched on a branch of a tree or a bush that was ecologically related to the individual bird à la Fuertes—these were different from much of what he had done before. His Barton-Cotton paintings tended to be folksy pictures of bird parents—house wrens, barn swallows, horned larks—feeding their begging young, images to warm the heart. Roger's Mill Pond vignettes showed birds, admittedly common or famous ones, in all their glory. Robins, cardinals, wood thrushes, Baltimore orioles, peregrine falcons, and more, posed front and center, haughtily modeling their fine plumage, seemingly declaring, "I'm an important creature. Just as important as you humans."

The Mill Pond prints had an educational component that made Roger's status as a Mill Pond artist a perfect extension of his field guide authorship. Laurie Lewin Simms says that the artists answered such questions as, "Why did you paint this? Where were you?" "[Mill Pond] . . . asked the artists interview-type questions which would elaborate on their thought process, their technical process, and the trials and tribulations of being a naturalist. . . . It really brought people face-to-face with—'What was it like to be in the great outdoors?'"

Accompanying the prints—sold as both nonlimited decorator prints plus signed, numbered, limited-edition prints on thick "all-rag imported paper"—were cards providing an overview of the artist's background and a statement about the painting. Roger explained his method of achieving the right red for the scarlet tanager's plumage: "To get the fiery glow in this painting I first laid in a wash of clear yellow, then the red, allowing the yellow to glow through. The white of the paper would have resulted in a cooler, less vibrant red." He drew the foliage the tanager was set against from twigs he "snipped" from tulip trees growing near home. Regarding the black-eyed Susans he had male and female bobolinks sitting in, he explained that the flowers, which moved east with the fragmentation of Appalachian forests, had lately "gone riot" around his studio, so he "could not resist" including them in his composition.

Roger offered a conservationist statement about his vignette of male and female eastern bluebirds. Early in the century, he noted, the introduced starling appropriated the nesting holes normally used by the bluebird and ate the berries the bluebird relied on to survive winter. The bluebird's "orchards were sprayed even more intensively, wiping out their insect food," Roger continued. "In tobacco growing areas several million bluebirds perished in the smokestacks of a new type of oil burner that came into use." He concluded by observing that the bluebird's numbers were now bolstered by the availability of nest boxes erected by birdwatchers. (He didn't mention that it was he who had recommended doing this nearly forty years earlier.)

Within several years Roger devoted time to some of that painterly painting he wanted to get his brushes around. There was the puffin scene with waves crashing over the rocks. Laurie Lewin Simms remarks: "As far as I'm concerned, his most artistically successful piece ever was his puffin painting. . . . If you look at that painting, you can feel the wind, you can feel the movement of the water, you can feel that you are right there as the puffins are interacting with each other and with the sea breeze." Other painterly paintings included two of the mystical snowy owl, as well as ones of stately raptors like gyrfalcons and golden eagles.

In 1976 John and Alice Forester of Wausau, Wisconsin, decided to convert their home into a public fine arts museum. Searching for ideas, they enlisted the help of local nature artist Owen Gromme, who suggested an exhibition focusing on birds. Realizing they needed assistance from someone with connections to organize the event, they contacted Wisconsin resident George Harrison.

"Of course, I was happy to do that. I organized the first show," says Harrison. "Because I was the managing editor of *National Wildlife,* I knew who the top bird artists were in the country—actually, the world. Roger Tory Peterson was one of them. After that first exhibition, which was enormously successful . . . , we decided to make it an annual event."

The initial event, at what would become known as the Leigh Yawkey Woodson Art Museum (named in honor of Alice Forester's mother), was dubbed Birds of the Lakes, Fields, and Forests; its permanent name became Birds in Art once it was transformed into an annual September affair, for which Harrison consulted another twelve times. Soon the organizers unveiled the Master Wildlife Artist Award. Owen Gromme was its first recipient. The following year, it was George Sutton. The third, Roger Tory Peterson. "I got to present [Roger] with the medal and give a speech about his life and his contributions and all that sort of thing in front of a crowd," says Harrison, proudly.

Roger was also a frequent presenter of the medal, draping it around the necks of Gromme, Robert Bateman, Guy Coheleach, and Kent Ullberg. "They had so much respect for him," says Marcia Theel, the museum's associate director and public relations coordinator.

It was tough being a bird artist. Human narcissism prevented bird art from being respected. Art depicting the natural world, without homo sapiens as the focus, was dismissed as "genre painting." Birds in Art became the place for like-minded artists to meet, share ideas, and commiserate. "There were not very many venues for this sort of exchange to take place," says Kathy Kelsey Foley, the museum's director. "These artists worked largely in a vacuum. Especially people like Dr. Peterson, Arthur Singer, who worked under some pressure from their publishers to produce, produce, and produce on deadline, and Roger talked about wanting to do real painting, his easel painting. . . . The opportunity for him to do what he considered a higher . . . calling of artwork and then come together with other artists who aspired to the same purer art form as opposed to scientific ornithology illustration work . . . , that was really, I think, a privilege."

Roger was the star attraction at Birds in Art. His active participation every year lent prestige to the event. "It brought together his two most favorite things," says Marcia Theel. "Birds and art. He had the stature in both fields."

"The people in the community, in the region, wanted to participate in our opening festivities," says Foley. "There's a huge bird-watching population out there and the public certainly wanted a piece of Roger while he was here. Roger, of course, thrived on that. . . . They wanted their catalogs signed. They wanted their field guides signed."

Prior to the exhibition's opening to the public on the first Saturday following Labor Day, the Woodson Art Museum hosts an informal gathering on Friday afternoon with the artists, which Roger enjoyed immensely. "We always had cookies and bars and coffee and Dr. Peterson had an incredible sweet tooth," says Theel.

Foley adds: "He was always with the cookie in the hand and the cup of coffee, talking in these little groups of artists."

The following day, after the Master Wildlife Artist of the year gave his presentation, the artists boarded a bus for a private event in northern Wisconsin. "I can remember Dr. Peterson always being the last person to get on the bus," Theel recalls. "People were stopping him all the way from the main gallery up to the bus. They were with him, step by step, all the way, wanting to talk, wanting to share ideas, hear what he had to say, talk about their own birding experiences. . . . He loved to chitchat."

Roger's association with Mill Pond Press facilitated his involve-ment with Birds in Art. Because of Mill Pond, he was painting again and had new works Birds in Art could show.

Bob Lewin was still acting as Roger's informal career adviser, regardless of any effect their decisions might have on Mill Pond. If Roger wondered if he should accept a project, he asked Bob and Bob gave him an honest, thoughtful answer. More frequently Bob had ideas for Roger, such as an art show requiring Lewin to locate people with rare pieces Roger might have sold decades earlier. Lewin also labored to get Roger the recognition he believed his friend deserved, whether it was an award or just favorable public-ity, and had Mill Pond assemble any materials necessary to sup-port a Peterson-centered event.

Lewin also looked after his friend's well-being. In 1976 the entrepreneur arranged an interview with Roger by Canadian art experts David and Ellen Lank to highlight Roger's artistic back-ground and philosophy, as well as his knowledge of art history. The talk dragged on for quite a while. Although Roger didn't complain, Lewin interrupted: "I think we ought to take a break for a while and let Roger eat."

Ellen Collard, now public relations director at Mill Pond, started with the company at its 1973 inception and was the per-son Bob Lewin relied on to do something difficult—and quickly. In October 1973 Roger was to receive the Joseph Wood Krutch Medal from the Humane Society of the United States. Lewin assigned Collard the last-minute task of ensuring that the event featured some of Roger's art. "The only way to get the artwork up there was for me to fly up and take it as baggage," says Collard. "These were prints. With frames. That's one of those times you don't really forget. Mr. Lewin called at nine o'clock in the morning. I had to go to the framer. I don't think he was normally open on Saturday. Anyway, he spent the day getting these four done. We . . . picked them up and had to pack them and get on the plane the next morning. That was kind of a Mr. Lewin schedule."

"We worked hard to burnish the star of any artist whom we published and believed had superior talent," says Laurie Lewin Simms. "In the beginning, we did all of that without any thought of what it might cost us in raw financial terms, what it might cost us in terms of time. Later on we started to become aware of that, but in the beginning, it was just fun. It was great fun to see wonderful honors come to somebody like Roger."

Dealing with somebody like Roger had its downside. "It was rare," says Ellen Collard, "to receive a new painting [from Roger]. We were very grateful for what we received." Bob Lewin often pestered Roger to get that latest painting out of Old Lyme and down to Venice. "I think it was when Roger was painting the barn owl," Collard remembers. "Mr. Lewin had flown up to Connecticut to pick up the painting. Roger was rather notorious for, 'I'll have it finished in two days.' 'I'll have it finished in a week.' 'I'll have it finished in another day.' Mr. Lewin went up, partly to put pressure on him . . . because it was kind of a situation where Roger could go on forever when he didn't need to. . . . I think Mr. Lewin ended up spending a week there. He was getting very exasperated!

"He gave him some kind of a hard time about what . . . he hadn't gotten done. Roger looked at him and said, 'Well, if you look at what I *have* done.' Roger turned it on him—of all the field guides that he'd been involved with, and the photography. That he had accomplished a lot." Roger was a stickler for detail and "very methodical about what he did," says Collard. "He would really labor over the concepts of the paintings. Yes, [he had] very high standards."

Despite Roger's typical immovability, Bob Lewin maintained a great affection for him. "Oh, yes," says Katie Lewin. "He did. And the patience to go with it. I wouldn't have been so patient."

Bob Lewin's devotion brought Roger and Arthur Klebanoff together. Not long after the fourth edition of Roger's eastern guide came out in 1980 and sold over a million copies, Lewin was approached by American Express and the Danbury Mint to feature Roger's Mill Pond art on collectible plates. Lewin didn't want to involve Mill Pond in licensing, so he phoned Klebanoff, then a law partner in Janklow, Traum & Klebanoff and also increasingly involved in Janklow's side vocation, that of being a literary agent.

Although Klebanoff wasn't a birder, he knew of Peterson because of the impressive numbers the eastern guide's fourth edition had sold. "It's not every day that [the business partner of] an author who sells millions of books . . . calls up," he says. "So I didn't need any briefing to know that this represented a major opportunity." Klebanoff got Roger a deal with American Express, which had outbid the Danbury Mint. Subsequently, he got Roger a contract with the Danbury Mint for large vases sporting Roger's work. The mint sold ten thousand vases at $125 each.

It was some years before Klebanoff also represented Roger in literary matters. Meanwhile, one licensing deal, complete except for all parties' signatures, died at the hands of truth telling. Klebanoff had spent several months negotiating a licensing agreement with the Franklin Mint for a line of bird figurines based on Roger's paintings. The exciting day arrived when everyone would meet face-to-face. This was also the day Arthur first met Roger. Klebanoff hired a limousine to take Roger and Ginny from New York to the Philadelphia suburbs. The trip began well enough. "While you would think that riding the New Jersey Turnpike is a horrible way to spend a couple of hours with anybody," says Klebanoff, "with him, he's looking out the window, testing Ginny on birds flying over, what's growing on the side of the road. It was really pretty amazing."

Franklin Mint representatives offered lunch and samples of other bird figurines the company had produced. "They put out their examples of the best things they'd ever done," Klebanoff remembers. "Some of them had cost $500. . . . And Roger takes one look at everything—it wasn't that he thought it was ugly or pretty. He just picked it apart for accuracy."

"I thought we were going to have a food fight," he laughingly continues. "The people at the other end of the table started turning color. The meeting was over before it started. . . . Roger didn't do it on purpose. He definitely didn't care whether the people at the other side of the table were happy or unhappy with him. His view was 'I will tell you what I think.' I never heard him raise his voice to anybody about anything. He was the lowest-keyed, most affable, positive guy you could possibly encounter."

Roger was concerned that Klebanoff would be angry with him for, essentially, sabotaging the deal. "No," Klebanoff says. "The position I took was, 'Look. My job is to make you happy. . . . Let's forget it. What are we supposed to do? Just write it off.'"

The two-hour return ride could have been awful, but it wasn't: "Out of that ride came the Easton project. And the Easton project is fifty times the size of whatever could have happened with the Franklin Mint." Klebanoff is referring to Easton Press, which signed on to publish leather-bound reissues of the entire Peterson field guide series in honor of the original field guide's fiftieth anniversary. Since then, Klebanoff has worked with Easton Press on other, non-Peterson-related transactions. The Franklin Mint debacle thus had a happy ending.

Mill Pond Press found Roger an audience he otherwise wouldn't have had. People who bought bird art prints, or bird plates or bird vases weren't necessarily birders. Associating with other bird artists at the Woodson Art Museum was at least pleasant for Roger and ought to have boosted his self-regard.

But was he really an artist or just an illustrator? Ohio art dealer Jay Brown, owner of ArtUSA.com, believes that Roger was a pioneer in bringing respectability to bird art. "Without Roger, I don't think the guys who are the collectible guys of today could have been there," says Brown. "Experts would say, 'This isn't really art. This is illustration!' Now some of the most collectible and respected artists in our industry are wildlife guys."

Did Roger convince the art intelligentsia that he was an *important,* or even *good,* bird artist? Jay Brown thinks that "talent is talent. If people want to create fabulous artwork that people want to hang in their homes, that they want to enjoy, that makes every day of their lives better, that perhaps provides collectibility, I think that's fine art."

But will Roger's work stand the test of time? "There's a special look to Roger's pieces," says Brown. "If I could put a piece of Roger's . . . on a wall, and put a piece by a dozen other great wildlife painters on the wall, and ask you . . . to stand back, don't see the artists' names, and tell me which one is the Roger Tory Peterson, you can do it. He's got his own look, . . . maybe because of the preciseness of everything. He did it his own way. . . . That's one of the reasons that some artists have staying power as collectible."

Michigander Earl Ryan, a longtime Peterson guide user, has all of Mill Pond's signed, limited edition Peterson prints. "We did not buy them as investments," he says. "We bought them because we liked them and we wanted to look at them and display them. If their value went down to zero, I wouldn't care."

Speaking with Roger's friends and fans can be instructive. To his sometime editor Les Line, his Mill Pond paintings are "absolutely magnificent." "Bob Lewin," he says, "gave Roger a chance to really show the world what he could do with fine art." Fleur Ng'weno regards Roger as an artist of genius. While art dealer and appraiser Russell Fink is not particularly taken with Roger's Mill Pond prints, he was taken aback by the beauty of the field guide paintings, all 2,600 plates, upon appraising them after Roger's death. "In the field guides, when they were printed, the birds were flat, lackluster," he says. "His originals are stunning. . . . [When I did the appraisals] Roger's status, in my mind, went up drastically. It took a big jump . . . . When you picked up the field guide, [and looked at] the same plate, . . . the publication just didn't do justice to it."

Canadian author-naturalist John Livingston admired Roger's field guide art, even on the printed page. "Look at one of the recent guides—Mexico, for example," he wrote in the 1970s. "These plates are more than collections of diagrams. Each, in its own right, is a delightful, attractive design. Peterson sometimes crams as many as thirty individual birds into a plate, and yet somehow contrives to have the plate maintain a design integrity of its own."*

(Indeed, plate 30 in *A Field Guide to Mexican Birds,* showing the jay species, is an exemplar of inspired Peterson design. Dominating is the black-throated race of the magpie jay, exceedingly long tail trailing down the page, effectively acting as support bar to the smaller jays' upturned tails. The plate became an early Mill Pond Press print.)

Yet some of Roger's biggest fans are not huge fans of his paintings. "Roger was terribly good at what he did," says Wildlife Conservation Society's Bill Conway. "But it doesn't take any expert to tell you that he was not a super-duper great artist, which he would not like to have heard. . . . That's not to say that he didn't, from time to time, come out with something quite wonderful. But there are some really marvelous natural history artists around. Let's not kid ourselves about that."

"He painted birds fine for a guide," says bird artist Richard Parks, who as a teen in 1936 first met Roger at an Atlanta Bird Club meeting. "The only thing you want to do is show the bird so you can identify it. Now, my object, and the object of most bird painters, is to paint the bird the way it is. . . . To make it really look

---

* The maximum number of birds on a plate in the Mexican guide is actually twenty-six; most have far fewer.

like a living bird . . . Make it look alive. Make it look like it's got feathers on it. Peterson never could do that."

Funny enough, Roger's main deficiency as an artist, in the eyes of the art intelligentsia, was that his birds looked *too* much like they really were. To them his paintings were too representational rather than not representational enough. This was the same hurdle sculptor Kent Ullberg faced as an art student dissuaded by teachers from sculpting true-to-life animals.

"His paintings were not necessarily wall-to-wall paintings with the bird playing a secondary role," observes Ullberg, who continues,

> *His paintings were more what we call vignettes, where the bird is prominent and he used foliage as a design element around the birds. But so did Audubon. And so did many of the great bird artists. . . . You mustn't forget the time, the period, that Roger worked in. . . . At that time in New York, and in academia, representational art was barely considered art and certainly not bird paintings or nature paintings. Those were considered illustration, period. They were not looked at as fine art. Neither was my work. . . . Roger, I must say, in all our discussions, was quite pained by that. . . . That the art scene and the art world . . . were somewhere else. I remember one expression that Roger had that he always brought up: "They're always looking for subconscious comment!"*

Ullberg remembers Roger's retort for the art establishment: "The subconscious comment here is our love for what we do—our love for nature!"

Roger often said: "If I were to paint like another bird artist I would choose Robert Bateman." Bateman was flattered, of course, but his approach to nature painting differs from Roger's in a way that suggests a major philosophical difference—his birds and other animals tend to fit into a landscape without necessarily being central to the picture. Bateman describes this as a "total environment painted in a fairly particular, detailed style, but not like a Hallmark card. It's a little more slice of life, chunk of the real planet, not prettied up." He sees Roger's paintings as decorative arrangements, perhaps influenced by the latter's early workaday experience decorating furniture. Roger would have agreed with that, declaring in 1976: "Frankly, I'm not as comfortable with the full environmental thing as I am with the open white background treatment. I think possibly this goes back to the old furniture decorating days when we simply used open Oriental designs on a solid tone, usually on a black background."

Bateman says even Roger's full environmental paintings are more like arrangements than slice-of-life scenes. (He is quick to note that Michelangelo's and da Vinci's paintings are too.) But Roger didn't care to be completely true to life, saying more than once that the "dilemma that a bird painter faces is how to handle the fact that nature, by pattern and so on, tends to obliterate form." Bateman doesn't worry about obliterating the bird's form, speculating that great art might be regarded as such because it has an "air of mystery," something Roger's work lacks. "To get a sense of mystery," Bateman acknowledges, "you have to destroy part of the beauty of the bird." Roger loved birds too much to omit something or mar a lovely or interesting characteristic. "It would go against the grain," says Bateman.

The conversation thus returns to the subconscious comment Roger thought his work contained—his love of what he did, his love for nature. And what did he love most about nature? Birds.

While Roger understood what he was painting and why, he remained dissatisfied with his painting career. "Poor old Roger, in latter years, became a little bit introspective and a little bit self-critical," says Keith Shackleton. "He was often saying, 'If only I'd spent my life painting lovely atmospheric pictures like Peter Scott does, and the sort of things that you do, then I would have been really happy.' And I said, 'You're talking absolute rubbish, because there is nobody who has done more to further an interest and an understanding of birds than you, through your art. So don't let's have any more of this nonsense about thinking you've wasted your time, because it's the very, very reverse!'"

Part Six:

BIRD MAN
OF BIRD MEN

Chapter Eighteen

Territory under Challenge

The 1970s were a tumultuous time for Roger Tory Peterson as his life went through major changes. Before his divorce from Barbara, before signing on with Mill Pond Press, before optimistically beginning revisions of *A Field Guide to the Birds* (for the fourth edition), the biggest change came at the decade's start, when James Fisher died at fifty-eight.

> *The International Ornithological Congress was held this past September in Holland. Roger attended and was pleased to see James Fisher so cheerful after his hip operation. He was looking forward to dispensing with his cane, but within a month we received the tragic news of his death in a car accident. Roger, who regarded James as his most intimate friend in the ornithological world, has been very much depressed.*

So wrote Barbara in the Petersons' January 1971 New Year's letter. But it was worse for Roger than she reported. She solemnly admits, shaking her head and pursing her lips, that he "never really got over that one."

Roger and James had planned to coauthor a field guide to the world's seabirds. The Old Lyme resident was gathering information for it during his 1965 Antarctic trip with penguin authority Bill Sladen. But, as Roger said at the July 1973 dedication of the Copinsay Islands* as a Royal Society for the Protec-

---

* The Copinsay, a small group of islands off the east coast of northern Scotland, are inhabited only by breeding pelagic birds.

tion of Birds nature reserve in James's memory, "we allowed too many other projects to have priority—and it never really got fully underway."

The depth of Roger's grief is sensed in his words at Copinsay. He revealed more of himself there than he tended to when paying tribute to departed friends. "The loss of one of my dearest friends has left me with a feeling of desolation," he said. "When I fly into London these days it hits me very hard. James was always at the airport to meet me." Their closeness wasn't a secret: "Many people wrote or telephoned me to express their sympathy, as though I had lost a brother."

Roger told Keith Shackleton: "It's like a light's gone from my life."

Although Roger had many enduring friendships, none would ever be as meaningful as his friendship with James.

Losing good friends did nothing to diminish Roger's wariness of mortality.

Bill Vogt died at sixty-six in July 1968. Roger was always sentimental about Vogt; the first through fourth editions of *A Field Guide to the Birds* included a dedication to him for his encouragement to do the guide. Roger considered himself the closest to Vogt of any ornithologist.

Allan Cruickshank retired from Audubon in 1972, dying two years later at sixty-seven. "Cruicky" wrote several books that featured his photography, in 1958 co-authoring with photographer wife, Helen, the enormously helpful *1001 Questions Answered about Birds,* perhaps the first bird book to presage the spirit, if not the format, of today's "idiots" and "dummies" guides.

Months before Cruickshank's death Roger had surprised him with an appearance at an event honoring him at the Indian River Bird Club in Florida, near the Cruickshanks' home. Roger waxed nostalgic about Cruicky as late as 1984 at the dedication of the Cruickshank Nature Trail at Florida's Merritt National Wildlife Refuge.

In 1977 came news of the drowning death of Roger's first wife, Mildred, in a Muscongus Bay, Maine, boating accident.

The reality of encroaching years was inescapable at a melancholy February 1978 reunion of the Bronx County Bird Club in Fort Myers, Florida. The club's barn owl maven, Irving Kassoy, was dying of cancer. Joe Hickey organized the fiftieth anniversary event, set up like a formal ornithological symposium with surviving members plus Helen Cruickshank giving papers and showing films on their preferred avian subjects. For old time's sake, each member was elected an officer; Roger was dubbed "permanent president." Helen became the club's first female member.

"It was a very emotional experience, yet deeply satisfying, being with Irv, you and the rest of the gang," Roger wrote Joe afterward. "For some strange reason we all seemed the same as we were in the heyday of our club. . . . We've always been a very cohesive group but there was that long gap after the various members scattered to distant places."

Kassoy died shortly thereafter, as did another original member, Dick Kuerzi.

A postdivorce letter from Roger to Barbara in Seattle mentioned the Bronx club reunion and wished her a happy fifty-ninth birthday. This sort of letter was rare. Although Barbara tried to keep in touch from time to time, it didn't seem he was hearing from her. Indeed, his November 1978 letter relating news of the Bronx club also reminded her that he turned seventy in August, and updated her on news from the previous year, as if they had had no contact in all that time.

The fact that Barbara, taking care of her elderly mother and working in the Department of Environmental Studies at the University of Washington, kept some of Roger's letters and accumulated newspaper clippings of his activities in later years suggests she maintained positive feelings about him and was still interested in how he was doing.

But Barbara wasn't the only one not hearing from him. Jimmy and Dolores Zaccaro, who early in Roger and Ginny's relationship regularly hosted the couple in their home, found themselves by the mid-1980s cut from the proceedings. "It was hard to get Roger on the phone," remembers Dolores. "I knew when Ginny went shopping. So I would always call on Saturday mornings because she was always out of the house. He always answered. I'd say, 'Roger, how about coming over for dinner?' And he'd say, 'Oh, that's great! That's terrific! I'll tell Ginny.' Then there was nothing she could say. If I got her on the phone, she'd say, 'Oh, I don't know. I don't think Roger's up to it. I don't think he wants to go out.'"

Even people who barely knew Roger and Ginny sensed that, as Dolores says, Roger's third wife was "a little controlling of him." William Zinsser, not even a Peterson acquaintance, noticed this.

Zinsser is a veteran journalist, a valued teacher of writing basics, and the author of the staple instructive work *On Writing Well*. He readily admits that birds are not his subject. In 1992 he was asked to write a profile about Roger for *Audubon* magazine and responded that he "didn't know enough about birds. The only one I can identify for sure is the pigeon, a frequent caller at my Manhattan windowsill." But Zinsser acquiesced after seeing a profile of Roger on PBS called *A Celebration of Birds.* What interested him was Roger the survivor, someone "still going strong" in his eighties, doing what he did best. Zinsser wrote the piece; it was published. This led to his being asked to double its length for use as the text in 1994's *Roger Tory Peterson: The Art and Photography of the World's Foremost Birder,* a Rizzoli Publications coffee table book and the brainchild of Arthur Klebanoff. For Zinsser the book project meant another interview with Roger.

While Roger had led a fascinating life and was clearly an expert in his field, it was "not really much fun" to interview him, Zinsser found. Roger seemed "dour" and "reticent"; getting usable material meant having to "pull everything out of him." Zinsser realizes now that it was much better talking to him on the phone (for follow-up questions) than in person. Then Roger "opened up." But why? The difference was Ginny. She was there for the in-person interviews and didn't let Roger fully answer Zinsser's questions, constantly interjecting her own comments, generally opening with, "What Roger means to say is. . . ." Zinsser considered her "very bossy, a very peremptory woman."

Nowadays Zinsser advises his students to "get rid of the spouse" when interviewing someone.

Roger's daughters-in-law, Janet and Courtney, were Tory's and Lee's advocates in trying to get face time with their Dad.

From 1980 to 1992 Janet and Tory lived just forty minutes from Old Lyme, but it was always an effort to see Roger. Ginny, in charge of Roger's social life, never invited them. Janet typically called to ask Roger and Ginny over, but Ginny, who usually answered the phone, continually declined. When Ashley, Tory's daughter from his first marriage (Roger's only biological grandchild), was visiting from Atlanta, Janet asked if the three of them—Ashley, Janet, and Tory—could visit. "I made every effort to ensure that Ashley would get to see her grandfather," Janet says, "and that her grandfather would know about her and see her develop through the years. But to do that, one had to make an appointment with Virginia." If it was "convenient," Ginny would invite them "to tea."

Janet remembers one weekend when they were in Old Lyme visiting friends and called to ask if they could drop by while they were in town. "We went by midmorning and we were sitting around the living room drinking coffee and chatting," says Janet. "Roger all of a sudden jumped up and said, 'I know what! Let's all go to lunch!' And Virginia said, 'No, no, dear. We've got something else we've got to do.'" Roger acquiesced.

It wasn't that Roger wasn't happy to see them. Janet found him warm and welcoming. He was obviously proud of his granddaughter too for being "academically successful."

Courtney and Lee lived in New Orleans for years, the former repeatedly reminding Ginny that she and Roger were invited to their home. But the in-laws only came once, while in town for an event. Since Courtney and Lee never resided near Old Lyme, making an "appointment" to see the couple was an impossibility. They succeeded with a different tack: If they were passing through Connecticut, Courtney simply called and announced: "Hi! We're coming by!" It would have been awkward for Ginny to respond: "Oh—today is not a good day."

Visiting wasn't comfortable. "We were all on our best behavior the few times we would be around them," says Courtney, adding, "Barbara had a way of talking to you and asking you things and making you feel like she was interested in what you had to say. Ginny didn't have to. Didn't need to. Didn't try to."

As Roger didn't seek an active family life while he was married to Barbara, it isn't surprising that he neglected his fatherly role during his third marriage too. Just as he had relied on Barbara to make proper arrangements concerning household matters, he trusted Ginny to do what was right. Unfortunately, for Ginny, doing what was right meant little time for his side of the family, unless it was somehow unavoidable.

Roger may have been worried about being properly recognized as a serious painter, but he couldn't have been concerned about the attention his work was receiving from educational, natural history, conservation, and ornithological groups. By the 1970s he was receiving awards with increasing regularity. It helped that he was a joiner and at one time or another served on the board of so many organizations. Eventually many of these groups would recognize him for his conservation, writing, and nature-teaching accomplishments. Receiving a fraction of these honors would make the average person lightheaded. Here are a few of his 1970s accolades:

- Frances K. Hutchinson Award from the Garden Club of America in 1970

- Audubon Medal from the National Audubon Society in 1971

- Gold Medal of the World Wildlife Fund, presented by Prince Bernhard of the Netherlands, in 1972

- Golden Key Award for Outstanding Teacher of the Year, from a consortium of teacher's organizations, in 1974

- Conservation Achievement Award from the National Wildlife Federation in 1975

- Linnaeus Gold Medal from the Swedish Academy of Sciences, presented by Swedish King Carl XVI Gustav, in 1976

- Order of the Golden Ark from the Netherlands in 1978

By the end of the 1970s, Roger had nine honorary doctorates to his name. His common public appellation as "Dr. Peterson" was all the more solidified in the general consciousness.

By then, friends were pushing for Roger to receive one very illustrious award absent from his mantel. Victor Emanuel, in 1979 visiting Roger and Ginny in Old Lyme, had had an epiphany one night while, unable to sleep, he wandered about their house. "I looked in their dining room, which, when I was there, they never used," says Emanuel. "They always ate in the kitchen. There were these paintings of wildflowers he'd done—these original plates—but there were also these honors he'd gotten, from people like the King of Sweden, and Prince Bernhard of the Netherlands. . . . I thought, 'He's gotten these honors in Europe! He hasn't gotten sufficient honor in the United States, on a national basis. . . . Well, this man is getting along in years and needs to be honored.'"

On the plane home, Emanuel wrote a "rather impassioned letter to President Carter saying . . . [just that], but in more words. That was sometime in the fall. I just forgot about it."

The following May, when Roger and Ginny joined Victor's tour of the Dry Tortugas, they excitedly pulled him aside to relay the news that Roger would be receiving the Presidential Medal of Freedom in June. "We don't know who nominated him or how this came about," Ginny remarked. Emanuel offered that he had written a letter the previous fall. "So they decided my letter had been responsible for starting the ball rolling. Whether it was true or not I have no idea. Some friend of mine was working at the

White House then and somehow gave me an indication that it might have been. Anyway, I don't know."

The Lewins helped also. Katie Lewin recalls her husband, Bob, working "behind the scenes" on Roger's behalf, through "friends of friends." It was most likely a confluence of forces that brought Roger to the White House on that sunny day of June 9, 1980. The honorees were a diverse group: besides Roger were Ansel Adams, Lucia Chase, Archbishop Iakovos, Clarence Mitchell Jr., Admiral Hyman Rickover, Beverly Sills, Robert Penn Warren, Eudora Welty, Tennessee Williams; plus four who had passed away—Rachel Carson, Hubert Humphrey, Lyndon Johnson, and John Wayne.

Said President Carter: "Roger Tory Peterson has achieved distinction as a consummate painter, writer, teacher and scientist. As an unabashed lover of birds and a distinguished ornithologist, he has furthered the study, appreciation and protection of birds the world over. And he has done more. He has impassioned thousands of Americans, and has awakened in millions across this land, a fondness for nature's other two-legged creatures."

Former Delaware governor Russell Peterson (no relation to Roger), then the head of the National Audubon Society, believes Roger was particularly touched by this award. "Roger was super, super pleased with that," says Peterson. "One reason was that Jimmy Carter was the best environmental president we ever had . . . . Roger thought that was the case, which made getting an award from him especially meaningful."

It was quite a day.

Among friends joining Roger in the Rose Garden were Joe Hickey and Lars Lindblad. "We had this wonderful lunch," remembers Victor Emanuel. "It was just done beautifully. The table settings, the food, the whole thing. Carter and [vice president Walter] Mondale were there in the receiving line."

After the ceremony, guests roamed through the White House and its grounds. String quartets played. Tennessee Williams requested show tunes of the U.S. Marine Band. "The most fun part was when I was in the men's room," says Roger's son Tory. "Admiral Rickover came in and I had to explain to him how to use the towel dispenser."

Looking back, Emanuel reflects: "It was just a wonderful feeling that this man had been honored by the president and by our country."

Nineteen eighty was far from a perfect year, though. It was instead a fitting conclusion to a tumultuous decade for Roger of loss and change. And the emphasis in 1980 was *change*.

Roger continued to rue aging. Of the 1978 Canadian Broadcasting Company documentary narrated by John Livingston and filmed by Rudi Kovanic, *Portrait of a Birdwatcher*, he wrote to journalist Roger Caras: "I wish, when I am filmed, the cameramen would give me some makeup or use soft focus and back lighting; I am beginning to look so damned old when shot in harsh sunlight. It is not the vision I have of myself!" In response, Caras recommended a bronzing lotion that would make him "just look good and outdoorsy," and pooh-poohed his friend's hangups about aging: "As far as your growing old, Roger, nonsense. You are just growing, period. Certain people never grow old because in the lives of the rest of us they are constants, anchor points, beacons. No one will ever think of RTP as old!"

Right around that time, Houghton Mifflin published *Penguins*, Roger's homage in photographs, paintings, and words to his favorite family of birds. "He has followed them to the remotest places in the Southern Hemisphere," wrote Frank Graham in *Audubon* magazine of *Penguins* and penguins. "He celebrates his infatuation in his latest book."

An old person wouldn't dare entertain an infatuation with blubbery birds sporting dangerously sharp beaks. An old person wouldn't go by the cutesy monicker King Penguin. This person wasn't old, but young of heart and mind, still full of pep and ambition.

Old? Bah! An old person wouldn't be busy brushing off a bunch of wannabes groping for his King Penguin throne. First came the *Golden Guide* in 1966. By 1979 it was selling 300,000 copies a year. In 1977 another competitor arrived, the *National Audubon Society Field Guide to North American Birds,* boasting multiple authors and photographers but no drawings. Audubon was selling 243,000 copies a year of its eastern edition alone. Annual sales of Roger's 1947 revision of his *A Field Guide to the Birds,* when combined with the 1961 *A Field Guide to Western Birds,* were a paltry 120,000 copies. For now his stature, simply in terms of annual sales of his U.S. bird guides, seemed threatened. But as long as he was on the job, this challenge would soon be settled—favorably, one assumed.

A new Peterson would have to bring a couple of key points up to date. First, it would have to acknowledge the human-caused eastern invasion of the house finch from the west, which had happened somewhat contemporaneously with the publication of Roger's 1947 volume. For over thirty years, his book didn't include the tiny bird, slightly smaller and less brightly colored than the east's purple finch, a close relative. One hoped Peterson users were not misidentifying every house finch as a purple. Then there was the cattle egret, a native of Africa, which Roger predicted in 1952 would begin nesting in the United States. Sure enough, by the following year, it had. The bird soon established a healthy American population, achieved without human encouragement, winging from Africa to northern South America and up from there. This bird too was absent from the 1947 guide.

Roger had been thinking about updating the guide since 1969. He always used his famous collegiality to accomplish anything of substance, including field guide revisions. For his last major revision, that of the western, published in 1961, Roger consulted about one hundred ornithologists and birders regarding everything from birdsong to field marks to ranges. "I shall not list again the mass of ornithological literature digested in the preparation of the 1st edition of this guide, nor the regional works, checklists, papers, and periodicals that went into the compilation of this revision," Roger wrote in the preface. "Assiduously I consulted them all and intentionally ignored none."

Stuart Houston of Yorkton, Saskatchewan, was among thirty ornithologists Roger consulted concerning ranges for the 1961 revision. Roger was loathe to rely on secondary sources, as he indicated to Houston in a November 1959 letter: "Rather than rely on the new A.O.U. Check-list I have gone back to whatever local publications are available (some are not too recent)." Interestingly, approaching one person such as Houston triggered the services of many more individuals. Upon receiving Roger's draft, Houston sent various associates questions of his own, such as:

Roger Tory Peterson wishes to know the status of the Ross' Goose in Saskatchewan. How many definite records have you for Kindersley?

Should you have unpublished [Arctic loon] records for Lake Athabaska of: a) nest, eggs or flightless young, or b) adults present in breeding season, please rush reply by airmail.

What evidence is there that the Greater Scaup breeds at Lower Souris Refuge?

Houston received detailed responses and incorporated them into his comments. In a December 1959 cover letter, Houston commended Roger: "I wish to congratulate you on your excellent 'geographical sense.' This is what so many ornithologists lack.

The A.O.U. Check-List errors are all basically errors of geography, not of ornithology per se." Nine days later, Roger responded that he had already integrated Houston's "suggestions" into the manuscript.

One doubts that Roger would have surrendered to sloppiness less than two decades later for the much anticipated fourth edition of the eastern guide. "As he works," wrote Joseph Kastner in a 1979 *New York Times Magazine* profile, "he refers to his notes, his photographs, museum specimens and his sharp memories of what he has seen in the field." He consulted about 130 ornithologists and birders. In April 1980, six months before the fourth edition's publication, he informed Frank Graham:

> *The new* Field Guide *is more than a revision. . . . This one is a completely new book; every illustration new and twice as many of them; plus hundreds of range maps (not thumbnail ones in the margin, but maps with state and provincial lines and additional detailed information). Ginny and I researched the maps together and she carried out their execution, having trained her hand and critical abilities at the Coast Guard while working out infra-red spectroscopy methods of analyzing oil spills. . . . My goal has been to make the new Eastern guide the most critically accurate and effective field guide yet produced on any region in the world. It has taken me three times as long as it did to produce the original book. The first edition now looks very primitive by comparison.*

The finished product was spectacular, the sort of work one would expect from Roger were he freed to give each bird its due in full color. Black-and-white sketches were limited to a new minichapter, "How to Identify Birds," adapted from Roger's old instructional volume *How to Know the Birds*. Bird plates were no longer relegated to a central section; each was found opposite full descriptive paragraphs of the birds. Descriptions were necessarily shortened. However, greater verbal discipline was never at odds with historically terse Peterson prose. (In 1947 Roger wrote that the snowy egret was the "heron with the 'golden slippers.'" In 1980 he simply said, "Note the *golden slippers*." In 1947 he declared the killdeer the "common noisy breeding Plover of the plowed fields and pasture-lands." In 1980 the killdeer was the "common noisy breeding plover of the farm country.")

While Roger avoided the more flamboyant (and distracting) aspects of, say, the *Golden Guide*—colorful foliage or whole habitat scenes behind the birds—he dramatically expanded depictions of birds in flight, particularly wading and marsh birds. One characteristic of the Peterson guide that remained unchanged was the prevalence of arrows pointing to salient field marks. Now, with generally fewer birds per plate, the arrows were easier to see.

The eastern guide's fourth edition got huge press and sold (and sold), with 550,000 copies in print by December 1980 and both hardcover and paperback versions on the *New York Times* best-seller list. Roger had brushed back the competition, not something an *old* person could easily do.

Wrote Richard Rogin for *Sports Illustrated:* "The drawings are often so lifelike that I half expected to see the marbled godwit fly off the page."

"For the beginner, intermediate, and teacher, the Fourth Edition of Roger Tory Peterson's *A Field Guide to the Birds* is the single field guide," commented Robert E. Budliger for *The Conservationist*. "The expert? He'll make his copy of Peterson's into his own field guide with its own character."

Ken Emerson of the *New York Times* praised Roger's color plates ("The great horned owl that used to look ungainly is now properly imperious") but mourned the pithier descriptions ("Even as the expanded and enlarged illustrations in Mr. Peterson's new 'Field Guide' breathe new life into birds, the clipped style drains the life out of them").

Acknowledged Robert Arbib in *Natural History:* "The new Peterson guide was not designed to solve those really difficult identification problems: all the immature gulls, cryptic flycatch-ers, problem raptors, juvenile pelagics, and uncommon hybrids. We need special, detailed field guides for those."

Roger's progeny had been itching for a different sort of Peter-son revision than they got. They were the "experts" Budliger mentioned, the ones obsessed with the "really difficult identifica-tion problems" referred to by Arbib. Divulged Tom Davis in *The Linnaean Newsletter,* the house organ of Roger's alma mater, as it were: "There is a continent-wide yearning among serious birders, their numbers vastly swollen since the mid 1930s, for a carefully-executed 'advanced' field guide. . . . While the new Peterson is superior to other current American guides it falls woefully short of fulfilling this burgeoning group's desires."

Seemingly annoyed, Davis wrote that Roger's "mistreatment of . . . *Sterna* terns and other problems belies his awareness of mod-ern day field techniques," adding, "truly interested persons will continue to get their advanced education in bird identification from more expert participants and sophisticated articles pub-lished in *American Birds, Birding, Continental Birdlife, British Birds,* and elsewhere."

Perhaps Roger had created a monster made of telescope-toting, proud authorities on every North American bird species, starved for a volume catering to their already prodigious knowledge.

In *The Auk,* Jon Dunn was also disappointed, tactfully start-ing off: "Most if not all of today's field experts began their stud-ies under the tutelage of the man known without dispute as the dean of American birdwatchers." Dunn proceeded—politely—to enumerate presumed inaccuracies regarding such things as color, field marks, bill shapes, and silhouette shapes. He said that the "Confusing Fall Warblers" section, meant to distinguish between warbler species in their winter plumage, contained the "worst plates" in the book. (*The Conservationist*'s Budliger had called the fall warblers section "exceptionally well done!") Ages of immature gulls were "mislabeled." While Dunn lauded the addition of range maps, he bemoaned Roger's alleged failure to have consulted the regional editors of the National Audubon Society's bird-sighting periodical, *American Birds* (notwithstanding Roger's statement that he had reviewed the magazine's files, plus a regional supplement prepared by Susan Roney Drennan). Worse, Dunn complained, the revised guide included none of the "wealth of new information" accumulated over the last thirty years. Roger should have, but didn't, consult "current experts on field identification." Also, he "ignored the literature."

Move over, bub. The new guys are in town.

The biggest smackdown came from several writers for *Birding*, the magazine launched by the American Birding Association, a group that probably owed its existence to Roger. (Just that year Roger had received the association's Ludlow Griscom Award for Outstanding Contributions to Field Birding. Presumably, these contributions had ceased in the eastern United States with the publication of the 1947 guide.) Birders Henry Armistead, Ron Naveen, Claudia Wilds, Will Russell, and—to a lesser extent—Lawrence Balch all lamented what they saw as the 1980 edition's chief deficiencies, which varied from person to person. For example, while Wilds criticized Peterson's bill shapes, and Russell Roger's overall "sense of shape," Balch allowed that his "feeling for shape, posture, bill-size, and other details is generally very good." But all agreed on the theme common to young birders reviewing the 1980 guide for different publications: Roger hadn't incorporated any of the knowledge accumulated by them and people like them in recent decades concerning what really mattered in the field identification of different species. Perhaps, heaven forfend, this failure evidenced a lack of knowledge on his part.

Maybe there is no God.

Kenn Kaufman, Roger's avid follower from boyhood, expressed bitter disillusionment over the guide in a review for the birding journal he had founded, *Continental Birdlife*. "Now the new Peterson is out," he wrote. "Compared to its own previous editions, it has a more convenient format—but the illustrations are less accurate and the text is more limited. Is this progress?"

Negatives permeated Kenn's essay: "badly bungled," "wildly atypical," "obscured or confused," "embarrassingly awkward," "shamelessly." More than some reviewers, he repeatedly returned to the irksome possibility—nay, likelihood—that Roger hadn't done his homework:

> *If only the book reflected* current *knowledge of field identification, instead of being thirty years out of date for most species. If only the expert birders of North America had looked at the book before publication (instead of looking through it, groaning with disappointment and disbelief, after publication). . . . I think it would be wrong to charge that the "go-it-alone" policy in the new edition was due entirely to arrogance on Peterson's part. It is quite possible he doesn't realize that much has happened in the field (aside from the appearance of a rival guide) since the time of his previous edition.*

If Roger's progeny were disturbed by what they perceived as his lackadaisical attitude toward advances in field identification techniques, Roger was more disturbed that anyone would think such a thing. The same issue of *Birding*, which featured the five reviews, provided Roger space at the end to rebut their statements. He used the opportunity to challenge negative reviews he'd also received elsewhere.

Roger cautioned: "I realize over the years I have spawned my own critics (or competition—call them what you will). There are always Young Turks out there ready to climb on my shoulders, but I can only hope that they do so wearing felt slippers and not with hobnailed boots." This was as personal as he got, thereafter calmly informing—or reminding—his critics of what he'd been trying to do from the very beginning: teach people who don't know how to identify birds how to identify them, while striking a balance between those who want "even simpler abstraction" and those who prefer "infinite detail." Then he recited some of the changes present in the guide's fourth edition made in response to outside pressures.

Happily, Houghton Mifflin budgeted enough money to place the text opposite the plates. However, image and color quality were still subject to limits in technology and economics. Most important of all was the reality that, were he to "cover all the subtle variations in immature gulls and buteos and the seasonal variations of certain shorebirds," his book would be a manual, "precisely the type of approach which I have been trying to get away from in my field guides."

Illustrating his point, Roger cited two examples of how extreme detail was antithetical to the concept of a helpful field guide. He mentioned a thirteen-page spread in a previous issue of *Birding* concerning the plumages of one species, the Thayer's gull. Its discussion was way too long for a field guide; its author stated he couldn't even guarantee accuracy. Next Roger mentioned a feature written by one group of hawk-banding experts for *American Birds* on the problem of distinguishing between Cooper's and sharp-shinned hawks. It was promptly questioned by another group of hawk-banding experts. Roger insisted he was "perfectly aware of modern field techniques and had read every specialized article on identification" in magazines such as *American Birds, Birding,* and Kaufman's *Continental Birdlife.* "But within the limits of a field guide," he warned, "one cannot devote a full page—let alone three or four—to a single species."

Finally, seventy-two-year-old Roger invited his critics to mail him comments about his treatment of different species in the eastern guide. Although he was already working on the third edition of *A Field Guide to Western Birds,* he promised that another revision of the eastern would be in the offing well before he was 105.

Privately, Roger was hurt. "It was a heartache for him to have his constituency seemingly turning on him," says Bob Bateman.

"Roger was so nice to so many people for so many years, young and old, particularly young, . . . and everybody loved him," recalls bird tour leader Peter Alden. "He'd never had a nasty review in his life of anything he wrote. . . . All those people who used to high-five Roger over good bird stories and so forth, one by one, every one of the young Turks came out, because they were . . . trying to carve a niche in the pecking order . . . [and] every one of them managed to find some faults. . . . He was livid."

Alden remembers being with Roger at Kennedy Airport en route to Alaska to lead a tour and the uncomfortable encounter they had with Linnaean Society's Tom Davis, whom Alden had invited unbeknown to Roger to sit with them and try to make amends. It didn't go well. "They used to be sort of friends," says Alden. "Roger was not in a forgiving mood. . . . He was not welcoming." Davis slinked off with a meek, "Nice to see you, Mr. Peterson," recalls Alden. Roger and Peter departed for Alaska. Uncharacteristically, and under his breath, Roger cursed the reviewers who had given him grief. *Goddamned this one, goddamned that one.*

All the negativity, says Alden, made these young birders consider an author's feelings when they wrote future reviews. It also made Roger seek their company and confer with them as much as possible to avoid a repeat of the unpleasantness attendant to the 1980 guide's publication.

"I've regretted that ever since," says Kenn Kaufman of his *Continental Birdlife* review. "It never dawned on me that he would actually read a review that I had written. When I found out that he had read it and had really been bothered by it I was mortified at the idea."

Kaufman says he has matured as a birder since the Peterson guide controversy. He used to believe that any beginning birder was going to become an expert and therefore required the greatest amount of detailed information about a bird. Something as arcane as the "timing of the molt of the tertial feathers" on a species of flycatcher might thrill some, but "there are vast numbers of people who just enjoy birdwatching. They don't want to become experts and are never going to. . . . If you take all the people who can identify a Hammond's flycatcher on sight, you won't have enough votes to elect a mayor, let alone to really effect [conservation] policy on a large scale. We really have to encourage lots of people to appreciate birds at some level." Even if it's not at an expert level.

By the early 1980s Roger and Kenn were friends. Together they bridged the gap between young and old, demonstrating that enthusiasm and knowledge can be shared at any age.

Roger had a lot of work to do to stay atop the heap. Field guide revisions would occupy more and more of his time, even with the deaths of friends and associates, even as he wished to do more writing, painterly painting, and traveling to far-flung places. The risk was that, despite Roger's mental vitality, his indefatigable ambitions were bound to surrender to physical age at some point. It happened to everyone.

Chapter Nineteen
Still All over the Range Map

In November 1982 seventy-four-year-old Roger Tory Peterson updated Joe Hickey on his recent doings:

> *I am just beginning to surface again after the last several weeks of adventure and travel to such disparate places and meetings as Long Point, Ontario where I sponsored the fundraising Birda-thon, the Owl Rehabilitation Center near . . . [Hamilton], and the affair at the Laboratory of Ornithology at Cornell where I presented Bill Gunn* with the Arthur Allen Medal. Following this came the New York State Outdoor Education Association convention in Buffalo where I acted as keynote speaker; Fredonia State College where I received another honorary award; the Phila-delphia Academy of Sciences where I took part in the opening of the Fuertes exhibition and the presentation of the new book on Fuertes for which I wrote the foreword; the A.O.U. meetings at the Chicago Field Museum; etc. Last night Ginny and I returned from Texas where we spent two days birding with Prince Philip; and tomorrow I will be presented with the great Swedish-American Heritage Award by the King of Sweden in New York.*

The 1980s were a heady time for Roger. He continued to receive more awards and honors. He was first nominated for the Nobel Peace Prize in 1983 and again in 1986, when he was a top-

---

* Bill Gunn was sound recordist for CBC's *The Nature of Things*. Roger received the Arthur Allen Medal, named for the founder of the Cornell Laboratory of Ornithology, in 1967.

four finalist. "Frankly, I cannot see any reason why I should have had it," he wrote to Bob Lewin. "Except for the birds, angels are the only beings with feathers in their wings. That is the only connection with peace I can think of." (His writing and conversations increasingly included references to angels.)

After the Presidential Medal of Freedom, Roger's most illustrious domestic honor was the Smithson Medal awarded toward the end of his friend Dillon Ripley's tenure as secretary of the Smithsonian. The occasion was the fiftieth anniversary of the first Peterson. A selection of his artwork—paintings, field guide illustrations, and black-and-white drawings—were on display at the Smithsonian from April 27 to September 3, 1984. Ripley, a much decorated ornithologist, said in his citation: "You have fostered the communion of amateur and professional, and you are uniquely adept at taking natural history and the philosophy of conservation to the people." Receiving an award from the Smithsonian was wonderful enough, but Roger also held Ripley in the highest esteem. "Roger held Dillon a bit in awe," says Paul Spitzer. "I'll never forget this. Roger got this slightly faraway look in his eyes and he said, 'He's the king.'"

The older Roger got, the more in demand he seemed to be for events sponsored by ornithological, natural history, birdwatching, and conservation groups. Judging from his 1982 letter to Hickey, he still got around. Susan Roney Drennan believes that, although Roger was accepting fewer speaking engagements by the 1980s, he was always a soft touch when the cause was conservation: "One of his old friends [in Maine] said to him, 'Please come and talk before this group.' Roger was kind of holding back, and . . . [the friend] said, 'We have so many conservationists here who could use some direction.' . . . And, man, he gave in instantly! He just caved! . . . I happened to be there, in the area, not because of Roger, but because I had other work for Audubon to do, so I decided, 'OK, I'll go that night.' Boy, he was just galvanizing, and got these people all excited. The question-and-answer period was twice as long as the talk itself."

Roger's presence at an event usually meant it was a roaring success. The organization holding the event attracted record numbers of people, raised money, and fostered greater awareness of its mission. One such event was the fiftieth anniversary celebration of the Federation of Ontario Naturalists in May 1981. "We wanted to have a successful conference," says Nathan Garber, the program chair. "We had a couple of previous conferences that had lost money ....I was determined... [to] make some money on this conference." Garber's persistence paid off; Roger would speak at the conference on condition that someone take him to Point Pelee beforehand to watch the spring migrants arrive. The conference was a sellout.

The April 1983 Royal Society for the Protection of Birds Members' Weekend in Coventry at the University of Warwick was similarly successful. The special treat was a reunion of the authors of *A Field Guide to the Birds of Britain and Europe,* timed to coincide with publication of a revision featuring thirty-seven new color plates by Roger. "Rob [Hume] and I came up with this idea that we should bring together Mountfort, Hollom, and Peterson . . . in one conference," Trevor Gunton, now retired from the RSPB, remembers. "Oh, it was a sensation—people were queuing for their autographs!" Midweekend, Roger gave the "celebrity lecture." His acclaim among RSPB members was as lofty as it would have been at a birding symposium in the United States. "He was sort of a legendary figure, so merely for him to stand on stage and to be there," explains Gunton, "it made the weekend for everybody."

Richard Parks, who as a lad of sixteen first met Roger in 1936, has fond memories of the Georgia Ornithological Society's fiftieth anniversary event in Macon, Georgia, on November 7–9, 1986. "It was the best meeting ever held in Georgia!" Parks declares. "We had over three hundred people. We didn't have that many people in the GOS, even!" It was terrific for the birders, who were able to listen to Roger speak, bird with him, and get his autograph. It was also terrific for Roger. "When we drove back to [the] Atlanta airport," says Parks, "he thanked me three times for inviting him."

Roger was much in demand by the younger generation. In the wake of the negative reaction by many "hotshot" American birders to the eastern guide's fourth edition, the sides achieved a kind of détente, opening an era of golden relations between generations.

Victor Emanuel remained a close friend; Roger frequently joined his team for the annual Texas Big Day when they would search for as many birds, by sight or sound, as they could find in a twenty-four-hour period. The more they found, the more money they raised for conservation. This activity required stamina as well as consistently sharp concentration. In his midseventies, Roger was decades older than his companions, but could still do it. Especially taxing were the plane rides across the state; any glitch in transportation meant a potential loss of species and a setback for the team. Greg Lasley, a member of the Austin police force, served on Victor's team with Roger and American Birding Association founder Jim Tucker and recalls a few anxious moments on their May 1, 1985 Big Day when their plane almost didn't clear the mesquite trees ahead of them.

A few minutes after the passengers had regained their composure, Lasley asked Roger to autograph his copy of *A Field Guide to Mexican Birds*. Roger replied: "I am so happy that I'm here to sign your book!"

Flight safety wasn't an issue at the Cape May Bird Observatory's first World Series of Birding in May 1984. As New Jersey was much more manageable than Texas to travel in a day, the automobile was the mode of transport. The main concern was keeping fans from Roger. Pete Bacinski, today director of the Sandy Hook Bird Observatory, remembers that when they reached Princeton's Institute Woods, birders not involved in the World Series started grabbing at the elder naturalist. "Our way around this was we surrounded him," says Bacinski. "We were like bodyguards!" Roger's protectors told gawkers to come to Cape May the next day upon the World Series's conclusion if they wanted an autograph.

It was to Roger's advantage to associate with young people like Bacinski. Doing young things with young people made him feel young. There was also an educational component to these forays. Roger could still teach his progeny, but perhaps his progeny had something to teach him that might be of value for the third edition of the western guide already in progress.

Californian Rich Stallcup had just written a major article on loon identification for the *Point Reyes Bird Observatory Newsletter*. Back in Old Lyme, Roger read it, and in 1984 surprised Stallcup with a call: "Can I come out and follow you around?" Roger asked.

"Of course, I was totally honored," says Stallcup, "and said, 'Why, yes!'"

Their plan was to surprise Stallcup's bird class by showing up for a daybreak breakfast at a Sausalito restaurant. Then everyone would board a boat and bird around piers, harbors, and islands. When the day arrived, so did torrential rains. The boat ride was canceled before Roger and Rich appeared.

"[The bird class students] were about the only people in this little restaurant having breakfast," remembers Rich, "and we walked in out of the rain. It was like a movie where everything is freeze-framed. Everyone just stopped with their mouths hanging open and their forks halfway up. . . . Usually, these people, they listen to me. They listen to what I say. Not that morning. After they knew who was there, it was like I was invisible. And mute. They were pretty awestricken, I must say."

Because of the rain, the group's first stop was the California Academy of Sciences in San Francisco. The bird students watched Roger and Rich pull loon and grebe study skins from museum drawers and compare field marks. "We were mostly comparing Pacific loons with Arctic loons, which, at that time, were thought to be the same species, but we knew better," says Stallcup. "We were having a tug-of-war with a red-throated loon specimen, just out of being anxious to learn and share and teach and listen."

The following day, Rich and Roger went out to watch loons and other birds at Tomales Bay. "There's fourteen thousand diving birds on that bay during a herring run," Rich says. "So we just went and birded. . . . I couldn't pinch myself enough to realize that I was actually just out knocking around with the Grand Master. And he was just—'Hey, Rich, look at this!' Acting like he was just another guy."

Roger had an eye on the competition. He noted in a 1983 letter to Bob Lewin that the *Golden Guide* was coming out with a new edition, the National Geographic Society was publishing a guide, and Knopf's Chanticleer Press, apparently building on its National Audubon Society guide, was about to issue a three-volume handbook. "My own strategy," wrote Roger, "inasmuch as these others have stepped on my shoulders, is now to step on theirs, taking advantage of whatever ideas or points are valid and also getting the advice of the most likely critics who will carefully comb these works and point out . . . what is . . . not entirely accurate."

Rich Stallcup was credited in the western guide's third edition with reviewing Ginny's maps and providing feedback regarding text revisions. Nineteen-eighty field guide critics Jon Dunn, Lawrence Balch, Ron Naveen, and Kenn Kaufman also helped.

Wrote Kenn in February 1990 correspondence: "I was happy to look at the range maps, Virginia, but as I recall they were already so accurate that I had little to suggest."

Initially, Roger thought that revising the eastern guide, yet again, would be an easy job. "Actually, there will be precious little work involved in updating the Eastern guide," Roger advised Lewin in that 1983 letter. "I can use several of the best of the Western plates. It will be basically a matter of name and map changes, and minor points in the text."

Another revision (1993) of *A Field Guide to the Birds of Britain and Europe* intervened. Roger painted nineteen new plates and modified many of the others to include female and immature plumages. Then he devoted his last years to the fifth edition of the eastern guide, researching field marks and ranges, leaving fifty-nine plates alone, revising eighty-five plates, and adding seven new ones.

"I think it was a pity that he spent so much time in his older age doing field guide revisions," Lars Jonsson says. "He was probably a bit annoyed by the young, upcoming ornithologists who really criticized his revised editions. . . . He was very competitive. . . . He felt like he wanted to try once again and get all the new things in, and so on. . . . I have pressure to revise my European field guide that came out in 1992."

Jonsson, now in his fifties, often wonders whether he should, telling himself: "Maybe I should just let it be as it is. I did it, and I [should] just go ahead and do other things."

Roger couldn't work as energetically as he had in his youth, or even as a younger senior citizen. The work did not go quickly.

"The thing about getting older is you can do everything you could do before," Roger told his old associate from the Canadian Broadcasting Company, Rudi Kovanic. "You just have to do it a lot more slowly, so you don't get to do as much. But you can still do it all."

It was getting lonely for Roger, who was outliving, if not outworking, his contemporaries. "The older he got," says Susan Roney Drennan, "the more disparity there was between the ages of the people who actually attended [ornithological] meetings and Roger. . . . Many, many years ago he was among contemporaries . . . . There was a big gap between the movers and shakers in these ornithological societies and Roger. . . . So many young people didn't have any history with him."

In the November 1982 letter that Roger wrote to Joe Hickey, he said:

> At the Chicago [American Ornithologists' Union] gala I was very moved when you talked about our long association. I realized that only three of us at the convention went back as far as the 1925 A.O.U. meeting in New York—you, [John] Emlen, and I. . . . I count my blessings that I was able to know the Bronx County Bird Club. . . . Today the American Museum [of Natural History] does not seem to have the vitality that it had when its halls were frequented by such giants as [Frank] Chapman, . . . [Robert Cushman] Murphy, . . . Griscom, Mayr, [Eugene] Eisenman [sic], [Dean] Amadon, etc. Amadon, however, still goes to his old office occasionally.
>
> Thinking back to former A.O.U. meetings, the thing I miss recently is the healthy mix of the advanced amateur and the professional or academic. Today they seem to be made up primarily of young academics who are struggling for their credentials.

The ranks of Roger's close friends were also thinning. Peter Scott, a year his junior, died a month shy of his eightieth birthday on August 29, 1989. Roger had a strange dream the day after he learned the news. He recounted to Keith Shackleton: "In this dream I saw Peter and James Fisher standing there facing me, amidst a tessellation of crystals—triangular, opalescent crystals shifting this way and that; glittering. They said nothing; they were just there. Half awake, I said[,] 'I must hold onto this dream.' And, I repeated to myself, 'I *must* hold onto this dream!' Then I awoke .... I miss them very much."

Joe Hickey followed Peter Scott four years later on August 31, 1993. Before the memorial service held September 4, Roger told Joe's daughter, Susi: "I remember when I used to come to Madison with the Audubon Screen Tours. Your father would stand up at the end of the talk at the back of the audience, and he'd be waving his hands. It was a signal for me that I was over the time limit and I should sit down and shut up. ... I never did that then, and I'll bet you're going to be waving your hands at me today, but I'm not going to listen to you, either!"

"That's what happened," Susi recalls. "He read his remarks, looked up from the paper, and talked some more, and everybody enjoyed it. It was great." She didn't signal Roger to stop. "I was just smiling. I didn't wave."

Roger believed he had lost the National Audubon Society too. After former Delaware Governor Russell Peterson took over in April 1979, he scuttled the old Audubon Screen Tours program, which, along with other educational efforts of the society, had been in a state of neglect for years before he arrived.

Russell Peterson says he "was interested in getting a much broader appeal. ... We didn't kill that program. It was just that we put our emphasis on ... television and radio. ... That illustrates why these old-timers who were the lecturers, people with tremendous experience in the natural world, had good stories to tell, why they got teed off. Because this new approach dominated our work and was reaching hundreds of thousands of people instead of dozens of people."

Roger disagreed with this change in direction, complaining to Frank Graham: "The screen tours . . . were a great loss which can never be made up even by television participation. They had direct bearing on the [Audubon] chapters. Television is fine because it reaches a great many people, but is not something the chapters can actively participate in [in] a local hands-on way."

Junior Audubon had been all but dead for years. The National Wildlife Federation's slick *Ranger Rick* magazine was popular, but Audubon offered nothing to compete with it for quite a while. "I presented the dilemma at an Audubon convention in Colorado back in the 1970's," Roger informed Frank Graham. "Russ Peterson then took the ball and decided to do something about it. It was after two or three false starts that you, Ada [Graham], and Marshall Case were pulled into the act and have succeeded famously." In June 1984, *Audubon Adventures,* a joint effort of Frank and wife, Ada, debuted. It was geared toward children in grades four through six and designed to encourage the formation of local Audubon Youth clubs. Roger was pleased with the newsletter's impact.

Remaining Audubon old-timers were horrified in the early 1990s by another development, this one courtesy of the society's new head, Peter Berle. In a move symbolic of the evolving direction of the National Audubon Society, Berle approved changing the organization's logo from an egret to a blue flag. But that was just the most visible evidence of the conversion of Audubon from a group concerned with the conservation of birds and other wildlife to one concerned about more general environmental questions. Roger was quoted in an article in *Harrowsmith Country Life* that, although he remained a special consultant to Audubon, "They never call me anymore." He wrote Frank Graham: "Let's hope the flack at National Audubon resolves itself and that wildlife will continue to have priority instead of being dismissed as secondary to the problems of human survival which are being addressed by dozens of other environmental organizations."

"He was quite outspoken," says Graham. "He felt that they were kind of turning their back on birds. And they were! He was absolutely right about it. . . . They had this real prestige within the ornithological movement. They were considered part of it by academics and so on. He felt that they had let the ball drop."

Roger's third wife, Ginny, made it difficult for his family to stay in touch, engendering disappointment and resentment. Some of his oldest friends and associates disliked her and wished for Barbara. The occasional outsider found Ginny too controlling of him. But she had fans among many of the young male birders who reverentially paid their respects to her husband in Old Lyme or invited him on Big Days or other adventures—Victor Emanuel, Peter Alden, Noble Proctor, Pete Dunne.

Gushed Dunne in *Feather Quest:*

Ginny is tall, willowy, and golden-haired. There is a part of her that skips across adversity like a stone across water—and this must be the Irish in her. There is a part that sees too deep, takes the world's hurts the way elms find lightning—and this is the Irish in her, too. Tempered by both natures is a wonderful, intelligent woman whose strengths can balance the gravitational pull of a star.

(That "star" was Roger.)

It was also evident that for all her faults, Ginny cared for Roger. Like Barbara, she babied him.

Rob Hume's job during the April 1983 RSPB Members' Weekend (and ensuing tour plus birding in England's northeast) was to get Roger and Ginny where they needed to go. At one point Ginny took Hume aside and asked him to go to Heathrow and collect a pair of Roger's eyeglasses. "She said, 'Don't ask Roger, because he'd say don't worry. It's nothing important. But please, if you could, it's very important to him. He's having real difficulties without them.' I was quite happy to do that," says Hume.

Ginny also didn't like leaving Roger alone. If she couldn't go on an excursion with him, or he wasn't interested in her travel plans, she had to find him a companion. "He went to Churchill [Manitoba] because Virginia was going to Italy and she wanted him to do something," says Victor Emanuel. "He didn't want to go to Italy . . . , so she called me and . . . said he wanted to go on this trip."

In his senior years, Roger suffered from a "sub-diabetic condition," as he put it. This gave Ginny a mission. In April 1992 Greg Lasley and wife, Cheryl, were Roger's guests for a trip to Hato Cedral, a ranch in the llanos—savannah—in Apure, Venezuela. Roger wanted to leave the "slavery" of field guide work for what he found most relaxing—photographing birds. Greg was to help Roger do this. But before the trip, Ginny "sent us a four-paged, single-spaced, typewritten letter that my wife likes to call 'The Care and Feeding of Roger Tory Peterson'! . . . It was very detailed," he says. "Everything Roger was allowed to eat, everything he was not allowed to eat, every medication he had to take at certain times, and it was very explicit. . . . Ginny really hovered over him like a mother hen with this sort of thing. But what was so funny about Roger, when he wasn't with Ginny . . . , he did what he damned well pleased. He did what he wanted to as far as eating things and drinking things and doing things. He would get upset if you tried to tell him not to. . . . When Ginny wasn't hovering over him, it was hard to get Roger to follow his diet. About sweets, especially."

In 1994, like his friend Victor Emanuel before him, Lasley received the Roger Tory Peterson Excellence in Birding Award from the Houston Audubon Society. Roger attended the dinner, accompanied by his stepson-in-law Seymour Levin, and presented the statue. Remembers Lasley: "They brought Roger, I believe it was something like a strawberry shortcake. . . . Some kind of cake and icing and strawberries and syrup. Roger [said], 'Um! Oh, boy!' You know? And Sy said, 'Now, Roger. Roger. You can't eat that.' He looked at Sy and said, 'I'm eighty-six years old. Ginny's not here. I'm going to eat it, so leave me alone! . . . And don't you tell Ginny!'"

All naughtiness aside, if he pondered death in the 1970s and 1980s, by the 1990s it was a philosophical mainstay. While admiring birds with Lasley in the Venezuelan llanos, he asked Lasley's opinion on more than just bird behavior. "I don't think Roger . . . was particularly religious in a Bible, church way," says Lasley. "His religion was life. Nature. [But] I still remember him one time asking me, 'What do you think happens when we die?' I said, 'I don't guess any of us know that. I guess we become part of the Earth.' He'd say, 'I know we're all going to die, . . . but I don't really want to. I have too much I want to do.'"

Roger had thwarted death before. He would again in his old age. Being with resourceful, alert, young people, as he often was in his seventies and eighties, kept him alive.

Michael Male and Judy Fieth were struggling natural history filmmakers when they first met Roger in the early 1980s. He had agreed to be interviewed for their first project, *Return of the Osprey*. Through their company, Blue Earth Films, they made other movies, including *Watching Warblers*, rough footage of which they showed Roger on some evenings in his studio. "He'd be excited about the fact that you'd brought it to show him, and it had birds, and they were closeups," says Judy. "Having Roger Tory Peterson telling us that what we were doing was really good was very—it was great! It was really nice of him."

Then the couple thought of making a movie about birds for *Nature*, the public television program. Maybe Roger could star. The proposition was all the more attractive to him because he knew they would be able to include quality bird footage. They began filming *A Celebration of Birds with Roger Tory Peterson* in January 1990 at the Ding Darling National Wildlife Refuge at Sanibel Island, Florida. After a break, they moved up the coast, stopping in Cape May for the spectacle of the red knots feasting on horseshoe crab eggs, and Old Lyme for the resurgence of the osprey. In July they departed for Maine.

"He'd just had a prostate operation," Michael recalls. "He was feeling kind of beat up and old and all of that."

But Roger was excited to be a participant. "He was set to rough it," says Judy. "There he was, eighty-two years old, and he was very excited about traveling up the coast in our Volkswagen van and camping out and staying in little motels in out-of-the-way places where there were birds."

In Maine they planned to camp on Eastern Egg Rock in Muscongus Bay for a few days so Michael and Judy could capture Roger filming the fruits of the National Audubon Society's Project Puffin, spearheaded by Steve Kress. Kress had restored Atlantic puffins, storm petrels, and three tern species, among other birds, to Eastern Egg Rock and other islands and national wildlife refuges off Maine's coast after the birds had been extirpated by human persecution nearly a century before. Initially Kress opposed taking the three out in a boat because of the fog. Roger's companions concurred. "But Roger was just chomping on the bit to get out there," Michael recalls.

"We cared," Judy says. "He didn't. He was fearless."

There was Ginny's admonition from afar: "You've got to look after Roger. He's a national treasure."

During the two or three days of downtime, the threesome drove around, investigating Roger's old haunts from summers in his twenties. He insisted on looking for sedge wrens in a familiar wetland, and guided his companions by the family bungalow of his first wife, Mildred, which they remember he called Lilac Cottage.

When the fog lifted enough for safe boating, Steve Kress arranged their transportation in a dory. Several productive but otherwise uneventful days ensued. Then the day came for leaving Eastern Egg; Roger was to speak at Hog Island Audubon Camp that night. In his early eighties, he was no longer sure footed, having to negotiate the rocks with a "monopod" down to the inflatable dinghy that would take them to the twenty-three-foot open boat with outboard engine awaiting them. Steve Kress, Jerry Skinner, and Captain Bob Bowman were their escorts back. On the dinghy, Judy and Michael kept their expensive equipment in waterproof cases, but it was such a warm, bright day they took it out again and started filming—and interviewing Roger—once on board the boat. It was, maybe, 4:00 p.m. Roger later wrote:

> Because our eyes were on the cormorants lined up on shore, only one of us was aware of the rogue wave—even momentarily—before our boat was rolled over a couple hundred yards off Western Egg Rock—in 15 or 16 feet of water. I was wrapped in eye dazzling foam one moment, in murky green depths the next, with dark objects sinking around me—thousands of dollars of camera equipment. But no time to panic; another gulp or two of seawater could send me choking to the bottom.

Everyone and everything was underwater. Some were thrust closer to Western Egg, others pushed farther seaward. If one ignored the dangerous power of the currents and the risk of drowning, the depths were peaceful and lovely with the sun shining through the ocean's surface.

Roger thought of Mildred, who had drowned in Muscongus Bay thirteen years earlier. She appeared to him in the water.

Then Roger snapped to reality, struggling to the surface to find his companions fighting their own battles. Michael was weighted down with a movie camera attached to his waist via a cable. Judy managed to disengage him from this thirty-five-pound anchor, defying the pull of the heavy, rubber boots stuck on her feet. Michael persuaded her to let the camera go, all $20,000 of it.

"Somebody's gotta help Roger!" Michael yelled. Their charge was desperately trying to keep his head above water. Captain Bob swam to Roger and dragged him back to the boat, now bottom up, and helped him climb atop it to join all the others.

They were on top long enough to catch their breath. Then the next comber came and flung them all into the waves again. Swirling around in the frothy water, Bob, then Judy, then the rest, were washed away from Roger, into surf crashing against Western Egg. Michael returned to the water to retrieve Roger, who was doing his best dog paddle but was in terrible shape.

They thought Roger was going to die; his eyes were rolling back in his head. Michael tried to swim him to the rocks. Judy plunged in to help. The water was so cold neither of them could close their hands, so they clung to Roger with bent elbows.

"We're gonna make it! We're gonna get there!" Michael screamed at Roger over the sea's roar. Bob, Steve Kress, and Jerry Skinner pitched into the water; it took all of them to drag Roger ashore and drape him upside down over a rock. Michael forced the water out of his stomach and lungs.

Roger wrote:

There I lay, sorely bruised, with arms scraped raw and bleeding by barnacles. Was my left hip broken? Or my ribs? It felt as though they were. Retching to get rid of the salt water, and shiver-

ing—shuddering—I was grateful for the wet garments that were put over me. Hypothermia was setting in and . . . had it not been for Michael Male who added his own body warmth and positive encouragement I might not have pulled through.

"You're gonna be all right!" Michael yelled at Roger. "You're gonna be all right!"

It was about 4:30 p.m. One of their tents had washed up. It was promptly placed on top of Michael who was lying on top of Roger in an effort to raise his body temperature. Articles of clothing they didn't need they piled onto this unusual stack of men and items. Despite exhaustion, the group searched the island—only four or five acres wide—for more things to place on top of Roger and Michael.

Bob, Steve, and Jerry lit multiple fires. Burning plastic lobster pot buoys that had washed up made ugly black smoke, just the thing to attract attention. Meanwhile, another of their tents had washed up. This they erected. When it heated up in the sun, they got Roger up, walked him over to it, and lay him inside. Each person took turns staying with him to make sure he was all right. He fell asleep.

When Roger awoke, he perceived a butterfly shadow showing through the canvas of the tent. *Is that a monarch I see? The shape is closer to that of a red admiral or an anglewing. No, it's too big. Could it be an optical illusion? An* angel *wing?*

Judy wept when she heard Roger's voice through the tent, mumbling about butterflies. He was going to be well. (Steve Kress says it was likely a monarch Roger saw, as they were migrating through at the time.) More things had washed up too. A cooler with food. Roger's medical bag.

They weren't alone. Besides the passing butterfly, the island was home to nesting cormorants and great black-backed gulls.

Around 6:00 p.m., the *Hardy II*, a boat filled with binocular-laden puffin watchers, passed within two miles. Passengers noticed the smoke; the vessel ventured closer to get a better look without risking crashing against the rocks. The castaways hollered and bellowed.

"Are you all right?" Came a voice through a bullhorn. "Do you want the Coast Guard to come?"

More hollering and bellowing: *Yes!* By 9:00 p.m., the U.S. Coast Guard vessel *Wrangell* had arrived on the island's bay side, diverted from its main duty of "Bush Patrol" off Kennebunkport. Four men whisked ashore on a Zodiac, trudged seaside where the rescue subjects were huddled, wrapped Roger in a blanket and strapped him into a stretcher, which they carried across to the Zodiac. Roger couldn't help birdwatching even then. He later wrote: "Lying on my back, helpless, unable to move and gazing straight up into the darkening heavens, I thought I saw a Leach's storm-petrel as it flew out of the mist." A crane mechanism lifted the stretcher-bound naturalist from the Zodiac to the main vessel. The group was transported to a hospital in Boothbay Harbor. All were examined, but only Roger was admitted, perhaps because of his age and his complaints of chest pains—which were really from the bruising he suffered, struggling on Western Egg's rough shore.

Roger had weathered the ordeal so well he reprimanded a doctor who condescendingly questioned everyone's failure to don life jackets before boarding the boat. "We're all alive," Roger argued. "We're all fine!"

When the *New York Times* phoned the hospital to learn what had happened, a nurse responded that Roger could not be bothered; he was resting. She later mentioned this to him. Shocked, he firmly requested she call the paper back: "This could sell books!"

Michael Male and Judy Fieth salvaged most of the footage they had filmed in Maine, but the sound from that leg of the trip was ruined. Later that year they went to Old Lyme to reinterview Roger over a two-day period. "He was gracious about trying to redo things for us," says Judy. They found a renewed Roger. Says Michael: "He got through this traumatic experience, and . . . came out of it feeling pretty vigorous, [judging] from the times we saw him afterward. He seemed pretty inspired by it."

Later that year, Roger gave a talk at a convention of the International Council for Bird Preservation in New Zealand, relaying his recent brush with death by way of praising the usefulness of ecotourism. "He talked about how ecotourism saved his life," Steve Kress says. "If that [boat of birdwatchers] hadn't been going by at that time of day, because there were no other boats on the water, then no one would have seen us."

"But thank heaven I was alive!" Roger wrote that fall. "I still have several books to finish."

Indeed, he did. But there was little time for much besides field guide revisions. Taking a break meant photographing birds rather than finishing manuscripts or painterly painting, which had slowed to a halt; Mill Pond Press got nothing from him in the 1990s. His last non-field-guide book was published by Abbeville Press in 1981, a gigantic volume on the art of John James Audubon called *The Audubon Society Baby Elephant Folio: Audubon's Birds of America*. It contained scholarly notes on the bird paintings from Audubon's massive *Double-Elephant Folio*.

In his senior years Roger revealed his Audubon expertise, reviewing the artist's life and critiquing his science, the questionable habitats Audubon's painted birds frequently found themselves in, and the lusty obsessiveness with which the explorer shot birds, killing dozens if not hundreds more of a given species than he needed for one portrait. The book also offered conservation lessons on various species and the challenges they faced in the present day. Sadly, heavy and huge as it was, Roger's new book wasn't the sort of thing even a bird lover could comfortably read, and more affordable smaller editions didn't showcase Roger's sweeping knowledge of Audubon and the history of North American bird art in general.

Much of Roger's new writing in the 1980s and 1990s showed up in *Bird Watcher's Digest,* although many of those pieces he recycled from *Birds Over America* and *Audubon* magazine articles, updating them to ensure their modern-day relevance. In 1994 William Zinsser disclosed in Rizzoli's *Art and Photography of the World's Foremost Birder* that Roger was writing four books simultaneously. One was called *Wild Islands;* Zinsser quoted from a passage on the Dry Tortugas, proclaiming the naturalist the "very model of a travel writer."

What happened to this project and other works? "Roger thought he was going to live to 150," says Noble Proctor. "He was always accumulating data in the files so that . . . when he could get away from doing field guides . . . he would have something to work on. He always wanted something to work on. . . . I would say, pretty much, he was a workaholic."

Roger never did escape the field guides.

But promoting nature education was always on Roger's mind. In July 1993 a stunning edifice was unveiled in Jamestown, a monument to his passion. This building and its purpose had their origins in a December 1975 gathering of Jamestown natives, led by Roger's high school classmate Lorimer Moe and Gebbie Foundation's John Hamilton, who considered forming a nonprofit organization in the naturalist's honor. The following year, Roger joined some of these same people for three days at Jamestown Community College. He excitedly reported to friend Roger Caras:

> The community college in my town (Jamestown) plans to start an environmental center or institute (to be named in my honor), one which will stress the wild world, which is my area of expertise. It would also be a place where my memorabilia, books, drawings, research material, manuscripts, films, etc. will eventually be housed and where environmental education will be the keynote.

In 1985 after years of sorting out finances and determining whether another city and an established institution of higher learning could better host an entity devoted to Roger's mission, the Roger Tory Peterson Institute of Natural History was incorporated. The following year Jamestown's Gebbie Foundation granted $2.5 million in startup money. The RTPI would be in Jamestown, after all. Explains Jim Berry, RTPI president since January 1996:

> So this group in Jamestown said, "We'll take it, and . . . we'll keep it in perpetuity, never to sell or dispose of any parts of it, and . . . we're fine with only owning the physical [not intellectual] property because all we will be doing is using it for educational purposes, anyway." The fourth point that drove it home and which garnered Roger's entire support was that it would be a separate entity, its own 501(c)3 agency. It wouldn't be part of a parent or get lost in the sauce of being a department that was part of a larger university or anything like that.

For years, the institute operated out of temporary offices on Falconer Street. "We accomplished a good bit . . . in terms of money, the land, the organization, the people, the sources of funds," says founding board member Howard Brokaw, who then laughs: "There was a lot of heavy labor involved in that thing!"

The designated twenty-seven-acre site was adjacent to Jamestown Community College on Curtis Street and the Hundred-Acre Lot where Blanche Hornbeck took young Roger and her other seventh-graders birdwatching in 1920. Additional grants from the Gebbie Foundation and the state of New York enabled the institute to hire architect Robert A. M. Stern and build a handsome structure. Roger wrote: "When it was in the planning stage someone suggested it should reflect Jamestown, the manufacturing town settled by Swedish immigrants where I grew up, but I thought otherwise. Rather than have it structured like . . . several of the classic furniture factories, it should, I felt, reflect the outdoor world, and fit into the gentle rolling landscape of Chautauqua County."

The result was a building of strong Norse quality, part fortress, part modern geometrics, using lines, arches, light, and space through the sensitive interaction of stone and wood. An opening ceremony in August 1993 saw Roger address dignitaries, high school classmates, and friends under a spacious tent. The crowd eagerly walked to the new building; Roger dutifully cut the ribbon. Lars Lindblad took the microphone and, perhaps taken by the Scandinavian atmosphere, launched into a Swedish folk song as Roger waited, his face betraying a tickled tolerance for his friend's eccentricities. The tune finished, Roger could turn and, with everyone else, partake of refreshments inside.

Before and since, the RTPI has focused on teaching the teacher about nature. The idea is to show "teachers how to use nature study to teach all the subjects, . . . where it's integrated in the language arts, and science, and everything else," notes Jim Berry, who adds that the goal is an "ecologically literate youth who then grow up to become . . . participating members in their community with the knowledge it takes to make decisions when it comes to land use, resource use, and things like that." To that end, education director Mark Baldwin and his staff have developed nature workshops and performed teacher and school district outreach on a national level with a variety of seminars. Baldwin also works with the State University of New York on programs for young people studying to be teachers. The RTPI too is a tourist attraction, functioning as a community center. Nature art exhibits change four times a year. The institute offers the public nature walks and classes.

In his eighties Roger knew his legacy would have a permanent home in Jamestown, and that this home would be the center of his lifelong objective, promoting nature education. But what *was* his legacy? He was still working to solidify it and defeat the competition. He dreamed of broadening old vistas and conquering new ones in art and words. Meanwhile, his health was worsening, making work and travel more difficult and affecting his mood. He regretted subjecting the Lewins to a bout of crabbiness one evening in July 1993, writing:

> *I want to apologize for being so negative the other night at Lars Lindblad's. I could hardly sleep that night thinking about it. I've been under so much stress lately because of the circulation problem in my legs and the pressure of work that I worry whether I'll ever be able to get back to the kind of painting that I'm capable of—the third dimensional painting for which I was trained.*
>
> *You and Katie have been very supportive of the things I've been doing and I am truly grateful to you both. Again, I apologize for seeming so grumpy and negative the other night.*

Despite his hope—however fanciful—that he might live to 110 or 150, Roger may have sensed a nearer end, writing to Bob Lewin later that year that the coming Lindblad Antarctic cruise "may be my last one." While his mother saw the start of the American Bicentennial, dying at age ninety-seven after a fall, his father had reached only seventy-six, the victim of a stroke. Roger had surpassed his father in longevity, but could he live to see his centenary? He lost Lars Lindblad in July 1994 to a heart attack—Lars was only sixty-seven—which could not have helped his morale.

At the Woodson Art Museum, Laurie Lewin Simms witnessed a conversation between Roger and George Harrison whose subject smacked of science fiction but seemed most meritorious. Simms remembers Harrison asking Roger what his "newest project" was and Roger answering, "The newest project is really in my mind. . . . How do we take all the data I have in my mind and put it on one of those little, round *somethings* so that it can record all the knowledge I have and the new person who wants to be an expert ornithologist doesn't have to reinvent the wheel?"

"George knew that Roger was talking about a CD," says Simms, "and they were talking about how someday somebody would invent a CD that would just record everything that's in the living person's mind."

Harrison recalls considering the issue, although not with Roger, remarking: "What a waste of a brain when it dies after living seventy, eighty, ninety years and collecting all that information and knowledge and so forth. Roger would be a prime example," he adds, of someone whose brain ought to have been preserved for all it contained.

CBC cameraman Rudi Kovanic filmed Roger for a program on protective coloration in nature. Roger apologized about his memory, Kovanic recalls: "He had to look up his own book to see the ranges of various birds that he was talking about." But Kovanic came away impressed: "I remember being surprised that in his late eighties he could even remember the names of all these different species."

By the 1990s Roger was embarrassed about losing his hearing's upper register. Birding with Pete Dunne and the others on the Guerrilla Birding team during the first Cape May World Series of Birding, Dunne was awed by the ears of this man who was nearly seventy-six. "There were three species of bird that he pulled out that none of us got," says Dunne. "One of them was actually very remarkable. We were driving through the Pine Barrens and the window was open, and we were tooling along. Not [at] a ridiculous speed, but the wind was whistling through the windows. Roger said 'mourning warbler' in the middle of the Pine Barrens. We stopped the car, and sure enough, there was a mourning warbler."

Nine years later, participating noncompetitively in Dunne's world series, it was apparent that Roger's hearing had lost some acuteness. "I . . . remember . . . being with him and standing in front of the bird observatory and there was a blackpoll warbler, and it was singing. Blackpoll is . . . one of the high sibilants, and he couldn't hear it. He was asking me, 'Tell me when it's singing.' 'Now.' 'Tell me when it sings again.' 'Now.' He wasn't hearing it. I know that was very hard for him."

Degraded hearing (for Roger) and, because of diabetes, the increasing difficulty he had simply walking—distressing for a man who prided himself on his physical prowess and could tirelessly walk for miles even a decade earlier—made him feel self-conscious and ashamed. "He was having trouble walking," says David Sibley. "He said something like, 'I wish people didn't have to see me like this.' He really wanted people to see him as the sharp birder . . . , still identifying everything. He said he was having trouble hearing. He was having trouble with his eyes. . . . I thought that was so sad . . . . The birders who were there didn't care about that. They wanted to see him and hear some of his stories, . . . just shake his hand, try to maybe absorb some of his wisdom, or just see this man who was such an icon."

On September 1, 1995, Roger and Seymour Levin arrived at McAllen Airport in Texas. Greg Lasley and friend Steve Bentsen collected them; they traveled to Santillana Ranch near where Bentsen had some blinds erected for wildlife photography. Roger was happy to connect his favorite pastime with a commitment, on September 8, to speak at the opening of the Connie Hagar Cottage, the first site on the central coast section of the Great Texas Coastal Birding Trail. After four days at Santillana Ranch, Roger, Seymour, and Greg departed for the Encino division of the King Ranch, where they met Lasley's friend, wildlife biologist Tom Urban, and spent another couple of days. Lesser goldfinches, screech owls, and deer were all photographic subjects.

It was hot. "In South Texas in September, it can be just like June, July, or August," says Lasley. "We were shoving water down Roger as much as we could get him to drink, but, of course, coming from the North, people don't think about drinking water as much as you need to in a hot time in south Texas." Nor did Roger complain about the heat.

They arrived in Rockport the night before the Hagar dedication. Roger spent two hours autographing people's field guides that evening. "Maybe we ought to be getting him back to the hotel—don't you think, Sy?" Lasley asked Seymour Levin.

"Yeah," Levin said, "but he's not going to leave."

Levin was right. Roger acted predictably. Says Lasley: "He would sit there until the last person was finished, until the last person brought their book. He would not disappoint anybody."

The morning of September 8, Roger participated in a meet-and-greet before he and other dignitaries assembled under a great tent for the dedication ceremony. Attendees sat in folding chairs under full sun. At 11:30 a.m., it was 91 degrees and extremely humid. Lasley wrote in his journal that evening:

> *Andy Sansome—director of Texas Parks & Wildlife spoke. As it became apparent that Andy was about to introduce Roger— Roger turned to me and asked what the man's name was who was speaking. I told him, then wrote Andy's name in red pen on Roger's speech. Andy introduced Roger—and I helped Roger onto the stage. . . . Roger spoke—said "Thank you Andy" from what I had written—then launched into an 8 to 10 minute speech about Connie Hagar.*
>
> *During the speech—Betty Baker showed me 2 of Connie Hagar's RTP Field Guides and was going to ask Roger to sign them on stage for the Sanctuary archives.*
>
> *After Roger finished—He started to step down. Betty and I asked him to wait a minute, and Betty showed the audience the RTP field guides that Connie had owned. Roger signed one—but I'm not sure if he signed them both. I then helped Roger off the stage. He seemed slightly unsteady. . . . He then helped remove the cover to one sign—then turned toward me and I helped him toward the wooden chairs. As I helped him to the chair he said "Oh boy, oh boy" softly—and I felt he was anxious to sit down. I felt he was tired or dizzy. A lady asked me if Roger would sign a book—I told her later. A TV crew—a lady—asked if she could do an interview. I was in the process of telling her no when I felt Roger's head on my right shoulder. I then saw his teeth clenched and he was making hissing noises. He began to slump from his chair. His eyes*

rolled back, his face contorted and his mouth fell slack. I started to
help him to the ground—I knew he was in trouble.

Lasley asked someone to call emergency medical services. He
took Roger's jacket off. Laying him on the grass, he propped up
Roger's head with the jacket. He wrote: "I thought he was going
to die in my arms. I thought he was having a stroke or a heart
attack." Lasley noticed a pulse in Roger's neck, but then "Roger
started gagging and having dry heaves. . . . Betty Baker was on the
PA System telling people to leave."

The medics took emergency measures and transported him
to Coastal Bend Hospital in Aransas Pass. Doctors said Roger
would be all right. To Lasley's surprise, "Basically, what they said
was that . . . Roger had gotten very dehydrated from not drinking
enough water in the past week." After a couple of days in the hospital, Roger and Seymour Levin left for Old Lyme. That was the
last time Greg Lasley saw Roger.

Robert Michael Pyle was at the RTPI not long after that. Pyle, who
noticed Roger standing alone amid an exhibit of his own paintings, recalls:

There was a meadowlark that was utterly stunning and . . . a
nude that he'd drawn in his youth. They had drawings from his art
school days as well as bird drawings. "I remember talking about
two or three of the paintings with him. . . . He said he had a real
affection for some of the drawings of his youth and their simplic-
ity. And how . . . , because of the many, many demands of the way
things had gone, he hadn't had a chance, in latter years, really,

to paint people or any of the subjects he thought he might have enjoyed continuing to paint. . . . I think he knew his days were drawing to a close. His hair was thinner. He definitely seemed much, much older. . . . I remember contrasting . . . [this meeting] with the first one in 1970 when it was pure energy. There wasn't nearly as much energy now. . . . But he wasn't drifting. His eyes were every bit as intense as they'd ever been. It's just—he was older. . . . And yet he was all there mentally. . . . He was completely attentive. . . . Not only to me, or whomever else he was speaking with, but also to what was around him.

That winter, Roger suffered a stroke. It was mild enough that he could still work, if only two to three hours a day—on the fifth edition of the eastern guide, which he wanted to make sure was just right.

It was around this time that Roger told Kent Ullberg that he would like to sculpt a king penguin. Roger had never sculpted before and was fascinated by Ullberg's creative process. Kent had a different idea: "As gratitude, or just in my admiration for you, let me be your hands in clay. You don't have the technique with clay, but you and I will do it together." This remained, for a little while, a plan for the future.

One day Steve Kress phoned Roger and asked if he would write the foreword for his book, *Project Puffin*. "I think toward the end he would ask people to write a draft . . . and then he would tweak it," says Kress. "He told me about his tumble at that event in Texas. How he wasn't feeling too good, but I should send him a draft of what I had in mind, and he would do it."

Kent never got to work with Roger in clay, nor did Steve send him a draft foreword in time.

In June and July 1996, Roger passed many hours photographing butterflies and birds from a picture window. This "took his mind off of his health problems," noted Jane Kinne. On the morning of July 28, a half-finished plate of accidental flycatchers sat on his drawing board. He was returning to the plate after postponing finishing it for several months while searching for more information about the La Sagra's flycatcher, a rare visitor to southern Florida from the Bahamas. "Roger's struggle to paint his final birds is evident," Ginny wrote in a preface to the fifth edition. By then, he had completed 85 percent of it.*

Roger was tired after working, but, as usual, relaxed by photographing butterflies flitting in the garden Ginny had built him. He retired to bed early. As always, she rubbed his feet and gave him a good-night kiss. He smiled, turned his head into the pillow, and died.

A year later, Ginny hosted a dinner celebrating Roger's life at the Mystic Aquarium in Connecticut where a penguin exhibit was being named in his honor and Kent Ullberg's sculpture, *King and Heir,* was unveiled. After Roger died, Kent had gone forward with a king penguin sculpture at Ginny's insistence. She made many of Roger's king penguin photos available to Kent for reference. "I did it monumentally. Several times lifesize, as a proper monument to Roger." The sculpture—eight feet high, fashioned of bronze on stone—depicts an adult king penguin with its chick, but Ullberg explains, "It's a portrait of Roger, and in a way, it's a subportrait of myself as the next generation, sitting on Roger's feet. . . . It's also a portrait of naturalists. . . . We are all heirs of Roger's, really."

---

* It was published in 2002, six years after his death and one year after Ginny's. A team effort, Noble Proctor finished the text, Paul Lehman consulted on bird distribution, H. Douglas Pratt completed the flycatcher plate, and Pete Dunne provided editorial and design feedback.

Ullberg and his wife were staying at a local inn while they were in town. Early the following morning, they received a frantic call from Ginny.

"Kent—you've got to come over right now to the house, to the studio. You've got to come right now."

"Ginny—what's up?"

"I can't tell you. Come right now!"

He says:

We jumped in the car . . . and drove over. And this sounds really freaky, but on the wall of Roger's studio was a big play of light going on and . . . , I swear to God, it was an image, a huge image, of a penguin on a wall. . . . And I do not know to this day where it came from. It was like a mystical experience. Everybody saw it. . . . Ginny [and] . . . her son-in-law were there. The family, several people were there, and saw it. . . . Of course, you can give a scientific explanation for it—the rising sun bouncing off a rearview mirror . . . in one of the cars. . . . It was like a greeting from Roger."

The King Penguin had said good-bye.

Acknowledgments

So many people have assisted in the genesis and evolution of this book that it will probably be impossible to acknowledge everyone's contributions, but I will try. At the top of the list are my agent, Russell Galen, and the fine people connected with The Lyons Press, particularly Mary Norris, Jeff Serena, Ellen Urban, Diana Nuhn, and Rose Marye Boudreaux. To say that Laurie Lewin Simms and Arthur Klebanoff put me on the right track would be an understatement; they were generous with so many things I wouldn't know where to begin. Thanks to Jim Berry and Marlene Mudge for allowing me to nose around in the archives at the Roger Tory Peterson Institute of Natural History and tolerating my innumerable follow-up questions. (For more information about the RTPI, go to www.rtpi.org, or call 1-800-758-6841.)

Of course, I am thankful to everyone who agreed to be interviewed for this book. I hope I made the process bearable for them. Their names are listed at the end, under Sources. Also, all who provided photographs deserve thanks. Photographic credits accompany each photo reproduced in this book. Additionally, I am beholden to those who shared their papers with me. I was especially touched by a few people—particularly Frank Graham Jr., C. Stuart Houston, and Susi Hickey Nehls—who entrusted me with *original* letters and other documents. The chapter-by-chapter bibliography identifies all documents and other sources I used in telling the Roger Tory Peterson story.

Susan Roney Drennan and Paul Spitzer reviewed the entire manuscript and offered helpful suggestions; Peter Ames and William J. L. Sladen also read portions of the manuscript and schooled me on scientific points. (Any errors that may remain are my own.)

My husband, Stan, was the first person to read my manuscript in its various stages. I couldn't have done without his wisdom.

Thanks to Roland Clement and Kenn Kaufman for kindly (but separately) treating me to lunch during hours-long interview sessions in Hamden, Connecticut, and Cape May, New Jersey. More thanks to Lee and Courtney Peterson, who opened their home to me to chat, leaf through old letters and articles, and bask in the attention of their friendly dogs. I felt honored to sit down twice with the warm and friendly Barbara Peterson, the most important person in Roger Tory Peterson's adult life.

Keith Bildstein, Sarkis Acopian director for Conservation Science at Hawk Mountain Sanctuary in Pennsylvania, opened up the sanctuary's archives to me, made me feel at home, and ensured the availability of photos and recordings. Thanks also to Andrea Zimmerman of the sanctuary.

Thanks to the professional, hard-working staff of the New York Public Library, Manuscripts and Archives Division, under whose watchful eyes, over many days, I sifted through the same decades-old letters, memos, and other documents handled by pioneering conservationists.

I appreciate the efforts of the staff of the Smithsonian Institution Archives who were welcoming and helpful.

Ellen Collard, public relations director at Mill Pond Press, worked hard to dig up old papers and photos and graciously weathered my frequent inquiries.

Exceptional efforts in securing photos were provided by Clem Fisher, curator of birds and mammals at the World Museum Liverpool, England; Tom Schaefer of the Hog Island History Project; and Gustave Yaki.

Also helping with photos were Lynda DeWitt, Audubon Naturalist Society; Coi E. Drummond-Gehrig, Denver Public Library; Nancy Greenspan, executor of the Shirley Briggs estate; David Hosking, Hosking Charitable Trust; Rudolf Koes; Judith Magee and Jamie Owen, British Natural History Museum; Karen Mason, curator of the Iowa Women's Archives, University of Iowa; Peter

Mott, president, New York City Audubon Society; Nancy Severance, director of marketing communications, National Audubon Society; Marcia Theel, associate director, Leigh Yawkey Woodson Art Museum; Dick Thomas, director, Alumni Relations, Chewonki Foundation; Dave Vargas, Lindblad Expeditions; and Melissa Watterworth, curator of Literary, Natural History, and Rare Book Collections, Thomas J. Dodd Research Center, University of Connecticut.

Thanks to James Ferguson-Lees, Fleur Ng'weno, and Keith Shackleton for their friendship, enthusiasm, and insight, and also to Jasper Shackleton for his thoughtfulness.

Others investing time to help include Nancy Archibald; Howard Brokaw; Pamela Fingleton, Lindblad Expeditions; Clifford Hence; P. A. D. Hollom; Robert Koenke, editor and publisher of *Wildlife Art*; Christine Lietch; Ursula Livingston; George McAfee; and Carmen Thorndike, executive assistant at the H. John Heinz III Center for Science, Economics and the Environment.

For answering some of my more obscure questions, thanks go to Walter J. Bock, professor of evolutionary biology, Columbia University; Paul Buckley, Royal Society for the Protection of Birds; Robert M. Chipley, international programs officer, American Bird Conservancy; Lisa Clark, World Wildlife Fund; Deborah Edge; Stephen Edge; Alistair Gammell, Royal Society for the Protection of Birds; Nancy Keeler, vice president for development, Academy of Natural Sciences; Charles Lee, Florida Audubon Society; Katie Clare Mazzeo; Alison Pirie, Department of Ornithology, Harvard University; Robert Risebrough, Bodega Bay Institute; Andrés Marcelo Sada; Ian Wallace; and John C. Wingfield, professor of biology, University of Washington.

Joe DiCostanzo and Alan Messer, Linnaean Society of New York; Lori Fujimoto and Bryan Patrick, the American Birding Association; and Peter Alden tracked down elusive printed matter for me.

These acknowledgments wouldn't be complete without mentioning my family, who continue to provide me with moral support and encouragement; my bosses Marge Schwartz and Hank Maurer, who granted me a leave of absence to write this book; and my Nanuet High English teacher, Karen Achille, who liked my writing and introduced me to the fundamentals of research and note taking.

Sources

It was exciting to interview people from all over the world about Roger Tory Peterson. I sensed that I was living through history as they shared their memories with me. It was clearly also exciting for my interview subjects to talk about Roger; many of them were surprised and pleased to have the opportunity. But his reach was at once so close and so far as to be unimaginably profound in bird study and conservation. To do his life justice, my search for Peterson friends and associates had to be global.

To give the reader a true flavor of Roger's worldwide impact, I have made the interviews the foundation of this biography. Therefore, the list of interviewees comes first, after which I include a chapter-by-chapter bibliography of my documentary sources.

Personal Interviews

Alden, Peter. Concord, Massachusetts. November 19, 2006.
Allen, Douglas. Salem, Massachusetts. September 7, 2006.
Ames, Peter. Gainesville, Florida. May 11, 2006.
Anderson, Daniel. Davis, California. June 29, 2006; July 17, 2006.
Archibald, George. Baraboo, Wisconsin. October 21, 2006.
Attridge, Barry. London, Ontario, Canada. August 10, 2006.
Bacinski, Pete. Fort Hancock, New Jersey. December 15, 2006.
Baldwin, Mark. Jamestown, New York. June 19, 2006.
Bateman, Robert. Salt Spring Island, British Columbia, Canada.
    September 7, 2006.
Berry, Jim. Jamestown, New York. June 19, 2006.
Blakstad, Rolph. Ibiza, Spain. March 11, 2007.
Borror, Art. Pittsfield, New Hampshire, October 23, 2006.
Brokaw, Howard. Greenville, Delaware. August 3, 4, and 5, 2006.
Brown, Jay. Strongsville, Ohio. July 31, 2006.
Burt, William. Old Lyme, Connecticut. December 15, 2005.
Cadbury, Betsy. Pittsfield, New Hampshire, October 23, 2006.
Cadbury, Peggy. San Francisco, California. December 15, 2006.
Cadbury, Virginia. Hanover, New Hampshire. October 28, 2006.

Cade, Tom. Boise, Idaho. September 26, 2006.

Chasko, Greg. Hartford, Connecticut. May 9, 2006.

Clement, Roland. Hamden, Connecticut. April 16, 2006.

Collard, Ellen. Venice, Florida. November 13, 2006.

Conway, William. Bronx, New York. August 29, 2006.

Copp, Allyn. Providence, Rhode Island. June 7, 2006.

Copp, Belton and Genie. Old Lyme, Connecticut. April 22, 2006

Copp, Genie. Old Lyme, Connecticut. December 5, 2006.

Dannen, Kent. Allenspark, Colorado. March 30, 2007.

Drennan, Susan Roney. Middlebury, Vermont. June 24, 2006.

Dunne, Pete. Cape May Court House, New Jersey. January 26, 2007.

Emanuel, Victor. Austin, Texas. June 12, 2006.

Fanshawe, John. Cambridge, UK. June 28, 2006.

Fenton, Jane. Cambridge, UK. November 14, 2006.

Ferguson-Lees, James. Somerset, UK. August 20, 2006.

Fieth, Judy. Locustville, Virginia. February 12, 2007.

Fink, Russell. Lorton, Virginia. August 28, 2006.

Fisher, Clemency Thorne. Liverpool, UK. July 4, 2006.

Foley, Kathy Kelsey. Wausau, Wisconsin. March 6, 2007.

Furmansky, Dyana. Denver, Colorado. October 15, 2006.

Garber, Nathan. London, Ontario, Canada. August 14, 2006.

González, Mauricio. Jerez, Spain. September 22, 2006.

Graham, Frank Jr. Milbridge, Maine. May 18, 2006.

Gunton, Trevor. Cambridgeshire, UK. July 22, 2006.

Hancock, Lyn. Lantzville, British Columbia, Canada.
     September 1, 2006.

Harrison, George H. Hubertus, Wisconsin. January 25, 2006;
     February 1, 2006; May 28, 2006; April 15, 2007.

Hernandez, Robert. Bethesda, Maryland. April 27, 2006; May 22, 2006;
     May 7, 2007.

Houston, C. Stuart. Saskatoon, Saskatchewan, Canada.
     January 14, 2007.

Hudson, Don. Wiscasset, Maine. July 27, 2006.

Hume, Rob. Bedfordshire, UK. June 5, 2006; June 13, 2006;
     June 17, 2006.

Humphrey, Philip. Lawrence, Kansas. November 21, 2006.

Jonsson, Lars. Burgsvik, Sweden. September 30, 2006.

Kaufman, Kenn. Rocky Ridge, Ohio. October 29, 2006;
     November 7, 2006.

Kellogg, Francis. New York City. February 28, 2006.

King, Warren. Ripton, Vermont. August 28, 2006.

Kinne, Jane and Russ. New Canaan, Connecticut. June 27, 2006;
    July 24, 2006; July 30, 2006.

Klebanoff, Arthur. New York City. December 4, 2006.

Kovanic, Rudi. Bowen Island, British Columbia, Canada.
    February 25, 2007.

Kress, Stephen. Ithaca, New York. January 30, 2007.

Lasley, Greg. Austin, Texas. February 1, 2007.

Lewin, Katie. Rye, New York. March 23, 2007.

Lindblad, Sven-Olof. New York City. September 12, 2006.

Livingston, Zeke. Victoria, British Columbia, Canada. March 4, 2007.

Line, Les. Amenia, New York. February 12, 2007.

Lovejoy, Thomas. Washington, DC. January 23, 2006; April 10, 2006.

Male, Michael. Locustville, Virginia. February 12, 2007.

McAfee, George. Toronto, Ontario, Canada. February 27, 2007.

McGivern, Andy. Wausau, Wisconsin. March 6, 2007.

Mott, Peter. Bronx, New York. January 10, 2007.

Nehls, Susi Hickey. Monticello, Wisconsin. August 22, 2006;
    September 8, 2006.

Ng'weno, Fleur. Nairobi, Kenya. May 12, 2006; May 17, 2006; May 18,
    2006; May 26, 2006; June 1, 2006; June 6, 2006; June 23, 2007.

Nicholson, Al. Bridgeton, New Jersey. March 11, 2007.

Parks, Richard. Atlanta, Georgia. January 8, 2007.

Pasquier, Roger. New York City. September 13, 2006.

Peterson, Barbara. Kennett Square, Pennsylvania. November 28, 2005;
    June 11, 2006.

Peterson, Courtney. Lincoln University, Pennsylvania. May 24, 2007.

Peterson, Janet. Tryon, North Carolina. May 24, 2007.

Peterson, Lee. Lincoln University, Pennsylvania. November 28, 2005;
    March 25, 2006; June 11, 2006; May 24, 2007.

Peterson, Russell. Breidablik, Delaware. December 9, 2006.

Peterson, Tory. Tryon, North Carolina. August 7, 2006; May 24, 2007.

Proctor, Noble. Branford, Connecticut. February 15, 2007.

Pyle, Robert L. Honolulu, Hawaii. October 18, 2006.

Pyle, Robert Michael. Grays River, Washington. September 13, 2006.

Radis, Rick. Rockaway, New Jersey. April 10, 2007.

Remington, Charles. Hamden, Connecticut. September 26, 2006.

Rivaud, Esperanza. Ibiza, Spain. July 2, 2007.

Robbins, Chandler. Laurel, Maryland. March 13, 2006.

Ryan, Earl. Northville, Michigan. August 9, 2006.

Scott, Philippa. Gloucestershire, UK. May 20, 2006.

Shackleton, Keith. Devon, UK. May 27, 2006; March 18, 2007.

Shannon, George. Worcestershire, UK. September 5, 2006;
    January 1, 2007.

Sibley, David Allen. Concord, Massachusetts. October 19, 2006.

Simms, Laurie Lewin. Bozeman, Montana. July 16, 2006;
    March 3, 2007.

Sitwell, Nigel. London, UK. August 3, 2006.

Sladen, William J. L. Warrenton, Virginia. June 16, 2006; July 4, 2006.

Snyder, Jim. Sonoma, California. December 5, 2006.

Spitzer, Paul. Trappe, Maryland. May 2, 2006.

Stallcup, Rich. Inverness, California. November 22, 2006.

Sutton, Clay and Pat. Cape May Court House, New Jersey.
    February 12, 2007.

Swiderski, John and Kate. Valdosta, Georgia. January 22, 2007.

Switzer, Frank. Regina, Saskatchewan, Canada. February 8, 2007.

Theel, Marcia. Wausau, Wisconsin. March 6, 2007.

Train, Russell. Washington, DC. November 14, 2006.

Turner, Donald. Naivasha, Kenya. July 22, 2006.

Ullberg, Kent. Loveland, Colorado. July 20, 2006.

Wake, David. London, Ontario, Canada. August 10, 2006.

Weber, William A. Boulder, Colorado. May 9, 2007.

Weidensaul, Scott. Schuylkill Haven, Pennsylvania.
    September 29, 2006.

Weinke, Jane. Wausau, Wisconsin. March 6, 2007.

Wessel, Janet. Walnut Creek, California. December 18, 2006.

Wilson, Edward O. Cambridge, Massachusetts. September 17, 2006.

Yaki, Gustave. Calgary, Alberta, Canada. July 12, 2006; July 24, 2006.

Zaccaro, Jimmy and Dolores. Old Lyme, Connecticut.
    September 6, 2006.

Zinsser, William. Niantic, Connecticut. August 21, 2006.

Chapter Notes

Part One: Fledgling
Chapter One: Boy Rebel to Boy Wonder

"A-Birding in the Bronx," by Frank Graham Jr., *Audubon* magazine, May 1982. Personal Papers of Joseph J. Hickey.

"A Birdwatcher Looks at Flowers," by Roger Tory Peterson, *Audubon* magazine, May/June 1968.

All Things Reconsidered: My Birding Adventures, by Roger Tory Peterson, edited by Bill Thompson III, Houghton Mifflin, Boston, New York, 2006.

"A Speech to the New York State Legislature," by Roger Tory Peterson, Albany, New York, June 17, 1987. Pamphlet. Roger Tory Peterson Institute Archives (hereafter cited as RTPI), Jamestown, NY.

Bird Guide: Land Birds East of the Rockies: From Parrots to Bluebirds, by Chester A. Reed, Doubleday, Page & Company, Garden City, New York, 1916.

"Bird Painting in America," by Roger Tory Peterson, *Audubon* magazine, May/June 1942.

Birds of the New York City Region, by Ludlow Griscom, the American Museum of Natural History, Handbook Series No. 9, New York, 1923.

Birds Over America, by Roger Tory Peterson, Grosset & Dunlap, New York, 1948.

Blanche Hornbeck letter to Roger Tory Peterson, May 10, 1950. RTPI, Jamestown, NY.

Carolina Low Country Impressions, by Alexander Sprunt Jr., Devin-Adair Company, New York, 1964.

Clarence Beal letter to Roger Tory Peterson, April 25, 1928. Lewis F. Kibler Papers, RTPI, Jamestown, NY.

Dean of the Birdwatchers: A Biography of Ludlow Griscom, by William E. Davis Jr., Smithsonian Institution, 1994.

"From the September-October issue of 'Bird-Lore,' 1910." Flyer. National Audubon Society Archives (hereafter cited as NAS), New York Public Library.

Handbook of Birds of Eastern North America, by Frank M. Chapman. D. Appleton and Company, New York and London, 1930.

Henrietta Peterson letters to Roger Tory Peterson, February 8, 1927, March 25, 1927, May 22, 1928, October 4, 1928, September 2, 1929, September 4, 1929, November 5, 1929. Kibler Papers, RTPI, Jamestown, NY.

"Introduction to the Dover Edition," by Roger Tory Peterson, December 1964. In *Bird Studies at Old Cape May: An Ornithology of Coastal New Jersey,* by Witmer Stone, Stackpole Books, Mechanicsburg, PA, 2000. Reprint of 1965 Dover edition. First published 1937 by the Delaware Valley Ornithological Club.

Jamestown, by Kathleen Crocker and Jane Currie, Arcadia Publishing, Portsmouth, NH, 2004.

"Memories of Ten Boys and an Era That Shaped American Birding," by John Farrand Jr., *American Birds,* Fall 1991. Personal Papers of Joseph J. Hickey.

"Notes Gleaned from the Editor's Mail," *Passenger Pigeon* 1, no. 4 (January/February [1927]). Kibler Papers, RTPI, Jamestown, NY.

Roger Tory Peterson letter to Charles Callison, August 22, 1968. NAS, New York Public Library.

Russell Walp letter to Roger Tory Peterson, n.d., late 1920s. Kibler Papers, RTPI, Jamestown, NY.

The Audubon Ark: A History of the National Audubon Society, by Frank Graham Jr., Knopf, New York, 1990.

"The Birds Were Glad," by Clarence E. Allen, *The Florida Naturalist* 42, no. 2 (April 1969). Mill Pond Press Papers, Venice, Florida.

"The Most Valuable Lesson I Ever Learned," by Roger Tory Peterson, *Guideposts* (March 1981). RTPI, Jamestown, NY.

The Race to Save the Lord God Bird, by Phillip Hoose, Farrar, Straus & Giroux, New York, 2004.

The World of Roger Tory Peterson, by John C. Devlin and Grace Naismith, Times Books, New York, 1977.

Transcript from "Tape recorder session between RTP and Carl Buchheister, October 21, 1975: History of the Audubon Society," RTPI, Jamestown, NY.

Transcript of Roger Tory Peterson's Talk at Memorial Service for Joseph Hickey, September 4, 1993. Personal Papers of Barbara Peterson.

Transcript, "Roger Tory Peterson Reminisces: The Banquet Address at American Birding Association's First Convention June 16, 1973, Kenmare, North Dakota." RTPI, Jamestown, NY.

Two Little Savages: Being the Adventures of Two Boys Who Lived as Indians and What They Learned, by Ernest Thompson Seton, Doubleday, Garden City, NY, 1911.

Two Park Street: A Publishing Memoir, by Paul Brooks, Houghton Mifflin, Boston, 1986.

"Roger Peterson's Bird's-Eye View: Louis Agassiz Fuertes," by Roger Tory Peterson, *Audubon* magazine, March/April 1956.

Roger Tory Peterson letters to Joe Hickey, July 30, 1927, September 2, 1927, October 2, 1927, n.d. (circa fall 1931). Personal Papers of Joseph J. Hickey.

Unpublished autobiographical essay by Joseph J. Hickey. Personal Papers of Joseph J. Hickey.

Wild Wings, by Herbert K. Job, Houghton Mifflin, Boston, 1905.

Chapter Two: The Boy Wonder and the Conservative Conservationist

"A-Birding in the Bronx," by Frank Graham Jr., *Audubon* magazine, May 1982. Personal Papers of Joseph J. Hickey.

A Field Guide to the Birds: A Bird Book on a New Plan, by Roger Tory Peterson, Houghton Mifflin, Boston and New York, 1934.

A Field Guide to the Birds, by Roger Tory Peterson, Houghton Mifflin, Boston, 1939.

Audubon Nature Camp. Writer/Director/Producer: Roger Tory Peterson, under auspices of National Association of Audubon Societies. VHS copy of 1935 celluloid film, courtesy of the Hog Island History Project, Tom Schaefer, Chair, Dayton, Ohio.

Birds Over America, by Roger Tory Peterson, Grosset & Dunlap, New York, 1948.

Flyers for annual National Association of Audubon Societies Conventions, 1935–39. NAS, New York Public Library.

Francis Lee Jaques: Artist of the Wilderness World, by Florence Page Jaques, Doubleday, Garden City, New York, 1973.

Handbook of Birds of Eastern North America, by Frank M. Chapman, D. Appleton & Company, New York, London, 1930.

John Baker Correspondance. Guy Emerson letters to John Baker, n.d. and n.d. "Tuesday"; John Baker letter to Carl Buchheister June 15, 1936; John Baker letter to Carl Buchheister, August 12, 1937; Carl Buchheister letter to John Baker, August 28, 1937;

John Baker letter to Carl Buchheister, November 5, 1937; Roger Baldwin letter to John Baker, February 5, 1936; John Baker letter to Roger Baldwin, March 27, 1936; Roger Baldwin letter to John Baker, March 30, 1936; Memorandum from John Baker to Robert Cushman Murphy, April 12, 1938; Robert Cushman Murphy letter to John Baker, April 15, 1938; and memorandum of Robert P. Allen, Irving Benjamin, William Vogt, Richard H. Pough, Roger T. Peterson, and Lester L. Walsh to John H. Baker, April 15, 1938. NAS, New York Public Library.

"Life's Pictures," *Life,* May 23, 1938.

Man's Dominion: The Story of Conservation in America, by Frank Graham Jr., M. Evans and Company, New York, 1971.

"Ornithological Literature: 'A Field Guide to the Birds,'" by J. V., *Wilson Bulletin,* June 1939.

"Recent Literature: Peterson's 'Field Guide to the Birds,'" by W. S., *The Auk,* July 1934.

"Report on the Association's Educational Activities: Annual Meeting 1939." NAS, New York Public Library.

Tape recording of Roger Tory Peterson keynote speech, October 13, 1984, Hawk Mountain Sanctuary Fiftieth Anniversary. Hawk Mountain Sanctuary Archives, Kempton, PA.

The Audubon Ark: A History of the National Audubon Society, by Frank Graham Jr., Knopf, New York, 1990.

"The Birds Were Glad," by Clarence E. Allen, *The Florida Naturalist* 42, no. 2 (April 1969). Mill Pond Press Papers, Venice, Florida.

The Diversity of Life, by Edward O. Wilson, Belknap Press of Harvard University Press, Cambridge, MA, 1992.

"The Evolution of a Magazine," by Roger Tory Peterson, *Audubon* magazine, January 1973. RTPI, Jamestown, NY.

The Junior Book of Birds, by Roger Tory Peterson, Houghton Mifflin, Boston, 1939.

"The True Story of the Wooden Dovekie Deception," by William A. Weber, January 11, 1990. Personal Papers of Joseph J. Hickey.

The World of Roger Tory Peterson, by John C. Devlin and Grace Naismith, Times Books, New York, 1977.

Transcript from "Tape recorder session between RTP and Carl
Buchheister, October 21, 1975: History of the Audubon Society."
RTPI, Jamestown, NY.
William A. Weber letter to Joseph J. Hickey, January 11, 1990. Personal
Papers of Joseph J. Hickey.

Chapter Three: Spreading His Wings
A Field Guide to the Birds, by Roger Tory Peterson, Houghton Mifflin,
Boston, 1947.
Alexander Wetmore letter to Commander Charles Bittinger, January
19, 1943 [month of January was probably a typo, date was
likely June 19, 1943]. Alexander Wetmore Papers, Smithsonian
Institution, Washington, DC.
Arizona and Its Bird Life, by Herbert Brandt, Bird Research Foundation,
Cleveland, Ohio, 1951.
Audubon Bird Guide: Eastern Land Birds, by Richard H. Pough,
Doubleday, Garden City, New York, 1946.
Barbara Coulter Peterson, handwritten biographical notes and
typewritten biographical profile, 1970s. Personal Papers of Barbara
Peterson.
Barbara Peterson's autobiographical handwritten notes. Personal
Papers of Barbara Peterson.
Birds in the Garden and How to Attract Them, by Margaret McKenny,
Reynal & Hitchcock, New York, 1939.
Birds Over America, by Roger Tory Peterson, Grosset & Dunlap, New
York, 1948.
Commander Charles Bittinger letter to Colonel Julian V. Sollohub,
June 23, 1943. Alexander Wetmore Papers, Smithsonian
Institution, Washington, DC.
Executive Committee Meeting of the Audubon Society, November
7, 1944. Audubon Naturalist Society Archives, Smithsonian
Institution, Washington, DC.
"Friends with Feathers," *Pathfinder,* April 5, 1950. RTPI, Jamestown, NY.
How to Know the Birds, by Roger Tory Peterson, New American Library,
New York, 1949.
"Letters," *Audubon* magazine, May/June 1944.
"Letters," *Audubon* magazine, May/June 1948.

Lieutenant Colonel Julian V. Sollohub letter to Commander Charles
    Bittinger, June 24, 1943. Alexander Wetmore Papers, Smithsonian
    Institution, Washington, DC.
Memorandum titled "Roger Tory Peterson, Private, Company 'C,'
    6th Battalion, ERTC, Fort Belvoir, Virginia." Alexander Wetmore
    Papers, Smithsonian Institution, Washington, DC.
"Mockingbirds," by Roger Tory Peterson, *Life,* April 8, 1946.
"Now It Can Be Told," *Audubon* magazine, January/February 1948.
"Ornithological Literature: 'A Field Guide to the Birds,'" by Harold
    Mayfield, *Wilson Bulletin,* September 1947.
"Preface," *A Field Guide to Western Birds,* by Roger Tory Peterson,
    Houghton Mifflin, Boston, 1941.
Road to Survival, by William Vogt, William Sloane Associates, New
    York, 1948.
Roger Tory Peterson letter to Eleanor King, April 28, 1948. RTPI,
    Jamestown, NY.
Roger Tory Peterson John Burroughs Medal Award acceptance speech.
    RTPI, Jamestown, NY.
"Roger Tory Peterson, 1908–1996, and the Audubon Naturalist
    Society," by Shirley Briggs, *ANS News,* September 1996.
"R. T. Peterson Wins Burroughs Award," *New York Herald Tribune,* April
    2, 1950. RTPI, Jamestown, NY.
Spring in Washington, by Louis J. Halle, Atheneum, New York, 1963. First
    published 1947 by Harper & Brothers.
"The American Bald Eagle: National Bird Wins Fight for Survival," by
    Roger Tory Peterson, *Life,* July 1, 1946.
The Audubon Guide to Attracting Birds, edited by John H. Baker, Halcyon
    House, 1943. First published 1941 by Doubleday, Doran &
    Company.
The Audubon Society of the District of Columbia 1944 Announcement
    of Spring Programs of Field Trips; Audubon Society of the District
    of Columbia postcard announcement. Audubon Naturalist Society
    Archives, Smithsonian Institution, Washington, DC.
The Birds of Newfoundland, by Harold S. Peters and Thomas D. Burleigh,
    Houghton Mifflin, Boston, 1951.
The Birds of Rocky Mountain National Park, by Fred Mallery Packard,
    Rocky Mountain Nature Association, Estes Park, Colorado, 1950.
"The Mockingbird's Wing-Flashing," by Francis H. Allen, *Wilson
    Bulletin,* June 1947, editorial footnote.

The Roseate Spoonbill, by Robert Porter Allen, Dover, New York, 1966.
First published 1942 as Research Report Number 2 by the
National Audubon Society.

The World of Roger Tory Peterson, by John C. Devlin and Grace Naismith,
Times Books, New York, 1977.

"300 Attend Banquet of Audubon Society," *Washington Evening
Star,* October 27, 1944. Audubon Naturalist Society Archives,
Smithsonian Institution, Washington, DC.

Two Park Street: A Publishing Memoir, by Paul Brooks, Houghton Mifflin,
Boston, 1986.

Wild America, by Roger Tory Peterson and James Fisher, Weathervane
Books, New York, 1955.

Wildlife in Color, by Roger Tory Peterson, Houghton Mifflin,
Boston, 1951.

William Vogt letter to Roger Tory Peterson, December 25, 1948.
RTPI, Jamestown, NY.

Part Two: Intercontinental Migration
Chapter Four: International Range

A Guide to Bird Watching, by Joseph J. Hickey, Anchor Books, Garden
City, New York, 1963. First published 1943 by Oxford University
Press.

"A Prairie Chicken at Old Wives Lake," by Roger Tory Peterson,
The Blue Jay, March 1960. Personal Papers of C. Stuart
Houston.

"Introduction," by Julian Huxley, *A Field Guide to the Birds of Britain
and Europe,* by Roger Tory Peterson, Guy Mountfort, and P. A. D.
Hollom, Houghton Mifflin, Boston, 1954.

Introduction by Roger Tory Peterson to Peter Scott's essay "The Aura"
in *The Bird Watcher's Anthology,* edited by Roger Tory Peterson,
Harcourt, Brace, New York, 1957.

"Joe Hickey, Birder," by Michael Harwood, n.d. Personal Papers of
Joseph J. Hickey.

"Obituary: Roger Tory Peterson (1908–1996)," by Guy Mountfort,
British Birds (December 1996). Personal Papers of James
Ferguson-Lees.

"President's Message," by Joe Taylor, *Hawk Mountain News,* Fiftieth
Anniversary Issue, September 1984.

"Roger Peterson's Bird's-Eye View: A Night in a Channel Lighthouse,"
  by Roger Tory Peterson, *Audubon* magazine, September/
  October 1952.
"Spread and Disappearance of the Greater Prairie-Chicken,
  Tympanuchus cupido, on the Canadian Prairies and Adjacent
  Areas," by C. Stuart Houston, *Canadian Field-Naturalist,* January–
  March 2002.
Transcript from "Tape Recorder Session between RTP and Carl
  Buchheister, October 21, 1975, History of the Audubon Society."
  RTPI, Jamestown, NY.
Unpublished autobiographical essay by Joseph J. Hickey. Personal
  Papers of Joseph J. Hickey.
"Views on Birdwatching," by Sylvia Sullivan, *Birds,* Autumn 1983.
  RTPI, Jamestown, NY.

Chapter Five: Anglo-American Mates in the U.S. Wild

Barbara Peterson letter to Maurice Brooks, September 2, 1963. RTPI,
  Jamestown, NY.
Copinsay speech by Roger Tory Peterson, July 7, 1973. RTPI,
  Jamestown, NY.
"Foreword," *The Bird Watcher's Anthology,* edited by Roger Tory Peterson,
  Harcourt, Brace, New York, 1957.
"Introduction," by Roger Tory Peterson, *Birds as Individuals,* by Len
  Howard, Doubleday, Garden City, New York, 1953.
James Fisher letter to Barbara Peterson, May 9, 1953. Personal Papers
  of Barbara Peterson.
Looking for the Wild, by Lyn Hancock, Doubleday Canada Limited,
  Toronto, Canada, 1986.
Return to Wild America, by Scott Weidensaul, North Point Press, New
  York, 2005.
"Reviews: 'The World of Birds,' " by Robert M. Mengel, *The Auk,* July 1966.
Roger Tory Peterson letters to Alexander Wetmore August 23, 1963
  and Pierce Brodkorb November 27, 1962. RTPI, Jamestown, NY.
The Appalachians, by Maurice Brooks, Houghton Mifflin, Boston, 1965.
The Birds, by Roger Tory Peterson and the editors of *Life,* Time, New
  York, 1963.
The World of Birds, by James Fisher and Roger Tory Peterson, Doubleday,
  Garden City, New York, 1965.

Watching Birds, by James Fisher, Penguin, Harmondsworth, Middlesex, UK, rev. ed., 1951. First published 1941 by Pelican.

Wild America, by Roger Tory Peterson and James Fisher, Weathervane Books, New York, 1955.

Part Three: Paradoxical Homo Sapiens
Chapter Six: A Super Pair and Their Habitat, Nest, and Brood

"A Letter from the Petersons," 1976. NAS, New York Public Library.

"A New Year's Letter from the Petersons," January 1961, January 1963, January 1964, January 1965. Personal Papers of C. Stuart Houston.

"Barbara Coulter Peterson" résumé. Personal Papers of Barbara Peterson.

Barbara Peterson letter to Edward Gruson, February 4, 1976. Personal Papers of Barbara Peterson.

Inside book cover flap, *The Bird Watcher's Anthology,* edited by Roger Tory Peterson, Harcourt, Brace, New York, 1957.

Roger and Barbara Peterson letter to the Alexander Wetmores, p. 3, circa late 1954, early 1955. Alexander Wetmore Papers, Smithsonian Institution, Washington, DC.

Roger Tory Peterson letter to Mrs. Charles W. Nichols Jr., September 15, 1975. Personal Papers of Barbara Peterson.

"The Story of Vera," flyer by Eleanor Harris Howard, Women's Committee, New York Zoological Society, Bronx, New York. Personal Papers of Barbara Peterson.

Chapter Seven: A Natural Obsession

"A Birdwatcher Looks at Flowers," by Roger Tory Peterson, *Audubon* magazine, May/June 1968.

A Field Guide to Ferns and Their Related Families, by Boughton Cobb, Houghton Mifflin, Boston, 1956.

"A New Year's Letter from the Petersons," January 1963. Personal Papers of C. Stuart Houston.

Birds Over America, by Roger Tory Peterson, Grosset & Dunlap, New York, 1948.

"Introduction," *A Field Guide to Wildflowers of Northeastern and North-Central North America,* by Roger Tory Peterson and Margaret McKenny, Houghton Mifflin, Boston, 1968.

Chapter Eight: Hidden Roger

Barbara Peterson letter to her mother, March 14, 1973. Personal Papers of Barbara Peterson.

"Foreword," by Roger Tory Peterson, *Looking for the Wild,* by Lyn Hancock, Doubleday Canada Limited, Toronto, Canada, 1986.

Roger Tory Peterson letters to Carl Buchheister, August 25, 1962 and September 6, 1962. NAS, New York Public Library.

"Three Conversations with Roger Tory Peterson, February 27, 1976, with David and Ellen Lank." Mill Pond Press Papers, Venice, Florida.

Part Four: Conservation Stories

Chapter Nine: Embryonic Conservationism

"A Report on Some Results of Airplane Spraying of Woodlands with D.D.T.," by Richard H. Pough, July 17, 1945. NAS, New York Public Library.

"Birds and Floating Oil," by Roger T. Peterson, *Audubon* magazine, July/August 1942. RTPI, Jamestown, NY.

Birds Over America, by Roger Tory Peterson, Grosset & Dunlap, New York, 1948.

"Burden of Proof: The Science Behind Conserving Shorebirds and Horseshoe Crabs in Delaware Bay," by David Mizrahi, *New Jersey Audubon* magazine, Spring/Summer 2007.

"Half a Mile Away: Field Characteristics of Eastern Gulls," by Roger Tory Peterson, *Nature* magazine, February 1932. RTPI, Jamestown, NY.

"Introduction," *Insecticides for the Control of Insects of Public Health Importance: Training Guide—Insect Control Series,* by Harry D. Pratt and Kent S. Littig, U.S. Department of Health, Education and Welfare, Public Health Service, Communicable Disease Center, Atlanta, Georgia, n.d. NAS, New York Public Library.

John H. Baker letter to Donald C. Peattie, September 9, 1942. NAS, New York Public Library.

"Report on ADTB Project G-50: 'Deleterious Effects of DDT on Wildlife,'" by Roger T. Peterson, Sergeant, Engineer Corps, n.d. NAS, New York Public Library.

"Returning Red Knots at Delaware Bay Number Only a Troubling 12,000," by Sandy Bauers, *Philadelphia Inquirer,* June 11, 2007. http://www.redorbit.com/news/science/963005/returning_ red_knots_at_delaware_bay_number_only_a_troubling/index. html?source=r_science.

"The Flight of Northern Birds," by Roger Tory Peterson, *Passenger Pigeon* 1, no. 5 (March/April [1927]). Kibler Papers, RTPI, Jamestown, NY.

"The Osprey: Endangered World Citizen," by Roger Tory Peterson, *National Geographic Magazine,* July 1969. RTPI, Jamestown, NY.

"The Pesticides Controversy," by Roland C. Clement, *Environmental Affairs* 2, no. 3 (Winter 1972). NAS, New York Public Library.

Wild Wings, by Herbert K. Job, Houghton Mifflin, Boston and New York, 1905.

Chapter Ten: Adventuresome Flights of Conservation

"A Letter from the Petersons," March 1966. Personal Papers of C. Stuart Houston.

All About Birds, "Swallow-Tailed Kite," http://www.birds.cornell.edu/ AllAboutBirds/BirdGuide/Swallow-tailed_Kite.html#conservation.

"A New Year's Letter from the Petersons," January 1965. Personal Papers of C. Stuart Houston.

An Eye for a Bird, by Eric Hosking with Frank W. Lane, Eriksson, New York, 1973.

Audubon News Release, National Audubon Society, "Contents This Release: 1. Audubon President Advises Navy on Albatrosses, 2. Dingell Bill would Change Predator-Control Policy," February 14, 1964. NAS, New York Public Library.

"Baharini," by Roger Tory Peterson, *Massachusetts Audubon,* December 1970. RTPI, Jamestown, NY.

"Birding," unpublished, autobiographical essay by William A. Weber. Personal Papers of William A. Weber.

"Birds and Aircraft on Midway Islands: 1957–58 Investigations," by Dale W. Rice, Branch of Wildlife Research, Bureau of Sport Fisheries and Wildlife, Special Scientific Report—Wildlife No. 44, U.S. Department of the Interior, Fish and Wildlife Service, Washington, July 1959. RTPI, Jamestown, NY.

Birds of East Africa: Kenya, Tanzania, Uganda, Rwanda and Burundi, by Terry Stevenson and John Fanshawe, Princeton University Press, Princeton, NJ, 2002.

Birds of Isla Grande (Tierra del Fuego), by Philip S. Humphrey, David Bridge, Percival W. Reynolds, and Roger Tory Peterson, Smithsonian Institution, Washington, DC, 1970.

Birds of Kenya and Northern Tanzania, by Dale A. Zimmerman, Donald A. Turner, and David J. Pearson, Princeton University Press, Princeton, NJ, 1999.

"Chronology of Events at Midway," Midway Atoll National Wildlife Refuge, n.d. http://www.fws.gov/midway/past/chronol.html.

Department of Defense News Release, No. 1227-59, "Navy Starts Project to Eliminate Aircraft Hazards on Midway Island," October 22, 1959. NAS, New York Public Library.

Draft, Antarctica Society Speech by Roger Tory Peterson, 1966. RTPI, Jamestown, NY.

"Foreword," by Roger Tory Peterson, *A Passion for Birds,* by Eric Hosking with Kevin MacDonnell, Coward, McCann, & Geoghan, New York, 1979.

E. E. Wyman, assistant to the president of Pan Am, letters to Robert Porter Allen, June 20, 1935, and July 24, 1935. NAS, New York Public Library.

"Farewell to Flamingos?" by Les Line, *National Wildlife* magazine, December/January 2004, http://www.nwf.org/nationalwildlife/article.cfm?issueID=65&articleID=875.

"Exploring Antarctica," by Roger Tory Peterson, *International Wildlife* magazine, November/December 1971. RTPI, Jamestown, NY.

H. E. Yarnell, rear admiral, U.S. Navy, commandant, 14th District (Pearl Harbor), letter to Robert Porter Allen, July 10, 1935. NAS, New York Public Library.

"High Seas in a Rowboat," by Roger Tory Peterson, *Audubon* magazine, January/February 1962. Personal Papers of Philip S. Humphrey.

"How He Became King," by William J. L. Sladen, *The Roger Tory Peterson Institute of Natural History Guide,* Spring 1997.

"How I Photographed All the Flamingos in the World," by Roger Tory Peterson, *International Wildlife* magazine [probably], n.d. RTPI, Jamestown, NY.

Humphrey Field Notes, "25 November, 1960: Chile: Tierra del Fuego: Ea. Cameron to Rio Grande (Argentina)." Personal Papers of Philip S. Humphrey.

"Introduction" by Roger Tory Peterson, *A Field Guide to the Birds of East and Central Africa,* by John G. Williams, Houghton Mifflin, Boston, 1963.

"In Quest of the Rarest Flamingo," by William G. Conway, *National Geographic Magazine,* July 1961.

John Aldrich letter to Roger Tory Peterson, January 10, 1962. NAS, New York Public Library.

"Nesting Behavior and Affinities of Monk Parakeets of Southern Buenos Aires Province, Argentina," by Philip S. Humphrey and Roger Tory Peterson, *Wilson Bulletin,* December 1978.

Penguins, by Roger Tory Peterson, Houghton Mifflin, Boston, 1979.

Portrait of a Wilderness, by Guy Mountfort, Hutchinson, London, 1958.

"Preface to the Revised Edition," *Portrait of a Wilderness,* by Guy Mountfort, David & Charles, Newton Abbott, Devon, UK, 1968.

"Rare Birds Flock to Spain's Marismas," by Roger Tory Peterson, *National Geographic Magazine,* March 1958.

"Render the Penguins, Butcher the Seals: The Antarctic's Bloody Past May Foretell Its Future," by Roger Tory Peterson, *Audubon* magazine, March 1973. RTPI, Jamestown, NY.

"Report of the Committee on Bird Protection to the American Ornithologists' Union, 1955," by Ira N. Gabrielson, chairman; Jean Delacour; Ludlow Griscom; Hoyes Lloyd; and Roger Tory Peterson; *The Auk,* January 1956.

"Roger Peterson's Bird's-Eye View: A Million Flamingoes," by Roger Tory Peterson, *Audubon* magazine, November/December 1957.

"Roger Peterson's Bird's-Eye View: Tragedy of the Albatrosses," by Roger Tory Peterson, *Audubon* magazine, November/December 1959.

Roger Tory Peterson letter to Barbara Peterson, n.d. (late 1965), McMurdo, Antarctica. Personal Papers of Barbara Peterson.

Roger Tory Peterson letter to John Aldrich, February 24, 1962. NAS, New York Public Library.

Roger Tory Peterson letters to Joe Hickey, August 16, 1927 and December 7, 1927. Personal Papers of Joseph J. Hickey.

Roland Clement Memorandum to Gene Eisenmann, October 20, 1959, Re: "Albatross Meeting." NAS, New York Public Library.

"Section 1: Penguins," "Penguins and Their Interactions with
Men," by Roger Tory Peterson, *International Zoo Yearbook 18,*
Zoological Society of London, 1978. Personal Papers of William
J. L. Sladen.

"Section 1: Penguins," "Penguins: Introduction," by William J. L.
Sladen, *International Zoo Yearbook 18,* Zoological Society of London,
1978. Personal Papers of William J. L. Sladen.

"Some Notes on Myiopsitta—R.T.P. October 28, 1960." Personal Papers
of Philip S. Humphrey.

"The Galapagos: Eerie Cradle of New Species," by Roger Tory Peterson,
National Geographic Magazine, April 1967.

"The Tourist as Conservationist," by Roger Tory Peterson, *Audubon*
magazine, March 1972. RTPI, Jamestown, NY.

Transcript from "Tape recorder session between RTP and Carl
Buchheister, October 21, 1975," History of Audubon Society.
RTPI, Jamestown, NY.

Chapter Eleven: DDT, the Osprey, and the Old Lyme Offspring

"All Things Reconsidered: The Osprey Story," by Roger Tory
Peterson, *Bird Watcher's Digest,* September/October 1988. RTPI,
Jamestown, NY.

"A New Year's Letter from the Petersons," January 1969. Personal
Papers of C. Stuart Houston.

Brief Reports: The Status of the Osprey: Population Trends of Ospreys
in the Northeastern United States," by Roger T. Peterson. In
Peregrine Falcon Populations: Their Biology and Decline, edited by
Joseph J. Hickey, University of Wisconsin Press, Madison, 1969.
Personal Papers of Paul Spitzer.

Carl Buchheister letter to Roger Tory Peterson, July 31, 1964. NAS,
New York Public Library.

"DDT Residues in Adélie Penguins and a Crabeater Seal from
Antarctica: Ecological Implications," by William J. L.
Sladen, *Nature,* May 14, 1966. Personal Papers of William J. L.
Sladen.

"Environmental News: For Release After 1:30 p.m. Friday, April 20,
1973: EPA Denies Use of DDT to Control Tussock Moth," U.S.
Environmental Protection Agency. NAS, New York Public Library.

"Foreword," by Roger Tory Peterson, *Peregrine Falcon Populations: Their Management and Recovery,* edited by Tom J. Cade, James H. Enderson, Carl G. Thelander, and Clayton M. White, Peregrine Fund, Boise, Idaho, 1988. Personal Papers of Tom Cade.

J. J. Hickey Audubon Medal Acceptance Speech, November 29, 1984. Personal Papers of Joseph J. Hickey.

"Joe Hickey, Birder," by Michael Harwood, n.d. Personal Papers of Joseph J. Hickey.

"Late News from the Fire Ant Front," by Harold S. Peters, Research Biologist, National Audubon Society, paper presented at Fifty-Fifth Annual Convention, National Audubon Society, New York, November 10, 1959. NAS, New York Public Library.

"Man's Role in Nature," by Roger Tory Peterson, speech at Symposium on Endangered Species, San Francisco, February 1974. RTPI, Jamestown, NY.

"Nature's Protector and Provocateur," by Frank Graham Jr., *Audubon* magazine, September/October 2007.

Pesticides and the Living Landscape, by Robert Rudd, University of Wisconsin Press, Madison, 1964.

Natural Resources Defense Council, "Healthy Milk, Healthy Baby: Chemicals: Heptachlor," http://www.nrdc.org/breastmilk/chem6.asp; "Chemicals: Chlordane," http://www.nrdc.org/breastmilk/chem1.asp; "Chemicals: Dieldrin, Aldrin, and Endrin," http://www.nrdc.org/breastmilk/diel.asp.

Rachel Carson at Work: The House of Life, by Paul Brooks, G. K. Hall, Boston, 1985.

Rachel Carson: Witness for Nature, by Linda Lear, Henry Holt, New York, 1998.

"Resurgent Bald Eagle's Comeback Is Complete," by H. Josef Hebert, *The Philadelphia Inquirer,* p. A7, June 28, 2007.

Roger Tory Peterson letters to Carl Buchheister, November 3, 1962, and August 13, 1964. NAS, New York Public Library.

Roger Tory Peterson letter to William Vogt, July 11, 1964. RTPI, Jamestown, NY.

"Ruckelshaus Takes First Steps to Ban Remaining DDT Uses," by E. W. Kenworthy, *New York Times,* January 16, 1971. NAS, New York Public Library.

Since Silent Spring, by Frank Graham Jr., Houghton Mifflin, Boston, 1970.

"Statement of Pesticide Hazards," by Dr. Roger Tory Peterson, to
  Subcommittee on Reorganization and International Organization,
  Senate Committee on Government Operations, presented in
  Washington, DC, April 22, 1964. RTPI, Jamestown, NY.
"The Osprey: Endangered World Citizen," by Roger Tory Peterson,
  National Geographic Magazine, July 1969. RTPI, Jamestown, NY.
The World of Birds, by James Fisher and Roger Tory Peterson, Doubleday,
  Garden City, New York, 1965.

Chapter Twelve: The Wilds of Lindblad

"A Letter from the Petersons," 1972. NAS, New York Public Library.
"All Things Reconsidered: Eco-Tourism: The New Buzzword," by
  Roger Tory Peterson, *Bird Watcher's Digest,* July/August 1991. RTPI,
  Jamestown, NY.
"A New Year's Letter from the Petersons," January 1969. Personal
  Papers of C. Stuart Houston.
"Indian Ocean Islands," by Tony Irwin, *Africana,* December 1969/
  January 1970. RTPI, Jamestown, NY.
Passport to Anywhere, by Lars-Eric Lindblad with John G. Fuller, Time
  Books, New York, 1983.
"The Tourist as a Conservationist," by Roger Tory Peterson, *Audubon*
  magazine, March 1972. RTPI, Jamestown, NY.

Part Five: Inspiring Flights
Chapter Thirteen: Worldwide Progeny

*A Field Guide to Advanced Birding: Birding Challenges and How to Approach
  Them,* by Kenn Kaufman, Houghton Mifflin, Boston, 1990.
A Field Guide to Mexican Birds, by Roger Tory Peterson and Edward L.
  Chalif, Houghton Mifflin, Boston, 1973.
A Field Guide to the Birds of Texas, by Roger Tory Peterson, Houghton
  Mifflin, Boston, 1960.
A Field Guide to Western Birds, by Roger Tory Peterson, Houghton
  Mifflin, Boston, 1990.
Birds of Europe, by Lars Jonsson, Christopher Helm, A & C Black,
  London, 2003. First published 1992 in English by Christopher
  Helm.
Birds Over America, by Roger Tory Peterson, Grosset & Dunlap, New
  York, 1948.

Edible Wild Plants: Eastern/Central North America, by Lee Allen Peterson, Houghton Mifflin, Boston, New York, 1977.

Kaufman Field Guide to Birds of North America, by Kenn Kaufman, Houghton Mifflin, Boston, 2000.

Kent Ullberg: Monuments to Nature, by Todd Wilkinson, International Graphics, Arizona, 1998.

Kingbird Highway, by Kenn Kaufman, Houghton Mifflin, 2000. First published 1997 by Houghton Mifflin.

Letter from Tom Lovejoy to Roger Tory Peterson, July 16 (no year indicated). RPTI, Jamestown, NY.

Pheidole in the New World: A Dominant, Hyper-Diverse Ant Genus, by Edward O. Wilson, Harvard University Press, Cambridge, MA, 2003.

"Remembering Roger Tory Peterson," by William Burt, *Bird Watcher's Digest,* August 2002.

Roger Tory Peterson's Dozen Birding Hot Spots, by George H. Harrison, Simon and Schuster, New York, 1976.

The Feather Quest: A North American Birder's Year, by Pete Dunne, Houghton Mifflin, Boston, New York, 1999. First published 1992 by Dutton.

The Sibley Field Guide to Birds of Eastern North America, by David Allen Sibley, Knopf, New York, 2003.

The Sibley Field Guide to Birds of Western North America, by David Allen Sibley, Knopf, New York, 2003.

The Sibley Guide to Birds, by David Allen Sibley, Knopf, New York, 2000.

Chapter Fourteen: Offerings

Birds of North America, by Chandler S. Robbins, Bertel Bruun, and Herbert S. Zim, Golden Press, New York, 1966.

Grace Murphy letter to Roger Tory Peterson, January 28, 1957. RTPI, Jamestown, NY.

"I Showed Roger Tory Peterson a New Bird," by Kent Dannen, *Backpacker,* 1974. Mill Pond Press Papers, Venice, Florida.

Roger Tory Peterson letter to Grace Murphy, January 14, 1957. RTPI, Jamestown, NY.

Roger Tory Peterson letter to Herbert Zim, May 24, 1962. RTPI, Jamestown, NY.

Roger Tory Peterson letter to Robert Lewin, March, 17, 1987. Mill Pond
    Press Papers, Venice, Florida.
Where to Find Birds in New York State: The Top 500 Sites, by Susan Roney
    Drennan, Syracuse University Press, New York, 1981.

Chapter Fifteen: Maturing with National Audubon

"A New Year's Letter from the Petersons," January 1963. Personal
Papers of C. Stuart Houston.
"A New Year's Letter from the Petersons," January 1965. Personal
    Papers of C. Stuart Houston.
"Announcing a New Feature by Roger Tory Peterson," *Audubon*
    magazine, July/August 1952.
Barbara Peterson letter to Bea Wetmore, October 20, 1964. Alexander
    Wetmore Papers, Smithsonian Institution, Washington, DC.
Connie Hagar: The Life History of a Texas Birdwatcher, by Karen Harden
    McCracken, Texas A&M University Press, College Station, 1986.
"In Memoriam: Roger Tory Peterson, 1908–1996," by Susan Roney
    Drennan, *The Auk*, April 1998. RTPI, Jamestown, NY.
Letter from Wayne Short "To Audubon Screen Tour Sponsors and
    Friends," n.d., 1957. NAS, New York Public Library.
Roger Tory Peterson letter to Maurice Broun, October 12, 1964. RTPI,
    Jamestown, NY.
Transcript from "Tape Recorder Session Between Roger Tory Peterson
    and Carl Buchheister, October 21, 1975," History of Audubon
    Society. RTPI, Jamestown, NY.

Chapter Sixteen: Shooting Birds

The Complete Book of Photographing Birds, by Russ Kinne, Amphoto, New
    York, 1981.

Chapter Seventeen: Painterly Birds

Birds in Art: The Masters, by Inga Brynildson and Woody Hagge, Leigh
    Yawkey Woodson Art Museum, Wausau, Wisconsin, 1990.
Draft of Roger Tory Peterson biographical essay by John Livingston,
    Summer 1973. Mill Pond Press Papers, Venice, Florida.
Roger Tory Peterson letter to Keith Shackleton, May 1, 1971. Personal
    Papers of Keith Shackleton.

The Agent, by Arthur Klebanoff, Texere, New York, 2001.

"Three Conversations with Roger Tory Peterson in Old Lyme Connecticut, February 27, 1976, with David and Ellen Lank." Mill Pond Press Papers, Venice, Florida.

Part Six: Bird Man of Bird Men
Chapter Eighteen: Territory under Challenge

"A-Birding in the Bronx," by Frank Graham Jr., *Audubon* magazine, May 1982. Personal Papers of Joseph J. Hickey.

"Abridged Too Far . . . ? An Objective Evaluation of the New Peterson Field Guide," by Kenn Kaufman, *Continental Birdlife,* February 1981.

"A Field Guide to Roger Tory Peterson," by William Zinsser, *Audubon* magazine, November/December 1992. RTPI, Jamestown, NY.

A Field Guide to the Birds, by Roger Tory Peterson, Houghton Mifflin, Boston, New York, 1980.

"A Field Guide to the Birds," by Tom Davis, *The Linnaean Newsletter,* October/November 1980.

A Field Guide to Western Birds, by Roger Tory Peterson, Houghton Mifflin, Boston, 1961.

"A Gathering of Birds," by Robert Arbib, *Natural History,* December 1980.

"A Letter from the Petersons," January 1971. NAS, New York Public Library.

"A New Bird Immigrant Arrives," by Roger Tory Peterson, *National Geographic Magazine,* August 1954.

"Battle of the Bird Books," by Joseph Kastner, *New York Times Magazine,* April 15, 1979. RTPI, Jamestown, NY.

"Behind the Best Sellers: Roger Tory Peterson," by Edwin McDowell, *New York Times Book Review,* December 7, 1980.

"Bird Book Wars: The Emperor Strikes Back," by Henry Armistead, Ron Naveen, Claudia Wilds, Will Russell, Lawrence Balch, and Roger Tory Peterson, *Birding,* August 1981.

"Book Reviews," by Robert E. Budliger, *The Conservationist,* January/February 1981.

"Booktalk," by Richard Rogin, *Sports Illustrated,* October 27, 1980.

"For Bird Watchers," by Ken Emerson, *New York Times Book Review,* October 26, 1980.

National Audubon Society Field Guide to North American Birds, Knopf, New York, 1977.

1001 Questions Answered about Birds, by Allan D. Cruickshank and Helen G. Cruickshank, Dover, New York, 1976. First published 1958 by Dodd, Mead and Company, New York.

On Writing Well, by William Zinsser, Thirtieth Anniversary Edition, Collins, New York, 2006.

"Reviews: A Field Guide to the Birds," by Jon Dunn, *The Auk,* July 1981.

Roger Caras letter to Roger Tory Peterson, September 18, 1979. RTPI, Jamestown, NY.

Roger Tory Peterson letter to C. Stuart Houston, November 22, 1959. Personal Papers of C. Stuart Houston.

Roger Tory Peterson letter to Frank Graham Jr., April 4, 1980. Personal Papers of Frank Graham Jr.

Roger Tory Peterson letter to Joe Hickey, February 13, 1978. Personal Papers of Joseph J. Hickey.

Roger Tory Peterson letter to Roger Caras, August 22, 1979. RTPI, Jamestown, NY.

Roger Tory Peterson letter to C. Stuart Houston, December 28, 1959, Personal Papers of C. Stuart Houston.

Roger Tory Peterson: The Art and Photography of the World's Foremost Birder, edited by Roger Tory Peterson and Rudy Hoglund, text by William Zinsser, Rizzoli, New York, 1994.

C. Stuart Houston letters to J. B. Gollop, December 12, 1959; Terry Shortt, December 12, 1959; Merrill C. Hammond, December 13, 1959; Roger Tory Peterson, December 19, 1959. Personal Papers of C. Stuart Houston.

"Worldviews: Peterson's Penguins," by Frank Graham Jr., *Audubon* magazine, 1980. RTPI, Jamestown, NY.

Chapter Nineteen: Still All over the Range Map

A Field Guide to the Birds of Britain and Europe, by Roger Tory Peterson, Guy Mountfort, and P. A. D. Hollom, Houghton Mifflin, Boston, New York, 1993.

A Field Guide to the Birds of Eastern and Central North America, by Roger Tory Peterson, Houghton Mifflin, Boston, 2002.

"All Things Reconsidered: The Roger Tory Peterson Institute," by
Roger Tory Peterson, *Bird Watcher's Digest,* September/October
1994. RTPI, Jamestown, NY.

"All Things Reconsidered: Whatever Happened to the Junior Audubon
Clubs?" by Roger Tory Peterson, *Bird Watcher's Digest,* September/
October 1984. Personal Papers of Frank Graham Jr.

"American Heroes: Roger Tory Peterson (1908–1996)," by Les Line,
National Wildlife, circa late 1996. RTPI, Jamestown, NY.

"Exile for the Egret," by Dyan Zaslowsky, *Harrowsmith Country Life,*
September/October 1991. RTPI, Jamestown, NY.

Kenn Kaufman letter to Roger and Ginny Peterson, February 15, 1990.
RTPI, Jamestown, NY.

Private journal of Greg Lasley, entry dated September 8, 1995. Personal
Papers of Greg Lasley.

Project Puffin: How We Brought Puffins Back to Egg Rock, by Stephen W.
Kress and Pete Salmansohn, Tilbury House Publishers, Gardiner,
Maine, 1997.

Roger Tory Peterson at the Smithsonian, by Richard L. Zusi, published
for the Smithsonian Institution by Mill Pond Press, Venice,
Florida, 1984.

Roger Tory Peterson letter to Joe Hickey, November 9, 1982. Personal
Papers of Joseph J. Hickey.

Roger Tory Peterson letters to Frank Graham Jr., December 11, 1987,
and November 13, 1991. Personal Papers of Frank Graham Jr.

Roger Tory Peterson letter to Keith and Jackie Shackleton, January 11,
1990. Personal Papers of Keith Shackleton.

Roger Tory Peterson letters to Robert Lewin, October 5, 1983, October
29, 1986, July 7, 1993, and November 11, 1993. Mill Pond Press
Papers, Venice, Florida.

Roger Tory Peterson letter to Roger Caras, November 4, 1976. RTPI,
Jamestown, NY.

"Rogue Wave," by Roger Tory Peterson, draft sent to Frank
Graham Jr. in letter of September 27, 1990. Personal Papers of
Frank Graham Jr.

The Audubon Society Baby Elephant Folio: Audubon's Birds of America, by
Roger Tory Peterson and Virginia Marie Peterson, Abbeville Press,
New York, 1981.

Further Reading

Broun, Maurice, *Hawks Aloft: The Story of Hawk Mountain,* Dodd, Mead
Company, New York, 1948, 1949.
Roger Tory Peterson wrote the foreword to this entertaining,
definitive account of how the Hawk Mountain Sanctuary came
to be.

Burt, William, *Rare and Elusive Birds of North America,* Universe
Publishing, New York, 2001.
Burt provides some Peterson anecdotes. The photos are
stunning too.

Carlson, Douglas, *Roger Tory Peterson: A Biography,* University of Texas
Press, Austin, 2007.
The first serious account of Roger's life since *The World of Roger
Tory Peterson* in 1977.

Carson, Rachel, *Silent Spring,* Houghton Mifflin, Boston, 1962.
A historic work by a courageous woman.

Diamond, Antony W., *Save the Birds,* Houghton Mifflin, Boston, 1989.
Roger wrote the introduction and most of the section "Saving
America's Birdlife."

Dunne, Pete, *Golden Wings and Other Stories about Birders and Birding,*
University of Texas Press, Austin, 2003.
Dunne's moving story about the death of Roger Tory Peterson,
"Golden Wings," is here.

Hume, Rob, *Life with Birds: Reflections of a Naturalist,* David & Charles,
Newton Abbott, Devon, UK, 2005.
Hume, a leader of the Royal Society for the Protection of Birds,
reminisces about his birding life while offering some Peterson
stories as well.

Kastner, Joseph, *A World of Watchers,* Knopf, New York, 1986.
The chapter "Revolution in the Bronx" is chiefly about the Bronx
County Bird Club and its mentor, Ludlow Griscom; the following
chapter, "The Guide," tells how Roger came to write the book that
changed birding.

Line, Les, editor, *This Good Earth: The View From Audubon Magazine,* Crown Publishers, New York, 1974.
Roger Tory Peterson's *Audubon* article, "The Evolution of Audubon Magazine," ends this beautiful, glossy, coffee table volume.

Montgomery, Sy, *Nature's Everyday Mysteries,* Chapters Publishing, Shelburne, Vermont, 1993.
Montgomery's charming collection of essays about aspects of nature the average person regularly encounters is endorsed by Roger in the foreword.

National Wildlife Federation, *Gardening with Wildlife,* Washington, DC, 1974.
Roger wrote the chapter "Your Guide to Garden Wildlife" especially for this volume.

Peterson, Russ, *Rebel with a Conscience,* University of Delaware Press, Newark, Delaware, 1999.
The autobiography of an American conservation leader who not only shares Roger's last name and Swedish ancestry, but is an admirer of his too.

Snyder, Jim, and Keith Shackleton, *Ship in the Wilderness,* Gaia Books, London, 1986.
A coffee table book featuring stories about the MS *Lindblad Explorer* and gorgeous art by Keith Shackleton.

Stefferud, Alfred, editor, *Birds in Our Lives,* U.S. Department of the Interior, Bureau of Sport Fisheries and Wildlife, Fish and Wildlife Service, Washington, DC, 1966.
This book includes Roger Tory Peterson's essay, "What Are Birds For?" and the carefully expressed "Birds and Pesticides" by Joseph J. Hickey.

Stroud, Richard H., *National Leaders of American Conservation,* Smithsonian Institution Press, Washington, DC, 1985.
A handy encyclopedia of conservation leaders.

Sutton, Clay, and Pat Sutton, *Birds and Birding at Cape May,* Stackpole
    Books, Mechanicsburg, Pennsylvania, 2006.
    Two storied naturalists tell their own stories about Cape May
    birding, past and present (which naturally means some Peterson
    tales along the way), and advise the reader on where to find birds.

Van Gelder, Patricia, *Wildlife Artists at Work,* Watson-Guptill, New York,
    1982.
    This book profiles ten wildlife artists, including Roger Tory
    Peterson, Robert Bateman, Maynard Reece, and Guy Coheleach.

Wood, J. Duncan, *Horace Alexander: 1889 to 1989: Birds and Binoculars,*
    William Sessions, York, UK, 2003.
    A biography of a British transplant to America who was among the
    first to appreciate viewing birds through binoculars rather than
    through a gunsight. He was also an acquaintance of Roger Tory
    Peterson; the book recounts birding before and after publication
    of *A Field Guide to the Birds of Britain and Europe,* by Roger Tory
    Peterson, Guy Mountfort, and P. A. D. Hollom.

Index